GERMANY AND EASTERN EUROPE SINCE 1945

From the Potsdam Agreement
to Chancellor Brandt's
"Ostpolitik"

KEESING'S RESEARCH REPORT

GERMANY AND EASTERN EUROPE SINCE 1945

From the Potsdam Agreement to Chancellor Brandt's "Ostpolitik"

CHARLES SCRIBNER'S SONS

New York

CONTENTS

INTRODUCTION

Winston Churchill said, in his speech at Fulton, Missouri, on March 4, 1946:

"From Stettin on the Baltic to Trieste on the Adriatic an iron curtain has descended across the Continent. Behind that line lie all the capitals of the ancient States of Central and Eastern Europe—Warsaw, Berlin, Prague, Vienna, Budapest, Belgrade, Bucharest and Sofia. All these famous cities and the populations around them lie in the Soviet sphere, and all are subject in one form or another not only to Soviet influence but to a very high and increasing measure of control from Moscow. . . .

"The Russian-dominated Polish Government have been encouraged to make enormous and wrongful inroads upon Germany, and mass expulsions of millions of Germans on a scale grievous and undreamed of are now taking place. The Communist parties, which were very small in all these Eastern States of Europe, have been raised to pre-eminence and power far beyond their numbers and are seeking everywhere to obtain totalitarian control. . . .

"An attempt is being made by the Russians in Berlin to build up a quasi-Communist party in their zone of occupied Germany by showing special favours to groups of left-wing German leaders. . . .

"If, now, the Soviet Government tries by separate action to build up a pro-Communist Germany in their areas this will cause new serious difficulties in the British and American zones and will give the defeated Germans the power of putting themselves up to auction between the Soviets and the Western democracies. Whatever conclusions may be drawn from these facts—and facts they are—this is certainly not the liberated Europe we fought to build up. Nor is it one which contains the essentials of permanent peace."

The "German Question", and especially the problem of Berlin, continued to be a cause of potential open conflict during the period of the "cold war" in the 'fifties and 'sixties, and it was almost 25 years after the end of World War II before tension in this area began to relax. The survey given in this book traces this development from the Potsdam Agreement of 1945 to the efforts of Chancellor Brandt of the German Federal Republic to find a *modus vivendi* for his country with those of Communist Europe.

ACKNOWLEDGMENTS

This research report is based on information contained in Keesing's Contemporary Archives and derived from a variety of sources, among which the following are the most important:

Frankfurter Allgemeine Zeitung—*Die Welt*, Hamburg—*Welt der Arbeit*, Cologne—*Frankfurter Rundschau*—*Der Tagesspiel*, West Berlin—*Federal Government Bulletin*, Bonn—*Neues Deutschland*, East Berlin—*Soviet Weekly*—*Times*, London—*Guardian*, London—*Manchester Guardian*—*Daily Telegraph*, London—*Neue Zürcher Zeitung*—*Le Monde*, Paris—*New York Times*—*New York Herald Tribune*.

Federal Press and Information Office, Bonn—U.S. Information Service—Soviet Embassy Press Department, London—Polish Embassy Press Department, London.

GERMANY AND EASTERN EUROPE SINCE 1945

From the Potsdam Agreement
to Chancellor Brandt's
"Ostpolitik"

I. FROM THE POTSDAM AGREEMENT TO THE ESTABLISHMENT OF THE TWO GERMAN STATES, 1945–49

1. THE POTSDAM AGREEMENT

World War II formally ended with Germany's unconditional surrender to the Allies on May 7, 1945.

Under an agreement reached at the Yalta Conference in early February 1945 and embodied in the "Crimea Declaration", the four major Allied Powers (the Soviet Union, the United States of America, the United Kingdom and France), each occupied a separate zone in Germany.

On June 5, 1945, the following joint statement was issued on the zones of occupation:

"1. Germany, within her frontiers as they were on Dec. 31, 1937, will, for the purposes of occupation, be divided into four zones, one to be allotted to each Power as follows:

An Eastern zone to the Union of Soviet Socialist Republics;
A North-Western zone to the United Kingdom;
A South-Western zone to the United States of America;
A Western zone to France. . . .

2. The area of Greater Berlin will be occupied by forces of each of the four Powers. An inter-Allied governing authority (in Russian, *Kommandatura*) consisting of four Commandants, appointed by their respective Commanders-in-Chief, will be established to direct jointly its administration."

The Allied Powers defined their policy on the treatment of Germany at the Potsdam Conference of July 17–Aug. 1, 1945, as shown in the following extracts from the Potsdam Agreement.

"The Allied Armies are in occupation of the whole of Germany and the German people have begun to atone for the terrible crimes committed under the leadership of those whom, in the hour of their success, they openly approved and blindly obeyed. Agreement has been reached at this Conference on the political and economic principles of a co-ordinated Allied policy towards defeated Germany during the period of Allied control. The purpose of this agreement is to carry out the Crimea Declaration on Germany. German militarism and Nazism will be extirpated and the Allies will take in agreement together, now and in the future, the other measures necessary to assure that Germany will never again threaten her neighbours or the peace of the world. It is not the intention of the Allies to destroy or enslave the German people. It is their intention that the German people be given the opportunity to prepare for the eventual reconstruction of their life on a democratic and peaceful basis. If their own efforts are steadily directed to this end, it will be possible for them in due course to take their place among the free and peaceful peoples of the world.

"I.   Political and Economic Principles governing the Treatment of Germany in the Initial Period of Allied Control

A.   Political Principles

1. In accordance with the agreement on control machinery in Germany, supreme authority in Germany is exercised, on instructions from their respective Governments, by the Commanders-in-Chief of the Armed Forces of the United States, the United Kingdom, the Soviet Union and the French Republic, each in his own zone of occupation, and also jointly, in matters affecting Germany as a whole, in their capacity as members of the Control Council.

2. So far as is practicable there shall be uniformity of treatment of the German population throughout Germany.

3. The purposes of the occupation of Germany by which the Control Council shall be guided are:

(i) The complete disarmament and demilitarization of Germany and the elimination or control of all German industry that could be used for military production. To these ends:

(a) All German land, naval, and air forces, the S.S., S.A., S.D. and Gestapo, with all their organizations, staffs and institutions, including the General Staff, the Officers' Corps, Reserve Corps, military schools, war veterans' organizations, and all other military and quasi-military organizations, together with all clubs and associations which serve to keep alive the military tradition in Germany, shall be completely and finally abolished in such manner as permanently to prevent the revival or reorganization of German militarism and Nazism.

(b) All arms, ammunition and implements of war, and all spe-cialized facilities for their production, shall be held at the disposal of the Allies or destroyed. The maintenance and production of all air-craft and all arms, ammunition and implements of war shall be pre-vented.

(ii) To convince the German people that they have suffered total military defeat and that they cannot escape responsibility for what they have brought upon themselves, since their own ruthless warfare and the fanatical Nazi resistance have destroyed the German economy and made chaos and suffering inevitable.

(iii) To destroy the National Socialist party and its affiliated and supervised organizations, to dissolve all Nazi institutions, to ensure that they are not revived in any form, and to prevent all Nazi and militarist activity or propaganda.

(iv) To prepare for the eventual reconstruction of German po-litical life on a democratic basis and for eventual peaceful co-operation in international life by Germany.

4. All Nazi laws which provided the basis of the Hitlerite regime or established discrimination on grounds of race, creed or political opinion shall be abolished. No such discriminations, whether legal, administrative or otherwise, shall be tolerated.

5. War criminals and those who have participated in planning or carrying out Nazi enterprises involving or resulting in atrocities or war crimes shall be arrested and brought to judgment. Nazi leaders, influential Nazi supporters and high officials of Nazi organizations and institutions, and any other persons dangerous to the occupation or its objectives, shall be arrested and interned.

6. All members of the Nazi party who have been more than nominal participants in its activities, and all other persons hostile to Allied purposes, shall be removed from public and semi-public office and from positions of responsibility in important private under-takings. Such persons shall be replaced by persons who by their political and moral qualities are deemed capable of assisting in devel-oping genuine democratic institutions in Germany.

7. German education shall be so controlled as completely to eliminate Nazi and militarist doctrines and to make possible the successful development of democratic ideas.

8. The judicial system will be reorganized in accordance with the principles of democracy, of justice under law and of equal rights for all citizens without distinction of race, nationality or religion.

9. The administration of affairs in Germany should be directed

towards the decentralization of the political structure and the development of local responsibility. To this end:

(i) Local self-government shall be restored throughout Germany on democratic principles, and, in particular, through elective councils, as rapidly as is consistent with military security and the purposes of military occupation.

(ii) All democratic political parties with rights of assembly and public discussion shall be allowed and encouraged throughout Germany.

(iii) Representative and elective principles shall be introduced into regional, provincial and State administration as rapidly as may be justified by the successful application of these principles in local self-government.

(iv) For the time being no central German Government shall be established. Notwithstanding this, however, certain essential central German administrative departments, headed by State Secretaries, shall be established, particularly in the fields of finance, transport, communications, foreign trade and industry. Such departments will act under the direction of the Control Council.

10. Subject to the necessity for maintaining military security, freedom of speech, press and religion shall be permitted, and religious institutions respected. Subject likewise to the maintenance of military security, the formation of free trade unions shall be permitted.

B. Economic Principles

11. In order to eliminate Germany's war potential the production of arms, ammunition, and implements of war, as well as all types of aircraft and seagoing ships, shall be prohibited and prevented. Production of metals, chemicals, machinery, and other items that are directly necessary to a war economy shall be rigidly controlled and restricted to Germany's approved post-war peace-time needs to meet the objectives stated in Para. 15.

Productive capacity not needed for permitted production shall be removed in accordance with the reparations plan recommended by the Allied Commission on Reparations and approved by the Governments concerned, or if not removed shall be destroyed.

12. At the earliest practicable date the German economy shall be decentralized for the purpose of eliminating the present excessive concentration of economic power as exemplified in particular by cartels, syndicates, trusts and other monopolistic arrangements.

13. In organizing the German economy primary emphasis shall be given to the development of agriculture and peaceful domestic industries.

14. During the period of occupation Germany shall be treated as a single economic unit. To this end common policies shall be estab-

lished in regard to: (a) mining and industrial production and allocation, (b) agriculture, forestry and fishing, (c) wages, prices and
rationing, (d) import and export programmes for Germany as a whole,
(e) currency and banking, central taxation and Customs, (f) reparations and removal of industrial war potential, (g) transportation and
communications.

In applying these policies account shall be taken where appropriate
of varying local conditions.

15. Allied controls shall be imposed upon the German economy,
but only to the extent necessary: (a) to carry out programmes of industrial disarmament and demilitarization, of reparations, and of
approved exports and imports; (b) to assure the production and
maintenance of goods and services required to meet the needs of the
occupying forces and displaced persons in Germany, and essential to
maintain in Germany average living standards not exceeding the
average of the standards of living of European countries. (European
countries means all European countries excluding the United Kingdom and the Soviet Union); (c) to ensure in the manner determined
by the Control Council the equitable distribution of essential commodities between the several zones so as to produce a balanced
economy throughout Germany and reduce the need for imports;
(d) to control German industry and all economic and financial international transactions, including exports and imports, with the aim
of preventing Germany from developing a war potential and of
achieving the other objectives named herein; (e) to control all German public or private scientific bodies, research and experimental
institutions, laboratories, etc., connected with economic activities.

16. In the imposition and maintenance of economic controls
established by the Control Council, German administrative machinery
shall be created and the German authorities be required to the fullest
extent practicable to proclaim and assume administration of such
controls. Thus it should be brought home to the German people that
the responsibility for the administration of such controls and any
breakdown in them will rest with themselves. Any German controls
which may run counter to the objectives of occupation will be
prohibited.

17. Measures shall be promptly taken: (a) to effect essential
repair of transport; (b) to enlarge coal production; (c) to maximize
agricultural output; (d) to effect emergency repair of housing and
essential utilities.

18. Appropriate steps shall be taken by the Control Council to
exercise control and the power of disposition over German-owned
external assets not already under the control of the United Nations
which have taken part in the war against Germany.

19. Payment of reparations should leave enough resources to
enable the German people to subsist without external assistance.

5

In working out the economic balance of Germany the neccessary means must be provided to pay for imports approved by the Control Council in Germany. The proceeds of exports from current production and stocks shall be available in the first place for payment for such imports.

The above clause will not apply to the equipment and products referred to in Para. 4 (a) and 4 (b) of the Reparations Agreement.

"II. Reparations from Germany

In accordance with the Crimea decision that Germany be compelled to compensate to the greatest possible extent for the loss and suffering she has caused to the United Nations, and for which the German people cannot escape responsibility, the following agreement on reparations was reached:

1. Reparation claims of the U.S.S.R. shall be met by removals from the zone of Germany occupied by the U.S.S.R. and from appropriate German external assets.

2. The U.S.S.R. undertakes to settle the reparation claims of Poland from its own share of reparations.

3. The reparation claims of the United States, the United Kingdom and other countries entitled to reparations shall be met from the Western zones and from appropriate German external assets.

4. In addition to the reparations to be taken by the U.S.S.R. from its own zone of occupation the U.S.S.R. shall receive additionally from the Western zones:

(a) 15 per cent of such usable and complete industrial capital equipment, in the first place from the metallurgical, chemical and machine manufacturing industries, as is unnecessary for the German peace economy and should be removed from the Western zones of Germany in exchange for an equivalent value of food, coal, potash, zinc, timber, clay products, petroleum products and such other commodities as may be agreed upon.

(b) 10 per cent of such industrial capital equipment as is unnecessary for the German peace economy and should be removed from the Western zones to be transferred to the Soviet Government on reparations account without payment or exchange of any kind in return.

Removals of equipment as provided in (a) and (b) above shall be made simultaneously.

5. The amount of equipment to be removed from the Western zones on account of reparations must be determined within 6 months from now at the latest.

6. Removals of industrial capital equipment shall begin as soon as possible and shall be completed within 2 years from the deter-

mination specified in Para. 5. The delivery of products covered by Para. 4 (a) above shall begin as soon as possible and shall be made by the U.S.S.R. in agreed instalments within 5 years of the date thereof. The determination of the amount and character of the industrial capital equipment unnecessary for the German peace economy, and therefore available for reparation, shall be made by the Control Council under policies fixed by the Allied Commission on Reparations, with the participation of France, subject to the final approval of the Zone commander in the zone from which the equipment is to be removed.

7. Prior to the fixing of the total amount of equipment subject to removal, advance deliveries shall be made in respect of such equipment as will be determined to be eligible for delivery in accordance with the procedure set forth in the last sentence of Para. 6.

8. The Soviet Government renounces all claims in respect of reparations to shares of German enterprises which are located in the Western zones of occupation in Germany, as well as to German foreign assets in all countries except those specified in Para. 9 below.

9. The Governments of the United Kingdom and the United States renounce their claims in respect of reparations to shares of German enterprises which are located in the Eastern zone of occupation in Germany, as well as to German foreign assets in Bulgaria, Finland, Hungary, Romania, and Eastern Austria.

10. The Soviet Government makes no claims to gold captured by the Allied troops in Germany. . . .

"III. Territorial Changes

With regard to territorial changes, the Potsdam Conference agreed to the transfer of territory to the Soviet Union and to Poland as follows:

A. Königsberg transferred to Russia

The Conference examined a proposal by the Soviet Government that, pending the final determination of territorial questions at the peace settlement, the section of the Western frontier of the U.S.S.R. which is adjacent to the Baltic Sea should pass from a point on the eastern shore of the Bay of Danzig to the east, north of Braunsberg-Goldap, to the meeting-point of the frontiers of Lithuania, the Polish Republic and East Prussia. The Conference has agreed in principle to the proposal of the Soviet Government concerning the ultimate transfer to the Soviet Union of the city of Königsberg and the area adjacent to it as described above, subject to expert examination of the actual frontier. The President of the United States and the British

Prime Minister have declared that they will support the proposal of the Conference at the forthcoming peace settlement. . . .

B. *Provisional Polish Western Frontier on Oder-Neisse Line*

The following agreement was reached on the western frontier of Poland:
'In conformity with the agreement on Poland reached at the Crimea Conference, the three heads of Government have sought the opinion of the Polish Provisional Government in regard to the accession of territory in the north and west which Poland should receive. The President of the National Council of Poland and members of the Polish Provisional Government have been received at the Conference and have fully presented their views. The three heads of Government reaffirm their opinion that the final delimitation of the western frontier of Poland should await the peace settlement.

The three heads of Government agree that, pending the final determination of Poland's western frontier, the former German territories east of a line running from the Baltic Sea immediately west of Swinemünde, and thence along the Oder river to the confluence of the western Neisse river, and along the western Neisse to the Czechoslovak frontier, including that portion of East Prussia not placed under the administration of the U.S.S.R., and including the area of the former Free City of Danzig, shall be under the administration of the Polish State, and for such purposes should not be considered as part of the Soviet zone of occupation in Germany.' "

The accompanying map, which was issued on Aug. 15 with the authority of the U.S. State Department, shows the final allocation of zones of occupation in Germany between Great Britain, the United States, the Soviet Union and France, reached in agreement among the four Powers. It also shows: (*a*) the provisional western Polish frontier and (*b*) the Soviet-Polish partition of East Prussia, as agreed upon at the Potsdam Conference.

The *British Zone* included the whole of the industrial Ruhr, the Northern Rhineland, Westphalia, Hanover, Oldenburg, Schleswig-Holstein, the great port of Hamburg, the German Frisian islands (Sylt, etc.) and Heligoland. The leading cities, in addition to Hamburg, included Cologne, Essen, Düsseldorf, Duisburg, Dortmund, Wuppertal, Hagen, Solingen, Aachen, Bonn, Münster, Hanover, Brunswick, Wilhelmshaven, Emden, Kiel and Lübeck.

The *Soviet Zone* included Brandenburg west of the Oder, Western Pomerania, Mecklenburg, Saxony, Prussian Saxony, Thuringia and Anhalt. The chief cities (excluding Berlin, which is garrisoned jointly by the four Powers) are Leipzig, Dresden, Halle, Chemnitz, Zwickau, Kottbus, Dessau, Weimar, Jena, Gotha, Magdeburg, Erfurt, Rostock, Wismar, Stralsund and Schwerin.

The delimitation of the Russian Zone implied the withdrawal of British and American troops from areas west of the Elbe, which at the time of Germany's surrender was in effect the line of demarcation between the Red Army and the Anglo-American armies. On July 1

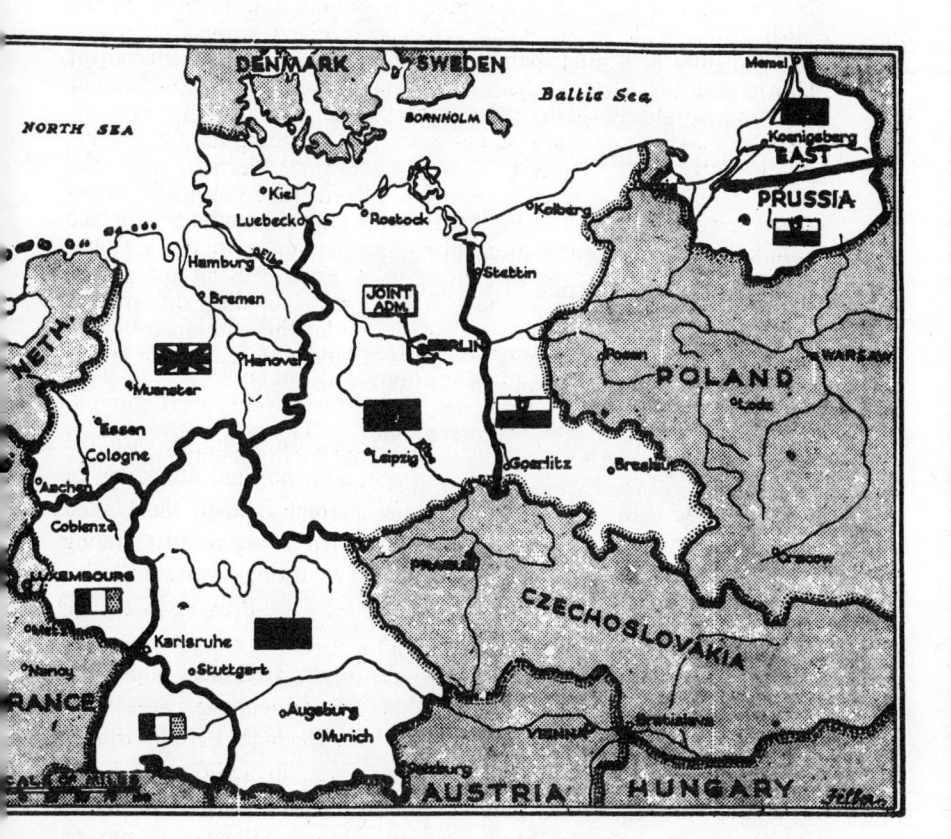

Germany, showing the Allied zones of occupation (indicated by the national flags), the provisional western frontier of Poland, and the Soviet-Polish partition of East Prussia. (*New York Times.*)

the British withdrew from Magdeburg and from part of Mecklenburg, including Wismar and Schwerin, in favour of the Russians.

On the other hand the Russians no longer administered those territories in Eastern Germany which, by the Potsdam decision, were placed within the provisional Polish western frontier and consequently under Polish administration; Breslau, Stettin, Görlitz and Danzig were the leading cities under Polish control, the last-named having had a Polish administration since its capture by the Red Army. The partition of East Prussia gave Königsberg, Insterburg and Tilsit to Russia and Elbing, Allenstein, and Marienburg to Poland.

Allied Control Commission's Declaration to German People— Implementation of Potsdam Decisions

The Allied Control Commission, meeting in Berlin under the chairmanship of Field-Marshal Montgomery on Sept. 25, 1945, issued a proclamation to the German people signed by Field-Marshal Montgomery, General Eisenhower, Marshal Zhukov, and General Koenig announcing "certain additional requirements arising from the complete defeat and unconditional surrender of Germany, with which Germany must comply". The main points of the declaration, a 3,000-word document consisting of a number of articles, were as follows:

Foreign Affairs: The German State ceased to have diplomatic, consular, commercial and other relations with other States, all these matters being in future regulated by the Allies. No foreign commitments of any kind might be entered into by German authorities or nationals without Allied sanction; all German diplomatic and consular officials abroad were recalled, their property and archives being at the Allies' disposal; and no German nationals might leave German territory without express authorization from Allied representatives.

Militarism and Totalitarianism: All military formations and organizations, including the General Staff and the National Socialist Party and all its organs, were "completely and finally" abolished.

Judicial: The German authorities were to furnish all information and documents necessary for the trial of Nazi leaders, and secure the attendance of witnesses; to comply with Allied directions for the repeal of Nazi legislation and for the reform of the German legal, administrative, police and educational systems; and to comply with all Allied directions concerning the property rights, titles and interests of all persons affected by legislation involving discrimination on grounds of race, colour, creed, language or political opinion. In any

10

proceedings before German courts Allied declarations and proclamations would override any provisions of German law inconsistent
therewith.

Finance and Commerce: The German authorities, and all German
nationals, were to hand over to the Allied authorities all gold and
silver in coin or bullion, and all platinum in bullion form, situated in
Germany or possessed by any German bank, company or cartel outside Germany, as well as all foreign notes and coins.

The Allies would exercise such control as they deemed necessary
over all or part of German finance, industry and commerce, detailed
statements of the subjects to which this provision applied being made
to the German authorities from time to time.

Internal Transport, Shipping, and Aircraft: All German merchant
shipping, and the entire German shipbuilding and repair industries,
were to be placed unreservedly at the Allies' disposal, as well as the
entire German inland transport system. The production, possession,
maintenance, or operation by Germans of aircraft of any kind were
prohibited.

War Material: Acquisition and possession of war materials were
forbidden, and the German authorities were to place at the Allies'
disposal "all research, experiment, development and design directly
or indirectly relating to the production of war material".

Evacuation of Germans Abroad: The Allied Control Commission
was to specify the times and conditions governing the evacuation of
German civilians and officials from territories both outside and inside
the 1937 frontiers of Germany, the German authorities making the
necessary arrangements for the reception and maintenance of the
persons evacuated. Withdrawals and evacuations were to be carried
out without damage to property, the Allied authorities to determine
what personal property and effects might be taken by the evacuated
persons.

Costs of Occupation: The German authorities were to comply with
all directions issued by the Allies for defraying the costs of the maintenance, accommodation and transport of the Allied forces and
agencies stationed in Germany, the costs of executing the requirements of unconditional surrender, and payment for relief in whatever
form it might be provided by the United Nations.

Reparations: "The German authorities will carry out for the benefit of the United Nations such measures of restitution, reinstatement,
restoration, reparation, reconstruction, relief, and rehabilitation as the
Allied representatives may prescribe. For these purposes the German
authorities will effect or procure the surrender of such property,
assets, rights, titles and interests; effect such deliveries; carry out such
repair, building and construction work, whether in Germany or elsewhere; and provide such transport, plant, equipment and materials

11

of all kinds, labour, personnel and specialist and other services for use in Germany or elsewhere, as the Allied representatives may direct."

2. DEVELOPMENTS IN THE SOVIET ZONE, 1945–46

In the Soviet zone of Germany, the most important developments during 1945 were (*a*) the admission of "anti-Fascist" political parties, among which the Communist Party and sections of the Social Democratic Party, in April 1946, merged as the Socialist Unity Party (SED), and (*b*) the land reform which ended the domination of agriculture by large land-owners.

Political Parties: Marshal Zhukov, Military Governor of the Russian zone, issued a proclamation on June 10, 1945, restoring political freedom to all anti-Fascist parties, whose programmes—as in the British, U.S., and French zones—had to be presented to the occupation authorities for approval. Free trade unions were also permitted. As a result, the Social-Democratic, Communist, Liberal-Democratic, and Christian Democratic parties emerged as the leading political organizations.

The Communist Party, meeting in Berlin on June 25, issued a manifesto, signed by Wilhelm Pieck and other Communist leaders, which said: "We consider it incorrect for Germany to open the path for implanting the Soviet system because such a path does not correspond with the conditions of the development of Germany at this moment. We consider that the real interests of the German people, under present conditions, dictate another path, that of establishing an anti-Fascist democratic régime and a democratic parliamentary republic with all democratic liberties."

Land Reform and Distribution: One of the most important developments in the Soviet zone was the introduction, under the direction of Herr Hörnle (Secretary for Agriculture in the zonal administration), of far-reaching measures of land reform, aimed primarily at destroying the power of the East Elbian *Junkers*. In a report on Dec. 8, Herr Hörnle announced that the land reform had been completed by the breaking up of great estates in Saxony, Brandenburg, and Mecklenburg (described as "the chief prop of Fascism and militarism"); that about 7,000 large estates aggregating 4,122,000 acres had been redistributed among 281,000 peasants, while 63,000 families deported from Poland and Czechoslovakia had also been settled; and that the average size of the new farms, of which there were over 220,000, was from 17-20 acres. The former *Junker* owners were, it was stated, under detention in camps on Rügen.

Formation of Socialist Unity Party
(Sozialistische Einheitspartei Deutschlands or SED)

A meeting of representatives of the Communist and Social Democratic Parties decided in Berlin on Dec. 21, 1945, to set up a committee to consider proposals for a fusion of the two parties.

A Social Democratic conference in Hanover on Jan. 8, 1946,
almost unanimously rejected such a fusion, and Dr. Kurt Schumacher,
the Social Democrats' leader in the U.S. zone, stated at the same
time that all Social Democrats would reject it, as they regarded the
Communists as the representatives of a foreign imperialist power.

Nevertheless the SED was formally set up in Berlin on April 22
with Wilhelm Pieck of the Communist Party and Otto Grotewohl of
the Social Democratic Party (SPD) as joint chairmen. This fusion
had been preceded by a plebiscite held in the U.S., British and French
zones of Berlin on March 31, 1946, when 82 per cent of the SPD
members taking part voted against fusion. No such plebiscite was
held in the Soviet sector.

3. PARIS CONFERENCES OF 1946

Divergent Views of Soviet Union and Western Powers

At a Conference of the Foreign Ministers of the United States,
the Soviet Union, Britain and France in Paris between April 25 and
May 16, 1946, the problem of Germany was placed on the agenda
at the special request of France.

Mr. Byrnes, the U.S. Secretary of State, criticized the present working of the Potsdam Agreement, saying that, while German industries
were being dismantled in fulfilment of one of the Potsdam decisions,
another important decision, to treat Germany as an economic unit,
was not being fulfilled. In view of the fact that Germany was at
present "split into four water-tight zones" and that the Powers had
"no clear picture before them of the political future of Germany", he
proposed: (1) that, with the aim of clarifying the policies and principles agreed on at Potsdam, the Ministers should appoint special
full-time deputies who would present to the Foreign Ministers at their
next meeting answers to the following questions—(a) whether the
industrial resources of the Ruhr and Rhineland, whatever the political future of those territories, would remain part of the German economic structure, (b) whether German industrial resources would be

used for the benefit of Germany as a whole and not restricted to the limits of the four Zones, (*c*) whether agreement could be reached within 90 days for setting up central German administrations to help keep Germany an economic unit, (*d*) whether the existing zonal boundaries would remain simply as boundaries between areas of military occupation and not as barriers to trade, and (*e*) whether tentative agreement could be reached as regards Germany's western frontiers; (2) that the special deputies should consider the preparation of a draft peace treaty for Germany, in which Germany would be treated as a whole, for consideration by an Allied conference in November next.

Mr. Bevin, the U.K. Foreign Secretary, who supported Mr. Byrnes' viewpoint, likewise declared that Germany should be treated as a whole, and that her frontiers, both eastern and western, should be considered together, adding that other countries, notably Holland and Belgium, should be consulted before any decision was reached as to the future of Western Germany in view of the fact that their economic life would be largely affected by the arrangements made in that area. He stressed in particular the need, when considering the Potsdam decisions in relation to the treatment of Germany as an economic unit, for an examination into German export and import capabilities and into the liability of the Allies for feeding Germany as a whole.

Mr. Molotov, the Soviet Foreign Minister, said he could accept neither Mr. Byrnes' nor Mr. Bevin's proposals, declaring that there was no need for the appointment of special deputies as suggested by Mr. Byrnes and that the Allied Control Council in Berlin was fully adequate to deal with the matters raised. He further stated that Poland, Czechoslovakia and Belgium should be heard in connection with any settlement for Germany. The subject was then dropped and the conference disbanded.

At a further meeting of the Allied Foreign Ministers in Paris between June 14 and July 13, 1946, the question of Germany was again considered.

Mr. Molotov held that 25 years was inadequate to secure Germany's disarmament and demilitarization, and suggested a 40-year period. "Experience," he said, "has shown that the short period of time during which restrictions on Germany's armaments were enforced after the first World War proved absolutely insufficient to prevent Germany's renascence as an aggressive force endangering Europe and the world. Only 20 years had passed since the end of the first World War when Germany unleashed a second World War. It is obvious that the peace-loving nations are interested in keeping her disarmed as long as possible." Continuing, Mr. Molotov demanded reparations from Germany to the Soviet Union to the amount of $10,000,000,000 (£2,500,000,000), declaring: ''The Soviet Government insists that this amount be exacted without fail, because it is but a small portion of the enormous damage suffered as a result of German occupation.'' Mr. Molotov also criticized conditions in the Western zones of Germany, declaring that land distribution had not, as in the Soviet zone, been carried out effectively, that German industrial cartels and monopolies were not being broken up, and that demobilization of the German forces was proceeding slowly; at the same time he protested against an order in the American zone stopping further reparations deliveries. He asked specifically that the Allied Control Council for Germany should set up two special committees, (1) to verify without delay the execution of the Allied Governments' decisions on the disarmament of the German armed forces, (2) to carry out, within a definite time limit, practical measures to eliminate all German industries which could be used for military production and arms manufacture. As regards the political structure of Germany, he argued against a loose federalism such as that advocated by France, pointed out that the Potsdam decision to set up a central German administration had so far not been implemented, and maintained that the Ruhr, though it should be placed under four-Power control, should not be detached from the Reich.

Mr. Bevin, on July 10, emphasized that policy towards Germany should be considered from a short-term and a long-term angle, and said that on the solution of short-term problems depended largely those of a long-term character. There was, he declared, no disagreement on the main purpose of keeping Germany demilitarized and permanently incapable of aggression. On short-term problems Britain stood by the Potsdam decision, and attached the greatest importance to the provision that Germany should, during the occupation period, be treated as a single economic unit. He pointed out that the failure to implement the economic conditions of the Potsdam agreement was costing the British Government $320,000,000 (£80,000,000), and the American Government $200,000,000 (£50,000,000), a year in their zones of occupation; emphasized, with respect to the British zone, that this state of affairs could not continue, and that the expenditure was incurred because the zone was not receiving surplus indigenous resources from other parts of Germany; declared that this was largely due to the refusal of the Soviet authorities to agree to a common export-import programme covering the whole of Germany; strongly criticized the present sharp division into zones, though upholding the principle of a long occupation of Germany; and urged (a) that Germany should be treated as an economic whole, with equitable distribution of indigenous resources throughout the four zones; (b) that surplus resources in any zone should be made available to meet requirements elsewhere in Germany; (c) that if such surplus from current production in any zone was not required, it should be exported as reparations, provided there was no deficit in payments in any other zone. Mr. Bevin strongly refuted Mr. Molotov's suggestion that disarmament was lagging in the British zone, pointing out that the British authorities had recently issued a report showing that demilitarization and demobilization were in fact proceeding apace.

The German question was further discussed at length on July 11, and again revealed fundamental disagreement on major issues, Mr. Molotov resisting suggestions by Mr. Byrnes and Mr. Bevin for an investigation in the Soviet zone, as well as the western zones, on the dismantling of German industrial plants, and for a special body of Ministers' deputies to consider the whole question of Germany. At the same time Mr. Molotov continued to insist on $10,000,000,000 reparations to Russia from Germany. In this connection Mr. Byrnes and Mr. Bevin pointed out that no such figure had been accepted in the past, at Potsdam or elsewhere; that, if it were seriously pressed, all previous estimates and policies about Germany's future would be shattered; and that Soviet insistence on this amount would leave little prospect that Germany could subsist otherwise than by some form of external assistance. Mr. Bevin again urged that Germany should be treated as an economic whole and that surplus resources in one zone should be used to make good deficits in others.

In a speech on U.S. policy towards Germany Mr. Byrnes said in Stuttgart on Sept. 6, 1946:

"The U.S.A. is firmly of the belief that Germany should be administered as an economic unit and that zonal barriers should be obliterated as far as economic life and activity in Germany are concerned. The conditions which now exist in Germany make it impossible for industrial production to reach the levels which the occupying Powers agreed were essential for a minimum German peace-time economy. Obviously, if the agreed levels of industry are to be reached, we cannot continue to restrict the free exchange of commodities, persons and ideas throughout Germany. The barriers between the four zones are far more difficult to surmount than those between normal independent States. The time has come when the zonal boundaries should be regarded as defining only the areas to be occupied for security purposes by the armed forces of the occupying Powers, and not as self-contained economic or political units. That was the course of development envisaged by the Potsdam Agreement, and is the course of development which the U.S. Government intends to follow to the full limit of its authority. It has formally announced its intention to unify the economy of its own zone with any or all of the other zones willing to participate. So far only the British Government has agreed to let its zone participate. . . .

"It is the view of the U.S. Government that the German people, under proper safeguards, should now be given the primary responsibility for the running of their own affairs. More than a year has passed since hostilities ceased. The German people should not be forced to live in doubt as to their fate. It is the view of the U.S. Government that the Allies, without delay, should make clear to the German people the essential terms of the peace settlement which they expect the German people to accept and observe. It is our view that the German people should now be permitted and helped to make the necessary preparations for the setting up of a democratic German Government which can accept and observe those terms. At Potsdam, specific areas which were a part of Germany were provisionally assigned to the Soviet Union and Poland, subject to the final decision of the Peace Conference. At that time, these areas were being held by the Soviet and Polish armies. We were told that Germans in large numbers were fleeing from them and that it would, in fact, because of the feelings aroused by the war, be difficult to reorganize their economic life if they were not administered as integral parts of the Soviet Union, and of Poland. The Heads of Government agreed to support at the peace settlement the Soviet proposal concerning the ultimate transfer to the Soviet Union of Königsberg and the area adjacent. Unless the Soviet Government changes its views on the subject, we will stand by our agreement. With regard to Silesia and other Eastern German areas, their assignment to Poland by Russia for administrative purposes had taken place before the Potsdam meeting. The Heads of Government agreed that, pending the final determination of Poland's western frontier, Silesia and other Eastern German areas should be under the administration of the Polish State and for such purposes should not be considered as part of the Soviet zone in Germany. However, as the Protocol of the Potsdam Conference makes clear, the Heads of Government did not agree to support at the peace settlement the cession of any particular area. The Russians and the Poles suffered greatly at the hands of Hitler's invading armies. As a result of an agreement at Yalta, Poland ceded to the Soviet Union territory east of the Curzon Line. Because of this, she asked for a revision of her northern and western frontiers. The U.S.A. will support such a revision in Poland's favour. However, the extent of the area to be ceded to Poland must be determined when the final settlement is agreed upon."

Mr. Byrne's speech was strongly assailed in France and Poland.

In France, the Press of all shades of opinion condemned it, declaring that the U.S.A. had forgotten the sufferings to which France and other occupied nations had been subjected by Germany and was apparently more concerned with helping Germany to become strong again.

In Poland, the semi-official *Rzeczpospolita* emphasized that Poland would not discuss any revision of her western frontier; the Socialist *Robotnik* declared that "Mr. Byrnes stands before our eyes not only as the champion of Germany but as our obvious adversary"; and the Polish Deputy Premier, Mr. Gomulka, declared on Sept. 8 that the former German territories now absorbed into Poland "are, and always shall remain, Polish". Whilst no official comment on Mr. Byrnes's speech was forthcoming from Moscow, it was strongly criticized by papers in the Soviet zone of Germany, *Neues Deutschland* (organ of the Socialist Unity Party) declaring that the federalization proposals would lead to a "breaking-up of Germany's anti-Fascist forces which would only benefit reaction".

In contrast to Mr. Byrnes's statements in his Stuttgart speech, Marshal Stalin, in an interview on Oct. 23, 1946, declared that the Soviet Union considered the Western frontiers of Poland permanent.

4. MOSCOW CONFERENCE OF MARCH—APRIL 1947

Allies' Failure to reach Agreement

The four Ministers (Mr. Bevin, M. Bidault, Mr. Marshall and Mr. Molotov) met in Moscow from March 10 to April 24, 1947, to consider Allied policy in Germany, including preparations for a German Peace Treaty. No agreement was reached in seven weeks of discussion.

Mr. Molotov, on March 11, alleged that in the Western, and particularly the British, zones the Potsdam decisions for the complete disarmament and demilitarization of Germany were not being implemented, saying that war industries were not being destroyed, that factories were not being dismantled for reparations, and that, especially in the British zone, German military formations were being maintained. He suggested that a plan for the elimination of all Germany's war potential should be drawn up by July 1.

Mr. Bevin, on March 12, strongly refuted these allegations, saying that Mr. Molotov was apparently referring to the *Dienstgruppen,* consisting of 80,000 men under British supervision, of whom 20,000 were employed in clearance of mines and 60,000 in timber work, road repairs, etc., adding that over 3,000,000 *Wehrmacht* members had been disbanded by the British authorities; the *Dienstgruppen,* he said, were being gradually replaced by ordinary civilian labour. He asked Mr. Molotov whether it was true that, as some reports had suggested, German prisoners of war in the Soviet Union ran into millions, and whether some had been induced to join the Soviet forces; also asked for precise information as to the rate at which prisoners in Russia were being repatriated; and drew attention to the steps taken in the British zone to destroy German cartels and monopolies and to bring basic industries under control of the zonal authorities. He also asked for an assurance that the German warships handed over to Russia for destruction had in fact been destroyed, and said that he could not agree to Mr. Molotov's proposal for a joint plan to eliminate German industrial war potential by July 1 until he knew whether Germany was to be treated as an economic whole or not, and until a fresh study had been made of the peace-time level which would be fixed for German industry. Mr. Molotov replied that the Soviet Union was willing to provide figures regarding German prisoners of war if the other Powers would do likewise, and agreed that the Allies should strive for the economic unity of Germany. He was not, however, satisfied as to the steps taken in the Western zones for the abolition of cartels and monopolies.

Statements on the progress of denazification in the British, American, and Soviet zones were made on March 13 by Mr. Bevin, Mr. Marshall, and Mr. Molotov.

During the following week the questions principally under discussion were the economic organization of Germany and reparations.

Mr. Marshall proposed on March 17 that the Foreign Ministers should issue a directive to the Allied Control Council to undertake the merger of the four zones into a single economic unit.

Mr. Molotov, on the same day (March 17), put forward the Soviet Union's reparations claims. After emphasizing that the Potsdam decisions required that Germany should be treated as a single economic unit, he declared that the economic fusion of the British and U.S. zones, and the French action in unilaterally separating the Saar from the rest of Germany, constituted an infringement of those decisions and presented the Allied Control Council with a *fait accompli.* He advocated that the Ruhr should be placed under four-Power control.

On March 18 the TASS Agency published a hitherto secret protocol on German reparations which was signed at Yalta by President Roosevelt, Mr. Churchill and Marshal Stalin.

19

This stated that reparations from Germany were to be exacted by the following methods: (1) "bulk removal within 2 years from the surrender of Germany of Germany's natural wealth (equipment, machine-tools, ships, rolling-stock, German investments abroad, shares of industrial, transport, navigation, and other German enterprises, etc.), these removals to be carried out chiefly for the purpose of destroying Germany's war potential"; (2) annual deliveries of goods from current production for a period to be fixed; and (3) the use of German labour. The protocol showed that the American and Soviet delegations agreed that the total sum for reparations under (1) and (2) should be $20,000,000,000 of which 50 per cent should go to the U.S.S.R. The British delegation, however, was of opinion that pending consideration of the reparations question by a Reparations Commission which, under the protocol, was to sit in Moscow, no definite figure should be mentioned.

The protocol was referred to by Mr. Molotov on March 18 when justifying Russia's reparations claims, but its validity was opposed both by Mr. Marshall and Mr. Bevin.

Mr. Marshall, in a short statement, declared that the U.S. Government held the view that the Yalta agreement on reparations had been superseded by the Potsdam agreement, which spoke only of reparations in the form of industrial capital equipment and German assets abroad. "At Potsdam", he said, "the idea of attempting to fix a dollar value on property to be removed from Germany was dropped."

On March 21 the Foreign Ministers turned to consideration of the German political structure.

Criticizing the British, American and French plans for the federalization of Germany, Mr. Molotov maintained that such plans aimed at the destruction of Germany as an independent State, which the Soviet Union could not approve.

The Soviet proposals were set forth as follows:

"The task of creating a provisional political organization for Germany must be solved on the basis of the following principles:

(*a*) The German political system must have a democratic character, and the organs of power must be formed on the basis of democratic elections.

(*b*) The Hitlerite centralization of the State administration, which destroyed the *Landtage* and the autonomous administration of the *Länder*, must be liquidated, and the decentralization of administra-

20

tion be restored which existed before the Hitler régime, with the restoration of the *Landtage* and the setting up of two all-German Chambers.

(c) A Provisional German Government must be set up which, while ensuring the political and economic unity of Germany, would simultaneously assume responsibility for the fulfilment of Germany's obligations to the Allies.

On the basis of the above it is proposed:

(1) As a first step toward the formation of a Provisional German Government, to establish central German administrative departments on finance, industry, transport, communications and foreign trade, in accordance with the Potsdam decisions.

(2) To charge the Control Council with working out a provisional democratic Constitution, drawing into the work the democratic parties, the free trade unions and other anti-Nazi organizations, and representatives of the *Länder*.

(3) To hold elections in accordance with the provisional German Constitution, after which a Provisional German Government should be formed.

(4) In accordance with the Potsdam decisions, to charge the German Government as one of its basic tasks with the eradication of the remnants of militarism and Fascism, the thorough democratization of Germany, and the realization of measures for the restoration of German economy, as well as the unconditional fulfilment of obligations to the Allies.

(5) A permanent Constitution must be approved by the German people."

On the State structure of Germany the proposals were as follows:

"(1) Germany should be restored as a unified democratic Republic, with an all-German Parliament consisting of two Chambers and an all-German Government, while ensuring the Constitutional rights of the *Länder* comprising the German State.

(2) The President of the German Republic should be elected by Parliament.

(3) Over the whole territory of Germany an all-German Constitution established by Parliament should operate, and in the *Länder* the Constitutions established by the *Landtage*.

(4) The German Constitution, as well as the Constitutions of the *Länder,* should be based on a democratic foundation.

(5) The all-German Constitution and the *Land* Constitutions should ensure the free formation and activity of all democratic political parties, trade unions and other public democratic organizations and institutions.

(6) All German citizens, without distinction of race, sex, language and religion, should be ensured democratic rights, including freedom

of speech, press, religion, public meeting and association, by the all-German Constitution and the *Land* Constitutions.

(7) The Parliament and the *Landtage* will be elected on the basis of a universal, equal and direct electoral law with secret voting and the proportional system.

(8) The local government organs, district and communal councils, will be elected on the same democratic basis as the *Landtage*."

On March 22, in view of the fact that no appreciable progress had been made on the German question, the Council of Foreign Ministers set up a sub-committee consisting of General Lucius Clay (U.S.A.), Lt.-Gen. Sir Brian Robertson (Britain), Mr. Vyshinsky (Russia), and M. Hervé Alphand (France) to co-ordinate and compare all the proposals which had been submitted by the different delegations. On March 25 the Foreign Ministers considered the procedure to be adopted for calling the peace conference with Germany, but failed to reach agreement on the procedure to be followed and the States to take part.

On April 10 the Council of Foreign Ministers turned to consideration of the German-Polish frontier.

Revision of the existing provisional frontier in Germany's favour was advocated both by Mr. Marshall and Mr. Bevin, who quoted statements by Marshal Stalin at the Potsdam Conference to show that he did not consider the present frontier as final and that the definitive settlement should be made at the Peace Conference. Mr. Marshall agreed that the southern part of East Prussia, and industrial Upper Silesia, should remain Polish; emphasized, however, that the division of the remaining territory, which was largely agricultural, required consideration of the needs of both the Polish and German peoples; and proposed that a Boundary Commission should be set up representing the "Big Four" and Poland which should recommend (1) revision of the pre-war Polish-German frontier which would compensate Poland fairly for the territory ceded to Russia east of the Curzon Line; (2) "economic arrangements appropriate for assuring that raw materials and heavy industrial resources from the area in question which are vital to the European economy shall fairly serve that need, including particularly the need of Poland." Continuing, Mr. Marshall emphasized that the final frontier should be drawn so as to avoid unnecessary and unjustified economic upset, to minimize irredentist pressure in Germany and to ensure that it would not be a cause of later international friction, and declared: "The new frontiers must be adequate to give Poland resources at least as great as she had before the war and capable of maintaining her peoples at a good standard of life. But the needs of Germany have also to be considered. Before the war the German area now under provisional Polish control contributed over a fifth of Germany's total food supply. If Germany must in the future import two-fifths or more of her food supply from abroad, the German economy will have to be industrialized to an even greater extent than before the war, or Germany will become a congested slum in the centre of Europe. The five to six million Germans who have been evacuated from areas in the east will, for the most part, have to depend on industrial employment for their livelihood. I agree with M. Bidault that there is danger in requiring an eventual German population of over 66,000,000 to live within the confines of a smaller Germany."

Mr. Bevin said that after the last war many people felt that the Polish frontiers were pushed too far east, that now there was a danger that they might be pushed too far west, and that the British delegation at Potsdam had felt "grave doubts" in agreeing even to the provisional Oder-Neisse frontier. Like Mr. Marshall, he drew attention to the danger of an overcrowded and over-industrialized Germany in a restricted area, and urged that Upper Silesia should be incorporated into Poland but that the agricultural area eastwards from Stettin should be returned to Germany.

Mr. Molotov declared that the Soviet Government, as stated by Marshal Stalin himself, considered the present Polish-German frontier as final; maintained that the Peace Conference should merely "formalize" the agreement made at Potsdam; pointed out that according to the Allied Control Council a total of 5,678,936 Germans had been removed from the disputed areas and replaced by 5,000,000 Poles; and asked how this could now be reversed.

The Polish Foreign Office, on the same day (April 10), issued a statement uncompromisingly rejecting the suggestions put forward by Mr. Bevin and Mr. Marshall and declaring that the contested territory was essentially Polish in spite of long years of attempted Germanization; that Poland must have priority over Germany in rehabilitation; and that concessions to Germany, so far from removing the danger of German aggressive aspirations, would only be a stimulus to Germany's spirit of revenge.

Mr. Marshall, on April 14, proposed that the Foreign Ministers should immediately appoint plenipotentiaries for the negotiation of a four-Power treaty to ensure German disarmament and demilitarization for a 40-year period after the signing of the peace treaty, as had been proposed by his predecessor, Mr. Byrnes. This was agreed to by Mr. Bevin and M. Bidault, but Mr. Molotov asked that the proposed treaty should be broadened to include a number of other matters, e.g., denazification, four-Power control of the Ruhr, land reform, the liquidation of cartels and reparations deliveries. Mr. Marshall argued that these matters had no place in the treaty proposed, which was intended only as a first and basic step to ensure the disarmament and demilitarization of Germany. After further discussion the Foreign Ministers' Council ceased consideration of German problems on April 15 without having arrived at any agreed decisions.

5. MUTUAL ACCUSATIONS BETWEEN SOVIET AND U.S. COMMANDERS, 1947

Colonel Tulpanov, a Soviet political official, in an address to a Socialist Unity Party conference in East Berlin on Sept. 21, 1947, stressed "the fundamental difference between our Socialist State and the capitalist character of the other occupation Powers"; called on the party to "fight ruthlessly its internal enemies and German reactionaries"; and also violently attacked Britain and the U.S.A., declaring that "American monopolistic capital" was "trying to whip up Germany into the bloody massacre of imperialist war".

General Lucius Clay, the American C.-in-C. in Germany, thereupon announced at a Press conference on Oct. 28, that the American Military Government would abandon its policy of avoiding political controversies and would launch a campaign against Communism throughout the U.S. zone of Germany.

Hitherto, General Clay explained, it had been the American practice to be silent in public on the subject of Soviet attacks against the U.S.A. However, the reply of Marshal Sokolovsky, the Soviet C.-in-C., to his (General Clay's) protest against Colonel Tulpanov's speech had been "unsatisfactory". "I do not intend," General Clay continued, "to enter into a series of recriminations and charges between the U.S.A. and the U.S.S.R., but I feel strongly about the U.S. form of democracy and its attributes of freedom of speech and the Press, and equally strongly that such freedoms do not exist under Communism. I intend to defend the principles in which we believe." Emphasizing that the new policy had been decided in Berlin and had not been discussed during his recent visit to Washington, General Clay declared: "I am not to be put in a position where the German people have the opportunity of hearing about only one system of Government. We have always tried to spread the advantages of our type of democracy. We have tried to avoid making unfavourable comparisons with other types of political philosophy, but we will no longer avoid them."

Colonel Gordon E. Textor, chief of the Information Control Division of the U.S. Military Government, stated the same day that the American propaganda offensive against Communism would be inaugurated within a week; that it would be directed through the Military Government newspaper *Neue Zeitung,* the three official magazines, and the five American-controlled radio stations at Berlin, Bremen, Frankfurt, Stuttgart and Munich; that the radio networks would be assisted by three short-wave transmitters capable of covering the whole of Germany, including the Soviet zone; and that the campaign would be directed by a central planning board.

On Nov. 9 it was authoritatively stated in Berlin and Düsseldorf that the British Military Government had decided against joining the U.S. campaign.

Marshal Sokolovsky's Attacks on Allied Policy in Western Germany

Marshal Sokolovsky, the Soviet member of the Allied Control Council, made a statement on Nov. 21, 1947, at a meeting of the Council strongly criticizing American, British and French policy in the Western zones of Germany. The statement, published in the *Tägliche Rundschau* (organ of the Soviet Military Government), was made on the eve of Marshal Sokolovsky's departure for London as a member of the Soviet delegation at the conference of the Council of Foreign Ministers meeting to consider the German and Austrian peace treaties.

The statement commenced by alleging that "practically no progress" had been made in the demilitarization of Western Germany by the American, British and French authorities, and went on to allege *inter alia* that "remnants of German military formations are being retained in the British zone under the guise of so-called labour corps"; that military training of German youth, by American instructors, was proceeding in the U.S. zone in various sports organizations despite the Allied Control Council's ban on all such training; that elimination of German military and naval bases was proceeding with slowness in the Western zones (Marshal Sokolovsky alleging in this connection that the British authorities had not demilitarized the Kiel naval base); and that "on the pretext of the need to develop peacetime economy" the American and British authorities had left intact important sections of German armaments plants scheduled for demolition, e.g., parts of the Bayerische Motorenwerke factory at Munich and of the Messerschmitt plant at Augsburg, declaring that "lists of factories scheduled by the American and British authorities for elimination consist mostly of enterprises of secondary importance". "The sabotage of demilitarization and the preservation of war potential in both the British and American zones," said the statement, "could have no other purpose than the conversion of these zones into a military base of Anglo-American imperialism in the heart of Europe" Allegations were also made that the decartelization measures decided on by the Allied Control Council were not being effectively implemented in the Western zones.

The statement was strongly critical of the bi-zonal economic fusion in Western Germany, maintaining that in effecting this arrangement the British and U.S. authorities had acted contrary to the decisions of Potsdam and Yalta, and saying that "the only explanation (of the bi-zonal fusion) is that the overriding purpose was to eliminate German industry from the world market as a rival of the British and American monopolies, while at the same time preserving Germany's war potential". Continuing, the statement said: "Viewed from the political aspect, all the above-mentioned separatist measures of the British and American authorities constitute nothing but the realization of a programme aimed at splitting Germany. These actions, which lead to the liquidation of Germany's unity, found their continuation in the Marshall Plan, which aims at subjugating the economy of the American, British and French zones to the American and British monopolies, and at converting these regions of Germany, primarily the Ruhr, into a military and industrial base of Anglo-American imperialism in Europe with a view to utilizing it as a means of pressure on European States which refuse to be enslaved by the American-British monopolies."

General Clay, the U.S. member of the Control Council, at a press conference on Nov. 23 before leaving for London to attend the Foreign Ministers' conference, said that he did not wish to make countercharges or to indulge in recriminations since he did not wish to add to the "strains and stresses" of the London Conference, but declared that the Russian statement constituted a "misrepresentation of known facts".

Establishment of German Economic Council and Executive Council

The establishment of a *German Economic Council,* in connection with the economic fusion of the British and U.S. occupation zones in Western Germany, in May 1947, and the subsequent setting up of an *Executive Council,* approximating to the status of a Cabinet, for the two zones, were strongly objected to by the Soviet Union.

The agreement on the economic fusion of the U.S. and British zones with effect from Jan. 1, 1947—which had been signed on Dec. 2, 1946—contained a preamble stating that the fusion "should be regarded as the first step towards the achievement of the economic unity of Germany as a whole" in accordance with the principles laid down at Potsdam, and that both the U.S.A. and Britain were ready to enter into discussions with the Soviet Union and France with a view to extending the arrangements to their zones.

At a meeting of the Allied Control Council in Berlin on Jan. 20, 1948, however, Marshal Sokolovsky insisted that the decisions were a contravention of the Potsdam Agreement, had been carried out without the consent of the Allied Control Council, and were a step towards the further splitting of Germany and the setting up of a West German State; he consequently asked for the abandonment of the scheme, and at the same time alleged that three German politicians in particular bore responsibility for the acceptance of the Anglo-American proposals—Dr. Konrad Adenauer, the Christian Democratic leader in the Western zones, Dr. Kurt Schumacher, the Social-Democratic leader in the West, and Herr Jakob Kaiser, chairman of the Christian Democratic Union. The U.S. and British members of the Council strongly denied Marshal Sokolovsky's allegations both in respect of the alleged political implications and of the alleged part played by the German politicians named, reiterating that the programme was purely economic in character.

The Economic Council, increased to 104 members in February 1948, was in effect an economic Government for the U.S. and British occupation zones, and its establishment was accompanied by that of a *Länderrat* (Upper House), in which each *Land* (or State) was represented by two members.

German *Länder* Governments had first been set up in the U.S. zone in September-October 1945, and in the British and French zones during 1946.

6. GROWING TENSION BETWEEN SOVIET UNION AND WESTERN POWERS, 1948

The Soviet delegation on the Allied Control Council for Germany, headed by Marshal Sokolovsky, walked out of the Council at its meeting in Berlin on March 20, 1948, after accusing the Western Powers of undermining the quadripartite control of Germany and of seeking to make the position of the Control Council impossible.

The walk-out arose from a memorandum presented to the Council by Marshal Sokolovsky in connection with a Conference of the Western Powers on Germany held in London in February. The memorandum protested at the fact that the conference had been called without the knowledge of the Control Council; complained that the Council had not been informed of the results of the conference despite the fact that it had dealt with such important subjects as the State structure of Germany, control of the Ruhr, reparations and the inclusion of Western Germany in the Marshall plan; emphasized that the questions discussed in London fell within the competence of the Council as the supreme authority for Germany set up by the Allies under the Potsdam Agreement; and called on the American, British and French representatives to state the directives they had received as a result of the London Conference.

The American, British and French members of the Control Council (Generals Clay, Robertson and Koenig), while agreeing that the Soviet request was legitimate, pointed out that the London Conference had made recommendations without taking decisions; stated that they had received no directives as a result of the London Conference; and emphasized that the Council had received no information regarding developments in the Soviet zone of Germany. Marshal Sokolovsky thereupon read a statement which, after describing the response to the Soviet request as "unsatisfactory", accused the Western Powers of pursuing a policy directed against the Potsdam Agreement and "contradicting four-Power decisions and the purposes of the occupation of Germany".

Despite the Soviet walk-out, the Soviet Military Government, on March 23, sent out notices convening meetings of the Control Council's sub-committees for the following day. The American, British and French authorities, however, announced that they could not participate in any further quadripartite meetings (excluding those of the four-Power *Kommandatura*, which was not affected by the Soviet action and continued to function normally as the Allied administering body for Berlin) until the Council had met to consider the position created by Marshal Sokolovsky's announcement of March 20. On March 30, when the Council was due to have met for a routine meeting, Marshal Sokolovsky made no attempt to convene such a meeting, it being stated in Berlin that the Council would not meet until April 10, when it would be convened by General Clay as chairman for the month.

Mr. Marshall, in a press statement in Washington on March 25, emphasized that the U.S.A. "intends to continue to fulfill its responsibilities as a member of the Control Council and as a joint occupant of the city of Berlin"; he added that for three years the U.S. Government had attempted to secure the effective political and economic unification of Germany, declared that these attempts had been frustrated to a large extent by the tactics of the Soviet representative on the Control Council, and said that the Soviet boycott of the Council "could only be construed as an intention, which the U.S.A. does not share, to renounce efforts to obtain four-Power agreement on policies for Germany".

The Soviet Military Government informed the U.S., British and French authorities in Berlin on March 31 that, as from April 1, new and more stringent traffic regulations would come into force with respect to road and rail traffic between the Western zones and Berlin.

It was stated that nationals of the Western Powers, whether military or civilian, would, with their families, have to present documents certifying their identity and the fact that they belonged to the Allied administration in Berlin; that these documents must be presented at the frontiers of the Soviet zone; that persons not connected with the Allied administration would, when entering or leaving the Soviet zone, have to be in possession of passes issued "in accordance with previously established procedure"; that goods belonging to the U.S., British, and French military authorities and intended for the Western zones would be allowed through specified "check points" only with the authorization of the Soviet authorities in Berlin; that all property, exclusive of personal property, would be examined at these "check points"; and that the new regulations would be applicable to traffic both entering and leaving Berlin, whether by road or rail. The U.S., British, and French authorities, in a reply the same evening, protested against the new regulations as a unilateral violation of established procedure.

In consequence of the new Soviet regulations, all Allied rail traffic between Berlin and Western Germany was cancelled on April 1 by

29

the U.S. and British authorities and replaced temporarily by special air services for passengers and freight, using the Gatow and Tempelhof airfields (by quadripartite agreement the American, British, and French authorities shared an international 10-mile-wide air "corridor" between Helmstedt, on the Anglo-Soviet zonal frontier, and Berlin). The previous night the Russian authorities had established "check points" at various places on the Helmstedt-Marienborn-Berlin *Autobahn* and at Marienborn, on the Soviet side of the zonal border, had held up 2 American and 1 British military trains after Russian officials had been refused permission to board the trains to inspect passengers' identification papers. In Berlin itself the Russians also instituted "check points" on roads leading into the U.S., British, and French sectors, traffic being stopped and papers examined.

The situation remained unchanged the following day, when the French authorities fell into line with the Americans and British and likewise cancelled all trains between the French zone and Berlin. Food trains, however, continued to reach Berlin from Western Germany without interference by the Soviet authorities, whilst U.S. and British *Dakotas*, also without interference, continued to fly quantities of foodstuffs to Gatow and Tempelhof for the British and American sectors of Berlin. Conferences took place in the latter city between Generals Clay and Robertson, whilst after a 10-hour meeting of the *Kommandatura* the Soviet representative, Colonel Yelisarov, announced that the "check points" between the Soviet sector of Berlin and the other Allied sectors would be abolished.

American troops in Berlin took their first retaliatory action on April 3 when they threw a cordon round the headquarters of the railway system for the Soviet zone (which is in the U.S. sector) and refused to allow any Russians to enter the building. In addition, U.S. troops established a "check point" on the main road between Berlin and Potsdam, where Marshal Sokolovsky, the Soviet Military Governor, had his residence, causing Russian officials to make a long détour. When the Soviet authorities protested to General Clay, the latter replied that he could take no note of the protest until the "free entry of American trains into Berlin" had been solved.

In correspondence with the Soviet Deputy Military Governor, released on April 4, Brigadier-General Gailey (U.S. Army) maintained that at a meeting in Berlin on June 29, 1945, between Marshal Zhukov and British and American officials, it had been "clearly understood that the U.S. forces in Berlin would have free and unrestricted use of the established corridors," and that it was only on this understanding that the American troops had withdrawn at the time from such areas as Saxony and Thuringia, subsequently incorporated in the Soviet zone.

A certain abatement of the tension occurred on April 4, when the U.S. cordon round the railway building in Berlin was withdrawn after Soviet guards had evacuated the premises, contacts between the U.S. and Soviet officers and officials being of an amicable nature. Furthermore, it was reported from Berlin that special British bus services between the city and Helmstedt were running normally, that road traffic was not seriously affected by the Russian traffic control measures, and that travellers on the *Autobahn* were encountering no delay provided their papers were in order. From Frankfurt-am-Main it was announced that the U.S. special air services to Berlin were being suspended since freight trains were getting through to the city without trouble.

7. GERMAN CURRENCY REFORM AND THE BERLIN BLOCKADE, 1948

Currency Reform in Western Zones of Germany

On June 18, 1948, in a proclamation by the British, French and U.S. Military Governors, currency reform measures were announced for the three Western zones of Germany.

The long-awaited reform was the result of discussions between the British, U.S., and French Governments, carried on almost continuously since Marshal Sokolovsky had walked out of the Allied Control Council on March 20, and followed previous long but fruitless efforts to obtain a four-Power agreement covering the whole of Germany. The new scheme, which had been discussed by Generals Clay, Robertson, and Koenig with the Prime Ministers of the *Länder* and the German Bi-zonal Economic Council and *Länderrat* in Frankfurt on June 14–15, followed the main lines agreed upon by the experts of the four Powers before the discussions ended with the Russian walkout for political reasons.

In his letter to Marshal Sokolovsky of June 18 informing the latter of the decision to introduce a new currency into the British Zone, Sir Brian Robertson, the British Military Governor, declared after referring to unsuccessful four-Power negotiations on currency reform: "The economy of the British Zone is suffering acutely from the evils of inflation and of economic stagnation which our quadripartite proposals for financial reform were designed long ago to eradicate, and I feel that I am not justified in waiting any longer before taking remedial measures." After stating that the British sector of Berlin remained unaffected "in view of the special circumstances of quadripartite government" in the city, which he had "no wish to disturb unless this becomes unavoidable", General Robertson expressed the hope that it would "be possible for the occupying Powers to agree at an early date to reintroduce a single currency for the whole of Germany, as well as to take the other measures of economic unity to which we have always attached so much importance". Similar letters had been sent to Marshal Sokolovsky by Generals Clay and Koenig.

On June 18 Marshal Sokolovsky, the Soviet Military Governor, issued a proclamation denouncing the separate currency reform in the Western zones; prohibiting the circulation of the new currency in the Soviet zone and in Berlin—which, the proclamation said, "lies in the Soviet zone and forms economically part of it"—and likewise prohibiting the import both of old and new notes from the Western zones into the Soviet zone and Berlin; and threatening punishment for any such imports, which would be regarded as "economic sabotage".

The Western currency reform, Marshal Sokolovsky declared, was being carried out "against the wishes and interests of the German people" and "in the interests of the American, British, and French monopolists", adding: "The separate currency reform completes the splitting of Germany. It is a breach of the Potsdam decisions and the control mechanism for Germany which envisaged the treatment of Germany as an economic whole. The Western Powers are trying to excuse themselves by claiming that it was impossible to agree on a four-Power currency reform for the whole of Germany. By this move they are simply trying to deceive public opinion. In the Control Council the Soviet representatives took every possible opportunity of reaching agreement on a common currency reform. It is clear that the Western representatives used the discussions in the Control Council as a cover, under cloak of which they prepared in secret for separate currency reform. The American, French, and British monopolists in the Western zones are supported in their policy of splitting Germany by the big German capitalists and the *Junkers* who helped Fascism to power and prepared the second world war. Separate currency reform strengthens the political and economic position of these reactionaries and harms the working people. The introduction of two currencies in Germany will mean that trade relations within the country will be destroyed. Inter-zonal trade will become in practice trade between two separate States, since two different currencies will be used. The prerequisites for free passenger traffic and goods traffic between the occupation zones will be destroyed."

Soviet Restrictions on Inter-zonal Traffic

Prior to the above announcement the Soviet authorities in Berlin had ordered that all passenger train traffic between the Soviet and the Western zones would be halted at midnight of June 18–19, that all motor traffic for Berlin on the Hanover-Berlin *Autobahn* (the only road link between Berlin and the West) would also be stopped, and that nobody would be allowed to cross the frontier into the Soviet zone on foot.

The German Economic Commission for the Soviet Zone, in a statement issued the same night, also denounced the separate currency reform in the Western zones as "a decisive step towards the splitting of Germany" and "the final breach of the agreement reached at Potsdam that Germany should be treated as an economic unit", declaring that the Western areas would as a result become "mere colonies of American capital"; it added that Berlin would "cease to be the capital of Germany" and that its "untenable position" could "only be resolved by a close link with the Eastern zone of Germany", and appealed "to the entire German people not to allow themselves to be misused for these anti-democratic and anti-German policies".

A meeting of the Allied *Kommandatura* in Berlin, which General Ganeval, the French Commandant, had called for June 18 to discuss the currency reform, was cancelled after the Russians had announced that they would not attend it.

The Berlin City Assembly, in an extraordinary session on June 19, approved a resolution, supported by the Social Democrats, Christian Democrats, and Liberal Democrats, and against Socialist Unity Party opposition, protesting against Marshal Sokolovsky's proclamation and the "*Diktat* of the Soviet military authorities", and asking that Berlin should not be included in a one-sided currency reform for either Western or Eastern Germany, and that only an agreed four-Power reform measure should be applied in the city; the resolution rejected the contention of Socialist Unity Party members that Berlin should be joined economically with the Soviet zone as the city's "natural hinterland".

General Robertson replied on June 31 to a letter by Marshal Sokolovsky of the previous date in which the latter had described the Western currency reform as "illegal", had claimed sole Soviet responsibility for currency matters in Berlin, and had announced a forthcoming currency reform in the Soviet zone, including Berlin.

On the same day the Russian-licensed German news agency reported that the German Economic Commission for the Soviet zone had, at a special meeting, passed a currency reform law for that zone and had submitted it to Marshal Sokolovsky for his approval. Mr. Maletin, chief of the financial division of the Soviet Military Government, in a statement published by the official *Tägliche Rundschau*, repeated Marshal Sokolovsky's contention that there could be only one currency in Berlin and that Berlin was economically part of the Russian zone, and declared that the attempt to introduce two currencies would meet with determined counter-measures from the Soviet authorities. Nevertheless, later the same night Marshal Sokolovsky informed General Robertson that he would accept the latter's invitation for four-Power talks on currency reform for Berlin. This conference, attended by financial experts from the four Allied Powers, took place on June 22, but subsequent U.S. and British statements said that it had "produced no positive results" and that no further meeting had been arranged.

As a counter-move the British, U.S., and French authorities in Berlin announced in proclamations later the same morning that the new *Deutsche Mark* would be introduced into the Western sectors of the city, and that Russian orders that the Soviet zone currency reform should apply to the whole of Berlin were "null and void" in the Western sectors, the announcement describing the action of the Soviet Military Administration as "an attempt to usurp for itself the authority to dominate the economic affairs of Berlin". At the same time all banks and shops in the Western sectors, except food and chemists' shops, were ordered to close and a temporary moratorium declared.

Soviet Decision to introduce New Currency into Eastern Zone and Berlin

In the early hours of June 23 Marshal Sokolovsky issued an order introducing currency reform both for the Soviet zone and for Greater Berlin.

In view of the acute conflict between the Western Powers and the Soviet Union, and the technical difficulties arising for the population out of the divergent measures of both sides, great tension prevailed in Berlin, especially since, through the Soviet restrictions on inter-zonal traffic, all barge traffic from the British to the Soviet zone had stopped since June 21, road traffic had remained completely blocked, and the movement of U.S. military freight trains to Berlin had been suspended since that date by orders of General Clay, following the Russian refusal to pass a train carrying U.S. army supplies. Only a small number of British goods trains were able to enter the Soviet zone at the Russian check-point at Marienborn, the city being other-wise completely isolated from the West except for air traffic, both the British and U.S. military authorities instituting on June 21 special air services to and from the city to maintain passenger traffic and the flow of army supplies.

Marshal Sokolovsky, in a proclamation to the people of Berlin on June 24, declared that the Allied *Kommandatura* in Berlin had "to all intents and purposes" ceased to exist as an organ for the administration of the city, as it was no longer a suitable intrument for the control of currency reform.

Meanwhile the situation grew more serious when rail traffic on the one-track line from Berlin to Helmstedt, the Western Allies' only rail link with the West, was cut off by the Russians in both directions early on June 24 on the pretext of "technical trouble", thus stopping even the limited movement of British goods trains to Berlin which had still been maintained, and cutting off all further supplies for the British, U.S., and French forces and the German population of their sectors. At the same time the Russian authorities in Berlin announced, ostensibly because of shortage of coal owing to "insufficient supplies from the West", that there would be no further deliveries of electric current from the Soviet sector and from the Soviet zone to the Western sectors, and stopped all coal, food, and other supplies from the Soviet sector to the three Western sectors, including deliveries of fresh milk.

The British authorities ordered on June 25 the complete cessation of all goods traffic between the British and Soviet zones, thus depriving the latter of all coal and steel supplies from the West; it was stated that this measure had been taken because the Russians had failed to return 16,000 goods trucks to the Western zones.

General Clay declared at Frankfurt on June 24, 1948, that "nothing short of an act of war can drive us out of Berlin", adding that no Soviet "pressure tactics" nor any new East German Government which might be created by the Russians would halt the U.S.-British-French project to develop Western Germany politically and economically.

Mr. Bevin gave a brief account of the events in Berlin in a statement to the House of Commons on June 25.

He confirmed that the Soviet decision to introduce a new currency into their zone and Berlin was acceptable to the Western Powers if the Soviet zone currency was to be issued in Berlin under four-Power control—a condition in accord with all the existing four-Power agreements—but that the Russians did not accept this and insisted that the issue should be under their sole control. "To have accepted this," Mr. Bevin declared, "would have been tantamount to the abandonment of our rights in Berlin. The Western Powers have had no alternative but to introduce a special currency in the Western sectors of Berlin distinct from the new currency in the Western zone. . . . There will therefore be very shortly two currencies in circulation in Berlin".

General Robertson on June 26, 1948, sent a letter to Marshal Sokolovsky calling on the latter to restore communications between the city and the Western zones immediately.

Saying that he had not hitherto protested against the various restrictions because they had been described by the Soviet military administration as temporary and as designed to protect the currency of the Soviet zone pending the introduction of currency conversion in the latter, General Robertson continued: "Now, however, I learn that the Soviet military administration has announced that all traffic on the railway between Helmstedt and Berlin is suspended on technical grounds and that no alternative route will be made available. Simultaneously, barge traffic on the canals has been stopped. Under arrangements in force among the occupying Powers, the British authorities are responsible for contributing supplies for the population of Berlin. I am able and willing to continue to discharge this responsibility provided that my freight trains and barges are free to pass between the Western zones and Berlin. The interruption of essential freight cannot be held to be a measure necessary to protect the currency position in the Soviet zone. I therefore request that arrangements be made by the Soviet administration to restore normal traffic communications to and from Berlin immediately. I wish to make it clear that if they are not so restored, and undue and avoidable suffering is thereby inflicted upon the German population, it will be because I have been deprived by you of the means to sustain them."

The Soviet authorities in Berlin issued on June 29 the text of Marshal Sokolovsky's reply.

Saying that the Soviet measures were only temporary, the letter, which was conciliatory in tone but was, on the other hand, modified by many qualifying passages, reiterated that the Soviet military authorities had been forced to take these measures to avoid endangering the economy of the Soviet zone; stated that the reopening of frontier traffic for Germans with valid inter-zonal passes had already been ordered; but insisted that the restrictions for motorcar traffic on the *Autobahn* must be maintained to prevent the illegal import of money from the West. With regard to railway traffic on the Helmstedt-Berlin line, Marshal Sokolovsky said that it had to be stopped because of technical difficulties, that the Soviet transport authorities would, however, take all measures to remove these difficulties, that Berlin's food supplies would last for several weeks, and that it was hoped that it would meanwhile be possible to restore railway communications "as soon as possible".

On June 30 Mr. Bevin made a further statement in the House of Commons on the situation in Berlin. In his speech he rejected the Soviet argument that the fault lay with the Western Powers who had repudiated the Potsdam agreement. Mr. Bevin stated *inter alia*:

"It is the Soviet Government which has consistently failed to operate the Potsdam agreement, and destroyed, up to the moment, the possible unity of Germany. . . .
"The Potsdam agreement provided for the economic unity of Ger-

many, but this was constantly rejected by the Soviet Union at conferences in Paris, Moscow and London. There is a claim by Russia that they should share in the administration of the Ruhr, and some people thought that this had been agreed upon at Potsdam. There is no agreement of the kind. We have declined to put the Ruhr under four-Power control while the rest of Germany is to be left to single-Power control. The Council of Foreign Ministers in London last year demonstrated to the full that while the Soviet Government kept up lip-service to German unity, they were determined to destroy it by continuing to insist on policies and programmes which made unity impossible. . . ."

On the same day Mr. Marshall issued the following statement in Washington:

"We are in Berlin as a result of agreements between the Governments on the areas of occupation in Germany, and we intend to stay. The Soviet attempt to blockade the German civilian population of Berlin raises basic questions of serious import, with which we expect to deal promptly. Meanwhile the maximum use of air transport will be made to supply the civilian population."

At a meeting of the Allied Chiefs of Staff on July 1 Colonel Kalinin, Soviet Chief of Staff in the Berlin *Kommandatura*, announced that Russian representatives would no longer attend any meetings of any organizations of the *Kommandatura*.

The main reason for the Soviet decision was the introduction by the Western Powers of the new Western currency in Berlin, "a city which is part of the economic system of the Soviet zone".

A statement issued by the British H.Q. in Berlin denied the validity of the Soviet contention that the introduction of the currency reform in the Western sectors gave the Russians the right to declare the *Kommandatura* to be dissolved.

After consultations between the Western Powers, British, U.S., and French Notes on the Russian blockade of Berlin, all in similar terms, were handed to the Soviet Ambassadors in London, Washington and Paris on July 8. The British Note, whose text was published on July 10, said *inter alia*:

"The rights of the U.K. as a joint occupying Power in Berlin derive from the total defeat and unconditional surrender of Germany. The international agreements undertaken in connection therewith by the

Governments of the U.K., U.S.A., France, and the Soviet Union defined the zones in Germany and the sectors in Berlin which are occupied by these Powers. They established the quadripartite control of Berlin on a basis of friendly co-operation, which H.M. Government earnestly desire to continue to pursue. These agreements implied the right of free access to Berlin. . . .

"Berlin is not a part of the Soviet zone but is an international zone of occupation. . . ."

The Note went on to declare that H.M. Government "will not be induced by threats, pressure or other actions to abandon" the right of free access to Berlin. The Note concluded:

"H.M. Government are ready . . . to participate in negotiations in Berlin among the four Allied Occupying Authorities for the settlement of any question in dispute arising out of the administration of the city of Berlin. It is, however, a pre-requisite that the lines of communication and the movement of persons and goods between the U.K., the U.S., and the French sectors in Berlin and the Western zones shall have been fully restored."

The Soviet replies, being in similar terms to the British, U.S. and French Notes, were delivered in London, Washington and Paris on July 14.

The Soviet Note reiterated its former statement that "the Berlin situation has arisen as a result of the violation by the U.S.A., Great Britain and France of the agreed decisions adopted by the four Powers in relation to Germany and Berlin, expressed in the carrying out of a separate currency reform, the introduction of special currency notes for the Western sectors of Berlin, and the policy of dismembering Germany. . . ."

The Soviet Note continued:

"The U.S. Government declares that it occupies its sector of Berlin by right deriving from the defeat and surrender of Germany, referring in this connection to the four-Power agreement in relation to Germany and Berlin. This only confirms that the existence of the abovementioned right in relation to Berlin is bound up with the obligatory fulfilment by the Powers of the quadripartite agreements concluded between them in relation to Germany as a whole. In accordance with these agreements, Berlin was envisaged as the seat of the supreme authority of the four Powers occupying Germany, and agreement was reached on the administration of Greater Berlin under the direction of the Control Council. Thus the agreement on quadripartite administration of Berlin is an inseparable part of the agreement on quadripartite administration of Germany as a whole. When the U.S.A., Britain and France, by their separate actions in Western Germany, destroyed the system of quadripartite administration of Germany and began to create in Frankfurt a capital for a Government of Western Germany, they thereby undermined the legal basis on which rested their right to participate in the administration of Berlin. . . ."

The Note concluded:

"As regards the declaration of the U.S. Government that it will not be induced by threats, pressure or other actions to abandon its right to participate in the occupation of Berlin, the Soviet Government does not intend to enter into a discussion of this declaration, for it has no need of a policy of pressure since, by violation of the agreed decisions on the administration of Berlin, the above-mentioned Governments are themselves reducing to nought their right to participation in the occupation of Berlin. The U.S. Government, in its Note of July 6, expresses readiness to begin negotiations between the four Allied Powers for an examination of the situation in Berlin, but passes over in silence the question of Germany as a whole. While not objecting to negotiations, the Soviet Government deems it necessary to declare that it cannot link the start of these negotiations with the fulfilment of any preliminary conditions, and that, secondly, quadripartite negotiations could only be effective if they were not confined to the question of the administration of Berlin, since this question cannot be separated from the general question of quadripartite control in relation to Germany."

The Soviet Notes thus made it clear that the Soviet blockade of the Western sectors of Berlin was entirely based on political grounds, dropping the reasons which had earlier been given, viz., "technical difficulties" and the necessity of "repairs" to rail and river communications.

On July 9 and 13 further Russian road traffic restrictions were announced. On July 20 the Soviet authorities declared that "in the desire to alleviate the position of the population" they would, on instructions from the Soviet Government, themselves accept responsibility for feeding the population of the whole of Berlin. The announcement also said that the Soviet Government had for this purpose made available 100,000 tons of bread grain and other foodstuffs from Russian stocks, and that measures had been taken by the Soviet military authorities to buy further food in Poland, Czechoslovakia, and other countries.

A British official statement on the same day described the Russian offer as "pure propaganda", and pointed out that there was no food shortage in the Western sectors, and that, on the contrary, the British and U.S. air lift was bringing in the equivalent of the entire consumption of these sectors.

The lack of understanding between the Government of the Soviet Union and the Western Powers was shown in a speech by Mr. Churchill on July 10 when he referred to the Berlin crisis as follows:

"The free democracies of the West are awaiting the Soviet reply to the joint Note that has been sent to the Kremlin. This Note makes it plain that we will not allow ourselves to be blackmailed out of Berlin by the inhuman attempts of the Soviet Government to starve the 2,500,000 Germans in the British and American zones. They were our enemies in the war, but we are now responsible that they should not be treated with cruel severity. If we were to yield on this grave issue we should, in my opinion, destroy the best chance now open to us of escaping a third world war. With Russia we are dealing not with a great nation that can expres sits free will, but with 13 men in the Kremlin who have made themselves the masters of the brave Russian people and who rule them with far more dictatorial authority than was ever shown by any Russian Tsar since the days of Ivan the Terrible. No one can tell what these 13 oligarchs in the Kremlin will do. . . . The safest course for us and other Western democracies is to pursue, as we are doing, a plain, fair and straightforward policy based on our undoubted rights and on those instincts of humanity which forbid us either to leave the Germans of Berlin, who have courageously stood with us, to Soviet vengeance or to let them all be starved to death."

Introduction of Eastern "Deutsche Mark"

A decree issued by Marshal Sokolovsky on July 23 announced that all stamped Eastern mark notes were to be exchanged on July 25–27 against notes in a new currency to be issued by the "German Issue Bank" (*Deutsche Notenbank*); the latter was the new name conferred on the German Issue and Transfer Bank (*Deutsche Emissions- und Girobank*) when the power to issue notes was vested in it by the German Economic Commission on July 22, its seat being at the same time transferred from Potsdam to Berlin.

The British, French and U.S. military authorities in Berlin announced on July 24 that they agreed to accept the new Soviet currency in the Western sectors of the city, but the policy followed by the Russians in carrying out the exchange operation led to serious financial and economic difficulties, both on the part of the Berlin city administration and of industrial and commercial undertakings situated in the Western sectors, and compelled the Western Commandants to take special financial emergency measures.

8. WESTERN POWERS' NEGOTIATIONS WITH THE SOVIET UNION ON THE BERLIN QUESTION, 1948

On July 26, 1948, Mr. Bevin presided at the Foreign Office in London over a conference of U.S. and British representatives to consider the joint reply to the Soviet Note of July 14 on the Berlin crisis.

It was announced on July 28 that complete agreement had been reached in the London discussions on the form and method of the three-Power reply to the U.S.S.R. and on the joint approach to be made to that country by Britain, the U.S.A. and France in connexion with the Berlin situation.

Following conversations at the Kremlin with Mr. Molotov on July 31 and with Marshal Stalin on Aug. 2 on the Berlin situation, Western envoys in the Soviet capital—Mr. Frank Roberts (personal representative of Mr. Bevin), General Bedell Smith (U.S. Ambassador) and M. Yves Chataigneau (French Ambassador)—on the instructions of their Governments, had a series of further meetings with the Soviet leaders at intervals during the ensuing six weeks.

As a result of these meetings, an agreed four-Power directive was sent to the Allied Commanders-in-Chief in Germany—Marshal Sokolovsky and Generals Clay, Robertson, and Koenig—instructing them to discuss certain technical problems. Accordingly, the Commanders-in-Chief and their deputies met on Aug. 31 at the Allied Control Council's H.Q. in Berlin for the first time since Marshal Sokolovsky walked out of the Control Council on March 20. It was authoritatively stated that the four-Power directive embodied an agreement that the blockade should be lifted and that the Eastern mark should be the single currency for Berlin, with the proviso that it should be subject to four-Power authority, the Commanders-in-Chief being given the task of transferring this agreement in principle into a workable technical arrangement. Until Sept. 7 the Military

Governors continued to meet daily, but on the latter date the talks were discontinued pending fresh instructions from the Governments concerned.

On Sept. 20 the Berlin situation was considered by Mr. Bevin, Mr. Marshall, and M. Schuman at a meeting at the *Quai d'Orsay*, and on Sept. 22 identical Notes, drawn up in Paris, were sent to the Soviet Ambassadors in Paris, London and Washington for transmission to Moscow.

The Soviet reply to these notes was presented in the Western capitals on Sept. 25. It said in part:

". . . As a result of negotiations held in Moscow in August, the four Governments reached an understanding that the following measures would be carried out simultaneously, provided the four Commanders-in-Chief in Berlin reached an agreement concerning their practical implementation.

"First, the recently introduced restrictions of transportation and trade between Berlin and the Western zones, as well as of movement of freight to and from the Soviet zone, would be lifted.

"Secondly, simultaneously with this, the German mark of the Soviet zone would be introduced as the only currency for Berlin, while the Western mark would be withdrawn from circulation in Berlin.

"At the same time agreement was reached to the effect that the introduction of the Soviet zone mark as the only currency for Berlin, and a number of functions in regard to the subsequent regulation of currency circulation in Berlin, would be under quadripartite control.

"The four Commanders-in-Chief were accordingly instructed to work out concrete measures for implementing the understanding achieved in Moscow, and the continuation of negotiations in Moscow on other issues connected with the situation in Germany was envisaged.

"Negotiations among the four Commanders-in-Chief, held in Berlin early in September, were not completed in view of the fact that the U.S.A., Britain and France referred certain differences that arose among the Commanders-in-Chief for joint examination with the Soviet Government in Moscow. The above-mentioned differences concerned three issues on which the Soviet Government's stand is as follows:—

"1. The Soviet Government insists on the establishment of control by the Soviet Command over the transportation of commercial cargoes and passengers by air between Berlin and the Western zones, and similarly over transportation by rail, water and highway. The air routes cannot remain outside this control, since the four Governments reached an understanding that the agreement should envisage the establishment of appropriate control over money circulation in Berlin and trade between Berlin and the Western zones.

"2. The Soviet Government believes it necessary strictly to adhere to the agreement reached by the four Governments in Moscow concerning the quadripartite financial commission and its functions with regard to the introduction and circulation of a single currency in Berlin. It cannot agree to such an extension of function of the financial commission as would result in the latter's intervention in the regulation of money circulation in the Soviet zone as a whole.

"3. The Soviet Government expressed consent to the wish of the Western Governments concerning the establishment of quadripartite control over Berlin's trade with the Western zones and third countries, including the issuing of appropriate licences, thus removing the difference which existed on this issue.

"All the above clearly shows the real attitude of the Soviet Government on the subject of the regulation of the situation in Berlin on a mutually acceptable basis. In these conditions it depends upon the U.S.A., Great Britain and France whether the negotiations will be disrupted or whether a satisfactory agreement will be reached by the four Powers."

On the following day (Sept. 26) Mr. Bevin, Mr. Marshall and M. Schuman met again at the *Quai d'Orsay* to consider the Soviet Note of Sept. 25, issuing a joint statement that in view of the fact that the Soviet Government, "in violation of the understanding between the four Powers, has chosen to make public unilaterally its version of the negotiations", and in view of the unsatisfactory nature of the Soviet Note, the Governments of the U.S.A., Great Britain and France had decided to refer the Berlin dispute to the U.N. Security Council.

A resolution, presented to the Security Council by its President on Oct. 25, 1948, received 9 votes in favour but was opposed by the U.S.S.R. and the Ukraine. The Soviet veto meant that the resolution could not be carried, and, after debate, the Council adjourned.

A comprehensive account of the Western Powers' negotiations with the U.S.S.R. on the Berlin question was contained in a U.S. White Paper—a 25,000-word document—issued on Sept. 27. It showed that after the envoys' first meeting with Marshal Stalin on Aug. 2 there was hope of reaching agreement; that these hopes, however, diminished at subsequent meetings with Mr. Molotov; that agreement in principle was reached, when Marshal Stalin was again consulted on Aug. 23, on the setting up of a four-Power Financial Commission in Berlin but that when the discussions moved to Berlin new Soviet demands were put forward which led to the final breakdown of negotiations.

9. ESTABLISHMENT OF SEPARATE MUNICIPAL GOVERNMENTS IN EAST AND WEST BERLIN, 1948

Six days before municipal elections were due to take place in the Western sectors of Berlin, Marshal Sokolovsky intervened personally for the first time in the Berlin crisis when, on Nov. 29, 1948, he addressed identical letters to Generals Robertson, Clay and Koenig, the text of which was published the same day by the Soviet News Bureau.

The letter said that the Soviet Command "cannot refrain from drawing attention to the dangerous measures which are being carried out in the Western sectors of Berlin to disorganize and split the City administration, and which are being supported by the Military Commandants of the Western sectors", and continued: "As you are aware, the Soviet military authorities have repeatedly drawn attention to the necessity of preserving the unity of Berlin, the capital of Germany, and have insisted on the carrying out of unified democratic elections in the whole of Berlin. These proposals have, however, been allowed to go unnoticed." The letter alleged that the elections of Dec. 5 would not be carried out "with due attention to democratic freedoms but under conditions of force and of police persecution of democratic organizations", and that they aimed at "the removal of the unified municipal adminstration and the creation of a separate City Council in the Western sectors so that the Western military authorities will be able to order and dictate as they please without control, and to support openly reactionary elements in the City". "Those elements in the *Magistrat*," it declared, "which are aiming at a split, and enjoy the support of certain occupation officials, have for a long time been attempting to disorganize the work of the *Magistrat* as a unified municipal organ. They are trying to exclude democratic representatives in close touch with the broad masses of the Berlin population. The Soviet Command does not intend to show tolerance to the anti-democratic elements of the Berlin *Magistrat* in their activities for the splitting of German administrative organizations in Berlin, and will continue to contribute to the preservation of the unity of Berlin and the creation of conditions which assure to all democratic representatives normal activity in the Berlin organizations of self-government."

On the same day Herr Ottomar Geschke, a vice-chairman of the City Assembly and one of the leaders of the Socialist Unity Party, issued a proclamation calling a meeting of the Assembly at the State Opera House (in the Soviet sector) for the following day (Nov. 30), and this meeting, attended by only the 26 SED members of the City Assembly, unanimously passed a resolution by the Berlin "democratic *bloc*" repeating the latter's allegations that the majority of the members of the *Magistrat* had disregarded the "most elementary vital interests" of the City and neglected their duties under the City Constitution, declaring the existing *Magistrat* "deposed", and setting up a new provisional *Magistrat* "to safeguard unified administration and supplies and to prepare general democratic elections in the whole of Berlin".

This new *Magistrat* elected Herr Fritz Ebert (son of the late Friedrich Ebert, the first President of the Weimar Republic) as provisional Chief Burgomaster, and took over the Berlin municipal headquarters in the Soviet sector.

The setting-up of this *Magistrat* in East Berlin was strongly condemned by the British and U.S. Commandants in Berlin as a "flagrant violation of the existing Constitution of Berlin and of quadripartite agreements pertaining to the City".

Generals Robertson, Clay and Koenig replied to Marshal Sokolovsky's letter on Nov. 30 in identical terms, strongly refuting the latter's charge that the Western Powers were responsible for the present situation.

In the municipal elections held on Dec. 5, 1948, in the Western sectors of Berlin, 86.2 per cent of the electorate took part, and the percentages gained by the three contending parties were

Social Democrats	64.4
Christian Democrats	19.4
Liberal Democrats	16.1

Only 3 per cent of the votes cast were invalid.

The elections thus represented an overwhelming vote of confidence in the anti-Communist parties, and in addition gave the Social Democrats, who had taken the most determined stand against Soviet policy, an absolute majority in the new City Council.

The Soviet authorities announced on the same date that they regarded the elections as "unconstitutional" and the election results as "invalid", and that they would not recognize the newly elected Western *Magistrat*.

The new City Assembly for the Western sectors on Dec. 7 elected Professor Ernst Reuter as Chief Burgomaster. With the setting-up of new administrative headquarters for the Berlin municipality in the American sector on Dec. 6, the division of the city into two separately administered parts was completed.

On Dec. 21 the three Western Commandants announced at a special meeting at the *Kommandatura* building in the U.S. sector of Berlin that the Allied *Kommandatura* would "resume its work forthwith", thus replacing the quadripartite *Kommandatura* by a "tripartite" one. This was the first meeting of the *Kommandatura* since the Soviet representative walked out of that on June 16, 1948.

10. THE 1949 "OCCUPATION STATUTE" FOR THE WESTERN ZONES OF GERMANY

The Foreign Ministers of the U.S.A., Britain and France announced in Washington on April 8, 1949, that they had reached complete agreement on "a whole range of issues now pending in Western Germany", and in particular on the text of an "Occupation Statute".

This Statute, published on April 10 and communicated the same day to the West German Parliamentary Council in Bonn, stated in its first paragraph:

"During the period in which it is necessary that the occupation continue, the Governments of France, the U.S.A. and the United Kingdom desire and intend that the German people shall enjoy self-government to the maximum possible degree consistent with such occupation. The Federal State and the participating *Länder* shall have, subject only to the limitations of this instrument, full legislative, executive, and judicial powers in accordance with the Basic Law and with their respective constitutions."

In its second paragraph, the Statute specified the areas reserved by the occupation authorities, notably disarmament and demilitarization; foreign affairs; and displaced persons and refugees.

The three Western Commandants in Berlin signed on May 14,

1949, a new charter, which came into immediate effect, granting wide legislative, executive, and judicial powers to the City Assembly of Western Berlin, and extending to the City Assembly a similar measure of responsibility to that conferred on the German Parliamentary Council in Bonn by the Occupation Statute for Western Germany.

11. ELECTIONS FOR "PEOPLE'S CONGRESS" IN THE SOVIET ZONE, 1949

Elections for a new "People's Congress" were held on May 15–16 in the Soviet zone of Germany and the Soviet sector of Berlin, voting being for a single list of candidates drawn up by the "People's Council", and no opposition candidates being permitted. The electors were required merely to give an affirmative or negative answer as to whether they were in favour of "German unity and a just peace", and to approve the single list of candidates presented. The candidates were drawn from the various Communist-dominated parties of the Eastern Zone, notably the Socialist Unity Party (SED), and included a number of nominees of the recently formed "National Democratic Party". The American, British and French authorities in Berlin, in a joint statement on April 22, declared that no facilities would be given in Western Berlin for the "People's Congress" elections, on the grounds that the results of these elections were "already settled in advance", that the various "parties" presenting candidates were in every case dominated by the Communists, and that the Soviet authorities had, in December 1948, declined the opportunity offered for a free election in which all Berlin citizens could participate.

The new "People's Congress" of 1,525 members, claiming to be "representative of the German people", met on May 29–30 at the State Opera House in the Soviet sector of Berlin. It approved a "Constitution" for the whole of Germany which had been passed by the "People's Council" on March 19, and issued a manifesto calling for a peace treaty based on the Yalta and Potsdam principles, the reestablishment of German unity through a Provisional German Government, participation by such a government in the peace treaty negotiations, and the abolition of zonal barriers to trade, currency, and transport.

12. SOVIET AGREEMENT WITH WESTERN ALLIES ON LIFTING OF BERLIN BLOCKADE AND OF WESTERN COUNTER-BLOCKADE, 1949

The Tass Agency announced on April 26, 1949, that the Soviet Government had made known to the U.S. Government its willingness to raise the blockade of Berlin if the Western Powers counter-measures were lifted simultaneously and a definite date set for a meeting of the Council of Foreign Ministers to discuss the whole question of Germany.

Dr. Jessup, the U.S. representative at the United Nations, who saw President Truman on the same day, confirmed reports that he had had conversations at Lake Success with Mr. Malik about the Russian blockade of Berlin, and said that the Russians had offered to end the blockade on certain conditions.

Following further diplomatic activities and after a meeting of the delegates of the four Powers in New York on May 4, it was officially announced that complete agreement had been reached "on all the main questions of principle"; that "all restrictions imposed in Germany which have been the subject of conversations" would be mutually lifted, though certain details were still under consideration; and that a meeting of the Council of Foreign Ministers would be held "after an interval" to "consider questions relating to Germany and problems arising out of the situation in Berlin, including also the question of currency in Berlin". The *communiqué* added that the four representatives were "hopeful that the remaining matters of detail can be adjusted in a very short period of time", and that if these details were speedily arranged a further *communiqué* embodying the agreement would be issued simultaneously in the four countries on the following day. Later it was officially announced that the blockade would be lifted on May 12 and that the Foreign Ministers would meet on May 23.

The final *communiqué* issued in London, Paris, Moscow and Washington on May 5 read as follows:

"The Governments of France, the Soviet Union, the United Kingdom and the United States have reached the following agreement:

"(1) All restrictions established since March 1, 1948, by the Soviet Government on communications, transport, and trade between

Berlin and the Western zones of Germany, and between the Eastern and Western zones, will be lifted on May 12, 1949.

"(2) All restrictions imposed since March 1, 1948, by the Governments of France, the U.K. and the U.S.A., or any of them, on communications, transport, and trade between Berlin and the Eastern zone, and between the Western and Eastern zones of Germany, will also be removed on May 12, 1949.

"(3) Eleven days subsequent to the removal of the restrictions referred to in paragraphs (1) and (2), namely, on May 23, 1949, a meeting of the Council of Foreign Ministers will be convened in Paris to consider questions relating to Germany and the problems arising out of the situation in Berlin, including also the question of currency in Berlin."

The Soviet blockade of Berlin, and the Western Powers' counter-measures, ended at one minute past midnight on May 12, 1949, when British and American lorries and military vehicles crossed the Soviet zonal frontier and proceeded to Berlin without interference along the Helmstedt-Marienborn-Berlin *Autobahn*. Soon afterwards the first British-U.S. train from Bielefeld and Frankfurt to Berlin likewise crossed the zonal border at Marienborn station.

The joint U.S.-British airlift, which had since June 26, 1948, carried more than 2,000,000 tons of essential supplies (mainly coal, food and liquid fuel) to West Berlin, did not end until Sept. 30, 1949.

13. ESTABLISHMENT OF FEDERAL REPUBLIC OF GERMANY, 1949

The German Parliamentary Council authorized under the London Six-Power Agreement of 1948 to draw up a Basic Law (Provisional Constitution) for a German Federal Republic comprising the 11 States (*Länder*) of the American, British and French zones, commenced its work in Bonn on Sept. 1, 1948, under the presidency of Dr. Konrad Adenauer, leader of the Christian Democratic Union in Western Germany.

The Council finally approved the Basic Law drafted by it on May 8, 1949, by 53 votes to 12 after the rejection of a Communist proposal that the Parliamentary Council should accept an invitation from the "People's Council" in the Soviet zone for conversations on the restoration of German unity. The Basic Law was specifically approved as a Constitution of a provisional character pending the adoption of a definitive Constitution for a unified Germany.

The Federal Republic of Germany was officially proclaimed by Dr. Adenauer at Bonn in the afternoon of May 23, 1949.

The Federal Republic was the first democratic State to emerge in Germany since the fall of the Weimar Republic and comprised about two-thirds of the population and about half the territory of the former German Reich, the population being about 45,000,000.

On Sept. 12, 1949, the Federal Convention (consisting of the members of the *Bundestag* and the *Landtage* of the German States) meeting in Bonn, elected Professor Theodor Heuss, the leader of the Free Democratic Party, as the first President of the Federal Republic.

The *Bundestag*, on the proposal of the Federal President, on Sept. 14 elected Dr. Adenauer, the leader of the largest Parliamentary party, as Federal Chancellor.

A Coalition Cabinet was formed by Dr. Adenauer from Christian Democrats, Free Democrats, and members of the German Party. After announcing the members of his Cabinet, Dr. Adenauer made a statement to the *Bundestag* on the Government's policy.

Turning to external affairs, Dr. Adenauer declared that Germany could not accept the Oder-Neisse line as its eastern border, this declaration being cheered by the whole House with the exception of the Communist members. Recalling that at Potsdam the U.S.A., Britain and Russia had decided to defer the final settlement of the western frontier of Poland until the peace conference, he declared: "In no circumstances can we agree to the one-sided annexation of this territory by Russia and Poland. . . . We shall never cease to prosecute, in a proper and legal manner, our claims to this territory." As regards Germany's relations with her neighbours, he said: "We are sincerely prepared to live in peace with our Eastern neighbours, particularly Russia and Poland, but we expect them to acknowledge our rights, and to allow our fellow-countrymen in the Soviet zone and Berlin, as well as further east, to live in freedom according to their tradition, upbringing and convictions."

Dr. Kurt Schumacher, the Social-Democratic leader, like Dr. Adenauer, declared that Germany could not accept the Oder-Neisse line as her definitive Eastern frontier.

Soviet and "Satellite" Protests to U.S.A., Britain and France

The Soviet Government presented a Note to the U.S., British and French diplomatic representatives in Moscow on Oct. 1, 1949, declar-

51

ing that the formation of the West German Government represented "not only a violation of obligations for preserving the unity of Germany, but also of obligations for the conclusion of a peace treaty with Germany, inasmuch as the formation of a separate West German State leads to delay in the conclusion of a peace treaty".

The Note recapitulated the decisions taken by the Western Powers in Germany since 1946 and reiterated the previously expressed Soviet view that all these developments constituted a violation of the Potsdam decisions. "For its part", the Note continued, "the Soviet Government has conducted an unswerving struggle against the splitting of Germany, insisting, in accordance with the decisions of the Potsdam Conference, on the setting up of all-German economic agencies as the first step in the formation of an all-German democratic Government. The Soviet Government considers it necessary to draw attention to the extremely serious responsibility which rests with the U.S. Government in connexion with the policy in Germany pursued by the U.S.A. jointly with Great Britain and France, which has led to the formation in Bonn of an anti-popular separate Government that adopted a hostile attitude to the decisions of the Potsdam Conference on the democratization and demilitarization of Germany. . . . The Soviet Government considers it necessary to state that a new situation has been created in Germany which renders of particularly great importance the fulfilment of the tasks for the restoration of the unity of Germany as a democratic and peace-loving State, and for ensuring the fulfilment by Germany of the obligations laid on her by the Potsdam Agreement of the four Powers."

The Hungarian Government on Oct. 4, and the Romanian, Czechoslovak, Polish, and Albanian Governments on Oct. 6, likewise sent Notes of protest to the Western Powers at the establishment of the Western German Government.

14. PROCLAMATION OF GERMAN DEMOCRATIC REPUBLIC

The decision to form a "German Democratic Republic" in Eastern Germany was announced in Berlin on Oct. 5, 1949, after a meeting of the Presidium of the Soviet-sponsored "People's Council" and leaders of the "bloc of democratic parties in the Soviet zone", held under the chairmanship of Herr Wilhelm Pieck, the veteran Communist leader and joint chairman of the Socialist Unity Party. The announcement issued after the meeting was as follows: "The formation of a separate Western German State, the Occupation Statute, the dismantling operations which are contrary to international law, the refusal of a peace treaty, and the control exercised by the High Commissioners . . . have revealed the serious national emergency brought about in Germany by the dictatorial policy of the Western Powers. To safeguard the national interests of the German people by national self-help, the German People's Council, which was elected by the German People's Congress on May 30, 1949, is hereby requested to declare itself a Provisional People's Chamber, under the articles of the Constitution adopted by the People's Congress and Council, and to create a constitutional Government of the German Democratic Republic. The Presidium of the German People's Council has decided to convene the Council in Berlin on Oct. 7, 1949."

The "German People's Council" accordingly met in the former Air Ministry in Berlin on Oct. 7 and unanimously adopted the following proclamation: "The German People's Council proclaims itself the Provisional People's Chamber (*Provisorische Volkskammer*) in accordance with the Constitution of the German Democratic Republic adopted by the Council on March 19, 1949, and approved by the German People's Congress, on May 30, 1949."

The Council also unanimously adopted a manifesto stating:

"On the basis of the Constitution approved by the German People's Congress in Berlin by all parties and mass organizations which participate in the German People's Council, the German Democratic Republic has been established unanimously. The Provisional German Government which will be formed in accordance with the Constitution will seek as its main aim the struggle for peace and the unity and sovereignty of Germany.

"Four and a half years have passed since the guns became silent. The hopes of the German people for the preservation of their economic and political unity, for the democratic anti-militarist transformation of Germany, and for the conclusion of a peace treaty, solemnly promised to them in the Potsdam Agreement, have been deceived. Germany has been split as a result of the imperialist policy of the Western Powers. . . . The German people has been refused a peace treaty. Instead, the Western zones have had foisted on them the Occupation Statute, which maintains the occupation for an indefinite period. By the creation of the separate Bonn State the splitting of Germany has been completed.

"The separate Bonn Government has the task of including Western Germany in the Atlantic Pact military *bloc*, and of converting the youth of the separate State into mercenary troops of American imperialism. In order to fulfil this task, German Fascism and militarism are openly increasing in Western Germany, and revanchist ideas are revived, a warning of which has been given by the first sittings of the Bonn Parliament."

Appealing to "every German man and woman, irrespective of party and outlook" and without regard to "political or social position", to support the aims of the "National Front of Democratic Germany", the manifesto outlined the aims of the Front *inter alia* as follows:

"(1) Restoration of the political and economic unity of Germany by the elimination of the separate West German State, . . . and the formation of an all-German Government of the German Democratic Republic.

"(2) The speediest conclusion of a just peace treaty with Germany. Withdrawal of all occupation troops from Germany within a short time after the signing of the peace treaty.

"(3) Complete and unconditional recognition of the Potsdam decisions on the democratization and demilitarization of Germany, as well as of Germany's obligations in regard to other peoples, stipulated in those decisions.

"(4) The restoration of the complete sovereignty of the German nation, with recognition of the right to an independent foreign policy and to independent foreign trade. Free and independent development of the German Democratic State and the German people after the conclusion of the peace treaty.

"(5) An irreconcilable struggle against the instigators of a new war in Germany. Prohibition of war propaganda in the press and radio and at meetings. Irreconcilable struggle against drawing Germany into aggressive military *blocs,* into the European Union and the North Atlantic Pact.

"(6) Merciless and active struggle against the traitors to the German nation—the German agents of American imperialism, the criminal supporters of the splitting of Germany and the enslavement of her Western regions—and the separatists who support the imperialist policy of splitting Germany.

"(7) Unlimited support for the forces throughout the world which are fighting for peace, equality, and friendship among the peoples. The co-operation and friendship of Germany with all peace-loving peoples and countries which recognize the national interests of democratic Germany.

"(8) Immediate re-establishment of the unity of the capital of Germany, Berlin, and immediate restoration of normal life in the city.

"(9) A single currency for the whole of Germany; unhindered trade and economic co-operation; free movement of the population and goods between all the *Länder* and zones of Germany. . . ."

Herr Pieck announced at the meeting that the *Landtag* elections which had been expected to take place this autumn would not be held, but that elections to a new *Volkskammer* would be held on Oct. 15, 1950.

A *Länderkammer*, the Upper House of the new Parliament, was elected at a meeting in Berlin of the members of the *Landtage* of the five *Länder* of the Soviet zone.

Following a notification by Herr Johannes Dieckmann (the newly-elected President of the Chamber) of the formation of the *Volkskammer*, General Chuikov, chief of the Soviet Military Administration in Eastern Germany, announced on Oct. 10 that the Soviet Government had decided to transfer to the "Provisional Government of the German Democratic Republic" the functions hitherto appertaining to the Military Administration, and that in place of the latter a Soviet Control Commission would be established "charged with exercising control over the fulfilment of the Potsdam and other joint decisions of the four Powers in respect to Germany".

At a joint session of both Houses on Oct. 11, which was attended by high Soviet officials and members of the military missions of the "satellite" States of Eastern Europe, Herr Wilhelm Pieck was unanimously elected first President of the "German Democratic Republic", and at the same time took the oath as prescribed in the Constitution of May 1949.

Addressing the joint session after his election, Herr Pieck claimed that the new Government had the right to speak for the whole of Germany, and called on the West German *Bundestag* and the West German Federal Government "to realize the danger in which the German people finds itself in face of the policy of the Western Powers", and not to give further support to the latter's measures. "If the *Bundestag* and the Federal Government do that," he added, "we will draw nearer each other, finally remove the division (of Germany), and create unity, so that Germany will not be made a colony and a deploying ground for a new imperialist war." He also appealed to the people of Western Germany not to allow themselves "to be misled by the agitation against the East" and to "unite with the people of the East in the creation of the National Front, the prerequisite for the victory in the common struggle". After attacking the Western Powers on the lines of the manifesto of Oct. 7, he praised the Soviet Government's decision to hand over to the new Government the administrative functions of the Soviet Military Administration.

Herr Grotewohl became head of the new East German Government and presented his Cabinet on Oct. 12, 1949, with Herr Walter Ulbricht as a Deputy Premier.

In his policy statement to the *Volkskammer* the same day, Herr Grotewohl reiterated the points laid down in the manifesto of the "National Front".

He stressed that the foreign policy of his Government would be based on friendship with the Soviet Union; declared that "the Oder-Neisse Line is a frontier of peace" and that it was "criminal to think of the possibility of plunging Germany into a war with a view to changing that frontier"; and strongly attacked the Western Powers, repeating the allegation that they were responsible for the "splitting" of Germany. Whilst not expressly claiming for the new Government jurisdiction over the whole of Germany, he declared that it would not accept the division of the country and would continue the struggle for Germany's reunification.

On Oct. 16 it was announced in Berlin that the Soviet Union and the new East German State would exchange diplomatic missions and subsequently diplomatic recognition was also extended to the latter by Poland, Czechoslovakia, Hungary, Romania and Bulgaria.

Dr. Adenauer protests at Establishment of German Democratic Republic

Dr. Adenauer, the West German Federal Chancellor, declared on Oct. 7 that the East German Republic was "without legal basis", since it had no backing from the people. In an official statement he said:

"The Eastern State was created without contact with the population of the Eastern zone, who received no opportunity to voice their will. The Eastern zone Government does not represent the will of the Eastern zone population, and it can even less claim to speak on the affairs of Germany as a whole. The Federal Republic of Germany, in face of the attempt to subjugate the 18,000,000 inhabitants of the Eastern zone in an even stronger degree to foreign influence, must do everything in its power to give the Eastern zone population spiritual and moral assistance."

General Robertson, Mr. McCloy and M. François Poncet, the Allied High Commissioners in Western Germany, issued a statement on Oct. 10 likewise denouncing the East German Republic as having no legal basis and no title to representation.

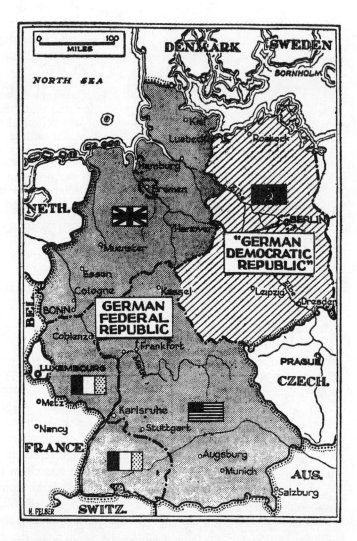

The map shows the areas under the control of the German
Federal Republic (the West German Government) and the
German Democratic Republic (the East German Govern-
ment). The Federal Republic of 1949 comprised the British,
American and French occupation zones, whilst the Democratic
Republic was established in the Soviet zone.—(*New York
Times*)

II. INTEGRATION OF WESTERN AND EASTERN GERMANY INTO WESTERN AND EASTERN BLOCS

1. EAST GERMAN AGREEMENTS OF 1950

Agreement on Oder-Neisse Frontier between Governments of Poland and German Democratic Republic (Zgorzelec Agreement)

It was announced in Warsaw and East Berlin on June 7, 1950, that a delegation from the German Democratic Republic, headed by Herr Walter Ulbricht, then Deputy Prime Minister, had visited Warsaw on June 5-6 for talks with the Polish Government, and that as a result the following agreements had been reached:

(1) An agreement on the demarcation of the Polish-German State frontier on the Oder-Neisse line;

(2) an agreement on trade and payments for 1950, providing for an increase in the volume of trade of over 60 per cent as compared with 1949;

(3) an agreement on the provision of Polish credits to the German Democratic Republic;

(4) an agreement in respect of technical and scientific co-operation, "providing for mutual utilization of experience in methods of production, and for the mutual provision of technical aid";

(5) a cultural agreement providing for "the exchange of achievements in the fields of science, exchange of scientific works and *belles lettres,* and co-operation in the spheres of the cinema and radio",

58

and for the exchange of "information on curricula and organization of education and physical training".

In addition, the *communiqué* said that both delegations had exchanged information concerning the Polish six-year plan and the five-year plan of the German Democratic Republic, and had decided to commence in August the negotiation of a long-term trade agreement "for the purpose of planned development of trade".

The agreement recognizing the Oder-Neisse line as the permanent frontier between Eastern Germany and Poland, and thus formally ceding to Poland the former German territories occupied by her since the end of the war, was published at the same time and said in part:

"The basis of the further development and strengthening of good-neighbourly relations and friendship between the Polish and German peoples lies in the demarcation of the inviolable frontier of peace and friendship existing between both States along the Oder-Neisse. In this manner the German Democratic Republic confirms the statement of Prime Minister Grotewohl made on Oct. 12, 1949 [when, on becoming Prime Minister, he had declared the Oder-Neisse line to be "a frontier of peace"].

". . . Both parties have decided within the space of a month to carry out the demarcation of the frontier along the Oder-Neisse, and likewise to regulate the questions of minor frontier traffic and of navigation in the waters of the frontier zone".

The agreement on the Oder-Neisse frontier aroused deep resentment in Western Germany, where the Federal Government issued a statement on June 9 strongly denouncing it.

"The German Federal Government," the statement said, "does not recognize the demarcation line laid down in the agreement which the present Communist Government, imposed on the population of the Soviet Zone, has concluded with the Polish Government. The so-called Government of the Soviet Zone has no right to speak for the German people, and all its agreements and arrangements are null and void. The decision on the Eastern territories at present under Soviet or Polish administration can and will be made only in a future peace treaty with the whole of Germany. The German Federal Republic, as the spokesman of the whole German people, will never agree to the alienation of these purely German territories against all principles of right and humanity. In future peace negotiations the Federal Government will seek a just solution of this question between a really democratic Poland and a democratic, united Germany."

However, a frontier demarcation agreement implementing the Oder-Neisse line agreement of June 6 was signed at Zgorzelec (Görlitz) on the Neisse River (Zgorzelec, the town's eastern part, being Polish, and Görlitz, its western part, German) on July 6, 1950, by Mr. Josef Cyrankiewicz and Herr Grotewohl, the Polish and East German Prime Ministers.

Delimitation Agreement—Further Frontier

Herr Dertinger, the Eastern German Foreign Minister, and Dr. Skrzeszewski, permanent head of the Polish Foreign Office, signed an agreement at Frankfurt-on-Oder on Jan. 27, 1951, finally delimiting the East German-Polish frontier. The agreement signified the East German Government's final acceptance of the Oder-Neisse Line as Germany's eastern frontier, and, speaking after the signature, Herr Dertinger declared that any attempt at revision of the Oder-Neisse frontier would mean war and would be as much against the national existence of Poland as against the vital interests of the German Democratic Republic.

In West Berlin it was reported that under the delimitation as finally agreed upon the Eastern German Government had ceded to Poland the four-mile-wide western strip of Usedom Island—in the Oder estuary north of Stettin (Szczecin)—the eastern part of which had already been taken over by Poland earlier. It was claimed by the West German press that the agreement contravened that section of the Potsdam Declaration under which the Soviet, U.S. and British Governments affirmed that the final delimitation of the western frontier of Poland should await the peace settlement with Germany.

1955 Reaffirmation of Agreement

A joint statement was issued on July 6, 1955, the fifth anniversary of the Zgorzelec Agreement, by the Polish and East German Governments declaring that the frontier between Poland and Germany had been "definitely and irrevocably" fixed on the rivers Oder (Odra) and Neisse (Nysa). The statement added that there was "complete unanimity" between the two Governments on this matter, and that both Governments had "recorded their unflinching determination to combat, in accordance with the provisions of the Warsaw Treaty, all attempts to disturb the friendly relations between them".

East German—Czechoslovak Declaration on Finality of
Expulsion of Sudeten Germans from Czechoslovakia—
East German—Hungarian Declaration of Friendship—
Cultural, Technical and Financial Agreements
with Czechoslovakia and Hungary

Following the arrival in Prague on June 21, 1950, of an Eastern
German delegation, led by Herr Walter Ulbricht and Herr Handke,
the Minister for Foreign Trade, it was announced on June 23 that the
following joint declaration had been signed by Mr. Zapotocky, the
Czechoslovak Premier, and Herr Ulbricht:

"Both Governments are convinced that their joint obligation to
maintain and secure peace is being helped and strengthened by the
fact that there are absolutely no disputes or open questions which
remain to be settled between the two countries. Our two States have
no territorial claims on each other, nor are there any claims for
alteration of the present frontier, and the two Governments desire to
emphasize that the resettlement of Germans from the Czechoslovak
Republic has been settled in an unalterable, just and permanent
manner".

In addition to the declaration, both countries signed (1) a cultural
agreement envisaging the exchange of scholars and writers; (2) a scientific and technical agreement providing for exchanges of scientific
knowledge and technical experts, and the interchange of processes,
patents, and technological methods; (3) a financial agreement under
which Czechoslovakia granted a short-term credit to Eastern Germany to enable the latter to buy certain Czechoslovak goods. A convention regulating frontier traffic would, it was stated, be signed within two months, and it was also agreed to negotiate a five-year trade
agreement in the autumn.

The declaration constituted the final acceptance by the Eastern
German Government of the expulsion of over 2,000,000 Sudeten
Germans from Czechoslovakia since the end of the war, of whom
the majority had gone to Western Germany, about 800,000 to Eastern Germany, and the remainder to Austria.

Immediately after the signing of the agreements, Herr Ulbricht and
the other Eastern German delegates left Prague for Budapest, where
it was announced on June 24 that the Eastern German and Hungarian

Governments had signed (1) a two-year cultural agreement; (2) a five-year scientific and technical agreement, both agreements being on the same lines as those concluded between Eastern Germany and Czechoslovakia; (3) a financial agreement; and (4) a trade agreement.

2. THREE-POWER CONFERENCE IN NEW YORK, 1950

The U.S., British and French Foreign Ministers, respectively Mr. Dean Acheson, Mr. Ernest Bevin and M. Robert Schuman met in New York on Sept. 12-18, 1950, to review the international situation.

The official statement issued in New York on Sept. 19, dealing with Germany announced important decisions on (1) the forthcoming ending of the state of war, (2) permission for the establishment of new mobile police formations in the Federal Republic, (3) a revision of the Occupation Statute, especially in the field of foreign affairs, and (4) modifications to the agreement on prohibited and limited industries in Germany, including the immediate removal of existing restrictions on shipbuilding for export and of the "ceiling" for steel production as far as required for the defence effort of the West. The statement also announced that any attack against Western Germany or Berlin from any quarter would be treated by the Western Allies as an attack upon themselves, but indicated that no decision had yet been reached on the question of integrating German forces within a unified Western army. The statement was in part as follows (with cross-headings inserted):

"Pending the unification of Germany, the three Governments consider the Government of the Federal Republic as the only German Government freely and legitimately constituted and therefore entitled to speak for Germany as the representative of the German people in international affairs. They reaffirm their desire, of which they have already given many proofs, to integrate the Federal Republic into the community of free nations. They are convinced that the overwhelming majority of the German people want to take part in building the European community and strengthening its common civilization. It appears to them that the time has now come to take a new step towards the attainment of these aims.

Ending of State of War.—In the spirit of the new relationship which they wish to establish with the Federal Republic the three Governments have decided, as soon as action can be taken in all three countries in accordance with their respective constitutional requirements, to take the necessary steps in their domestic legislation to terminate the state of war with Germany. This action will not affect the rights and status of the three Powers in Germany, which rest upon other bases. . . .

Western German Security.—The three Ministers have given serious consideration to the problem of the security of the Federal Republic in both its external and its internal aspects. They recognize the fact that outright military units have been created in the Soviet zone of occupation, and this fact together with recent events in Germany and elsewhere have given rise to a situation of great concern. The Allied Governments consider that their forces in Germany have, in addition to their occupation duties, also the important role of acting as security forces for the protection and defence of the free world including the German Federal Republic and the Western sectors of Berlin. To make this protection more effective the Allied Governments will increase and reinforce their forces in Germany. They will treat any attack against the Federal Republic or Berlin from any quarter as an attack upon themselves.

The Ministers are fully agreed that the creation of a German national army would not serve the best interests of Germany or Europe. They also believe that this is the view of the great majority of the German people. The Ministers have taken note, however, of sentiments recently expressed in Germany and elsewhere in favour of German participation in an integrated force for the defence of European freedom. The question raised by the problems of the participation of the German Federal Republic in the common defence of Europe is at present the subject of study and exchange of views.

As regards internal security, the Foreign Ministers recognize the necessity for ensuring that the German authorities are enabled effectively to deal with possible subversive activities. To this effect the three Ministers have agreed to permit the establishment of mobile police formations, organized on a *Land* provincial basis, but with provisions which would enable the Federal Government to have adequate powers to make effective use of all or part of this force in order fully to meet the exigencies of the present situation. The High Commission and Allied forces in Germany will render such assistance as may be feasible in the rapid establishment of this force.

Revision of Occupation Statute.—The new phase in the relations between the Allies and the Federal Republic will be marked by major extensions of the authority of the Federal Government. To make this possible, the occupying Powers are prepared to amend the Occupation Statute while maintaining the legal basis of the occupation, and the Federal Republic will be expected to undertake certain commitments and other actions consonant with its new responsibilities.

In the field of foreign affairs the Federal Government will be authorized to establish a Minister of Foreign Affairs and to enter into diplomatic relations with foreign countries in all suitable cases. In other fields, and particularly in relation to internal economic matters, far-reaching reductions will be made in existing controls, and the present system of review of German legislation will be modified. In certain cases the Allied powers will cease as soon as the Federal Government has given undertakings on taking suitable action. The High Commission will promptly begin discussions with the Federal Government to work out the necessary agreements for such undertakings.

Prohibited and Limited Industries.—The Foreign Ministers have also agreed that a review of the prohibited and limited industries agreement shall be undertaken in the light of the developing relationships with the Federal Republic. Pending this review the High Commission has been instructed to remove forthwith all restrictions on the size, speed, and number of commercial cargo ships built for export and to allow steel to be produced outside the present limitation where this will facilitate the defence effort of the West."

3. PRAGUE MEETING OF COMINFORM MINISTERS, 1950

A meeting of the Foreign Ministers of the Cominform countries and the East German Republic was held at Prague on Oct. 21-22, 1950, on the initiative of the Soviet Union to discuss questions arising out of the decisions on Germany taken by the New York conference of the British, U.S. and French Foreign Ministers. A communiqué was issued on Oct. 22 strongly attacking the tripartite statement of Sept. 19 and putting forward counter-proposals.

The communiqué declared that it was "clear . . . that the principal question at the Conference of the three Ministers was the question of the re-creation of the German Army and of the remilitarization of Germany", and said that the New York decisions contained "a threat to Europe", that they were "another gross violation of the obligations which these nations assumed under the Potsdam Agreement", and that they were "contrary to the interests of all peace-loving peoples, including the national interest of the German people".

(1) Termination of the State of War.—Dealing with the principal points in the New York statement, the Prague communiqué described the decision to end the state of war as "hypocritical through and through". It asserted that the stipulation that the termination of the state of war should not affect the rights and status of the three Powers in Germany meant that the validity of the Occupation Statute was intended to be prolonged "for a period of indefinite

length, in order to extend their (the Western Powers') rule in Western Germany as long as possible". Referring to the New York announcement that the Western Powers would increase their forces in Germany, the statement said that there was "no need to prove" that this decision had been "evoked by nothing less than the ever-growing aspirations of these Powers in Europe", and continued: "It is clear that the false phrases about the so-called 'termination' of the state of war with Germany are merely a screen to conceal the policy of the Powers who head the aggressive North Atlantic Alliance. These Powers want to untie their hands so that they may use Western Germany, its manpower and material resources, in their imperialist interests for the realization of their strategic plans, behind which are the aspirations of the U.S. ruling circles for world supremacy. On the pretext of terminating the state of war with Germany they strive to create the conditions for the open inclusion of Western Germany in the aggressive grouping of the so-called North Atlantic Alliance, and to transform Western Germany completely into an instrument of their aggressive military strategic plans in Europe."

It was also evident, the statement went on, that the question of terminating the war with Germany had been "dragged in, in order to delay as long as possible the conclusion of a peace treaty . . . and thus to postpone the unification of Germany", and it was "not fortuitous" that nothing about a peace treaty had been mentioned in the New York statement, although the four Powers had at Potsdam assumed the obligation to prepare such a treaty, which was now being "evaded on all kinds of pretexts". This, the communiqué affirmed, showed that "the present policy of the United States, Britain and France, grossly violating the Potsdam Agreement, runs directly counter to the interests of all peace-loving peoples of Europe".

(2) Level of Industry.—Dealing with the New York decision to review the agreement on prohibited and limited industries, the communiqué noted that "not a single word is said about prohibiting the restoration of war industry as required by the Yalta and Potsdam Agreements, as well as by subsequent four-Power agreements", and that the New York statement permitted steel production outside the established limits for the purpose of war production. "Thus," the Prague statement went on, "in the communiqué of the three Ministers the ban on German war industry, regarding which firm decisions of the four Powers were unanimously adopted, is in fact lifted."

On the question of German armed forces the communiqué said: "The principal question discussed at the New York conference of the Foreign Ministers of the United States, Britain and France was the question of the re-establishment of the German Army". Alleging that there were "456,000 men in German and foreign military formations in the Western zones of Germany and the Western sectors of Berlin, including displaced persons, and in various police units", and that most of them were "former soldiers and officers of the Hitlerite army", the communiqué continued; "The arming of these units and formations, their organizational structure and army training, the training of officer personnel for them in special schools, their participation in military manoeuvres together with the occupation troops of the Western Powers, proves that these formations and units are in fact army formations."

The Prague communiqué closed by making the following proposals "for the speediest possible conclusion of a peace settlement for Germany":

"(1) The publication by the United States, Great Britain, France and the Soviet Union of a statement that they will not permit the remilitarization of Germany, nor permit her to be drawn into any kind of aggressive plans, and that they will unswervingly carry out the Potsdam Agreement for the formation of a united, peace-loving, democratic German State.

(2) The removal of all restrictions in the path of the development of German peace economy and the prevention of the restoration of German war potential.

(3) The immediate conclusion of a peace treaty with Germany involving the restoration of the unity of the German State in accordance with the Potsdam Agreement, and with the provision that the occupation troops of all Powers be withdrawn from Germany within one year after the conclusion of the peace treaty.

(4) The creation of an All-German Constituent Council on a parity basis, consisting of representatives of Eastern and Western Germany, to prepare the formation of a provisional democratic peace-loving all-German sovereign Government, and to submit corresponding proposals for joint approval by the Governments of the U.S.S.R., the U.S.A., Great Britain and France, and which, until the formation of an all-German Government, is to be taken into consultations on the working out of the peace treaty. Under certain circumstances a direct questioning of the German people regarding this proposal may be carried out."

On Nov. 3, Mr. Gromyko, the Soviet Deputy Foreign Minister, handed to the British, U.S. and French Ambassadors in Moscow (Sir David Kelly, Admiral Alan Kirk and M. Chataigneau) identical Notes proposing another session of the Council of Foreign Ministers to discuss the demilitarization of Germany.

The Western Powers, replying to the Soviet Note on Dec. 22, 1950, suggested that four-Power discussions should deal not only with the question of Germany but also "the principal problems whose solution would make possible a real and lasting improvement" in relations between the Powers.

The Soviet Government, however, insisted on Dec. 30 that such talks should be confined to the demilitarization of Germany and "other questions concerning Germany".

4. ELECTIONS TO EAST GERMAN "VOLKSKAMMER", 1950

Elections to the East German *Volkskammer* (Lower House) were held in the Soviet Zone of Germany, excluding the Soviet sector of Berlin, on Oct. 15, 1950. On the following day Dr. Steinhoff, the Minister of the Interior, announced that an overwhelming majority of votes had been cast for the single list put forward by the "National Front".

The elections had been strongly denounced by the Federal German Government and the *Bundestag* in Bonn.

In a White Book published by the Western German Government on Sept. 8 it was declared that the East German elections would be "faked from top to bottom". Specifically, the White Paper pointed out that a voter had no choice but to vote for the "single lists", as his only alternative was not to drop the ballot paper into the urn, thus risking observation; that a candidate could be declared ineligible after his election if he was accused of an offence against "the political foundations of the anti-Fascist democratic order"; that the nominating party or organization could then automatically name a new candidate who would be officially considered elected; that the new Parliament could at any time elect by simple majority vote as many "supernumerary" members as it liked; that the inter-party agreement for a single party list was a direct breach of the East German Constitution, which laid down that elections should be carried out according to the principles of proportional representation; and that the new electoral law omitted a previous provision for the supervision of the elections by representatives of all parties.

In a statement approved by all parties except the Communists, the *Bundestag* on Sept. 14 denounced the elections as "neither free nor democratic"; appealed to all democratic countries to help the German people in its fight against Communism; charged the Soviet Union with crimes against humanity by her attitude towards the treatment of German prisoners of war and deportees, and her disregard for the sufferings of refugees; and put forward the following five requests to the Federal Government:

"(1) To keep the German people and the world continuously and accurately informed of the state of lawlessness under the Communist dictatorship in the Soviet Zone;

(2) formally to ask the Occupation Powers to sponsor free, general, equal, secret, and direct elections to an all-German Parliament in all four Zones, under international control;

(3) to initiate criminal proceedings in the Federal Republic against all persons participating in crimes against humanity committed in the Soviet Zone;

(4) to take action against all persons who are engaged in carrying out the decisions of the third party congress of the Communist-controlled Socialist Unity Party and of the 'National Congress', which aimed at violence against the Federal Republic;

(5) to strengthen by all economic and political means the resistance of Berlin to Communist dictatorship, as evidence of the determined and unremitting resolve of the Federal Republic to secure the unification of the whole of Germany in a free country based on law (*Rechtsstaat*)."

Prior to the adoption of the resolution. Dr. Adenauer, on behalf of the Federal Government, had declared that both the preparation and the execution of the East German elections were "not only in contradiction to genuine democratic conditions but also in defiance of the Constitution of the so-called Democratic German Republic itself". He affirmed that the "single list" of the "National Front" had only been brought about through pressure and compulsion; announced that the elections would not be recognized by the Federal Republic; and declared that the Federal Government would support by every means in its power "the will of the people of the Soviet Zone to free themselves from the yoke of the Socialist Unity Party and to express by means of a free vote their membership of the Federal Republic". At the same time he appealed to the world to support the re-unification of the whole of Germany and the recognition of democratic fundamental rights in all parts of Germany, and added: "We appeal to all Germans to stand together in determination and unity for the unification and freedom of Germany, against all attempts at Communist domination by violence".

Herr Jakob Kaiser (the Federal Minister for All-German Affairs) emphasized the need for actively defending the Federal Republic against the Communist aim of conquering the whole of Germany. In this connection he suggested that as an answer to Communist infiltration the laws against illegal Communist activities should be strictly applied.

Both Dr. Adenauer and Dr. Schumacher, the leader of the Opposition, broadcast on Oct. 13 messages of goodwill and encouragement to the Germans of the Eastern Zone.

Describing the East German elections as a "swindle", the Federal Chancellor said that a voting system which did not allow the citizen to express his political opinions freely and without danger to life and limb was no election at all, but a "shocking violation both of civic rights and of human dignity". The election result, he declared, could never be interpreted as giving the present rulers the right to speak in the name of the population of the Zone, let alone in the name of the German people, nor could it be regarded as an acceptance by the inhabitants of the Communist system. The election was "an act of political blackmail which neither bound nor inculpated its victims", and he was convinced that in unfettered elections the overwhelming majority would vote against the Communist system and for a free democratic Germany. The Federal Government, he said, would spare no effort to achieve the unity of the nation in freedom and justice, and was conscious of its special responsibility to the "oppressed inhabitants of the East".

The new East German *Volkskammer* met for the first time in the Soviet sector of Berlin on Nov. 8 and re-elected as its president Herr J. Dieckmann (Liberal Democrat), with Herr Hermann Matern (Socialist Unity Party), Herr Ernst Goldenbaum (Democratic Farmer), Lt.-General Vincenz Müller (National Democrat), and Herr Gerald Götting (Christian Democrat) as vice-presidents.

Herr Grotewohl, the outgoing Premier and leader of the Socialist Unity Party, was empowered to form a new Government.

In his policy statement to the *Volkskammer* Herr Grotewohl stressed the close political and economic co-operation between the East German Democratic Republic and the Soviet Union; denounced the North Atlantic Treaty, the Council of Europe, and the Schuman Plan (for the integration of West European coal and steel resources, which led to the establishment of the European Coal and Steel Community—the first of the three European Communities), confirmed the agreements with Poland and Czechoslovakia concerning the Oder-Neisse line and the Sudetenland; opposed any remilitarization in Western Germany as "a threat to the Soviet bloc"; and reiterated the support of his Government for the Prague declaration [see above], adding that they intended to take the initiative in arranging consultations between representatives of Eastern and Western Germany on all questions connected with the formation of a Constituent Council, on which both parts of the country would be equally represented.

5. DR. ADENAUER REJECTS
HERR GROTEWOHL'S PROPOSAL, 1950

It was announced in Berlin on Dec. 3 that Herr Grotewohl, the East German Prime Minister, had written to Dr. Adenauer, the Western German Chancellor, on Nov. 30, 1950, proposing conversations between the two Governments on the formation of an all-German Constituent Council as proposed in the Prague Declaration [see page 66]. Herr Grotewohl's letter was worded as follows:

"In view of the fact that the maintenance of peace, the conclusion of a peace treaty, and the restoration of the unity of Germany depend primarily on mutual understanding among Germans themselves—and we consider that such mutual understanding is possible since the whole of the German people desires a peaceful settlement —all peace-loving Germans would welcome the formation of an all-German Constituent Council, on the basis of parity, consisting of representatives of Eastern and Western Germany, which would prepare for the establishment of an all-German sovereign democratic and peace-loving Provisional Government and would submit to the Governments of the U.S.S.R., the United States, Great Britain and France appropriate proposals for joint approval. At the same time it would consult those Governments pending the establishment of an all-German Government, in the period of the working out of a Peace Treaty. Under certain conditions a referendum could be held among the German people on this proposal. We consider that an all-German Constituent Council could take upon itself the preparation of the conditions for the holding of all-German elections to a National Assembly. The formation of an all-German Constituent Council would create the pre-requisites for the immediate commencement of negotiations on the conclusion of a Peace Treaty, and at the same time the Council could carry out preparations for the formation of a Government.

"The German Democratic Republic is prepared to enter into negotiations in the spirit of honest mutual understanding on all questions connected with the formation and tasks of an all-German Constituent Council. Wide circles of the population of Eastern and Western Germany consider that the next step in deciding national and vitally important questions of our people must be to submit a joint German proposal for the consideration of the four occupying Powers. Proceeding from this desire of the peace-loving population, the Government of the German Democratic Republic is ready to begin negotiations between the two Governments on the formation of an all-German Constituent Council. We propose, for this purpose, that each Government appoint six representatives. Agreement on the place and time could be reached between the Secretaries of State of the Prime Ministers."

As no immediate reply was forthcoming from Bonn, Herr Grotewohl's letter was followed on Dec. 11 by an invitation to Dr. Adenauer from the East German radio to speak over that network to the Germans in Eastern Germany; on Dec. 24 by another appeal from Herr Grotewohl to Dr. Adenauer for joint negotiations on the unification of Germany, published in an article signed by Herr Grotewohl in *Neues Deutschland* (organ of the Socialist Unity Party); and on Dec. 30 by a letter from Herr Dieckmann, President of the East German *Volkskammer,* to Herr Ehlers, chairman of the West German *Bundestag,* likewise appealing for negotiations and urging that a reply should be made to Herr Grotewohl's offer.

It was not until Jan. 15 that Dr. Adenauer, in a statement approved by the Federal Government and all the parties in the *Bundestag* except the Communists, replied to the proposal at a press conference which was attended by other Western German Ministers, including Herr Jakob Kaiser, the Minister for All-German Questions. In his statement, which was broadcast, Dr. Adenauer, while avoiding any direct reply to the East German Government, indirectly rejected Herr Grotewohl's proposal and re-stated the conditions under which, in the Federal Government's view, Germany should be unified and all-German elections held.

After recalling that the West German Government had "since its formation worked for the restoration of the unity of Germany in peace and liberty", Dr. Adenauer referred to the two "practical and precise" proposals which had been made, first in its declaration of March 22, 1950, on the holding of all-German elections for a Constituent Assembly, and later in the similar *Bundestag* resolution of Sept. 14, 1950, which had been handed to General Chuikov on Oct. 9 through the intermediary of the Western High Commissioners but had so far remained unanswered; Herr Grotewohl himself, he pointed out, had not replied to either of these proposals, and could not therefore complain if the Federal Government had taken some weeks to answer his letter of Nov. 30.

Dr. Adenauer went on to say that ten days after the receipt of Herr Grotewohl's letter the East German Government had passed the so-called "law for the protection of peace", which was contrary to all principles of justice and democracy and was an instrument of "mental and physical terror", and that no régime executing such legislation could be willing to have free elections. Dr. Adenauer also declared that those who had renounced the German areas east of the Oder-Neisse line were not qualified to speak of re-uniting Germany; denounced the People's Police in the Soviet Zone—whose number, he said, were continually increasing—as "a menace to the German people" because of its military character and because it was "a tool serving foreign designs"; and affirmed that no such police formation existed in Federal territory, and that "any freely-achieved all-German solution has no room for a party instrument guided by a foreign Power".

The Federal Government, Dr. Adenauer continued, agreed with all Germans that "nothing should be left undone to re-establish German unity in liberty and peace", but it could enter into discussions only with those "willing to recognize and guarantee a form of government which respects liberty, the protection of human rights and the preservation of peace". Therefore, he declared, the following conditions must be fulfilled for the holding of all-German elections for an all-German Constituent Assembly; (1) German citizens in the Soviet Zone must be guaranteed personal liberty and security consonant with the rule of law; (2) political liberty, including the right to hold meetings, to form political associations and to carry on political activities, must be re-established in the Soviet Zone; (3) the People's Police in the Soviet Zone must be disbanded.

Finally, Dr. Adenauer rejected the allegation in Herr Grotewohl's letter that "the re-militarization of Western Germany and its inclusion in the plans for war preparations" had widened the division of Germany. This division, he said, was due only to the introduction in the Soviet Zone of a system of government which was "contrary to German tradition and to the German character, which robs the population of the Zone of any possibility of freely shaping its political, economic and social life, and by which it has been cut off from mixing freely with its kin in the West". Although the division of Germany had been still more aggravated through the formation of a strong "People's Police" force, the Federal Government—as was well known to the authorities in the Soviet Zone—had hitherto refrained from any similar measures.

Dr. Schumacher (the Social Democratic leader), in a broadcast on Jan. 21, defended the Federal Government's attitude towards Herr Grotewohl's offer; condemned the Grotewohl letter as a propaganda move timed to produce all-German talks before a possible four-Power conference; and described the proposals as being not in the interests of Germany but in those of the Soviet Union. "The real aim of the Soviet Union," he added, "is to get reparations from Western Germany. The Soviet Union wants these reparations out of Western Germany's current production after having plundered its own zone."

6. FOUR-POWER MEETING IN PARIS, 1951

Further Note exchanges were continued during January and February, 1951. On Feb. 6 the Soviet Government presented identical Notes to the Ambassadors of France, Great Britain and the U.S.A. in Moscow in reply to the Western Powers' Notes of Jan. 23, in which it again charged the Western Powers with "remilitarizing" Western Germany, but, subject to conditions, expressed willingness to consider matters other than Germany and agreed to a preliminary conference in Paris to discuss the agenda for the proposed meeting of the Council of Foreign Ministers.

The principal points of the Soviet Note were as follows:

(1) The Soviet Government considered that there should be no further delay in summoning the Council of Foreign Ministers.

(2) At the same time it referred to the "dangerous significance" of the "far-reaching negotiations" which had taken place in recent months between the Western Powers and the Bonn Government of Dr. Adenauer"; attacked what it described as "General Eisenhower's negotiations with the Government of the revanchist Adenauer" on the inclusion of a "revived German Army" in the North Atlantic Pact; and declared that General Eisenhower's appointment as Supreme Commander in the West "in no way tallies with the official declarations of a striving for peace" by the Western nations. It went on to declare that "revanchists of the type of Adenauer and Schumacher and militarists from among Hitler's followers" were "strengthening their influence and domination" in Western Germany, and added that "the increase in the armed forces and the armaments race" taking place in the U.S.A. and many European countries "much increased the tension in the international situation".

(3) Regarding the Western Powers' inquiry whether the U.S.S.R. would agree to discuss questions other than that of the demilitarization of Germany, the Soviet Government considered it possible that the Council of Foreign Ministers could discuss such questions "in the order stipulated by the Potsdam Agreement".

(4) It was suggested that the preliminary conference of representatives of the four Powers should confine itself to drafting an agenda for the subsequent meeting of the Council of Foreign Ministers, and to deciding upon the order in which the items should be considered.

(5) No objection was made to the convening of such a preliminary conference in Paris.

The British, U.S. and French replies to this Soviet Note, couched in identical terms, were presented in Moscow on Feb. 20. After repudiating the accusations contained in the Soviet Note, and repeating the Western view that the present international tension was caused primarily by "the existence of the huge armaments maintained by the Soviet *bloc,* which includes forces in Eastern Germany", the three Powers emphasized their willingness to commence preparatory four-Power discussions in Paris without delay.

The Soviet reply was handed to the British, U.S. and French Ambassadors on March 1. It was announced at the State Department in Washington that it constituted an acceptance of the Western Powers' proposals that preliminary four-Power discussions should commence in Paris on March 5.

The preliminary conference of representatives of the four Powers accordingly opened in Paris on March 5.

At the commencement of the Paris discussions the representatives received a request from the Eastern German Government asking that the question of a German peace treaty be placed on their agenda. Prior to the commencement of the discussions, the Allied High Commissioners in Bonn had announced on Feb. 22 that Dr. Adenauer would be informed "to the fullest possible extent" of any four-Power discussions on Germany, and that consideration would be given to any views that the German Federal Government might wish to present.

However, on June 21, 1951, after 74 meetings the Paris conference broke down owing to failure to reconcile the proposals put forward by the Western Powers on the one hand and those of the Soviet Government on the other.

7. NEW SOVIET PROPOSALS
FOR GERMAN PEACE TREATY, 1952

On March 10, 1952, the Soviet Government presented identical Notes to the British, French and U.S. diplomatic representatives in Moscow, urging immediate four-Power talks to draw up a draft peace treaty with Germany.

After pointing out that, although seven years had passed since the end of the war, "Germany still has no peace treaty, is partitioned, and remains in a position of unequal rights in relation to other States", the Soviet Government declared that "the need to expedite a peace treaty with Germany is dictated by the fact that the danger of the restoration of German militarism, which has twice precipitated world wars, has not been eliminated as the decisions of the Potsdam Conference still remain unfulfilled"; that the peace treaty must "ensure the elimination of the possibility of a revival of German militarism and aggression", and at the same time "establish for the German people lasting conditions of peace which will facilitate the development of Germany as a united, independent, democratic and peace-loving State"; and that the framing of the treaty "must be carried out with the participation of Germany, as represented by an all-German Government". The Notes added that, "in proposing this draft for discussion, the Soviet Government at the same time expresses readiness to consider other possible proposals on the question".

The attitude of the German Federal Republic towards the Soviet Note was defined by Dr. Adenauer in a speech at Siegen (North Rhine-Westphalia) on March 16.

Whilst saying that the Soviet Note marked "a certain progress", and emphasizing that no possibility of achieving a peaceful understanding should be ignored, the Federal Chancellor declared that in no circumstances should the building up of Western defence and of European integration be delayed. "The aim of German policy," said Dr. Adenauer, "is, now as hitherto, that the West should become so strong that the Soviet Union will enter into reasonable counsel with it. I am firmly convinced—and the latest Soviet Note is fresh proof of it—that, if we continue along this road, the time is not so distant when Soviet Russia will declare herself ready for such reasonable counsel."

After stating that he would have an opportunity of discussing the Soviet Note with the Western allies in Paris, Dr. Adenauer went on to say that he would like, from the Russian side, three clarifications of particular points raised in the Note, viz., (1) what the Soviet Government means by "an all-German Government", (2) how the problem of "German territories beyond the Oder-Neisse line" was intended to be solved, and (3) the question of German national armaments. As regards the first question, he declared that an all-German Government could only be brought about as a result of free and secret elections, while, as regards the second question, the Soviet answer would be "very illuminating". On the third point, the Russian proposals were, he said, impracticable in view of the development of arms technique; since 1945 such great progress had been made in military research that Germany could not, if only for financial and material reasons, build up for herself a national armament, and this part of the Soviet Note was accordingly "a scrap of paper".

In conclusion, Dr. Adenauer declared that the major aims of his policy were the preservation of peace in Europe and the world, the reunion of Germany, and "the new order in Eastern Europe", by which he meant a peaceful settlement of the disputed Oder-Neisse frontier in co-operation with Poland, and the clarification of Germany's contacts with the other East European States.

The East German Parliament (*Volkskammer*), meeting on March 18, unanimously adopted a resolution approving the proposals contained in the Soviet Note, and calling on the West German Government to accept those proposals. Herr Grotewohl, the East German Premier, declared that all-German elections should be preceded by the convening of an all-German commission; described the impending visit of the U.N. Special Commission on Germany as an "unjustified interference in German internal affairs"; interpreted the Potsdam decisions as having fixed the German-Polish frontier on the Oder-Neisse line, and as having envisaged the return of the Saar to Germany; and described the Oder-Neisse frontier as a "permanent frontier of friendship", declaring that his Government was pledged to prevent any "chauvinistic agitation" against it.

8. FOUR-POWER EXCHANGES ON GERMANY, 1952–53

Replies of the British, French and U.S. Governments drawn up in identical terms to the Soviet Note of March 10 were presented in Moscow on March 25, 1952. The Soviet Government's reply to the Western Powers' Notes was presented to the British, French and American Ambassadors in Moscow on April 9.

It rejected a Western proposal that the special U.N. Commission on Germany should "verify the existence of conditions" for the holding of all-German elections, on the ground that the U.N. Charter precluded United Nations "interference" in German affairs, but proposed, instead, that the question of all-German elections should be studied by a four-Power commission consisting of representatives of the four occupation Powers—Great Britain, the United States, France and the Soviet Union. In other respects the Soviet Note reiterated the original Soviet proposals of March 10, maintaining *inter alia* that Germany should possess her own national forces, that she should be forbidden to enter into any "coalitions or alliances" with other Powers, and that the Oder-Neisse frontier should be regarded as definitive. In proposing a four-Power investigation into all-German elections, the Soviet Government declared that "the question now being decided is whether Germany is to be established as a united, independent, peace-loving State . . . or whether the split in Germany, involving the danger of war in Europe, shall remain in force".

The replies of the Western Powers to the above Soviet Note on Germany were presented in Moscow on May 13. The principal points of the Western Notes were that the U.S., British and French Governments were ready to begin negotiations on German unity, the election of a free all-German Government, and the conclusion of a peace treaty with that Government when understanding had been reached on the scope of the negotiations and the fundamental problems to be examined; that they would prefer the inquiry to be held by the U.N. Commission on Germany and not, as proposed by the Soviet Government, by a four-Power Commission; that they were, however, willing to consider alternative suggestions; and that they would not be deflected from their purpose of establishing a European Defence Community which would include the German Federal Republic.

The series of Note exchanges between the Western Powers and the U.S.S.R. on Germany was continued on May 25, on which date the Soviet Government handed to the U.S., British and French Ambassadors in Moscow its reply to the Western Notes of May 13. The Soviet Note, which was presented on the eve of the signing of the contractual agreements between the Western Powers and the German

Federal Republic, was divided into three sections: (1) a section on what was described as "the urgency of solving the German problem" and "the dragging out by the Western Powers of the exchange of Notes on this question"; (2) a section concerning "separate agreements of the Western Powers with Western Germany and their attempts to evade the conclusion of a peace treaty with Germany"; and (3) the proposals of the Soviet Government on the German question.

The first section consisted essentially of a complaint that the U.S., British and French Notes of May 13 showed that the Western Powers declined to discuss without further delay the question of a German peace treaty and the formation of a united Germany, and that those Powers desired to delay the conclusion of a peace treaty and German unification. The second section was devoted to a denunciation of the contractual arrangements between the Western Powers and the German Federal Republic, in which connexion the Soviet Note alleged, *inter alia,* that those arrangements constituted a violation of the Potsdam Agreement, that they in fact continued the Allied military occupation while ostensibly abolishing the Occupation Statute, that they had paved the way for a renewal of German militarism and "revanchism", and that the objective of the European Defence Community was to include the Federal Republic in the "aggressive North Atlantic Treaty Organization". In the third and final section, the Soviet Government again proposed immediate four-Power meetings on the German question, and reiterated its previously expressed view that such meetings should be based on the Potsdam Agreement, that the Oder-Neisse frontier should be recognized as final, that Germany should be permitted to have her own armed forces, and that she should not be allowed to form alliances with any countries with which she had formerly been at war.

The Note exchanges between the Western Powers and the Soviet Government on the subject of Germany continued throughout the summer of 1952, both sides reiterating their former proposals and repudiating each other's arguments.

West German Six-Point Programme for German Unification, July 1953

Prior to a Washington conference of the Foreign Ministers of Great Britain, France and the United States, the German Federal Government handed to the Allied High Commissioners in Bonn the text of an "immediate programme" which, it was suggested, should form the basis of discussions on the unification of Germany. The programme was handed to the Allied High Commissioner on July 9, 1953, with the request that it should be forwarded to the Foreign Ministers in Washington and also to the Soviet Government, and consisted of the following six points:

(1) The opening of the zonal frontiers between East and West Germany.

(2) The abolition of the "no-man's-land" established by the Communists along the East German zonal frontier.

(3) Free movement of German citizens throughout the territory of Germany.

(4) Freedom of the Press and of public assembly throughout the country.

(5) Freedom for political parties to operate in all parts of Germany.

(6) Guarantees of personal liberty for all citizens, and protection against arbitrary power and terrorism.

Washington Conference of Western Foreign Ministers, 1953

The U.S. Secretary of State (Mr. John F. Dulles), the British Acting Foreign Secretary (Lord Salisbury) and the French Foreign Minister (M. Georges Bidault) met in Washington from July 10-14, 1953, to discuss the international situation.

A communiqué issued on July 14 contained the following passages:

Unification of Germany.—"The three Ministers have given further consideration to the problem of the reunification of Germany. The grave events which took place recently in Berlin and in the Soviet Zone once again gave proof of the will to independence and the indomitable determination for freedom of the inhabitants of these areas. These developments have confirmed the view of the Ministers that the early reunification of Germany, in accordance with the legitimate aspirations of the German people, would be a great contribution to the easing of international tension.

"The three Powers have made sustained efforts to reach this goal. They have, in recent years, addressed several Notes with constructive proposals to the U.S.S.R., the last dated Sept. 23, 1952, to which no reply has yet been received. These Notes responded to the over-whelming desire of the German people to see unity re-established in freedom, as reflected most recently by the resolution of the German *Bundestag* of June 10 of this year."

Proposed Four-Power Meeting on Germany.—"Early and orderly progress in this direction requires the co-operation of the Soviet Government. Mindful of the special urgency which recent events have given to the question of the unification of Germany, the three Powers have resolved to make a new effort to bring to an end the division of Germany. The three Governments have therefore decided, in consultation with the German Federal Government, to propose a meeting in the early autumn of the Foreign Ministers of France, the United Kingdom, the United States and the U.S.S.R. to discuss directly the first steps which should lead to a satisfactory solution of the German problem, namely, the organization of free elections and the establishment of a free all-German Government."

Soviet Proposals for Peace Conference and All-German Government, August 1953

A Soviet Note on the subject of the unification of Germany was presented to the United States, Great Britain and France on Aug. 15, 1953, in which it was suggested that a peace conference should be convened within the next six months to draw up a peace treaty for Germany, and that a provisional all-German Government should be formed to hold free elections.

The Note, a 14-page document, recapitulated at great length the previous Note exchanges on Germany between the Western Powers and the U.S.S.R.; asserted that the Western Powers had not yet replied to the Note of March 10, 1952, in which the Soviet Government had suggested certain basic conditions for a draft peace treaty with Germany [see above]; and attributed responsibility for this delay to the Governments of the U.S.A., Great Britain and France.

The Soviet Note urged that "practical steps aimed at the settlement of the German problem" should be taken "immediately" by the four Powers concerned, and in this connexion put forward the following proposals:

Convening of a Peace Conference.—"The Soviet Government is of the opinion that such a conference, with the participation of all the States concerned, could be convened within the next six months. . . . All preliminary work to prepare a peace treaty with Germany could be carried out within this period. It it important to ensure the participation of representatives of Germany at all stages of the preparation of a peace treaty and at the peace conference. Until the establishment of a provisional all-German Government, representatives of the existing Governments of Eastern and Western Germany could take part in the preparation of a peace treaty."

Establishment of Provisional All-German Government.—Holding of All-German Elections.—"With the object of restoring the unity of Germany on a peace-loving and democratic basis, the Soviet Government proposes that the Parliaments of the German Democratic Republic and the German Federal Republic, with the broad participation of democratic organizations, should form a provisional all-German government. Such a government could be formed by direct agreement between Eastern and Western Germany, so as to replace the existing Governments of the German Democratic Republic and the German Federal Republic. Should this be difficult at the present time, a provisional all-German government could be formed with the retention for a period of the Governments of the German Democratic Republic and the German Federal Republic. In this case, the provisional all-German government would in the first stage possess only restricted functions. Even in such a case, however, the formation of a provisional all-German government would be a real step forward on the road to the unification of Germany, which should receive its full completion in the establishment of an all-German government on the basis of really free all-German elections."

Tasks of a Provisional All-German Government.—"(1) The provisional all-German government should be able to solve such urgent questions of all-German importance as the representation of Germany at the preparation of a peace treaty, and its representation in international organizations; the prevention of the drawing of Germany into coalition or military alliances directed against any Power whose armed forces took part in the war against Hitlerite Germany; questions of German citizenship, of ensuring the free activity of democratic parties and organizations, and of preventing the existence of Fascist, militarist, and other organizations hostile to democracy and the preservation of peace; the expansion of trade relations between Eastern and Western Germany; questions of transport, postal and telegraphic communications; questions of the free movement of persons and goods, irrespective of established zonal frontiers; the development of economic and cultural relations between Eastern and Western Germany; and other questions affecting the interests of the whole German people.

"(2) The main task of a provisional all-German government should be the holding of free all-German elections, as a result of which the German people themselves, without the intervention of foreign Powers, would solve the question of a social and State system

81

for a democratic Germany. The provisional all-German government should draw up a draft electoral law which would ensure the truly democratic nature of the all-German elections, the participation of all democratic organizations in the elections, and the prevention of pressure on the electors from the big monopolies. The recognition of the advisability of verifying the existence throughout the whole of Germany of the conditions necessary for the carrying out of democratic elections, as well as the adoption of measures to ensure such conditions, would depend upon this free settlement.

"The Soviet Government deems it necessary that France, the U.S.A., Great Britain and the U.S.S.R. should take steps to hold the all-German elections in conditions of real freedom, excluding any pressure whatsoever from foreign Powers during the holding of these elections."

In reply to the Soviet Note of Aug. 15, and also to an earlier Note of Aug. 4, the British, American, and French Governments presented identical Notes in Moscow on Sept. 2 inviting the Soviet Union to a four-Power meeting at Lugano (Switzerland) on Oct. 15 to discuss both the German and the Austrian treaties.

In a statement in Bonn on Aug. 17, Dr. Adenauer commented that the latest Soviet Note was essentially the same as that of March 10, 1952. Whereas, however, the earlier Note had been directed against the alleged "aggressive" designs of the NATO, that of Aug. 15 had concentrated against the E.D.C. treaty, a move which, Dr. Adenauer said, was designed to influence the forthcoming elections in the Federal Republic. The Federal Chancellor added that a peace treaty on the lines desired by the Soviet Union might lead to the reunification of Germany but would leave her with a restricted national army and with no guarantees either of neutrality or security. To accept such a treaty would mean "suicide" for Germany, which, within a short time, would inevitably be "drawn under by Russian suction". As regards the Soviet suggestion that a provisional all-German Government might be formed by the West and East German Governments, Dr. Adenauer declared that neither the Federal Government nor any of the democratic parties in the *Bundestag* recognized the régime in the Soviet zone as representative of the popular will, and rejected all contact with it. He nevertheless supported the holding of a four-Power conference, if only to learn the "real intentions of the Kremlin" on the future of Germany.

9. BERLIN CONFERENCE, 1954

After further Note exchanges, the proposal for a four-Power meeting of Foreign Ministers at Lugano was ignored by the Soviet Union in Notes published on Nov. 4, 1953, when the Soviet Government reiterated its previous demands.

On Nov. 24, however, it expressed readiness for such a conference and suggested Berlin as its venue. Following acceptance of this proposal by the Western Powers on Dec. 7, meetings eventually took place in Berlin from Jan. 25 to Feb. 18, 1954.

At these meetings Mr. Molotov proposed a Collective Security Treaty, which was, however, declared to be unacceptable by the Western Foreign Ministers—primarily because in their view it relegated a settlement of the German problem to the indefinite future, and because it implied the abandonment of the European Defence Community and the North Atlantic Treaty.

Three-Power Statement on Berlin Conference

The following agreed statement on the Berlin Conference was issued simultaneously in London, Washington and Paris on Feb. 19 by the British, U.S. and French Governments:

"The major problem facing the Berlin Conference was that of Germany. The three Western delegations urged that the reunification of Germany should be achieved through free elections leading to the creation of an all-German Government with which a peace treaty could be concluded. They put forward a practical plan to this end. Their proposals were not accepted by the Soviet delegation, even as a basis for discussion, and they were forced to the conclusion that the Soviet Government is not now ready to permit free all-German elections or to abandon its control over Eastern Germany.

"The three Western Governments will continue their efforts to achieve German reunification in freedom and by peaceful means. In the meantime they have suggested certain measures which could reduce the effect of the present division of Germany and its consequences for Berlin. They have proposed that the three Western High Commissioners should study these questions with the Soviet High Commissioner.

"The three Governments reaffirm their abiding interest in the security of Berlin, as expressed in the tripartite declaration of May 27,

1952. They will do all in their power to improve conditions in Berlin and to promote the economic welfare of the city."

West German Reaction to Berlin Conference—Dr. Adenauer's Support for Western Proposals—Bundestag Debate and Resolution

The West German Federal Chancellor, Dr. Adenauer, addressed a mass meeting in Berlin on Feb. 23, 1954, following the ending of the four-Power conference of the British, American, French and Soviet Foreign Ministers.

Dr. Adenauer, whose speech was broadcast to Eastern Germany, said that the four-Power conference had shown (1) that the Soviet Union intended to maintain the *status quo* in Germany and, "in due course", to dominate the whole of Europe; (2) that an isolated solution of the German problem, without reference to other world problems, was impossible at the moment; (3) that the four Powers' agreement to hold talks on the Far East and disarmament could help to end the "cold war" and might thus benefit Germany indirectly, even if by a "roundabout route"; and (4) that the unity and determination of the Western Powers were even greater at the end of the conference than at its beginning.

After expressing his belief that "the future is not hopeless if we have the unshakable conviction that in the end good will triumph over evil, if we have patience and endurance, and if the German people achieve moral unity and are helped by the free world", the Federal Chancellor declared that the Soviet refusal to make any concessions on Germany was based not on strength but on fears for the future of its "satellite empire" in Europe and on its belief that "any loosening of the pressure within the sphere of its power constitutes a risk". It was necessary, he continued, to get rid of any "self-deception", and those who maintained that more should have been offered to the Soviet Union "completely misunderstood" the situation.

After declaring that the "positive success" of the negotiations lay in the fact that the Western allies had "never before been so firm and united as now", Dr. Adenauer said: "Germany has every reason to be grateful to the three Western Foreign Ministers. They presented our case so clearly, so logically, and with such warmth that German negotiators could have done no better. . . . In every way they served the cause of peace and freedom." Mr. Molotov's proposal for the neutralization of Germany, he added, would in fact lead to the Sovietization of Germany, and the Soviet Foreign Minister had "deliberately demanded the impossible to exclude the possibility of any positive result".

"Nothing forces us more to build up a genuine security system in Western Europe", Dr. Adenauer continued, "than the very conceptions of the Soviet Foreign Minister. . . . The purely defensive security system represented by the E.D.C. . . . contains elements from which we can develop a collective security system covering the whole of Europe and giving the Soviet Union the security desired by it. We must remove any doubt that Germany will ever get accustomed to the existence of two separate German States. In particular, we must make it quite clear to the Soviet Union that the Pieck-Grotewohl régime has not the slightest prospect of preserving its existence in an all-German future by such methods as the formation of a provisional Government or all-German committees." In conclusion, the Federal Chancellor emphasized that Germany remained "at the side of the West", that she would continue to adhere to the policy of European integration, and that "we stand for a policy which by every means and every path, even indirectly, aims at the reunification of Germany in freedom and peace".

The Federal Chancellor made a further statement in the West German *Bundestag* on Feb. 25, when opening a debate on the Berlin Conference.

Dr. Adenauer drew five conclusions from the conference, which he listed as follows: (1) To check the Soviet aim of achieving hegemony in Europe, it had become more than ever necessary to unify Europe, to integrate her resources, and to establish the E.D.C. (2) The Federal Republic "must consolidate its internal structure based on freedom and law, and develop the spiritual and material strength needed to prevent the Sovietization of the whole of Germany". (3) The Federal Government must "demonstrate by word and deed" that the German people would never resign themselves to the partition of Germany. (4) As the Berlin conference had shown that the German problem could not be solved in isolation, the Federal Government should welcome any attempts at removing conflicts in other parts of the world, since any relaxation of international tension resulting therefrom would also affect the German question. The Federal Government would itself endeavour to contribute to a general *détente* leading to new negotiations on Germany, and, specifically, would advocate the development of a collective security system, based on the free consent and equality of all its members, which would lead the U.S.S.R. to relax its control over Eastern Germany. (5) All possible measures would be taken by the Federal Government to ease the burdens borne by the population of Eastern Germany and Berlin.

Analysing the results of the conference, Dr. Adenauer said it was "the bitter truth that German reunification had been prevented by the Soviet Union", and declared that all the Soviet proposals had been aimed at undermining the United Nations and setting up in its place a "directorate" of the great Powers, including Communist China. He described Mr. Molotov's proposal for the formation of an all-German Government before the holding of free elections as an attempt to "insinuate a Trojan horse" into the all-German State; reiterated that the Soviet proposal for Germany's neutralization would mean her eventual Sovietization; and paid a tribute to the Western Foreign Ministers and to the solidarity of the Western allies in terms similar to those of his Berlin speech.

Herr Erich Ollenhauer, the leader of the Socialist Democratic Opposition, declared that the Russians knew that free all-German elections would mean the end of the Socialist Party and of Communist influence in the Soviet Zone, and they therefore sought to link the holding of elections with Germany's position in such a system.

At the end of the debate the *Bundestag* unanimously approved an all-party resolution which regretted that no progress had been made towards solving the German problem at Berlin, and attributed this failure to the intransigence of the Soviet Government. It also declared that the *Bundestag* would do everything possible to free the 18,000,000 inhabitants of Eastern Germany and to secure the country's reunification in peace and freedom.

10.   INTEGRATION OF WESTERN GERMANY INTO WESTERN BLOC, 1952–55

The gradual recognition of the German Federal Republic as a partner in the Western European Union and the Atlantic Alliance (NATO) during 1952–55 led to increasingly hostile reactions by the East European bloc, including the German Democratic Republic.

The steps by which the Federal Republic was integrated in the Western Alliance were:

(1) The replacement of the Occupation Statute by contractual arrangements in May 1952.

(2) The signing of the European Defence Community Treaty and related protocols in Paris in May 1952.

(3) The ratification of the European Defence Community Treaty by the Federal Government in March 1953 and February 1954.

(4) The signing of a treaty of friendship between Western Germany and the United States in October 1954.

(5) The agreements on the entry of Western Germany into the Western European Union and NATO in October 1954.

(6) The ending of the occupation régime and the recognition of the full sovereignty of the Federal Republic in May 1955.

(1) Occupation Statute replaced by Contractual Arrangements between Federal Republic and Western Powers

At a meeting in Bonn on May 22, 1952, between Dr. Adenauer and the Allied High Commissioners agreement was reached on the contractual arrangements ending the Occupation Statute, restoring sovereignty to the German Federal Republic and bringing Western Germany into the European defence system to be established through the European Defence Community.

The contractual arrangements, known as the Bonn Conventions, were signed in Bonn on May 26 by Dr. Adenauer, Mr. Eden (the U.K. Foreign Secretary), M. Schuman (the French Foreign Minister) and Mr. Dean Acheson (the U. S. Secretary of State).

(2) The European Defence Community Treaty

The European Defence Community (E.D.C.) Treaty was formally signed in Paris on May 27, 1952, by Dr. Adenauer and the Foreign Ministers of France, Italy, Belgium, the Netherlands and Luxemburg, together with a treaty of guarantee between the E.D.C. and the United Kingdom, also signed by Mr. Eden, and a tripartite declaration signed by Mr. Eden, Mr. Acheson and M. Schuman (for Britain, the United States and France respectively).

The E.D.C. was defined as a "supra-national community . . . with common institutions, common armed forces and a common Budget . . . within the framework of the North Atlantic Treaty Organization". The E.D.C. would have a Council of Ministers; a Board of Commissioners; an Assembly; and a Court of Justice. The duration of the treaty would be 50 years, unless a "new situation" arose which would necessitate a review by the contracting parties.

Hostile Reactions in Eastern Germany

A violent campaign against the contractual agreements between the German Federal Republic and the Western Powers was launched in Eastern Germany during the weeks immediately preceding the signing of those agreements in May 1952, this campaign being marked by denunciations of Dr. Adenauer and the Federal Government, by appeals to the Parliament and people of Western Germany not to conclude the agreements, and by calls for mass demonstrations in the Federal Republic against Dr. Adenauer's Government and the "Western imperialists". The East German President (Herr Wilhelm Pieck) declared in a May Day speech in Berlin that it would "become necessary for the German Democratic Republic to organize the armed defence of our country" if the West German population did not prevent "the conscription of youth for the service of American imperialism", whilst the East German Premier (Herr Grotewohl) declared in a statement on May 8 that the signing of the contractual agreements would "produce in Germany the same conditions as exist in Korea" and might involve the "danger of a fratricidal war of German against German". A still more violent denunciation of the then impending contractual agreements was made on May 12 by the East German Vice-Premier, Herr Ulbricht, who threatened Dr. Adenauer and his Cabinet Ministers with "reprisals at the hands of the German people" if they signed the agreements, and declared that all members of the West German Parliament supporting the agreements would be "blacklisted" and would one day be "suitably punished"; asked what consequences the signing of the agreements would have for Berlin, Herr Ulbricht (who was speaking at a press conference) declared that the consequences would be apparent in the city "on the very day after they are signed".

Immediately following the signing of the contractual agreements in Bonn on May 26 the East German Government took a number of measures designed, in effect, to "seal off" the Soviet Zone from Western Germany and also to hamper communications between the Western sectors of Berlin and the Federal Republic. These measures, taken on May 27, comprised (*a*) the creation of a "security zone" five kilometres (about three miles) in width, along the entire 350-mile frontier of Eastern Germany with the Federal Republic, extending from the Baltic Sea to the Czech border; (*b*) the establishment of a similar "security zone" of the same width along the Baltic coast; and (*c*) the cutting-off of telephonic communications between the Soviet Zone and the Western sectors of Berlin. In announcing these measures, the East German Government declared that entry into the "security zones" would be permitted only to residents of Eastern Germany in possession of special permits issued by the "people's police" (*Volkspolizei*); that these measures were aimed at making it more difficult for "agents and spies" from Western Germany to enter the territory of Eastern Germany; and that the measures were "transitional" in character and would be withdrawn when Germany was reunited. At the same time it was announced that persons resident in Western Germany or Western Berlin who wished to enter the Soviet Zone (for visits to relatives, etc.) would in future need special permits issued by the East German authorities. (Hitherto West Germans could travel to Eastern Germany on inter-zonal passes issued in the Federal Republic, whilst Berliners—whether resident in the Western or Eastern sectors—could enter the Soviet Zone provided they carried their normal identity papers.) These restrictions were further tightened on June 24, when the East German authorities, without previous warning, suspended the issue of passes to West Berliners wishing to visit the Soviet Zone; although this measure was described as "temporary", all existing passes were declared invalid and the three offices in East Berlin which had previously issued these passes were closed down. No restrictions, however, were placed on the movement of persons from West to East Berlin, or on road travel between the Western sectors and the Federal Republic along the Berlin-Helmstedt *Autobahn*.

The national committee of the East German "National Front" (the organization representing all the political parties in the Soviet Zone) issued a statement on May 21 accusing the Western Powers of "provocations" along the zonal frontier, and declaring that it had become "unavoidably necessary" to form a national army in Eastern Germany "for the defence of the democratic achievements of the German Democratic Republic".

The establishment of the so-called "security zone" along East Germany's frontier with the West, carried out by the *Volkspolizei*, was accompanied by the ruthless eviction of people from their homes and farms, their deportation to other parts of Eastern Germany, the felling of trees, hedges and other "obstacles" along the frontier, and in many cases by the ploughing-under of crops and fertile agricultural land; as a result of these measures, there had been created by the end of June a "no-man's-land" between Eastern and Western Germany extending from the Baltic to Czechoslovakia. Despite intensive patrolling of the frontier by armed *Volkspolizei*, many thousands of East Germans living in the "security zone" managed to cross the frontier into Western Germany, where they were temporarily accommodated in camps.

Addressing the West German *Bundestag* on June 18, 1952, Dr. Adenauer denounced the "brutal terror" exercised by the Russians and their East German "puppets" against the inhabitants of the "security zone"; announced that 7,500 refugees had already arrived in the Federal Republic and were being cared for; and said that many thousands of others who had been unable to escape were being deported to the interior of Eastern Germany. He also denounced as "plain lies" the East German excuse that the "security zone" had been established as a defence against West German "saboteurs" and American military "threats"; emphasized that these allegations were "completely baseless and untrue"; and declared that the Soviet and East German measures had two purposes, (*a*) to complete the separation of Eastern Germany from the free world and incorporate it politically and economically in the Soviet bloc, and (*b*) to repress the resistance of the East German people by acts of terror. After the Chancellor's speech, all members of the *Bundestag* (except the Communist deputies) joined in adopting a resolution protesting strongly against the measures which had robbed Germans in the frontier zone of their homes and means of livelihood; calling on the free world to take note of these events; and asking the free nations to assist the Federal Republic in giving succour and support to the refugees.

It was stated in Bonn on June 25 that the Federal German Government were appealing to the British and U.S. High Commissioners to station troops on the zonal frontier with Eastern Germany, in view of the fact that the Federal police were too few in numbers to give full protection in the frontier areas. This appeal was reinforced by the West German Minister for All-German Affairs (Herr Kaiser), who, after a visit to the frontier districts, urged on June 27 that British and American armoured and infantry units should be moved to the frontier to prevent the East German people's police from creating conditions bordering on civil war.

(3) Ratification of E.D.C. Treaty by Western Germany

After lengthy debates in the various national Parliaments, the treaty establishing the European Defence Community was ratified during the early months of 1954 by the Parliaments of Western Germany, the Netherlands, Belgium and Luxemburg—that is, by four of the six E.D.C. countries.

In the Federal Republic, two Bills ratifying the Paris agreement on the E.D.C. Treaty and the Bonn Conventions were approved by the *Bundestag* on March 19, 1953, and the required amendment to the Federal "Basic Law" (Constitution) on Feb. 26, 1954, against the votes of the Social Democrats but, in the case of the constitutional amendment, with the necessary two-thirds majority (334 votes to 144).

Legislation for the ratification of the E.D.C. treaty and the Bonn Conventions had been introduced in the *Bundestag* on July 9, 1952, by Dr. Adenauer. In his speech, the Federal Chancellor declared that the E.D.C. aimed at making war impossible between the European peoples, that the automatic assimilation of the foreign and economic policies of its member-States would lead to a European federation, and that Germany was faced with three choices: (1) acceptance of the treaty and union with the West, (2) rejection of the treaty and union with the East, or, alternatively, the "neutralization" of Germany, and (3) deferment of a decision with a view to starting new negotiations—a course which, he said, would be regarded by Germany's E.D.C. partners as a "veiled rejection" of the treaty. After emphasizing that Germany could not be a "no-man's-land" in the prevailing tension between East and West, Dr. Adenauer refuted the argument that German ratification of the treaty would dispose Russia to a "hot" war in place of the existing "cold" war; a highly armed totalitarian State, he argued, would not be deterred from aggression by the weakness of others, and Hitler would never have risked a war if the other Powers had looked to their defences in time. Germany, because of her geographical position, needed allies, as Bismarck had recognized, and today, more than ever before, she must look to allies for the preservation of her freedom. "By acceptance of the treaties," the Chancellor declared, "we shall serve the creation of a new Europe, the reunion of Germany, and, above all, the cause of peace and freedom."

(4) West German Treaty with United States

On Oct. 29, 1954, Dr. Adenauer and Mr. Dulles signed in Washington a new treaty of friendship, commerce and navigation between Western Germany and the United States. On the same day Dr.

Adenauer addressed the National Press Club in Washington, and in the course of his speech gave a warning against early negotiations with the Soviet Union. At the same time, however, he outlined a four-point programme, based on the strength and unity of the Western nations, aimed at an eventual non-aggression agreement with the Soviet bloc.

"The peoples of the West," said Dr. Adenauer, "must first secure their peace and freedom by combining for their common defence. They must create sound and stable economic conditions, and guarantee human freedoms and social security to everyone. They should prepare for the future by giving their forms of association a purely defensive character, endowing them with all the elements requisite for collective security. Finally, as a regional group . . . they should jointly enter into a relationship to be settled by arrangements (*Abmachungen*) with the Soviet bloc, a relationship which would offer security against aggression to all those participating in it. In this connexion we must make it quite clear that any continuation of the Soviet attempts to bolshevize by force whole nations and parts of nations against their expressed will are not designed to bring about that relaxation of tension which the Soviet leaders describe as their foremost aim. . . . The free world will find Germany able and ready to co-operate with all her strength in the realization of this programme, and for the preservation of peace and freedom."

"We in Germany," the Federal Chancellor said, "have a special interest in the normalization of the free world's relations with the Eastern bloc, because only through such a normalization can Germany's reunification in peace and freedom be brought about. But let us beware of illusions. We in Germany are particularly well informed about the difficulties that must be surmounted before there is an easing of tension with the Communist-dominated world." In this connexion he dwelt at length on the recent elections in Eastern Germany and said that on the day before the elections the East German Ministry of Information had issued a directive to the Press in the Soviet Zone to the effect that commentators should be prepared for 97.3 per cent of all the votes going to the "National Front" list, though "certain deviations" might be expected. He referred also to the fact that no provision had been made on the ballot-papers for the electors to register a "yes" or "no", and to the marching of people to the polling stations *en bloc*; denounced the East German elections as an "electoral fraud" of "unheard-of proportions"; and added: "Here we have the most recent example of what the Russians mean when they talk of 'free and democratic' elections."

Speaking of the mass emigration of refugees from Eastern to Western Germany, the Federal Chancellor stated that a total of 2,300,000 persons had left Eastern Germany and East Berlin for the West, of whom 1,149,973 had done so between the establishment of the Federal Republic and Sept. 30, 1954, whilst 420,890 had done so between the death of Marshal Stalin and Sept. 30, 1954. After dealing with the reasons for this exodus, Dr. Adenauer declared: "You will understand now why Germany is largely immune to the temptations of Communism, and why an overwhelming majority of all Germans sharply condemn any political adventures with the East. We know very well that the normalization of our relations with the Eastern bloc is one of the great unsolved problems, and that we must constantly seek a solution. But we also know that extreme caution and vigilance are essential."

(5) West German Accession to W.E.U. and NATO

Following decisions taken at a Nine-Power Conference in London from Sept. 28 to Oct. 3, 1954, agreements were signed in Paris on Oct. 23, 1954, *inter alia* admitting the German Federal Republic to the Western European Union (previously known as the Brussels Treaty Organization) and to NATO.

These agreements included:

(*a*) a protocol on the termination of the occupation régime in Western Germany;

(*b*) a convention on the presence of foreign forces in the Federal Republic, providing for the continued stationing on Federal territory of European and United States armed forces, and containing a protocol on "control of armaments", noting *inter alia* the West German Government's declaration "not to manufacture atomic, biological or chemical weapons" and listing a large number of armaments, the manufacture of which in Western Germany would be subject to control; and

(*c*) a protocol on Western Germany's accession to NATO.

The Paris Agreements were finally agreed to by the German Federal President, Dr. Heuss, on March 24, 1955, after they had been approved by the *Bundestag* on Feb. 27 against the votes of the Social Democrats.

(6) Ending of Occupation Régime in Western Germany

On May 5, 1955, the occupation régime in Western Germany was ended and the German Federal Republic attained full sovereignty and independence as a result of the agreements signed in London and Paris.

At the same time the Federal Republic became a member of the North Atlantic Treaty Organization and of the Western European union.

At an open-air ceremony held on May 5, Dr. Adenauer read the following proclamation:

"Today, nearly ten years after the military and political collapse of National Socialism, the occupation régime has ended in the Federal Republic. With profound satisfaction the Federal Government confirms that we are a free and independent State. What has long been in preparation on a basis of growing confidence has now become a legal reality. We are free among the free, joined in genuine partnership with the former occupying Powers.

"Together with the Federal Government, 50,000,000 free citizens of the Federal Republic remember at this moment the millions of Germans who are forced to live separated from us, deprived of justice and the rule of law. We say to them: 'You belong to us. We belong to you. Our joy at our regained freedom will be marred until that freedom is granted to you also. You can always rely on us, for we and the free world will not relax our efforts until you, too, have regained your human rights and are able to live with us peacefully, reunited in a single State.'

"In this hour we recall the many Germans who still have to endure the hard lot of prisoners-of-war. We shall do all in our power to bring about the hour of their release.

"Freedom carries with it responsibilities. At home there can be only one path for us—the path of a State based on the rule of law, democracy and social justice. In the world there is only one place for us—at the side of the free peoples. Our aim is a free and united Germany in a free and united Europe."

The German Federal Republic thereby gained the right to rearm within the framework of NATO, all prohibitions on armaments being lifted except those on weapons which the Federal Republic had voluntarily undertaken not to manufacture.

East German Reaction to Paris Agreements

The East German Government issued a declaration on March 25, 1955, announcing that it had begun to take "measures to protect the

94

German Democratic Republic" as a result of the ratification of the Paris agreements by the West German Government.

The East German declaration stressed that the unification of Germany could only be attained by the cancellation of the Paris agreements. It continued: "The [West German] Federal Parliament, by ratifying the Paris agreements, and President Heuss, by signing them, have ignored the demand of the German people for unity and peace. At the same time the Adenauer Government seeks to create the impression that ratification of the agreements is favourable to the reunification of Germany, and that negotiations will shortly be held on the solution of the German problem. The Government of the German Democratic Republic cannot permit this misleading statement to go unanswered. . . .

"The German people must realize that the Western Powers, Dr. Adenauer and the Federal Parliament, by ratifying the agreements, are destroying the possibility of negotiations on the peaceful reunification of Germany. . . . By pressing the Paris agreements through, the Western Powers and Dr. Adenauer have proved that they reject the reunification of Germany on a democratic and peaceful basis, and that they are ready to sacrifice reunification for the inclusion of Western Germany in an aggressive pact system.

"Exactly contrary action has been taken by the Soviet Union and the People's Democracies, with their declarations on the ending of the state of war with Germany . . . and with their proposals for the creation of a system of collective security in Europe. The Governments of the U.S.S.R. and of the German Democratic Republic have repeatedly declared their readiness to negotiate. They have at the same time announced that the ratification and implementation of the Paris agreements would make negotiations on the reunification of Germany impossible. . . ."

Herr Grotewohl, speaking at a Berlin demonstration on May 8, 1955, to celebrate the 10th anniversary of the overthrow of Nazism, reiterated that the cancellation of the Paris agreements was "the necessary pre-condition for the reunification of Germany". He announced at the same time that the *Volkspolizei* [the para-military police force in Eastern Germany, estimated at 100,000 to 120,000 strong] would be "developed into an effective instrument of defence".

Herr Grotewohl outlined his Government's policy for the reunification of Germany as follows: (1) annulment of the Paris agreements; (2) "an immediate understanding between the two parts of Germany on the removal of militarism, and on the preparation of free all-German elections to a National Assembly"; (3) a joint request to the four Powers (Britain, France, the U.S.A. and the U.S.S.R.) by the East and West German Governments for "the speedy conclusion of a peace treaty and the withdrawal of all occupation troops"; (4) continuous consultations between East and West Germany on "all questions of economic, social, and cultural co-operation".

After declaring that Eastern Germany would "take all necessary measures to defend herself against the West German militarists and neo-fascists", Herr Grotewohl referred to the Warsaw Conference which had been convened for May 11. "The pact to be concluded in Warsaw," he said, "will serve peace and bar the way to aggression in Europe. The history of the last few decades will not be repeated. This time the military expansion of the American and West German militarists will be brought to a decisive halt in its very first stages. . . ."

Herr Grotewohl said that the conclusion of the Austrian State Treaty—defining Austria's independence and neutrality and signed on May 15, 1955, by the Foreign Ministers of the four Powers—had "shown the way to the solution of the German problem", adding in this connexion: "Austria will tolerate no foreign military bases on her territory and will enter into no unilateral military alliances. . . . The solution of the German problem on this basis is possible if the right conditions are created. This means for Western Germany the steering of an independent course and the removal of the Paris agreements."

11. INTEGRATION OF EASTERN GERMANY INTO EASTERN BLOC, 1956

Soviet Recognition of East German Sovereignty

Even before the Paris agreements of October 1954, it had been announced in Moscow on March 25, 1954, that the Soviet Government recognized the German Democratic Republic as a sovereign and independent State conducting its own internal and external affairs; that the functions of the Soviet High Commissioner in Eastern Germany would be limited to security questions and to liaison with the Western Allied authorities on all-German questions; and that Soviet occupation forces would remain in Eastern Germany under four-Power agreements.

Mr. Georgi Maximovich Pushkin, a former Ambassador in Budapest, was appointed Soviet Ambassador to the German Democratic Republic and High Commissioner in Germany on July 19, 1954, in succession to Mr. Semeonov, who had assumed ambassadorial status in September 1953. On Aug. 6, 1954, the Soviet Government annulled all decrees and ordinances issued by the Soviet military authorities in Eastern Germany between 1945 and 1953.

The West German *Bundestag* unanimously adopted a resolution on April 7, 1954, refusing to recognize the right of the Soviet Union "to create an East German State", and emphasizing that the Federal Government was the only freely-elected body of its kind in Germany and therefore had the sole right to represent the German people.

On April 8, 1954, the three Western High Commissioners in Bonn, on behalf of the British, French and U.S. Governments, issued a declaration in connexion with "the statement issued on March 25 by the Soviet Government purporting to describe a change in its relations with the Government of the so-called German Democratic Republic". This stated (1) that the Soviet statement "does not alter the actual situation in the Soviet zone", where the Soviet Government "still retains effective control"; (2) that Britain, France and the U.S.A. would continue to regard the U.S.S.R. as the Power responsible for the Soviet zone of Germany, but would not recognize the sovereignty of the East German régime nor deal with it as a Government; (3) that they would continue to regard the German Federal Government as "the only freely elected and legally constituted Government of Germany".

Conclusion of Warsaw Treaty, 1955

The Soviet Union reacted to the conclusion of the Paris agreements by sending out invitations, on Nov. 13, 1954, to 23 European countries and the U.S.A. to attend a conference on "the safeguarding of peace and collective security in Europe". The only countries to accept the invitation, however, were the Communist States of Eastern Europe, whose representatives attended a conference in Moscow from Nov. 29 to Dec. 2.

The conference ended with the signing of a declaration stating that the creation of a West German Army and the inclusion of Western Germany in NATO would constitute a threat to the security of the eight countries represented at the conference, and that, if the Paris agreements were ratified, these countries would meet again "to adopt measures for safeguarding their security".

Ministers from eight countries—the Soviet Union, Poland, Czechoslovakia, Eastern Germany, Hungary, Romania, Bulgaria and Albania—subsequently held a three-day conference in Warsaw on May 11–13, 1955, which resulted in (1) the signing of a 20-year treaty of friendship, co-operation and mutual assistance between these countries, and (2) the creation of a unified military command for the armed forces of all these countries except Eastern Germany, whose participation would be "examined later". Marshal Ivan Koniev, of the Soviet Army, was appointed Commander-in-Chief of the joint armed forces.

The major speech at the conference was made by Marshal Bulganin, Prime Minister of the U.S.S.R., who strongly denounced the remilitarization of Western Germany under the London and Paris agreements. Extracts from his speech are given below:

"At the Moscow Conference (of November–December 1954) the Governments of the countries represented here agreed to reconsider the situation in the event of the Paris agreements being ratified. Now this necessity has arisen. The ratification of the Paris agreements has become a fact. As a result, the West German militarists have been given the right to recruit a standing army and to supply it with all types of modern weapons. . . .

"The Paris agreements, therefore, are putting means for new aggression into the hands of yesterday's aggressors. . . . Ten years after the end of the Second World War, Western Germany with the help of the United States, Britain and France, is becoming the main seat of war danger in Europe. It is becoming a member of the aggressive North Atlantic bloc and also of the West European military union directed against the Soviet Union and the people's democracies. . . ."

Formation of "People's Army" and Ministry of National Defence
in Eastern Germany

A law creating a "National People's Army" in Eastern Germany, and at the same time setting up a Ministry of National Defence, was unanimously passed by the East German *Volkskammer* on Jan. 18, 1956. The official text stated that the National People's Army would consist of "ground, sea and air forces necessary for the defence of the German Democratic Republic", and that the army's numerical strength would be "limited in accordance with the tasks of defending the territory of the German Democratic Republic, defending its frontiers, and air defence".

The law was introduced in the *Volkskammer* by Herr Willi Stoph (Deputy Premier in the East German Government), whose appointment as Minister of National Defence was announced on Jan. 20. Herr Stoph declared that the "strengthening of the defences of the German Democratic Republic" had become necessary as a result of Western Germany's entry into the "aggressive North Atlantic pact", the establishment in Western Germany of "a mercenary army under the supreme command of U.S. NATO generals", and the "transformation of Western Germany and West Berlin into a NATO war base".

A proposal that the two German States should formally pledge themselves to refrain from the use of force against each other was made in the *Volkskammer* on the same day (Jan. 18) by Herr Grotewohl.

After declaring that "both parts of Germany must realize the danger of the policy of NATO and of military pacts", Herr Grotewohl called upon the "progressive forces" in Western Germany "to join with us immediately in seeking a way to release Germany from the deadly policy of American militarism". He put forward the following proposals:

(1) Both German States should (*a*) support a European Collective Security Treaty; (*b*) urge a reduction in the number of foreign troops; and (*c*) "pledge themselves in treaty form to refrain from all use of force against each other, and to use only peaceful methods in their efforts for the reunification of Germany".

(2) All "propaganda and preparations for atomic war on German soil" should be brought to an end. The two German Governments should reach "joint agreement on the renunciation of the atom bomb and on the mutual renunciation of the manufacture of atomic weapons".

(3) The German Democratic Republic and the German Federal Republic should "make efforts to normalize their relations with each other, and conclude relevant agreements in the various fields of economic and cultural life".

Herr Grotewohl reiterated his Government's earlier proposal for the formation of an All-German Council in which these matters could be discussed.

East German Army admitted to Joint Military Command of Warsaw Treaty Powers, 1956

Following the creation of a "National People's Army" in Eastern Germany, a formal request for the admission of the German Democratic Republic to the joint command of the Warsaw Treaty Powers was made by Herr Ulbricht to the Prague meeting of the Political and Consultative Committee of the Warsaw Treaty which took place on Jan. 27-28, 1956.

The Prague meeting decided in favour of Herr Ulbricht's request and announced in a communiqué that contingents of the new East German Army would be incorporated in the unified command of the Warsaw Treaty Powers, and the East German Defence Minister would become a deputy commander under Marshal Koniev.

12. THE EAST BERLIN RISING OF JUNE 1953

Prior to these developments, serious disturbances amounting to an anti-Communist rising had taken place in East Berlin and other cities in Eastern Germany.

In a statement on June 11, 1953, the East German Government announced a series of measures "designed to correct the mistakes made by the Government and the administrative services in various fields, and to improve the standard of living of the workers and intellectuals, together with the farmers, craftsmen and other sections of the middle class". It was admitted that "mistakes" in the distribution of ration cards, the collection of agricultural produce and the collection of taxes had resulted in a "difficult situation" which, however, would be "immediately corrected".

Demonstrations on June 16, 1953, by East Berlin workers protesting against an increase in their working "norms" developed on the following day into mass demonstrations against the Soviet occupation authorities and the Communist régime, in which tens of thousands of workers took part. Strong forces of Soviet tanks and infantry were called out, a curfew and martial law restrictions imposed by the Soviet Commandant in East Berlin and many arrests made. Similar anti-Soviet and anti-Communist demonstrations occurred at the same time in many East German cities, a number of demonstrators being killed and injured in clashes with Soviet troops and the Communist "People's Police".

When it was becoming apparent that the People's Police were losing control of the situation, the Soviet Commandant in Berlin

(Major-General Dibrova) sealed off the Eastern sector from the rest of the city and called out strong forces of Soviet tanks, armoured cars and lorry-borne infantry to restore order. Later in the day he imposed a curfew from 9 p.m. to 5 a.m., banned all demonstrations and announced that groups of more than three persons would be liable to arrest and immediate punishment under martial law regulations. The curfew and other restrictions were maintained by the Soviet authorities for nearly a month, being lifted on July 13, 1953.

The East German News Agency announced on June 25 that 25 people had been killed and 378 injured in the disturbances.

Reports of mass arrests of anti-Communists, and of the execution of many demonstrators by the Soviet military authorities, continued to reach Western Germany during the last fortnight of June. No statements on these reprisals were issued either by the Soviet zonal authorities or the East German régime, except for an official announcement by the East German News Agency (June 18) that the Russians had executed a West Berliner, Willi Goettling. It was stated that General Dibrova had ordered Goettling's execution on the ground that he had acted "on the orders of a foreign Power as an active organizer of provocations and disturbances in the Soviet sector of Berlin".

Economic Concessions by East German Government

In a speech on June 24, 1953, Herr Grotewohl said that "fascist bandits and Western provocative elements" could not have met with success in East Berlin "if the dissatisfaction of the working masses had not provided the inflammable material". After declaring that "the guilt for the events of the past days rests with us", and not solely with "Western agents", he admitted that serious food shortages had been caused by the flight of "hundreds of thousands" of farmers to Western Germany; that the Government had pursued a mistaken policy in concentrating on industrial production at the expense of consumer goods; and that there was widespread and justified dissatisfaction with the existing economic conditions. Herr Grotewohl added the Government had "drawn the necessary conclusion" from its mistakes and would take immediate measures to ameliorate the condition of the people.

West German Reactions to Uprising in Eastern Zone

The Soviet suppression of the East Berlin uprising aroused intense indignation in the German Federal Republic.

The *Bundestag* decided on July 1, 1953, to commemorate the East Berlin uprising by making its anniversary (June 17) a memorial day each year. During the debate, Dr. Adenauer said that although definite figures were not available, there was reason to believe that 62 people in Eastern Germany had been sentenced to death and 25,000 imprisoned after the uprising.

Dr. Adenauer, Herr Kaiser (Federal Minister for All-German Affairs) and members of both Houses of the Federal Parliament visited West Berlin on June 23, 1953, to attend the funeral service of seven victims of the uprising of July 17. Dr. Adenauer, in a funeral oration at the graves of the victims, gave a solemn pledge "in the name of the whole German people" that the Federal Government "will not rest or desist until Germans behind the Iron Curtain are free and united with us in freedom and peace".

U.S. Food Aid for Eastern Germany

In a message to Dr. Adenauer on July 10, 1953, President Eisenhower offered $15,000,000 of American foodstuffs (grain, sugar, lard, and other commodities) to relieve the serious food shortage in Eastern Germany, and simultaneously appealed to the Soviet Government to co-operate in its distribution. The offer was rejected by the Soviet Government and also by the East German Government.

In response to President Eisenhower's message, Mr. Molotov presented a Note to the U.S. Embassy in Moscow on July 12 saying that the President was "incorrectly informed about the situation in Eastern Germany" and had obtained his information from "sources such as the U.S. High Commissioner in Germany and Adenauer, the Bonn Chancellor, who are among those chiefly responsible for the violation of public order in East Berlin". The offer of U.S. foodstuffs for the East German people was described as "behaviour which would offend even the population of a colony, let alone the people of a lawful democratic government", and as "a propaganda manoeuvre which has nothing in common with the true interests of the German people".

Herr Grotewohl issued a statement on the same day describing President Eisenhower's offer as "an insult", "a provocation", and an attempt "to use U.S. aid in order to organize espionage rings" in Eastern Germany.

Despite the Soviet rejection of his offer, President Eisenhower nevertheless ordered large quantities of foodstuffs to be despatched by sea and air to Germany, for distribution by the authorities in West Berlin. Depots and stockpiles were accordingly established by the West Berlin City Government, which invited people in East Berlin and in the Eastern zone to collect food parcels from the Schöneberg Town Hall and other distributing centres.

The food distribution programme was launched on July 27 and ended on Oct. 10, 1953, during which period over 3,000,000 people from East Berlin and other parts of Eastern Germany crossed to the Western sectors and collected food parcels for themselves and for their families. At the end of the 11-weeks' programme a total of 5,000,000 food parcels had been distributed, and it was estimated that 80 per cent of the people of East Berlin had obtained two rations per person. Of the total number of East Germans crossing into the Western sectors to collect parcels, 34 per cent were from East Berlin and 68 per cent from other parts of Eastern Germany.

13. ADENAUER GOVERNMENT'S STATEMENTS ON REUNIFICATION, 1953

The Adenauer Government had meanwhile repeatedly declared its insistence on the ultimate reunification of Germany on the basis of free elections to be held in Western and in Eastern Germany.

Five-Point Declaration of German Foreign and International Policy

A five-point declaration of the aims of the Federal Government's foreign and international policy, drawn up by the Government parties, was approved by the *Bundestag* on June 10, 1953, with the support of all Opposition parties except the Communists. The five points were as follows:

(1) Free and democratic elections for the whole of Germany.

(2) The subsequent formation of an all-German Government.

(3) The conclusion of a peace treaty between the Allied Powers of the last war and a reunited Germany.

(4) The settlement of all territorial questions in this peace treaty.

(5) Freedom for an all-German Government to enter into any arrangements with other countries which were consistent with the aims of the United Nations.

The Federal Chancellor denied rumours that he had tried to "torpedo" four-Power talks, and stressed that he was in favour of such talks if they offered a reasonable prospect of success. However, he said, the Soviet Union wished to draw up a peace treaty on the basis of the Potsdam Agreement, which would mean (1) that Germany would not be able to take part in the peace negotiations, (2) that the four Powers would retain permanent economic, political and military control over Germany, (3) that Germany would be barred from entering into international alliances, and (4) that the present German frontiers would be regarded as permanent and unchangeable.

Re-election of Dr. Adenauer

The *Bundestag* was dissolved on July 29, 1953, in preparation for general elections, which were held on Sept. 6 throughout the Federal Republic.

The election campaign was fought predominantly on questions of foreign policy and, in particular, on the question of European unity and Germany's role therein. On Sept. 4, shortly before polling day, the Federal Chancellor submitted a memorandum to the Western Powers proposing (1) the conclusion, within the framework of the United Nations, of a general security pact between Russia and her European allies on the one hand and the European Defence Community, in alliance with the North Atlantic Treaty Organization, on the other; (2) the development of trade relations between Western and Eastern Europe.

Dr. Adenauer said that he recognized that Russia might feel the need for some form of security against the possibility of an attack from the West, and suggested that such security could best be obtained by a European pact along the lines he had proposed. Refuting the Soviet contention that the E.D.C., linked with NATO, would constitute a threat to the Soviet Union, he emphasized that the armaments of the E.D.C. member-countries would be circumscribed and internationally controlled, and that Germany herself, as a member of the E.D.C., would have only 12 divisions. "The Soviet Government," he added, "has itself described its fear of an attack on the U.S.S.R. and its desire for peace as the mainspring of its policy. It is not credible that Russia can really feel herself threatened by the creation of the European Defence Community, including 12 German divisions. It is possible that she fears the U.S.A. and the world-wide influence it exercises. If for this reason there is really a subjective Russian need for security, the West is ready to meet it—without prejudice to the West's own need to remember its own security." To satisfy the "possible security needs" of the U.S.S.R. Dr. Adenauer therefore suggested that the alliance of the six E.D.C. countries, after being linked to NATO, should "enter into treaty relations with the regional alliances of the Eastern bloc, within the framework of a superstructure to be developed within the United Nations". After such a relationship had been achieved, trade between Eastern and Western Europe should be expanded to the greatest possible extent, since "economic development and political security go hand in hand".

The Social Democrats—the principal Opposition party—opposed what they described as the "little Europe" concept advocated by Dr. Adenauer, asserted that the Federal Republic was in a position of inequality both in the European Defence Community and the Coal and Steel Community, and maintained that full British and Scandinavian participation was essential in any projects of European co-operation and integration. Herr Ollenhauer, the party leader, declared during the election campaign that the reunification of Germany was the overriding consideration, and that a unified Germany should not commit herself to an alliance with either the East or the West.

These proposals were denounced by Dr. Adenauer, who declared that they would mean "the end of Germany", said that to leave it to the four Powers alone to determine Germany's future place in the world would be tantamount to saying that "Germans should mount the gallows with bowed heads", and criticized equally strongly the proposal that West German representatives should "sit down at the council table with the Pankow persecutors of their German brothers and sisters in the Soviet Zone". Replying to Dr. Adenauer's criticisms on Aug. 31, Herr Ollenhauer stressed that the Social Democrats continued to reject the participation of the East German Government as an equal partner in the discussions on the future of Germany, but maintained that the holding of free elections in all four Zones required "certain technical arrangements" for which it was indispensable to have discussions with East German representatives, just as the two sides had already discussed railway and postal questions and interzonal traffic. He added that the elections themselves must be placed under international control and denied that there had been any change in his party's policy, saying that its aim remained the holding of free elections and German co-operation with the four Powers in any negotiations for reunification.

The elections in the Federal Republic, which were held in a calm and orderly atmosphere, resulted in an overwhelming victory for the Christian Democrats headed by Dr. Adenauer, whose majority was the greatest in German parliamentary history.

Speaking later in the evening from the balcony of the Bonn *Rathaus,* from which he addressed a torchlight procession in his honour, Dr. Adenauer declared that his aims for his new term of office were "a happy and more prosperous future for Germany", "a better Europe for our youth", and the reunification of Germany. "We have always spoken", he said, "of the reunification of Germany, but should we not rather speak of the liberation of our brothers in the Eastern zone? Our aim must be the liberation of the 18,000,000 Germans in the East who are at present under the yoke of Soviet oppression and slavery . . . . Let us close our ranks and work together for this aim. Our policy is the peaceful achievement of German unity, the liberation of our brothers in the East, and a united Europe. . . . When the 18,000,000 Germans in the Soviet Zone have been liberated, a free and united Germany will be able to take her place in a united Europe."

In a further press statement on Sept. 8, Dr. Adenauer stressed that the main purpose of the E.D.C. was to make any future war between Germany and France impossible and that the E.D.C. was in no way directed against the Soviet Union. He also declared that the question of the former German territories in Eastern Europe must never lead to a war between Germany and Poland, and added: "It must be the aim of German policy to restore friendly relations with a free Poland. The German Eastern territories could then possibly be administered under a German-Polish condominium or placed under the United Nations."

The Federal Government's Press Office in Bonn announced on Sept. 9, 1953, that Dr. Adenauer would retain the post of Foreign Minister in the new Government to be formed concurrently with the Chancellorship.

At a summit conference of the Heads of Government of the Four Powers (President Eisenhower, Marshal Bulganin, Sir Anthony Eden and M. Edgar Faure) in Geneva, the four leaders agreed *inter alia* on July 23, 1955, that "the reunification of Germany by means of free elections shall be carried out in conformity with the national interests of the German people and the interests of European security".

III. FROM DR. ADENAUER'S VISIT TO MOSCOW TO DR. ERHARD'S POLICY STATEMENTS, 1955–65

1. DR. ADENAUER'S VISIT TO MOSCOW, 1955

The Soviet Government issued a declaration on Jan. 15, 1955, expressing its readiness to "normalize" its relations with the German Federal Republic on condition that the Paris agreements were not ratified. This declaration was followed on Jan. 25 by a decree, issued by the Presidium of the Supreme Soviet, ending the state of war between the U.S.S.R. and Germany, which had existed since the German invasion of the Soviet Union on June 22, 1941.

The Soviet declaration made the following three points:

(1) "The most important and urgent matter for settling the German problem is to solve the task of restoring German unity. In order to carry out this task, talks are necessary between the U.S.A., Britain, France and the Soviet Union, on the question of restoring the unity of Germany on the basis of free all-German elections. Such talks would lose all point and would become impossible if the Paris agreements were ratified."

(2) The Soviet Union, which had "good relations with the German Democratic Republic" was "likewise prepared to bring about normal relations between the U.S.S.R. and the German Federal Republic" with the aim of "promoting better mutual understanding and the search for more successful ways of carrying out the task of restoring German unity".

(3) "If the Paris agreements are ratified, a new situation will be created in which the Soviet Union would concern itself, not only with further strengthening friendly relations with the German Democratic Republic, but also, through the joint efforts of the peace-loving European States, with helping to strengthen peace and security in Europe."

The declaration said that the ratification of the Paris agreements would "draw the German Federal Republic into adventurist plans for preparing a new war", "establish the division of Germany for long years to come", and "be an obstacle in the way of the peaceful restoration of German unity". It added: "There are still possibilities, which have not been utilized, of reaching agreement on the question of German unification with due consideration for the legitimate interests of the German people, and for the holding in 1955 of free all-German elections with this end in view. Such possibilities exist if the main obstacle that now stands in the way of German reunification—the plans for the remilitarization of Western Germany and its inclusion in military groupings—is removed. The German people should be given the opportunity, by free general elections throughout Germany, including Berlin, to express their will freely, so that a united Germany can again arise as a great Power occupying a worthy place among the other Powers. . . .

"The Soviet Government considers it possible, in the event of assent by the German Democratic Republic and the German Federal Republic, to come to an understanding on the establishment of appropriate international supervision over the holding of all-German elections. In this connexion, no section of Germany must be bound by any conditions of separate agreements regarding its participation in military groupings. . . .

"The German people must make a choice. They must choose the road they are to follow. One road leads to the restoration of German unity and the establishment of normal relations with all European States. This road precludes participation by any section of Germany in military groupings directed against other States, and can best be ensured by Germany's participation in a system of European collective security. The other road, on to which the Paris agreements are dragging the German people, leads to the division of Germany, the restoration of militarism in Western Germany, and the inclusion of Western Germany in the plans for preparing a new war."

An official statement issued in Bonn on Jan. 16 described the Soviet declaration as a new move in the "continuing struggle of the Soviet Union" to prevent the unity of the Western world. It denied *in toto* the allegation that the Paris agreements would mean the remilitarization of Western Germany; declared that negotiations with the Soviet Union on the reunification of Germany had no chance of success unless it were based on an "alliance of free peoples"; and recalled that the Soviet Government itself, at the Berlin Conference of 1954, had refused free all-German elections and had blocked "every step towards the reunification of Germany in peace and freedom".

The decree issued on Jan. 25, 1955, by the Presidium of the Supreme Soviet, ending the state of war between Germany and the U.S.S.R., contained the following passages:

"Having in view the strengthening and extension of peaceful and friendly mutual relations between the Soviet Union and the German Democratic Republic, based on the recognition of the principles of sovereignty and equality; taking into consideration the opinion of the Government of the German Democratic Republic; and taking into account the interests of the population of both Eastern and Western Germany, the Presidium of the Supreme Soviet declares:

(1) The state of war between the Soviet Union and Germany is terminated, and peaceful relations are being re-established.

(2) All judicial restrictions occasioned by the war in respect of German citizens who were regarded as citizens of an enemy State are abolished.

(3) The declaration on the ending of the state of war with Germany does not alter her international obligations, and does not affect the rights and obligations of the Soviet Union which derive from existing international agreements of the four Powers concerning Germany as a whole."

Great Britain had terminated the state of war with Germany on July 9, 1951, France on July 13, 1951, and the United States on Oct. 24, 1951. Many other Allied countries had taken similar action, but the Soviet Union and East European countries had remained technically at war with Germany.

It was officially stated in Bonn on Jan. 26 that the Soviet termination of the state of war would be a practical step towards the restoration of normal Russo-German relations only if the Soviet Government were to agree to "really free elections for the whole of Germany", and to the negotiation of a peace treaty with a free all-German Government. The hope was expressed that the Soviet

Government, as a first step towards the normalization of relations, would release all German prisoners of war and civilians still in its custody.

Soviet Invitation to Dr. Adenauer to visit Moscow

The Soviet Government presented a Note to the Federal German Government on June 7, 1955, (transmitted by the Soviet Embassy in Paris to the West German Embassy in that city) inviting Dr. Adenauer to visit Moscow, and proposing the normalization of relations between the U.S.S.R. and the Federal Republic.

After declaring that the interests of peace and European security, as well as those of the Soviet and German peoples, called for the normalization of relations, the Note continued: "The experience of history shows that the preservation and strengthening of peace in Europe depends to a decisive degree on the existence of good relations between the Soviet and German peoples. . . . In the years when friendly relations and co-operation existed between our peoples, it was of great benefit to both countries. Conversely, hostile relations and wars between our peoples have brought them untold misery, privation and suffering. It was the Soviet and German peoples that suffered most of all in the two World Wars. . . .

"The Soviet Government cannot fail to draw the attention of the Federal Republic to the fact that certain aggressive circles in some countries are harbouring plans to set the Soviet Union and Western Germany against each other, and to prevent an improvement in their relations. Another war would turn Germany into a field of battle and destruction. Such a war on German territory, involving modern means of mass destruction, would be even more cruel and devastating in its results than any past war. Developments must not be allowed to follow this course. The impending danger can be averted if normal relations, based on mutual confidence and peaceful co-operation, are established between our countries. The Soviet Union, in spite of all the sufferings inflicted upon her during the recent war, has never let herself be guided by feelings of revenge against the German people. . . .

"The Soviet Government proceeds from the premise that the establishment of normal relations between the Soviet Union and the German Federal Republic will contribute to settling outstanding issues concerning the whole of Germany, and thereby help to solve the principal national problem of the German people—the re-establishment of the unity of a democratic German State. . . .

"The Soviet Government also attaches great importance to more stable relations between the Soviet Union and the Federal Republic in the field of trade. It is appropriate to recall that the Soviet Union and Germany carried on extensive and mutually advantageous trade in the past, with the commodity turnover amounting at times to one-fifth of the total foreign trade of both countries. The Soviet Union has extensive trade relations with the German Democratic Republic. Trade between the U.S.S.R. and the Federal Republic of Germany is of a limited and unstable nature. However, the pre-requisites exist for the development of extensive trade and the establishment of mutually advantageous economic relations between the Soviet Union and the Federal Republic provided there are normal relations between them. The Soviet Union, with its highly developed industry and expanding agriculture, considers it possible to enlarge substantially its volume of trade with Western Germany.

"Cultural interchange can also play an important part in normalizing relations between our countries. Scientific, cultural and technical ties between the peoples of the U.S.S.R. and Germany are of long standing. They have enriched the intellectual life of both peoples and have had a favourable effect on European cultural development as a whole. These traditions can serve to promote scientific, cultural and technical co-operation between the two countries.

"The Soviet Government believes that the abolition of the Occupation Statute in Western Germany, and the decree of the Supreme Soviet ending the state of war between the U.S.S.R. and Germany, provide the necessary conditions for establishing normal and direct relations between the Soviet Union and the German Federal Republic. In view of this, the Soviet Government proposes to the Government of the German Federal Republic that direct diplomatic, trade and cultural relations should be established between the two countries.

"Considering it desirable for personal contact to be established between the statesmen of the two countries, the Soviet Government would welcome a visit to Moscow, in the near future, of Chancellor Adenauer and any other representatives whom the Federal Government might wish to send, in order to discuss the establishment of diplomatic and trade relations between the Soviet Union and the German Federal Republic, and to examine the relevant issues."

An official statement in Bonn said that the Federal Government welcomed the Soviet Union's proposal to establish diplomatic, trade, and cultural relations between the U.S.S.R. and the German Federal Republic. It added that the Note "raises various questions which require prior examination", and that it was hoped that an eventual meeting between Dr. Adenauer and the Soviet leaders would "appear appropriate". No statement was issued by Dr. Adenauer himself.

The Federal Government's reply to the Soviet proposal for the normalization of relations between the U.S.S.R. and the German

Federal Republic was presented on June 30, 1955, to the Soviet Ambassador in Paris (Mr. Vinogradov) by the Federal German Ambassador (Herr von Maltzan). After stating that the Federal Government was "in agreement" with the Soviet proposal for discussions on the establishment of diplomatic, commercial, and cultural relations between the two countries, it added: "In present circumstances, it appears to the Federal Government advisable that the subjects which are to form the basis of this discussion should first be defined and their order clarified. It proposes, therefore, that informal discussions should take place between the Embassies of the two countries in Paris on these questions."

It was pointed out in Bonn that the Federal German Government did not propose to make any preconditions for a meeting with the Soviet Government (e.g., on the question of German prisoners of war still held in the Soviet Union); that, although the German Note had made no mention of the invitation extended to Dr. Adenauer to visit Moscow, this did not mean that the Federal Chancellor had declined the invitation; and that the text of the German Note had been made known beforehand to the British, American and French Ambassadors in Bonn.

A Soviet Note welcoming the German Federal Government's willingness to discuss the establishment of diplomatic, trade and cultural relations between the U.S.S.R. and the Federal Republic was transmitted to the German Ambassador in Paris on Aug. 3 by the Soviet Ambassador. It suggested that the talks between the Soviet Government and the German delegation headed by Dr. Adenauer should be held in Moscow "at the end of August or the beginning of September"; said that the Soviet Government "proceeds from the premise that establishment of diplomatic, trade and cultural relations between the two countries will naturally not be bound by any preliminary conditions on the part of one side or the other"; and added that the Soviet Government had no objection to the German suggestion that Herr von Maltzan and Mr. Vinogradov should have informal discussions in Paris "for the purpose of specifying the questions which are to be discussed and studied during the talks in Moscow".

The German reply, presented to Mr. Vinogradov by Herr von Maltzan on Aug. 12, suggested that the Soviet-German talks should

113

begin in Moscow on Sept. 9. It accepted the agenda suggested by the Soviet Government (i.e. the establishment of diplomatic, trade and cultural relations) but, in addition, proposed that the two Governments should also discuss (1) the question of German unity, and (2) the release of those Germans who were still held in the U.S.S.R. or in "the Soviet Union's sphere of influence". The German Note stressed that the Federal Government was of the opinion that these two questions could not be separated from the question of establishing diplomatic relations between the two countries.

In a further Note on Aug. 19, the Soviet Government agreed that the Moscow talks should begin on Sept. 9. It added: "As regards the question of Germany's national unity . . . the Soviet Government sees no obstacles to an exchange of views on this issue or on other international questions of interest to both parties". No specific mention was made of the question of German prisoners of war.

Adenauer-Bulganin Discussions in Moscow—Agreement on Establishment of Diplomatic Relations—Soviet Undertaking to return 10,000 German Prisoners

Discussions between the Chancellor of the German Federal Republic, Dr. Adenauer, and the Prime Minister of the U.S.S.R., Marshal Bulganin, were accordingly held in Moscow from Sept. 9-13 and resulted in an agreement on the establishment of diplomatic relations between the two countries. Marshal Bulganin also gave an undertaking that the Soviet Government would return to Germany nearly 10,000 prisoners who, he stated, had committed war crimes on Russian territory during the Second World War.

The first day's discussions (Sept. 9) were devoted to statements by Marshal Bulganin and Dr. Adenauer, summaries of which are given below.

Marshal Bulganin said: "The Soviet Government has agreed to an exchange of views on the question of establishing German unity. In doing this we must take note of those serious obstacles which have arisen as a result of the ratification of the Paris Agreements, under which the German Federal Republic has undertaken certain military alignments and the remilitarization of Western Germany is being carried out. The Soviet Government has always recognized that the solution of the problem of reuniting Germany must be first and foremost the affair of the Germans themselves. In this respect account should

114

be taken of the actual conditions which have arisen with the existence of the German Federal Republic and the German Democratic Republic. . . . The Soviet Government has supported, and continues unswervingly to support, the establishment of a united Germany as a peaceful and democratic State. It expresses the hope that the establishment of diplomatic relations between the U.S.S.R. and the German Federal Republic will help to solve unsettled questions in which both sides are interested. It proposes the establishment of such diplomatic relations and an agreement on the setting-up of a Soviet Embassy in Bonn and a Federal German Embassy in Moscow."

An agreement on the establishment of diplomatic relations, Marshal Bulganin added, would "greatly contribute to the development of trade between our two countries on the basis of appropriate long-term agreements".

Dr. Adenauer urged that the talks should be held in "an atmosphere of unreserved frankness" and that the delegates should make every effort "to get at the heart of matters". He did not think that normal relations could be achieved only by outlawing war, creating security systems, and establishing "so to speak, in a mechanical way, diplomatic, economic, and cultural relations", but by examining the causes which rendered the present relationship between the two countries abnormal, and by making all possible efforts to remove those causes.

Raising the question of German prisoners of war still in Soviet hands, "a question by which hardly any German family remains unaffected", Dr. Adenauer emphasized that he was raising the issue solely from humane considerations. He declared in this connexion: "The thought is intolerable that, more than ten years after the end of hostilities, men who in one way or another were drawn into the whirlpool of warlike events should be kept from their homes, families and normal peaceful occupations. Do not think I want to be provocative if I say that the establishment of normal relations between our States is inconceivable as long as this question is unresolved. It is not a precondition that I am setting—I am speaking of normalization itself. Let us end a situation that is a daily source of remembrance of a sorrowful and dividing past".

Turning to the question of German unification, the Chancellor said that both delegations were agreed that the division of Germany created an intolerable situation, that German unity must be restored, and that this was the responsibility of the four great Powers. He added: "Here also I must repeat that I propose no conditions but speak of normalization itself. The division of Germany is abnormal; it is contrary to divine and human right and against nature. . . . I know that I am speaking for all Germans, not only for the population of the Federal Republic, in requesting you to dedicate all your energies to a rapid solution of this problem. . . . There can be no real security in Europe without the restoration of German unity. We must eliminate this dangerous potential crisis in which passions can so easily be inflamed". The four great Powers, Dr. Adenauer continued, would be discussing this question at the forthcoming Geneva meeting of Foreign Ministers in October, and he had no intention of confusing the Geneva discussions by bilateral talks independent of the four-Power negotiations. "But I am in duty bound," he added, "to avail myself of the opportunity offered by this meeting to represent to you urgently the full seriousness of this question, and to discuss it with you so as to facilitate your task at Geneva."

Referring to the objection that a reunified Germany might be regarded as a source of danger to the Soviet Union, Dr. Adenauer pointed out that it must be left to the free decision of an all-German Government and an all-German Parliament whether Germany should join any alliance. He added: "If the Soviet Union, as a result of the reunification of Germany, should anticipate an impairment of her security, we are perfectly willing to collaborate in a security system which will do away with such preoccupations. It would appear to be right to consider, simultaneously with the deliberations on the re-establishment of German unity, a security system for Europe."

Dr. Adenauer emphasized that neither NATO nor the Western European Union were instruments of aggression; that peace was the primary objective of the entire German people; and that all Germans were fully aware, from their own experiences, of the terrible destruction which modern warfare entailed. They were also aware that atomic warfare "gives mankind the possibility of complete destruction, of which we can only think with a shudder". The Chancellor added: "You will find no one in Germany, neither responsible politicians nor among the people, who even toys with the idea that the great political problems of today can be solved by a war. New means to overcome conflicts and differences must be found—means based on international solidarity and international co-operation."

In conclusion, Dr. Adenauer said that his Government shared the Soviet view that the establishment of diplomatic, economic and cultural relations would be of advantage to the two countries.

The discussions on Sept. 10 centred on the question of Germans still held in the Soviet Union. Marshal Bulganin declared in this connexion that no German prisoners of war remained in Soviet territory, but that 9,626 "convicted war criminals from the former Hitlerite Army" were serving sentences for crimes committed in the U.S.S.R. during the war. He emphasized that if the question of these men was to be examined, it was essential that the German Democratic Republic (Eastern Germany) should be represented in the discussions equally with the Federal Republic.

Marshal Bulganin, after dwelling on the sufferings caused by the Nazis during the war, said that the Soviet people could not understand why attempts were being made in Western Germany to represent these war criminals as "innocent martyrs". If this question was to be examined, representatives of both parts of Germany would have to participate in the discussions. "But," Marshal Bulganin added, "since it seems that the German Federal Republic does not consider it desirable to discuss this matter with representatives of the German Democratic Republic, it is clear that discussion of this question is inappropriate during these negotiations."

Dr. Adenauer said that no one would deny the enormity of the crimes committed by the Nazis in the Soviet Union during the war, nor the sufferings and privations inflicted upon the Soviet people. The overwhelming majority of Germans felt disgust at the crimes committed by the *Wehrmacht* in Russia, but it should also be borne in mind that Soviet troops had "committed certain acts" on German soil, and that "terrible things" had happened during the Soviet advance into Germany.

Mr. Khrushchev intervened at this point to protest at Dr. Adenauer's "offensive" allegation that Soviet troops had committed acts of brutality in Germany, which he denied categorically. Declaring that the Soviet Army had performed a "sacred duty" in carrying the war into Germany after driving the German armies from the U.S.S.R., he added: "We fully understand the sufferings and sorrows of millions of German people who have heard nothing of the fate of their relatives. But who is to blame for the fact that these people have not returned to their families? Many Germans were killed in the war, but even more Soviet citizens perished. Who is to blame? We are not guilty. It was not we who crossed the border. It was not we who started the war." Mr. Khrushchev added, however, that bitterness and revenge were "bad counsellors" and that "we must look to the future, which demands the establishment of friendly and normal relations between the German and Soviet people". As regards the reunification of Germany, he said: "You [Dr. Adenauer] must understand our position. We honestly and repeatedly warned you that the Paris Agreements and the entry of the German Federal Republic into NATO would block a solution of this problem in the near future."

Mr. Molotov said that the German people had not been able to overthrow Hitlerism by themselves, and owed Hitler's downfall to the Soviet Union's prosecution of the war.

At a further session on the same day, Dr. Adenauer made an explanatory statement on his reference to "certain acts" committed by the Soviet forces in Germany. According to Moscow Radio, the Federal Chancellor spoke as follows:

"Mr. Khrushchev and Mr. Molotov have said that I stated that the Soviet Army, after arriving in Germany, committed crimes. I state categorically—I have checked it from notes taken by the Secretary of State, Dr. Hallstein—that I did not use this word deliberately and intentionally. I said that during the entry of the [Soviet] troops terrible things happened. It would be proper not to delve more deeply into these matters."

Dr. Adenauer continued: "Mr. Molotov said that the Germans were incapable of ridding themselves of Hitlerism. Do not take offence at what I am going to say now. It does not concern the Soviet Union alone, but a number of other countries also. Why, after 1933, did the Great Powers make it possible for Hitler to grow in strength? That is the crucial question. When I think of the honours accorded to Hitler by the Great Powers—for instance, at the Berlin Olympics —I ask you to understand that I really cannot control my feelings. I will never forget how Hitler, with impunity, got away with every violation of international treaties. This turned Hitler into a hero in the eyes of certain stupid Germans, while others were reduced to despair. They must have seen, as I saw from 1933 onwards, how this man was allowed to grow to such dimensions. We—I mean the Federal Government and our Parliament—are the unfortunate heirs to all that. Since Germany suffered much from the war, we must try to rebuild Germany. We must try once more to win the confidence of foreign Powers, as well as your confidence. I know it is a difficult task, but it must be solved."

As regards NATO, Dr. Adenauer was quoted as saying: "I am convinced that, providing the Great Powers conduct negotiations in the future in a sober manner, everything that has been achieved in NATO can—indeed must—become an instrument of a European security system. I think that this should be the aim of a comprehensive and soberly-pursued policy."

Appealing for an on-the-spot survey of the problem of prisoners of war, Dr. Adenauer said: "We think that we know quite a few cases where Germans taken as prisoners of war were sentenced for crimes committed after the cessation of hostilities. We wish for nothing more than that you should study this question together with us. Do not let us return home with a statement that the Soviet Union altogether refuses to discuss this question with us."

Referring to the Soviet insistence on East German participation in the P.O.W. question, the Chancellor added: "As soon as we are convinced that we are meeting the representatives recognized by the population of the Soviet zone, we shall sit down with them at the same table. . . . We hold that the Government of the German Democratic Republic cannot claim to represent the 17 or 18 million Germans living in the Soviet Zone. . . ."

After further discussions on Sept. 12-13 a communiqué was issued in the evening of Sept. 13 announcing that agreement had been reached on the establishment of diplomatic relations between the Soviet Union and the German Federal Republic, and that letters to this effect had been exchanged between Dr. Adenauer and Marshal Bulganin.

The communiqué said that the talks had taken place "in an atmosphere of mutual understanding" and that there had been "a broad and frank exchange of views on the question of the mutual relations between the U.S.S.R. and the German Federal Republic". It continued: "Agreement was reached . . . on the establishment of diplomatic relations between the two countries, and, to this end, on the setting-up of Embassies in Bonn and Moscow, and on the exchange of Ambassadors. Both delegations agreed that the establishment of diplomatic relations will contribute to the development of mutual understanding and co-operation between the Soviet Union and the German Federal Republic in the interests of peace and security in Europe. The parties start from the assumption that the establishment and development of normal relations between the Soviet Union and the German Federal Republic will further the settlement of pending problems affecting the whole of Germany, and must thus help the solution of the principal national problem of the German people—the re-establishment of a unified, democratic German State. In confirmation of the agreement reached, the Chairman of the Council of Ministers of the U.S.S.R. and the Chancellor of the German Federal Republic have exchanged letters, the text of which is annexed. The parties also agreed that negotiations between the German Federal Republic and the Soviet Union on the development of trade should be opened in the near future."

The text of the letters exchanged between Dr. Adenauer and Marshal Bulganin was released at the same time. In identical terms, they recapitulated, in effect, the wording of the communiqué and stated that the agreement on the establishment of diplomatic relations would take effect after ratification by the Presidium of the Supreme Soviet and by the Federal German *Bundestag.*

On the same day (Sept. 13) Moscow Radio broadcast the text of statements made by Marshal Bulganin and Mr. Molotov at the final session of the conference. Marshal Bulganin's statement related to Soviet displaced persons in Western Germany, whilst that of Mr. Molotov related to the distribution of anti-Communist literature in

119

the U.S.S.R. and Eastern European countries by balloons released in Western Germany, allegedly by U.S. organizations.

Marshal Bulganin's statement was worded as follows: "Hundreds of thousands of peaceful Soviet citizens were forcibly deported to Germany during the war by the Hitlerite Army from the territories of the Soviet Union it temporarily occupied. Many perished in compulsory labour camps in Germany. After the defeat of the Hitlerite Army, the majority of the captured Soviet citizens returned home. But a not inconsiderable number were retained, mainly in Western Germany.

"According to existing information there remain on the territory of the German Federal Republic over 100,000 such Soviet citizens, in many cases described as being without nationality. The majority of these unhappy people, separated by force from their homeland and families, have no permanent occupation, residence or means of subsistence. They suffer from serious privations and destitution. They remain in a foreign land as dependent men without rights. Many cases are known to us of displaced Soviet citizens who do not accept their lot of being gaoled on the territory of the German Federal Republic.

"Certain organizations hostile to the Soviet Union, supported by the relevant authorities, are waging spiteful propaganda and impeding the repatriation of these persons, frightening and terrorizing those who wish to return home. At the same time inadmissible attempts to make use of these persons for politically criminal purposes are continuing. We consider that the position which has arisen in the German Federal Republic in connexion with displaced Soviet citizens is abnormal and is opposed to the principles of humanity and of freedom of the individual.

"The Soviet Government considers it a duty to take up the defence of these Soviet citizens, who in certain cases have misbehaved against their country. We hope that they will reform, and we will not call them to account severely for offences committed by them. In drawing attention to this matter, we hope that the Government of the German Federal Republic will take the necessary measures and afford its co-operation for the return home of displaced Soviet citizens."

Mr. Molotov's statement was worded: "According to reports by Soviet airmen flying both on internal and international routes, there are uncontrolled flights of large balloons with loads attached to them. The balloons are about eight metres in diameter and 16 metres high. Investigations of balloons picked up on the territory of the Soviet Union show that the weight of the loads attached reach up to 300 kilograms. It is known that such balloons are released from Western

Germany with the aim of spreading in the Soviet Union and in a number of other European countries leaflets and propaganda literature hostile to those States.

"According to the findings of competent Soviet aviation experts, such balloons are dangerous to air transport. . . . According to information to hand, these balloons are released from Western Germany by American organizations. This was openly stated on Aug. 16 by the American radio station in Munich, which said that a large number of such balloons had been released on Aug. 15 by the American 'Crusade for Freedom' organization.

"In drawing the attention of the Federal Chancellor to this matter, the Soviet Government expects that the necessary measures will be taken in the German Federal Republic for the cessation of these activities and for the elimination of the danger created by the balloons to aircraft flying on the internal lines of the Soviet Union and on international lines over the territories of the U.S.S.R. and a number of European States."

Before leaving Moscow for Bonn on Sept. 14, Dr. Adenauer gave a press conference at which he announced that he had sent a second letter to Marshal Bulganin stressing (1) that the establishment of diplomatic relations had in no way changed the Federal Government's opinion that a final settlement of Germany's frontiers must await the conclusion of a peace treaty; and (2) that the Federal Government had not changed its position that the German Federal Republic was the only legitimate Government of all Germany. He also announced that both Marshal Bulganin and Mr. Khrushchev had given him assurances that the repatriation of the 9,626 Germans still held in the Soviet Union would begin immediately.

The relevant paragraphs of the Chancellor's second letter to Marshal Bulganin were as follows:

"The establishment of diplomatic relations between the German Federal Republic and the U.S.S.R. constitutes no recognition of the existing territorial situation on both sides. The final definition of the frontiers of Germany remains reserved to the peace treaty.

"The establishment of diplomatic relations with the Soviet Union implies no change in the juridical position of the Federal Government in relation to its right to represent the German nation in international affairs, and in regard to the political conditions in those German regions which lie at present outside its effective sphere of sovereignty."

Dr. Adenauer said at his press conference that the establishment of diplomatic relations would be a stabilizing influence for peace in

Europe, and would end a state of affairs which had been a marked factor of insecurity in the European situation and which could not have continued indefinitely. He added: "I want to declare very emphatically that no secret agreements or understandings of any kind have been arrived at between the Soviet Union and ourselves. Nor was any suggestion made to us during the negotiations that we should abandon our treaty obligations under NATO and the Western European Union."

A "very important and welcome result" of the talks had been the assurances of Marshal Bulganin and Mr. Khrushchev that the 9,626 Germans held in the U.S.S.R.—"as they put it, war criminals"—would be immediately repatriated. Some of these men would be granted an amnesty by the Soviet Government and returned to Germany in freedom, whilst others, in so far as the Soviet Government believed them to have been guilty of grave crimes, would be handed over to the German authorities so that the Federal Government could deal with them under German law. "I believe," Dr. Adenauer said, "that much suffering, misery, and pain will thereby be alleviated, not only for the 10,000 persons here in the Soviet Union but also for their numerous dependents at home. Marshal Bulganin has authorized me to tell you that already, before we arrive in Bonn, this operation [the repatriation of the P.O.W.s] will be set in motion."

The Chancellor went on to say that the German delegation believed that a fairly large number of Germans—over and above the 10,000 to be repatriated—still remained in the Soviet Union. Marshal Bulganin and Mr. Khrushchev had said that they knew nothing of such persons, but had added, however: "If you [the Chancellor] are in a position to give lists of them, we promise you that we will investigate the matter and that we will deal with these Germans in the same way as with the prisoners of war." Dr. Adenauer added: "We shall now have to examine the lists again. They are prepared from letters which the persons in question have sent to relatives in the Federal Republic, giving their camp, number and other details. After the declarations which we have received, I do not doubt that the Soviet Government will fulfil this solemnly-given promise."

As regards German reunification, Dr. Adenauer said: "It was declared from the Soviet side that the four Powers—that is, including Russia—had the obligation to bring about the restoration of German unity. The three Western Powers take the same view." After stressing that nothing had been done to anticipate the forthcoming four-Power talks in Geneva, he expressed the hope that the Geneva conference, and others that might follow it, would consider and decide upon the restoration of German unity "with all speed".

The establishment of diplomatic relations between the German Federal Republic and the Soviet Union was unanimously approved by the Federal German Cabinet on Sept. 19, after Dr. Adenauer's return from Moscow.

Dr. Adenauer gave another press conference in Bonn on Sept. 16 at which he reiterated his conviction that it would have been wrong to refuse to enter into diplomatic relations with the Soviet Union. The Soviet leaders, he said, had shown themselves extraordinarily sensitive on questions of prestige, not for themselves but for their country, and would have regarded the rejection of diplomatic relations as an insult. In view of the fact that the U.S.S.R. was "one of the most powerful States on this earth", covering one-sixth of the globe, he believed that the German delegation had done right in agreeing to diplomatic relations between the two countries.

Regarding the reputation of prisoners of war, the Chancellor said that both Marshal Bulganin and Mr. Khrushchev had given their word of honour that these men would be immediately returned to Germany. That had been "a great human success". "Throughout the entire negotiations," he added, "and in the internal discussions in our delegation, the thought of the prisoners affected us continually —often oppressively. What would have happened if we had ended the talks without an understanding, if none of the prisoners could have returned to their homeland and their relatives? That was for us a very essential aspect of the entire negotiations."

After stressing that the Soviet Union, like the three Western Powers, had accepted the restoration of German unity as an obligation. Dr. Adenauer expressed his conviction that the Soviet leaders earnestly desired a period of peace. He declared in this connexion: "They are concerned whether, while carrying the monstrous burden of armaments, they can master the great domestic tasks before them. They want a period in which they can spend less on armaments. They remain Communists; they believe they are right; we cannot convince them, nor they us."

Dr. Adenauer repeated that the establishment of diplomatic relations between the Federal Republic and the U.S.S.R. had in no way changed the Federal Republic's loyalty to its treaty obligations under NATO and the W.E.U. Moreover, the Soviet representatives had not asked that the Federal Republic should leave these organizations.

An official announcement was issued in Moscow on Sept. 15 declaring that the Soviet Government regarded Germany's present frontiers as final. It was worded as follows: "At a press conference in Moscow on Sept. 14, the Chancellor of the German Federal Republic made a statement on questions relating to the frontiers of Germany. The Soviet Government regards the German Federal Republic as a part of Germany. The other part of Germany is the German Democratic Republic. In connexion with the establishment of diplomatic relations between the Soviet Union and the German Federal Republic, the Soviet Government deems it necessary to state that the question of the frontiers of Germany was solved by the Potsdam Agreement and that the German Federal Republic is carrying out its jurisdiction on the territory under its sovereignty."

The Moscow agreement was unanimously approved by the German Federal Government on Sept. 19 and by the *Bundestag* on Sept. 23, 1955, and ratified by the Presidium of the Supreme Soviet two days later.

Dr. Adenauer, opening the debate in the *Bundestag* on Sept. 22, reiterated that the Federal Republic's loyalty to the West was undiminished. "Germany's partnership with the West," he declared, "goes beyond politics. It is rooted in her indissoluble membership in the circle of Christian Western culture. Speaking for myself, and for the populations of Western and Eastern Germany, I solemnly declare: Germany is part of the West, of its spiritual and social structure and its historical traditions. The Government will not relax its efforts towards European integration and the defence of freedom. Rather will it intensify these efforts."

After reviewing the background of the Moscow negotiations, the Chancellor declared that his decision to exchange Ambassadors with the Soviet Union was "not to be put on a level with a friendly treaty relationship". The Soviet leaders, he said, had pointed out to him that they maintained diplomatic relations with States with which they had substantial political and ideological differences, and the absence of relations between Bonn and Moscow was an "anomaly" which made it impossible to represent German interests *vis-à-vis* the Soviet Union. The German delegation, he emphasized, had told the Soviet leaders that a normalization of relations between the two countries could "on no account mean the legalization of the anomalous state of Germany's present partition". The Federal Chancellor added: "There is no inconsistency between our decision to establish diplomatic relations and the line of our foreign policy, which we are determined to pursue under all circumstances."

Moreover (Dr. Adenauer continued), the exchange of Ambassadors with the Soviet Union did not mean any change in the Federal Government's attitude to the East German régime, which was not formed on the basis of truly free elections, had no real popular mandate, and was rejected by the overwhelming majority of its own people. "The Federal Government alone is authorized to speak for all Germany," he declared. "The member-States of NATO have adopted this position in a joint declaration, and all other States of the free world have adopted it expressly or by implication. . . . The treaty of Sept. 20 between the Soviet-zone Government and the Soviet Union [see below] changes nothing in the existing position. The Soviet-zone Government has no sovereignty, and there is no question of recognizing it. I must make it clear that in the event of recognition of the so-called German Democratic Republic by third parties with whom the Federal Government has official relations, we should consider this as an unfriendly act calculated to intensify the division of Germany."

The Chancellor went on to refer to the exchange of letters between the East German and Soviet Foreign Ministers which accompanied the East German–Soviet Treaty of Sept. 20, 1955, under which responsibility for surface communications between Berlin and Western Germany, except for the traffic of Western forces, was assigned to the German Democratic Republic. Dr. Adenauer said that this was contrary to the four-Power agreement of June 20, 1949, ending the Berlin blockade, under which the Soviet Government had undertaken specific responsibilities for inter-zonal traffic and Berlin traffic. The new Russian move was intended to force the Federal Government to negotiate with, and eventually to recognize, the East German régime, but this it was not prepared to do. Dr. Adenauer said that the Federal Government had drawn the attention of the three Western Powers to this matter, and had asked them "to take the necessary steps".

In conclusion, Dr. Adenauer claimed that "in extraordinarily difficult negotiations" they had "made what was humanly and politically possible out of a given situation", adding: "I am not unmindful of the complex problems raised by the Moscow decisions. It is not by avoiding risks, however, that the difficult political problems of our country can be solved or the reunification of Germany achieved."

Herr Ollenhauer (the Social Democratic leader), speaking for the Opposition, welcomed Dr. Adenauer's efforts to secure the release of German prisoners in the Soviet Union, and announced that his party had decided to approve the Moscow Agreement because they wished "to exploit the possibilities of an active reunification policy offered by the normalization of relations between Bonn and Moscow".

Herr Ollenhauer maintained that the Moscow talks had shown that the Paris Agreements were not the key to German reunification, and that the Russians would refuse to allow Germany to become united as long as the Federal Republic adhered to NATO. "This is exactly the situation," he added, "which we Social Democrats warned you would arise even before the Paris Agreements were ratified." The Federal Government's argument that membership in the Atlantic alliance would force the Soviet Union to abandon Eastern Germany had been "utterly disproved", and, far from facilitating the reunification of Germany through alliance with the West, Dr. Adenauer's policy had resulted in a Soviet victory and the worsening of the prospects for German reunification.

The Social Democrats, Herr Ollenhauer continued, were disturbed over the future relationship between the two German Governments in the new situation. They disputed the "democratic legitimacy" of the East German régime, and agreed that no diplomatic contacts should be established with it. "All-German talks", as proposed by the Soviet Union, would involve the risk of Germany being treated in the same way as Poland and Czechoslovakia, and perhaps of sharing their fate. Herr Ollenhauer expressed regret, however, at the Chancellor's statement with regard to the Federal Government's attitude towards third countries recognizing the East German regime. "The Chancellor himself has said often enough," he declared, "how long and hard is the way to the recovery of the world's confidence in the German nation. When he now says, almost in the manner of an ultimatum, that the Federal Government will regard the establishment of diplomatic relations by third Governments with the German Democratic Republic as an unfriendly act, I ask myself who is served by such strong language. Certainly not the German nation. Such words are liable to open old wounds and endanger new friendships. . . ."

In conclusion, Herr Ollenhauer called for a more determined Western initiative to restore German unity; suggested that the Federal Republic should withdraw from NATO, and that the Great Powers should agree on a European security system satisfactory to all member-countries; and declared: "The Chancellor has taken in Moscow a step towards greater freedom of action in German foreign policy. The Paris Agreements gave him the right to do so, and we approve this step. Our attitude towards the Government's foreign policy in the new period now opening will be determined by the use he is going to make of this freedom."

In unanimously approving the Moscow Agreement, the *Bundestag* also adopted two all-party resolutions.

The first resolution took note of Marshal Bulganin's personal promise to release German prisoners of war still in the Soviet Union, and expressed the "certain expectation" that this promise would be kept.

The second resolution (*a*) endorsed the Chancellor's statement that the establishment of diplomatic relations with the Soviet Union did not imply West German recognition of the present frontiers of Germany pending their determination in a peace treaty; that the German Federal Republic was the only legitimate German régime in international affairs; and that there would be no recognition of the East

German régime; (*b*) reiterated the demand for the reunification of Germany.

Soviet Repatriation of German Military and Civilian Prisoners

In accordance with Marshal Bulganin's promise to Dr. Adenauer, the repatriation of 9,626 Germans imprisoned in the U.S.S.R. on charges of war crimes began in October 1955, a total of 5,863 being returned between Oct. 6 and Oct. 20, comprising 3,890 former prisoners of war and 1,973 civilians. Of those repatriated, 1,256 were sent to Eastern Germany, but some of them succeeded in escaping later to Western Germany.

On Oct. 20, however, the repatriation of the P.O.W.s was suddenly stopped, and was not resumed until Dec. 11. Although no official announcement was made on the German side attributing any blame to the Soviet authorities, the hold-up was attributed in the West German press partly to delays in the Soviet-German discussions on the detailed arrangements connected with the establishment of embassies in Bonn and Moscow, and partly to Soviet demands for the repatriation of 100,000 Soviet nationals allegedly held in Western Germany. This assumption was confirmed by the fact that, following German agreement to the proposed appointment of Mr. Valerian Zorin as Soviet Ambassador, and a German statement on the repatriation of Soviet nationals, it was announced by the Soviet authorities on Dec. 8 that further transports of prisoners were on the way.

Earlier Soviet Releases of German Prisoners

Between Sept. 25, 1953, and Nov. 27, 1953, about 4,500 Germans who had been imprisoned on charges of war crimes had been returned by the Soviet Union to Eastern and Western Germany, under an agreement between the U.S.S.R. and the East German Government. About 5,000 more were released between Dec. 28, 1953, and the beginning of January 1954.

The most prominent German general released during 1953 was the former Field-Marshal von Paulus, commander of the German Sixth Army at Stalingrad, and leader of the Free German Movement formed in Moscow amongst German officers in captivity. His release was announced on Oct. 26, 1953.

On Jan. 19, 1955, the Soviet High Commission officially announced the release of Field-Marshal Ferdinand Schörner, who commanded the German forces in Czechoslovakia at the end of the war, and of Vice-Admiral Hans Voss, chief naval liaison officer at Hitler's wartime headquarters.

The mass release of German prisoners from Soviet prison camps was not resumed until September, 1955, in which month nearly 1,100 soldiers and civilians returned to Eastern or Western Germany. These releases immediately preceded those under Marshal Bulganin's promise to Dr. Adenauer.

It was officially announced in East Berlin on Dec. 22, 1955, that the East German Government had granted an amnesty to 2,616 war criminals whom the Soviet authorities had handed over a considerable time earlier to the custody of the authorities in Eastern Germany.

Soviet Demand for Return of Soviet Refugees in Western Germany

Following Marshal Bulganin's allegation that more than 100,000 Soviet nationals were "detained" in Western Germany, the Soviet Committee for Return to the Homeland (which had its offices in East Berlin) requested the German Federal authorities on Oct. 31, 1955, to assist in repatriating these Soviet citizens. The East German News Agency announced that Major-General Michailov, chairman of the committee, had written to that effect to the Federal Minister of the Interior, Dr. Schröder.

In a statement on Dec. 2, Herr von Brentano, the West German Foreign Minister, told the *Bundestag* that the Federal Republic would not hold back any Soviet citizens who wanted to return to the U.S.S.R.

"It is beyond dispute," Herr von Brentano declared, "that no Soviet citizen will be hindered by us from returning to the Soviet Union if he wishes to go. If the Soviet Union doubts this, we shall gladly let them see for themselves that no Soviet citizen or any one is prevented from returning if he wishes to do so." The statement was made in reply to a question by Dr. Gille (Refugee Party), who quoted an article in *Izvestia* suggesting that the return of Soviet citizens from Germany was a condition for resuming the repatriation of German prisoners from the Soviet Union, which had stopped suddenly on Oct. 20 [see above].

In reply to a Soviet Note of March 9, 1956, which alleged that large numbers of Soviet citizens were being held against their will in camps and prisons in the Federal Republic, the German Federal

Government completely denied this allegation but stated that it was prepared to release 31 Russians who were at present serving sentences in West German prisons, and to hand them over to the Soviet authorities for repatriation.

The German reply said that 51 Russians serving sentences in the Federal Republic had asked to be repatriated; that in 31 cases the judicial authorities of the *Länder* concerned had agreed to the release of the Russians before completion of their sentences; and that the other 20 applications were still under consideration.

With regard to displaced persons and refugees from the U.S.S.R. now living in Western Germany, the German Note pointed out that all such persons enjoyed the protection of the U.N. High Commissioner for Refugees; that they had been given rights equivalent to those of German nationals; that they possessed international travel permits enabling them to leave Germany at any time; and that the Federal Government would "respect" the request of any foreigner for repatriation and would help him to leave Germany. The Note also offered that if any of these displaced persons or refugees were undecided and wished to talk the matter over with a Soviet representative, a meeting could be arranged. It declined, however, a Soviet request for a complete list of all these refugees, and for the visit of Soviet representatives to refugee camps, without the individual refugees' consent.

According to the authorities in Bonn, there were about 30,000 refugees from the Soviet Union in Western Germany, as well as 50,000 refugees from the former Baltic States and those areas of Poland annexed by the U.S.S.R. after the Second World War.

2. THE "HALLSTEIN DOCTRINE", 1955

Dr. Adenauer's remarks in the *Bundestag* on Sept. 22, 1955, on the consequences of any establishment of diplomatic relations with the East German régime by third countries (see above) were followed by the decision, officially announced in Bonn on Dec. 9, 1955, that the German Federal Republic would break off diplomatic relations with all countries which recognized the East German régime, and would refuse to enter into diplomatic relations with any Communist country except the Soviet Union.

This decision later became known as the "Hallstein Doctrine"—after Dr. Walter Hallstein, then State Secretary in the Federal Foreign

Ministry. Before 1967 the "Hallstein Doctrine" was enforced three times:

(1) In 1956 the German Federal Government recalled its Chargé d'Affaires from Damascus on learning that Syria had agreed to the opening of a Consulate by the East German Government.

(2) In 1957 the Federal Government broke off diplomatic relations with Yugoslavia when that country recognized Eastern Germany. (The diplomatic relations were resumed in January 1968.)

(3) In 1963, when the Government of Cuba had agreed to establish full diplomatic relations with the Government of the German Democratic Republic, the German Federal Government broke off diplomatic and consular relations with Cuba.

In addition the German Federal Government withdrew its economic aid to the United Arab Republic in 1965, after an official visit to Egypt by Herr Ulbricht.

The "Hallstein Doctrine" was for the first time tacitly abandoned when the Federal Government decided on Jan. 31, 1967, to establish diplomatic relations with Romania.

However, it was still applied in June 1969, when the Federal Government suspended its relations with Cambodia after the latter had established full diplomatic relations with the German Democratic Republic. The Federal Republic reacted similarly in July 1969, when the new Government of South Yemen recognized Eastern Germany.

On the other hand the Federal Government merely recalled its Ambassador for consultations when in April 1970 Somalia established diplomatic relations with the G.D.R. Later, the West German Government ignored the establishment of such relations with Eastern Germany by a number of other Governments, the first of which was that of the Congo (Brazzaville) in January 1970.

3. RENEWED SOVIET CRITICISM OF FEDERAL POLICIES, 1957

Letter by Marshal Bulganin to Dr. Adenauer, February 1957

The text of a personal letter sent by Marshal Bulganin to Dr. Adenauer was published in Bonn on Feb. 10, 1957.

"More than a year has passed," wrote Marshal Bulganin, "since extensive and frank negotiations took place in Moscow between the

Soviet Union and the German Federal Republic, as a result of which diplomatic relations were established between our two countries . . . I would like to tell you, with the same frankness which marked our talks in Moscow, that my colleagues and I are not satisfied with the course which relations between our two countries have taken since then . . . I will also not conceal that we watch with anxiety how, in the German Federal Republic, a strengthening is taking place of those forces which, with support from abroad, are preventing better relations between our countries, and which desire to impel the Federal Republic on to the dangerous path of military adventures.

"You may point out to me, as did the German delegation during the Moscow negotiations, that in Western Germany there are neither the forces nor the politicians who want an aggressive war. We see, however, the role which is contemplated for the German Federal Republic and its armed forces by the organizers of the North Atlantic Pact. They wish to use the Federal Republic for an aggressive war against the interests of the German people. . . .

"We are aware of the fact that there are forces which, with all the means at their disposal, are preventing the normalization of relations between the Soviet Union and the German Federal Republic. For the sake of their narrow and selfish interests, these forces are trying to incite a policy which would lead to a military conflict with the Soviet Union and other Socialist countries. This may be seen very clearly from the constant demands addressed to the Federal Republic for a speedy establishment of strong armed forces, and for increased expenditure on rearmament and the maintenance of foreign troops. . . . In addition, the use of West German territory as a concentration area for an atomic war is being prepared quite openly. . . .

"The policy of the Soviet Government is based on peace and co-operation with all States. . . . We are convinced that all international problems can be settled peacefully through negotiations between the interested countries. The Soviet Union adheres inviolably to these principles in its relations with the Federal Republic and other countries. We are convinced that Germany's greatness, and the full unfolding of the creative genius of the German people, can be achieved only in peaceful development.

"To a large degree there are sufficient prerequisites for an extensive development of mutually advantageous economic relations between the Soviet Union and the Federal Republic. The Federal Republic has an industry developed in all fields, and may count on big and favourable orders from the Soviet Union. On the other hand, the Soviet Union can sell goods to the Federal Republic in which West German industry and agriculture are interested. We raise the question of trade relations with the Federal Republic because the Soviet Union believes that they provide a solid basis for the improvement of political relations between States. . . .

131

"The strengthening of trust and of friendly co-operation between our countries would without doubt facilitate the unification of Germany, which the German people regards as its most urgent national task. . . . We sympathize with these justified desires, and are ready as always to support the German people in solving this all-German task. The reunification of Germany will not, however, be brought nearer if people ignore the fact of the existence of two German States. A solution of the German problem can be found only through a *rapprochement* between the German Democratic Republic and the German Federal Republic. It is equally clear that the remilitarization of Western Germany, the limitation of the democratic rights of its peoples, and the continuation of an unfriendly policy toward neighbouring peace-loving countries, are not serving the reunification of Germany.

"Before the day of reunification comes nearer, many difficulties will have to be overcome. All interested States will have to unite their efforts. The sooner this happens, the better. The Soviet Government for its part, is ready to lend its support to the Governments of both German States in solving the problem of reunification. An improvement in relations between our countries will be very useful in this respect . . .

"We are of the opinion that the time has come for the Governments of both our countries to undertake definite steps for an improvement of relations between the Soviet Union and the German Federal Republic, in conformity with the agreed decisions taken during the Moscow talks in 1955, and on the basis of the modest but nevertheless useful experiences of mutual relations in various fields since then.

"In particular, the following urgent questions should be discussed: (1) a substantial increase in trade between both countries, and the conclusion of a trade treaty; (2) the conclusion of an agreement on cultural and scientific co-operation; (3) a consular agreement which would lay down the rights of both sides in the protection of the interests of their nationals, thus facilitating the solution of questions concerning the repatriation of nationals of both countries.

"I would like to emphasize that we obviously do not consider it proper to limit our relations to economic, cultural and scientific co-operation. We attach great importance to the opinion of the German people in the discussion of important international problems. In talks with the German Democratic Republic we have already reached mutual understanding on such important questions as rearmament, European security and other problems in which both the Soviet and the German peoples are equally interested. We are of the opinion that a *rapprochement* in the standpoints of the Soviet Union and the German Federal Republic in these questions would be very profitable.

"We hope that the points of view outlined above will be examined by the Federal Government in a spirit of friendly and constructive co-operation. It goes without saying that I and the other members of the Soviet Government will gladly and carefully examine any proposals which you may care to make toward the strengthening of our relations . . ."

In a broadcast on Feb. 13, Dr. Adenauer said that although discussions between the U.S.S.R. and the Federal Republic might profitably be held on certain subjects, it was essential for the German people to bear in mind "clearly and distinctly" (1) that there was "only one German State", and that the "so-called Democratic Republic" was "not a State but an occupation zone under Soviet rule, whose people must have their freedom restored to them"; (2) that the Federal Government had no aggressive intentions whatsoever, and none of its allies had attempted to encourage any such intentions. If this were understood by the Soviet Union, as the German people sincerely hoped, "many difficulties could be overcome more easily".

Soviet Denunciation of NATO Bases in Western Germany and of Provision of Atomic Arms for West German Forces— Dr. von Brentano's Attack on Soviet Policy

The Soviet Government again attacked Western Germany's participation in the Atlantic Pact in a strongly-worded Note sent to the German Federal Republic on April 27, 1957.

After referring to the "concentration by the Western Powers of various types of nuclear weapons on the territory of the Federal Republic", and to the "preparations for equipping the West German Army with atomic weapons", the Soviet Note spoke of the "justified anxiety" among the population of Western Germany at the consequences which an atomic war would entail "for the German people, for the neighbours of Germany, and for Europe as a whole". It went on:
"The equipping with atomic weapons of the Army of the German Federal Republic—the only European State whose Government demands a revision of the present frontiers in Europe—would sharply aggravate international tension and increase the danger of war. . . .
"The atomic arming of the German Federal Republic is sometimes claimed to be necessary for ensuring the security of the country. Such assertions have nothing in common with the real state of affairs.

133

Instead of exerting efforts to ease international tension, and to facilitate agreement on disarmament and the prohibition of weapons of mass destruction, attempts are being made to ensure the security of the Federal Republic on the basis of the 'policy of strength'. . . .

"It is quite obvious that the conversion of the Federal Republic into a NATO atomic base is bound in the event of war to make Western Germany the immediate object of retaliation by all types of modern weapons, including rocket weapons. There is no need to dwell in detail on the consequences this would entail for the Federal Republic, which has such a density of population and concentration of industry that the vital centres of the country could be paralysed by a single hydrogen bomb . . . Germany would become one vast graveyard. . . .

"One cannot evade the question of the consequences which the equipping of the West German Army with atomic weapons would have for the restoration for Germany's national unity. If the policy pursued by the Federal Republic—a policy of remilitarization, accession to aggressive military blocs, and suppression of democratic freedom—has created great obstacles to the unification of Germany, the equipping of the *Bundeswehr* with atomic weapons and the conversion of Western Germany into a centre of atomic war in Europe would strike an irreparable blow at the national reunification of the German people. . . ."

The tone of the Soviet Note, and in particular the threats and menaces contained therein, aroused intense anger and indignation in the Federal Republic, which was expressed by Dr. von Brentano (the Foreign Minister) in a press statement on April 29.

Dr. von Brentano described the Soviet Note as "grotesque", "incomprehensible", and "an unparalleled interference in West German affairs", saying that the references to the catastrophic effects of atomic weapons could only be regarded as "a massive threat and an attempt at intimidation with a view to separating the Federal Republic from its allies". He declared that the Soviet Union's objective was to "obtain a monopoly of nuclear weapons so that it can hold this continent in everlasting servitude", referring in this connexion to the "savagery" with which the Soviet Army had crushed the people's uprising in Hungary in November 1956.

After stressing that the Federal Republic was the only country in the world which had voluntarily renounced the right to manufacture atomic weapons, Dr. von Brentano called upon the Soviet Union to make constructive proposals for disarmament instead of threatening the Federal Republic. In this connexion he declared that the U.S.S.R. " has not made one single serious effort in all these years to solve this problem on a basis acceptable to freedom-loving people". He reiterated that the Federal Republic would provide for its own security with atomic weapons if Russia continued to block an international agreement for all-round disarmament. Refuting the allegation that Western Germany had become the "main weapons depot of Europe", Dr. von Brentano contrasted the 20 NATO divisions (including the five half-formed West German divisions) with the 22 Soviet divisions in Eastern Germany, the 75 "satellite" divisions, and the 153 divisions in the Soviet Union itself. He added: "It simply defies comprehension that anyone possessing such superiority can talk about the Federal Republic having become 'Europe's main weapons depot'."

In reply to the Soviet Note of April 27, the German Federal Government sent a sharp Note to Moscow on May 22 declaring that it would not accede to "a one-sided, completely unjustified demand by a foreign Government to render accounts". It rejected all the allegations contained in the Soviet Note, and reiterated that the Federal Republic had the "legitimate right" to ensure its national security with atomic weapons if the U.S.S.R. continued to block an international agreement for controlled disarmament.

After drawing the Soviet Government's attention to a unanimous *Bundestag* resolution of May 10 calling on all nations possessing nuclear weapons to discontinue tests and to agree to a controlled disarmament system, the West German Note observed that the U.S.S.R.'s attitude at the London disarmament talks was "hardly encouraging" and that it was the only Government which had "up to this day refused any really effective control". Emphasizing that the NATO forces in Western Germany had a purely defensive mission, it declared that "only those who would irresponsibly risk attacking that [Atlantic] community have any reason to fear it or the weapons in its possession". In addition, the Note "emphatically repudiated" the allegation that West German policy would unleash an arms race; stressed that the Federal Government rejected any idea of changing Germany's present frontiers by force; and rejected the Soviet assertion that the provision of atomic weapons for the *Bundeswehr* would make German reunification impossible.

The West German Note again emphasized that the Federal Republic had voluntarily renounced the manufacture of atomic weapons, and stressed the Federal Government's desire for a ban on all nuclear and thermo-nuclear weapons as part of an all-round disarmament plan, and its willingness to do all in its power to promote that objective.

A further Soviet Note was presented in Bonn on June 27, being to a large extent a recapitulation of the earlier Note of April 27. It was described by an official German spokesman as "impossibly sharp and polemical" in tone and as approaching "the limit of what is customary in diplomatic exchanges".

This Soviet Note accused the Federal Government of "striving to obtain atomic arms from abroad" for the *Bundeswehr,* and of "evasive statements intended merely to calm the West German electors so that the country may later find itself confronted with the *fait accompli* of atomic armaments". It also accused the Federal Government of taking "a negative view of the proposals on disarmament which have a direct bearing on Germany, such as the creation in Europe of a zone of inspection to include both parts of Germany . . . and the reduction and subsequent withdrawal of foreign troops from German territory". After reiterating at great length the allegations contained in the earlier Soviet Note, the Note stated that those who pursued the policy of arming the *Bundeswehr* with atomic weapons "run the risk of going down in history as the grave-diggers of German unity".

Bulganin-Adenauer Correspondence on Relations between Western Germany and Soviet Union

In a letter to Marshal Bulganin on Feb. 28, 1957, the Federal Chancellor agreed that talks should be held between the two countries at an early date for an expansion of trade relations, increased scientific and cultural co-operation and a consular convention.

The Federal Chancellor defended Western Germany's membership in NATO against Marshal Bulganin's allegations of the allegedly "aggressive" character of that organization, and emphasized that its role was entirely defensive. As regards German citizens in the U.S.S.R., he pointed out that the Soviet Government had agreed in 1955, during his (the Chancellor's) talks in Moscow, to repatriate all German nationals still in the Soviet Union. While this had been done in the case of prisoners of war, it had not been carried out in the case of civilians—in which connexion Dr. Adenauer referred particularly to German scientists who were working at the nuclear experimental station at Sochum, on the Black Sea. On the question of German reunification, he reiterated that free all-German elections must be held in preparation for an all-German Parliament and Government, and appealed to Marshal Bulganin to "liberate 17,000,000 Germans" in the Eastern Zone. By doing so the Soviet Government would render "an inestimable service to the cause of friendly co-operation between our two countries" and would best serve the cause of peace and European security.

In reply to this letter, Marshal Bulganin informed Dr. Adenauer on March 18 that the U.S.S.R. was ready to enter into negotiations with the German Federal Government on the subjects of trade relations, cultural and scientific co-operation and a consular convention, and proposed that talks should open at an early date in Moscow or Bonn. As regards Western Germany's membership in NATO, Marshal Bulganin observed that "we continue to adhere to different viewpoints". On the question of reunification, he reiterated the Soviet view that the unity of Germany could be achieved only by direct negotiations between Western and Eastern Germany and a *rapprochement* between the two German States.

A West German Note to the Soviet Government, presented on April 17, agreed that negotiations on trade, cultural, scientific and consular matters should be held in Moscow "forthwith", and proposed that any agreements reached should be signed in Bonn. It was accompanied by a further letter from Dr. Adenauer to Marshal Bulganin in which the Federal Chancellor pointed out that the Soviet Premier had made no reference in his latest letter to the repatriation of Germans in the U.S.S.R., despite the fact that he (Dr. Adenauer) had raised this matter in his letter of Feb. 28.

After saying that he would "not go into the unfounded, severe accusations that have repeatedly been made against the Federal Republic in official declarations of the Soviet Government and are continually being repeated", Dr. Adenauer stated: "The aspirations of the entire German people for the re-establishment of its national unity cannot be nullified by a reference to the alleged existence of two German States. It is unrealistic to describe the so-called German Democratic Republic, whose governmental power was not established by legitimate means and which is rejected by the overwhelming majority of the population, as a reality in the life of the German people".

A Soviet Note of May 23 proposed that negotiations on the above-mentioned subjects should open in Moscow on June 15. As regards repatriation, the Note said: "The U.S.S.R. has fully completed the repatriation of German subjects who had been convicted in the

Soviet Union and of whom mention was made in the [Moscow] talks with the Federal German delegation in 1955. This does not preclude the possibility of discussing certain practical questions affecting undertakings to repatriate individual German subjects from the Soviet Union, and also the connected question of the repatriation of Soviet displaced persons who are still in the Federal Republic".

The West German reply, published on June 10, did not reject the Soviet proposal for the opening of talks on June 15 but made the Federal Government's acceptance conditional on the simultaneous holding of discussions on the repatriation of German civilians still held in the U.S.S.R. The Note maintained that Dr. Adenauer had been given a firm assurance by Marshal Bulganin, during the Moscow talks in 1955, that all German nationals in the Soviet Union who could be traced on the basis of German lists would be repatriated. It pointed out, however, that only 9,600 prisoners of war had been returned to Germany, and expressed the Federal Government's conviction—based on its researches and the repatriation applications received—that "many thousands" of German civilians were still held in the U.S.S.R. against their will.

As a result of the *impasse* between the West German and Soviet points of view on the repatriation question, no further proposals were made by either side during 1957 for talks on trade, cultural, scientific and consular matters.

Joint Soviet and East German Communiqué on West German Remilitarization and German Reunification

A delegation of the Soviet Government and Communist Party visited Eastern Germany from Aug. 7-14, 1957, for discussions with the East German Government and leaders of the Socialist Unity Party.

A joint communiqué which was published on Aug. 14 said in part:

West German Remilitarization.—"The Soviet Union and the German Democratic Republic consider it essential to declare that the stationing of American atomic weapons in Western Germany and other countries of Western Europe, and the decision of the organs of the North Atlantic bloc to equip European member-countries of NATO with atomic weapons, intensify the threat to peace and to the security of the countries of Europe. . . . The Government of the German Federal Republic, by tolerating and encouraging the disposition of atomic weapons of the Western Powers in Western Germany and by preparing the arming of the *Bundeswehr* with atomic weapons, is transforming the territory of the German Federal Republic into a main base of NATO for the waging of atomic war in Europe. Such actions of the German Federal Republic not only threaten the security of the peoples of Europe but are also fraught with mortal danger for the population of Western Germany itself, which in the event of war being unleashed by the NATO bloc would inevitably, as a result of the irresponsible policies of their ruling circles, be exposed to destruction by the concentrated blows of up-to-date nuclear weapons.

"The Government of the German Democratic Republic, in the name of peace in Europe and in the name of the future of millions of Germans, appeals to the Powers to renounce the introduction of atomic weapons in Germany. Once again it offers to the Federal Government an agreement to ban atomic arms from the armies of both German States and not to permit the manufacture of nuclear weapons in Germany. The Soviet Government fully understands and supports these proposals of the German Democratic Republic. . . ."

German Reunification.—"Both sides unanimously agree that the vital question affecting the German nation is the restoration of its unity, and is first and foremost a matter for the German people themselves. With this object in view the German Democratic Republic considers it essential first of all to come to an agreement with the Federal Republic over a common policy on the following matters:

(1) A ban on stationing or manufacturing any kind of atomic bomb or weapon on German territory, and banning all atom war propaganda.

(2) The withdrawal of both German States from NATO and the Warsaw Pact, the mutual abolition of compulsory military service, and an agreement on reciprocal limitation of the strength of their forces.

(3) A joint or separate appeal to the four Powers for the early withdrawal of their forces from the whole of Germany by stages.

Agreement between the German Democratic Republic and German Federal Republic on these matters would create the basis for the setting up of a German Confederation.

"The Soviet Union supports these proposals. . . . The Soviet delegation declared that the U.S.S.R. was willing in all ways to contribute to a *rapprochement* and achievement of mutual understanding between the German Democratic Republic and the German Federal Republic, bearing in mind especially that the Soviet Union is the only great Power which has diplomatic relations with both German States. . . .

"The present German Federal Government, ignoring the interests of the German people, hinders the establishment of good relations between the German Federal Republic and the U.S.S.R. . . . The main obstacle to the reunification of Germany as a peace-loving and democratic State is the present policy of remilitarization in Western Germany and her conversion into a military atomic base of the aggressive North Atlantic bloc. This policy of militarization is accompanied by the suppression in Western Germany of the democratic forces opposing preparations for a new war, as is strikingly illustrated by the banning of the German Communist Party [on orders by the Federal Constitutional Court in August 1956]. This policy deepens the rift between the two German States and threatens European peace and the security of the German people itself.

"Both sides consider it necessary to declare that there can be no question of the reunification of Germany at the expense of the interests of the German Democratic Republic and the social gains of its working people. There is only one way of peacefully solving the German problem—that of *rapprochement* and talks between the two German States now in existence. There can be no settlement of the questions affecting Germany as a whole without the participation of the German Democratic Republic . . . The peoples of the Soviet Union see in the German Democratic Republic an impregnable bastion of European peace. In view of the situation obtaining at present in Western Germany, the German Democratic Republic is called upon to play a particularly important role in the maintenance of peace in Europe. . . ."

4. TRADE AND CONSULAR AGREEMENTS OF 1958

Following further protracted negotiations, agreements on trade, shipping, and consular relations were initialled in Moscow on April 8, 1958, between the German Federal Republic and the Soviet Union. Informal arrangements were also concluded on the repatriation of certain groups of German nationals in the U.S.S.R. and of Soviet nationals in Western Germany.

Talks between a German delegation led by Dr. Rudolf Lahr and a Soviet delegation headed by Mr. Vladimir Semeonov (a Deputy Foreign Minister and formerly High Commissioner in Eastern Germany) had opened in Moscow on July 23, 1957. In a Note of July 6, however, the Soviet Government said that while the number of German nationals still in the Soviet Union was "quite insignificant", and while the repatriation question would be better left to the Red Cross organizations of the two countries, this "does not exclude the possibility that some practical questions might arise . . . with regard to the carrying-out of measures for the repatriation of individual German citizens from the Soviet Union or of the return of displaced

Soviet nationals from the Federal Republic, and these questions could be the object of specific discussions during the forthcoming talks". This statement was regarded by the Federal Government as implying that the U.S.S.R. would no longer insist on the exclusion of the repatriation question from the agenda.

Nevertheless, when the talks opened on July 23 the Soviet delegation refused to discuss repatriation, and the discussions were suspended on July 31 after the West German Government had recalled Dr. Lahr for consultations. Following an exchange of Notes between Mr. Gromyko and Dr. von Brentano the talks were resumed on Aug. 14, but in view of continued Soviet insistence on excluding the subject of repatriation Dr. Lahr was again recalled to Bonn on Aug. 16. The talks were again resumed on Aug. 26, but a further breakdown occurred when Mr. Semeonov, in a letter to Dr. Lahr published on Sept. 3, stated that the Soviet Union was prepared to discuss a trade and consular agreement but maintained her original assertion that no repatriation problem existed. Mr. Semeonov added that if Western Germany insisted on its proposal to suspend the talks on trade and consular questions because of the Soviet attitude on the repatriation question, the Federal Government "would have to bear full responsibility for the breakdown of the talks and the attendant consequences".

After a prolonged deadlock, which coincided with Federal elections in Western Germany, the talks were resumed on Nov. 14, 1957, and from then onwards continued without interruption.

The agreements initialled on April 8, 1958, comprised (*a*) a three-year trade and payments agreement; (*b*) a protocol on trade exchanges in 1958; (*c*) a general agreement on commerce and navigation; (*d*) a consular convention; (*e*) an agreement on repatriation. In addition, the two delegations made verbal declarations giving further details of the repatriation arrangements, but it was stated in Bonn that it had been agreed that these declarations would not be published in the Soviet Union.

The joint communiqué gave the following details of the various agreements:

Long-term Trade and Payments Agreement.—This was concluded for the three-year period 1958-60, and laid down lists of goods for Soviet-West German trade exchanges, as well as the procedure for trade and payments between the two countries. Aimed at making the commercial relations between the two countries "more stable and lasting", it provided for a considerable annual expansion of mutual trade, which by 1960 would amount to some 1,200,000,000 roubles, or about 1,260,000,000 Deutsche Marks—approximately double the 1957 figure. The total volume of deliveries agreed for the period 1958-60 would amount to 3,000,000,000 roubles, or about 3,150,000,000 DM. The lists of goods would be specified and extended each year by supplementary agreements between the two countries, and it was therefore expected that total trade exchanges would exceed the above-mentioned amounts within the three years.

The lists of goods annexed to the agreement provided that the Soviet foreign trade organizations in the German Federal Republic would place large orders for various kinds of machinery and equipment for supply to the U.S.S.R. within the three-year period. These orders would include equipment for the mining and steel industries, heavy forges, automation machinery, heavy machine-tools for the metallurgical industries, equipment for chemical industries (in particular for the manufacture of artificial fibres), equipment for whaling ships and floating factories, cables, chemical products, certain steel products, and other goods, including certain consumer goods. In return, the Soviet Union would supply Western Germany with timber, cellulose, oil and oil products, wheat, coal, asbestos, manganese and chrome ores, machinery and equipment, cotton, flax, hemp, tobacco, certain chemical products and a number of raw materials.

Trade Protocol for 1958.—This laid down the exact lists of commercial exchanges for the current year.

Agreement on General Questions of Commerce and Navigation.— This provided for most-favoured-nation treatment in Customs and other matters connected with the export and import of merchandise. It also regulated shipping questions, and provided for the setting-up of a Soviet trade representation in Western Germany, defining its legal status.

Consular Convention.—This placed consular relations between the two countries on a treaty basis, ensuring the effective protection of nationals of both countries, as well as of their trade and shipping interests. It was stated that its practical effect would be confined for the time being to the consular departments of the Federal German Embassy in Moscow and the Soviet Embassy in Bonn, but it would form the basis of the activities of any consulates which might be set up in future.

Repatriation.—The communiqué said: "During the talks on questions relating to the reciprocal repatriation of nationals of the two countries, it was agreed that the Soviet authorities would give favourable consideration to applications by individual German nationals for exit permits from the U.S.S.R. to the German Federal Republic. Conversely, the German Federal authorities would give the same treatment to applications from Soviet nationals now in the Federal Republic and wishing to leave for the Soviet Union. Both sides declared . . . that they supported the principle of reuniting families separated by the Second World War, and agreed that they would act in accordance with their respective legislation. They also agreed that co-operation between the two Red Cross societies would be continued."

The verbal Soviet declaration on the repatriation question said that, in addition to the arrangements mentioned in the communiqué, the Soviet authorities would examine and decide "in a positive way" the "practical questions arising in connexion with applications of those German nationals who possessed German nationality on June 21, 1941 [the date of the Nazi invasion of the Soviet Union], were still in the Soviet Union, and wished to leave for the German Federal Republic with their wives and children". The sole "decisive criterion" for these people would be their possession of German nationality at the above date.

It was added (a) that the Soviet delegation had "taken note" of the statement made by the German delegation that the German Federal Republic was likewise willing to examine "in a positive manner" the practical questions arising from applications by Soviet nationals in Western Germany wishing to be repatriated to the Soviet Union; and (b) that this arrangement would apply to all Soviet nationals who were at present in Western Germany owing to the war, as well as to their spouses and children.

The Soviet declaration reiterated that both sides would try to reunite families separated by the war; would act in accordance with their legislation; and had agreed to continued co-operation between the Soviet and West German Red Cross societies.

The verbal German counter-declaration took note of the Soviet statement and confirmed the willingness of the German Federal Republic to accede to applications by Soviet nationals wishing to leave Western Germany for the Soviet Union.

Mr. Mikoyan's Visit to Western Germany—
Signing of Trade and Consular Agreements

Mr. Anastas Mikoyan, the First Vice-Chairman of the Soviet Council of Ministers, arrived in Bonn on April 25, 1958, to sign the Soviet-German trade agreements and consular convention at the Federal Foreign Ministry. Dr. von Brentano signed for the German Federal Republic. During his stay in Bonn (April 25-26) Mr. Mikoyan had discussions with Dr. Adenauer, Dr. von Brentano, Professor Ludwig Erhard (Federal Minister for Economic Affairs), and Dr. Eugen Gerstenmaier, president of the *Bundestag*.

Mr. Mikoyan said on April 25 that the Soviet Union was ready to guarantee that if the territory of the Federal Republic were free of nuclear and rocket weapons, the Soviet Union would refrain from using such weapons against objectives in Western Germany, even in the event of a military conflict in which the Federal Republic participated. He repeated this statement at a press conference on April 26 and also expressed the view that the opportunities presented by the "Rapacki Plan" [see below] were seriously under-estimated in Western Germany.

A communiqué issued in Bonn on April 28 stated that Mr. Mikoyan and the German Ministers had re-emphasized that they would do all in their power to ensure the implementation of the agreements signed in Moscow, and also of the verbal agreement on repatriation. It had also been agreed that talks would be held later in the year to place cultural, scientific, and technical relations between the two countries on a firmer footing. Soviet-West German relations in general and the present international situation had also been discussed, and both sides had emphasized that their respective Governments would do their utmost to ensure that existing problems were solved in a spirit of mutual understanding and by peaceful means, on the basis of non-interference in each other's internal affairs.

5. THE "RAPACKI PLAN", 1958

A proposal for an "atom-free" zone in Central Europe had been put forward by the Polish Foreign Minister, Mr. Adam Rapacki, in the U.N. General Assembly on Oct. 3, 1957. In a debate on disarmament Mr. Rapacki declared that "if the two German States agree to impose a ban on the production and stockpiling of atomic and thermo-nuclear weapons on their territories, the Polish People's Republic is prepared simultaneously to impose a similar ban on its own territory". The Czechoslovak Government subsequently associated itself with this proposal and announced its willingness to ban nuclear weapons on its own territory on the same conditions—i.e. that both Western and Eastern Germany should agree to such a ban on the territories of the two German States.

The so-called "Rapacki Plan" was discussed by the Polish and Soviet Foreign Ministers (respectively Mr. Rapacki and Mr. Gromyko), who met in Moscow on an initiative by Poland, from Jan. 28 to Feb. 1, 1958.

The communiqué issued afterwards said that both sides agreed that Mr. Rapacki's proposal constituted "an attempt to take a real step forward towards an understanding between East and West, the relaxation of tension and the lessening of the danger of war".

After saying that Poland and the Soviet Union regarded as "without foundation the argument put forward by some circles . . . that an alleged short-coming of the [Rapacki] plan was its lack of clarity on the question of controls", the communiqué went on: ". . . The Soviet Government . . . declares its readiness to participate in the examination and implementation of an effective control system in the proposed zone."

The Polish proposals for an "atom-free" zone in Central Europe, covering the territory of Poland, Czechoslovakia, Eastern Germany and Western Germany, were amplified in a memorandum issued in Warsaw on Feb. 15 and handed by Mr. Rapacki to the Ambassadors of the United States, the Soviet Union, Great Britain, France, Czechoslovakia and Eastern Germany, and also to the Chargés d'Affaires of Canada and Denmark. The memorandum was also conveyed to the West German Government through the intermediary of the Swedish Government.

The memorandum contained a "more detailed elaboration" of Mr. Rapacki's proposals originally made at the U.N. General Assembly, and expressed the hope that they might "facilitate the opening of negotiations and the reaching of an agreement on this subject".

Full agreement with the new proposals was notified to the Polish Government by Czechoslovakia on Feb. 27, and by the Soviet Union on March 3. A spokesman for the Soviet Foreign Ministry (Mr. Leonid Ilyichev) had previously stated that the Soviet Union was willing to undertake all the commitments in the Rapacki Plan, provided that the U.S., British and French Governments "do the same". No replies from the Western Powers were received in Warsaw by the end of March.

By May 1958, however, the Rapacki Plan had been rejected by Britain, the U.S.A. and France, as well as by other NATO countries and by the Defence and Armaments Committee of the Western European Union Assembly.

The Rapacki Plan was discussed in Bonn during a four-day

Bundestag debate on foreign affairs and defence on March 20–25, 1958.

While Dr. Erich Mende, chairman of the Free Democratic parliamentary group, said that the second Rapacki Plan should receive serious consideration, Dr. Adenauer took the line that the Rapacki Plan should not be discussed at a time when the decisive question was whether or not the Federal Republic wanted to remain a member of NATO.

Dr. Adenauer pointed out that the Soviet Union—the potential enemy of NATO—was equipped with nuclear weapons and guided missiles. If an important section of NATO did not have equally strong arms, NATO itself would "lose its importance and its purpose". If the Federal Republic were to refuse to participate in these developments in armament techniques, contrary to a request by NATO, the Federal Republic would for all practical purposes have left the North Atlantic Treaty Organization.

A country with the economic potential of Western Germany, and in her geographical position, could not remain in isolation; if a world catastrophe occurred, she would be involved irrespective of whether she was armed or unarmed. "In the interests of our self-preservation," he added, "we have the duty to do all we can to prevent any such catastrophe. This we can do only if we remain in NATO and strengthen the Organization—but not if we weaken it by refusing to fulfil obligations arising from our membership."

Dr. Arndt, for the Social Democrats, said that to equip Western Germany with atomic weapons would entail the danger of an increased concentration of Soviet atomic weapons in Eastern Europe, and especially in Eastern Germany, and would also result in intensified Soviet pressure on the European peoples and the population of Eastern Germany. German reunification could be achieved only by way of a limitation of armaments, and a decision for equipping the *Bundeswehr* with nuclear weapons would almost certainly be a decision against reunification.

It was his party's conviction, he said, that Western Germany should contribute to the creation of a "zone of relaxation" in Central Europe.

At the conclusion of the debate on March 25 the *Bundestag* adopted, by 270 votes to 165 (mainly of the Social Democrats), a resolution which said *inter alia*:

"In conformity with the requirements of this defence system [within NATO] and having regard to the armament of the possible

146

enemy, the armed forces of the Federal Republic must be equipped with the most modern weapons so that they may be able to carry out the obligations assumed by the Federal Republic within NATO, and to make an effective contribution to the safeguarding of peace."

The resolution reiterated that free elections must form the basis of German reunification; and rejected the proposals for the conclusion of separate peace treaties with Eastern and Western Germany, as well as negotiations with the present régime in the Soviet Zone or a Confederation with that régime.

Revised Rapacki Plan

On Nov. 4, 1958, at a press conference attended by Polish and foreign journalists, Mr. Rapacki announced changes in the "manner of introducing a denuclearized zone in Central Europe". He explained that the modifications were intended to meet the objections raised against the proposals contained in his original plan and the revised proposals made on Feb. 14, 1958, and that they had been agreed to by the other Warsaw Treaty countries.

Mr. Rapacki suggested that there would be two stages in the implementation of his Government's plan. These were as follows:

"1. A ban would be introduced on the production of nuclear weapons in the territories of Poland, Czechoslovakia, the German Democratic Republic and the German Federal Republic. . . . At the same time, appropriate measures of control would be introduced. . . .

"2. The implementation of the second stage would be preceded by talks on the reduction of conventional forces. This reduction would be effected simultaneously with the complete denuclearization of the zone, and would be accompanied by appropriate measures of control."

Following Mr. Rapacki's statement on Nov. 4, Mr. Selwyn Lloyd, then British Foreign Secretary, stated in the House of Commons on Nov. 19 that, while he thought that the Polish Government and its Foreign Minister were "absolutely sincere" in putting forward these proposals, "the factor which must govern our view of this matter is whether any plan for disengagement will be acceptable if it changes the balance of military security to the disadvantage of either side".

Thereafter, no further exchanges took place on the Rapacki Plan between the Governments concerned.

6. THE BERLIN CRISIS OF 1958–59

An international crisis over the status of West Berlin and the occupation rights of the Western Powers in that city arose during November 1958, following M. Khrushchev's announcement that the U.S.S.R. intended to transfer all its functions and responsibilities connected with the City of Berlin to the East German Government, and his suggestion that the Western Powers should do the same. The crisis developed as follows.

Bundestag Resolution on Reunification

The *Bundestag* unanimously passed on July 2, 1958, an all-party resolution calling for the appointment by the U.S.A., the Soviet Union, Great Britain and France of a four-Power working group to prepare joint proposals for the solution of the German question. The resolution was based on a suggestion made by the Austrian Federal Chancellor (Dr. Raab), who had disclosed at a press conference on April 25 that he had proposed to the U.S. and Soviet Ambassadors the creation, at a "Summit" conference, of a four-Power commission charged with examining the conditions for all-German elections and drawing up a draft electoral law.

East German and Soviet Notes on Reunification

The East German Government issued a declaration on Sept. 5, and at the same time sent Notes to Britain, the U.S.A., France, the Soviet Union and the German Federal Government, proposing (1) the setting-up by the four Powers of a commission to start work on the terms of a peace treaty with Germany; (2) the establishment by Eastern and Western Germany of a second commission which would be charged with working out a common German attitude on this question.

The Soviet Government sent identical Notes on Sept. 18 to the U.S., British and French Governments, as well as Notes to the East German and West German Governments. In all of these it supported the East German proposal for the immediate conclusion of a peace treaty with Germany, which, it said, the U.S.S.R. had itself previously advocated. It also approved the East German proposal for the

148

setting-up of a second commission consisting of representatives of the two German States, and expressed the Soviet Government's willingness "to give such a commission any assistance it requires".

Western Replies to U.S.S.R. and Western Germany

In identical replies to the Soviet Government, delivered on Sept. 30, Britain, France and the U.S.A. expressed their willingness to discuss the question of German reunification with the Soviet Union within a four-Power working group, as suggested by the German Federal Government.

The Notes reiterated the Western view that German reunification through free elections and the setting-up of an all-German Government should precede the negotiation of a peace treaty. They accordingly rejected the Soviet proposal to entrust the question of German reunification to a commission of East and West German representatives. In this connexion the Western Notes said that only a Government set up in accordance with the wishes of the German people could "undertake obligations which inspire confidence in other countries and are regarded by the German people themselves as just and binding". Moreover the Notes said, the German representatives who would participate in discussions on a peace treaty preceding reunification could never bind a future all-German Government to carry out their decisions.

New Bundestag Resolution

The *Bundestag* and most members of the Federal Government held a three-day session in Berlin in Oct. 1-3, 1958, at which the following resolution was unanimously approved:

"(1) The *Bundestag* formally protests against the continued persecution of the people of Eastern Germany, a persecution which has led to more than 3,000,000 of them seeking refuge in the Federal Republic. It would be an act of political reason as well as of common humanity to give the people of Eastern Germany the right to decide their own future and to return to the German community.

"(2) The *Bundestag* protests in particular against the cold-blooded refusal of the East German régime to allow free movement across the inter-zonal frontier. Because of this, traffic has declined by 85 per cent since last year.

"(3) The *Bundestag,* in company with the Governments of the *Länder* and of Berlin, will continue to ensure a humane reception of East German refugees and their swift integration into the life of the Federal Republic. It appeals to every West German to give East Germans the welcome they deserve, so that the world may realize that they support the ideal of unity by deeds as well as words.

"(4) The Federal Republic will continue to regard itself as the guarantee of German democracy and the German right to reunification. This does not absolve the great Powers from their responsibility for promoting reunification, which can only result from the freely expressed wishes of the whole German people.

"(5) The *Bundestag* reaffirms its proposal for a standing four-Power committee on the German question, which can work out what steps have to be taken to reunify Germany."

Dr. Adenauer stated in a broadcast on Oct. 2 that the Federal Government would try to find a solution to the German question by means of diplomatic negotiations with the Soviet Union. The Federal Chancellor accordingly had a meeting on Oct. 14 with Mr. Andrei Smirnov, the Soviet Ambassador in Bonn, but their talk produced no result.

Mr. Khrushchev's Proposal for Change in
Status of Berlin—Soviet Responsibilities in East Berlin
transferred to East German Government

In a speech on Nov. 10, 1958, at a reception for a Polish Government delegation led by Mr. Wladyslaw Gomulka, which was visiting Moscow for Soviet-Polish discussions, Mr. Khrushchev made the following statement on the Soviet Union's intention to transfer control of East Berlin to the East German Government:

". . . At present the Western press writes a lot about the fact that the German Federal Republic is about to propose to the Soviet Union, the U.S.A., Britain and France a new four-Power conference to solve for the Germans—and despite the Germans—the question of unifying their country. But this is the continuation of the old, unrealistic policy which contradicts common sense and has no legitimate basis. No Powers have the right to interfere in the internal affairs of the German Democratic Republic, or to dictate their will to it.

"We quite understand the natural desire of the German people

150

for reunification of their motherland. But the German military and their American patrons only use these national sentiments for a purpose which has nothing in common with German unity or with ensuring a stable peace in Europe. In fact, the military circles of Western Germany are following the road of deepening the division of the country, and of preparing military adventures. If the West German Government tried to solve the question of German unity, not by words but by deeds, then it would take the only road which leads to that goal—the road of establishing contacts with the German Democratic Republic. . . .

"The German question—if this means unification of the two German States now in existence—can be solved only by the German people themselves through the *rapprochement* of those States. The conclusion of a peace treaty with Germany is another matter. This is a task which must be solved in the first instance by the four Powers which were members of the anti-Hitler coalition, in co-operation with Germany's representatives. The signing of a German peace treaty would help the normalization of the whole situation in Germany and in Europe as a whole. The Soviet Union has been proposing, and still proposes, to tackle this matter without delay.

"When one speaks of the four Powers' obligations with regard to Germany, one must speak of the commitments emanating from the Potsdam Agreement. . . . The Powers taking part in the anti-Hitlerite coalition undertook clear-cut and definite commitments to eradicate German militarism, to prevent its revival for ever, to take all measures to ensure that Germany should never again threaten her neighbours or the maintenance of world peace. The parties to the Potsdam Agreement also recognized the need to put an end to German fascism, to bar for ever the road to its revival in Germany, and to put an end to all fascist activity or propaganda. An important part of the Potsdam Agreement was the commitment to liquidate the dominance of cartels, syndicates and other monopolies in the German economy— i.e., those forces which had brought Hitler to power and which encouraged and financed his military adventures. . . .

"What have we got now, more than 13 years after the Potsdam Conference? Nobody can deny that the Soviet Union has been observing all these agreements irreproachably. They have been carried out fully in the Eastern part of Germany, the G.D.R. Let us now look at the way in which the Potsdam Agreement is being implemented in Germany's Western portion, the G.F.R., responsibility for whose development rests with the three Western Powers. One must say straightaway that, far from being eradicated in Western Germany, militarism is rearing its head higher and higher.

"The Powers which should have fought against the rebirth of German militarism drew Western Germany into the aggressive military bloc created by them—NATO. They are doing everything to aid the growth of German militarism and to create in Western Germany a large army . . . which, according to the calculations of the German militarists, will become stronger than the armies of Britain and France. . . . The German Federal Republic already has U.S. rockets which can be equipped with nuclear warheads. In the economic aspect, too, Western Germany is literally flying at the throat of its West European allies. All its economic resources are being placed at the service of rising German imperialism.

"To whichever of the basic propositions of the Potsdam Agreement we turn—those concerning the demilitarization of Germany, and the prevention of a resurgence of fascism—we unavoidably come to the conclusion that these propositions, to which were attached the signatures of the U.S.A., Britain and France, have been violated by those countries.

"What then has remained of the Potsdam Agreement? Virtually one thing only has remained: the so-called four-Power status of Berlin—that is, that Article according to which the three Western Powers have the possibility of holding sway in West Berlin; of turning that part of the city into a kind of State within a State; and of making use of this to carry on from West Berlin subversive activity against the German Democratic Republic, the Soviet Union and other Warsaw Pact countries. On top of everything, they enjoy the right of unhampered communication between West Berlin and Western Germany by air, rail, road and the waters of the German Democratic Republic, which they do not even wish to recognize. . . .

"The question arises: Who profits from such a situation and why do not the United States, France and Britain violate also this part of the four-Power treaty? The matter is quite clear. . . . They are clinging to it in every possible way because the agreement on Berlin is beneficial to the Western Powers . . . The Western Powers would naturally have nothing against extending such Allied privileges *ad infinitum*, although they have long ago abolished the legal basis on which their presence in Berlin rested.

"Has not the time come for us to draw the necessary conclusions from the fact that the most important points of the Potsdam Agreement relating to the securing of peace in Europe . . . have been violated, and that certain forces continue to direct German militarism against the East, as before World War II. Is it not time to revise our attitude to this part of the Potsdam Agreement and to reject it? The time has evidently come for the Powers which signed the Potsdam Agreement to abandon the remnants of the occupation régime in Berlin and thus make it possible to create a normal atmosphere in the capital of the German Democratic Republic. The Soviet Union, for its part, will hand over to the sovereign German Democratic

Republic those functions in Berlin which are still wielded by Soviet organs.

"Let the United States, France and Britain form their own relations with the German Democratic Republic and come to an agreement with it if they are interested in certain questions relating to Berlin. As for the Soviet Union, we shall observe as sacred our obligations which stem from the Warsaw Treaty and which we have confirmed to the German Democratic Republic many a time. Should any aggressive forces attack the German Democratic Republic, which is an equal partner of the Warsaw Treaty, we will consider it as an attack on the Soviet Union and on all the parties to the Warsaw Treaty. We shall rise to the defence of the German Democratic Republic, and this will mean the defence of the basic security interests of the Soviet Union, of the entire Socialist camp and of the cause of peace throughout the world."

Mr. Khrushchev's statement of Nov. 10 confirmed an earlier statement made on Oct. 27 by Herr Ulbricht (First Secretary of the East German Socialist Unity Party), in which Herr Ulbricht said: "The whole of Berlin lies within the territory of the German Democratic Republic. The whole of Berlin belongs to the area under the sovereignty of the German Democratic Republic. The authority of the Western occupying Powers no longer has any legal basis in Berlin." The East German Foreign Ministry had asserted on Oct. 30 that the present system of guaranteed communications for the Western Powers between Berlin and Western Germany depended on "a temporary and exceptional agreement".

A *Pravda* article of Nov. 18 rejected the firm stand which the Western Powers had taken up in defence of their rights in Berlin [see below]. "In the post-war period," *Pravda* wrote, "the occupation of West Berlin has been constantly used by the Western Powers as a venomous weapon with which to poison the atmosphere in Europe. It is now high time for a radical solution of the Berlin problem in the interests of strengthening peace and international security. . . . Even if the agreements on occupation—which are no longer valid—are recalled, it must be said that Berlin was never regarded as a special fifth zone of occupation. The Western Powers created in Berlin an artificial situation . . . in order to take advantage of the unlawful presence of their troops in the city and to create there a base for subversive activity against the German Democratic Republic, the Soviet Union, and the other Socialist countries. Such a situation is . . . intolerable. . . ."

153

Reactions in Western Germany

The Federal Government issued a statement on Nov. 12 saying that any unilateral renunciation by the U.S.S.R. of international agreements on the four-Power status of Berlin would dangerously increase political tensions, affect Soviet-German relations and involve a breach of international law which would seriously put in question the value of Soviet contractual undertakings. After recalling the repeated guarantees of the defence of Berlin given by the Western Powers, the statement said that "the Federal Government, the German people, the population of Berlin, and the entire free world have confidence in these declarations and in the effective protection which they pledged".

Dr. Adenauer said on Nov. 16 that Mr. Khrushchev's threats had created "a dangerous situation not only for Western Germany but for the whole world". He added, however, that he did not wish "in any way to respond to Mr. Khrushchev's provocation", and that the West German Note to Moscow would be left as drafted and would not be sharpened. After thanking the Western allies for their prompt reaction to the Soviet challenge, he gave a warning against doing anything which might create the impression that the four-Power status of Berlin was to be "whittled away" from the West German side; in this connexion he deprecated the demand of Herr Brandt (then Chief Burgomaster of West Berlin) that the deputies representing the city in the *Bundestag* should receive full voting rights. The Chancellor added that the question of counter-measures would arise only in the case of an actual blockade of Berlin, either by the Soviet or the "zonal" (i.e. East German) authorities; in such an eventuality inter-zonal trade would "run into difficulties".

Mr. Smirnov had a further meeting with Dr. Adenauer on Nov. 20, at which the Federal Foreign Minister (Dr. von Brentano) was also present.

An official statement said that the Ambassador had informed the Chancellor of the intentions of the Soviet Government with regard to the status of Berlin; the Soviet Embassy, however, issued a separate statement in which it was claimed that Mr. Smirnov had informed Dr. Adenauer "of the steps his Government intends to take to liquidate the occupation statutes concerning Berlin". This, however, was denied by a Federal Government spokesman, who said that Mr. Smirnov had merely explained Mr. Khrushchev's statement.

Asked if the meeting had helped to relax tension, the spokesman replied in the negative but said that there was no cause for alarm while the matter was still under discussion. He described the political and diplomatic offensive against West Berlin as "very serious", but did not think that the situation would become "acutely dangerous".

Dr. Adenauer said in Munich on Nov. 21 that Mr. Smirnov had expressed the belief that Western Germany would welcome the freeing of Berlin from occupation forces. He (Dr. Adenauer) had answered that the Allied troops were regarded by the people of West Berlin as protectors of freedom, and that it was most important that they should remain in the city.

The Chief Burgomaster of West Berlin (Herr Brandt) made the following statement in the City Assembly on Nov. 20:

"We shall master what lies ahead of us with determination and confidence. Our daily work and our free order are secured. Let me reiterate to the world that 3,500,000 people live here—2,250,000 of them in West Berlin—who want only to live in freedom and to complete their work of peaceful reconstruction. We have no weapons, but we have a right to live and we have good nerves. Presumably there will be some further tests of our nerves, but that will neither confuse nor disconcert us.

"Free Berlin belongs to the free West. We Berliners will not allow ourselves to be parted from our friends, just as our friends will not allow themselves to be parted from Berlin. . . . We are not made of the stuff that is blown over by a gust of wind. For this the people of Berlin have had too many experiences."

Dr. von Brentano flew to West Berlin on Nov. 23 for discussions with Herr Brandt, whilst on Nov. 25 he presided over a meeting of the West German Ambassadors in London, Washington, Paris, Moscow and Rome, who had been summoned to Bonn for consultations.

Reactions in Eastern Germany

Herr Grotewohl, the East German Prime Minister, said in a press statement on Nov. 12 that Mr. Khrushchev's speech had "further paved the way for a settlement of the German problem", but refused to make any "sensational comment". He added that the major task of his Government was the securing of peace and that "the problem of the status of Berlin is not the major problem; it is a problem, but only one of many in Germany today".

On the same day (Nov. 12) the East German Government sent Notes to 60 other countries, through the East German Embassy in Moscow, asking them to recognize the German Democratic Republic and to reject the suggestion that the Federal Republic was the only legitimate government in Germany.

Herr Ulbricht said in an interview on Nov. 25 that Eastern Germany was prepared to negotiate with the Western Powers about their right of access to West Berlin; there was no point in fearing that the Communists would blockade the city because "the possibility of negotiations exists".

Soviet Notes on Revision of Status of Berlin—Proposed "Free City" Status for West Berlin

The Soviet proposals for Berlin were formally handed to the British, French, U.S. and Federal German Ambassadors by Mr. Gromyko on Nov. 27, after the latter had visited East Berlin for discussions with Herr Grotewohl, Herr Ulbricht, and Dr. Bolz, the East German Foreign Minister.

The principal Soviet proposal was that West Berlin should become a demilitarized Free City, with Britain, France, the Soviet Union and the U.S.A., and possibly the United Nations, guaranteeing its status. Under a separate agreement, Eastern Germany would guarantee communications between West Berlin and the outside world, in return for an undertaking by West Berlin not to tolerate "subversive activity against Eastern Germany". If by the end of six months no agreement had been reached on this proposal between the Soviet Union and the Western Powers, the Soviet Government would carry out its plans in agreement with Eastern Germany, which would then be able to exercise full sovereignty by land, sea and air over the approaches to West Berlin.

At a press conference in Moscow on Nov. 27, Mr. Khrushchev denied that the six-months' period mentioned in the Soviet Notes constituted an "ultimatum". He added, however, that a Western refusal to agree to the Soviet proposal "will not stop us from executing our plans" since there would be "no other way out".

156

West German Reply to Soviet Note

The German Federal Government's reply to the Soviet Note was delivered in Moscow on Jan. 5, 1959. It rejected a "free city" status for West Berlin and denied the right of the Soviet Union to change the city's existing status by unilateral action.

After rejecting the idea of a "Confederation" between Western and Eastern Germany, the Federal Government strongly repudiated the Soviet allegations that West Berlin was being used as a "spy centre" by the Western allies and that the Federal Republic was pursuing a policy of "militarism" and "revanchism" *vis-à-vis* the East European countries and the Soviet Union. In the latter connexion it stressed the great disparity between the strengths of the Soviet armed forces and the West German *Bundeswehr*, and recalled that the Federal Republic had solemnly renounced the use of force to achieve political ends. Apart from its justified desire that a future peace treaty should bring about a just and reasonable settlement of Germany's eastern frontiers, the Federal Republic had no political objectives in the East and desired only to establish good-neighbourly relations with the countries of Eastern Europe.

Statement by Chief Burgomaster of West Berlin

In West Berlin itself, Herr Brandt had previously issued a statement on Nov. 27, 1958, making the following points:

(1) The Soviet plan for "free city" status "aims at having West Berlin cleared of Allied troops but remaining surrounded by Soviet divisions. It means, further, that the legal, financial and economic attachment of Berlin to the Federal Republic would be cut away and replaced by dependence on the Eastern bloc. This is unbearable."

(2) The Western Powers had "on repeated occasions given solemn assurances that they would exercise their rights and duties in Berlin until the division of Germany has been removed".

(3) There was "no isolated solution" of the Berlin question, which could only be solved in the context of an overall German settlement, including that of reunification.

(4) It was "the recognizable goal of Communist policy to make the whole of Berlin part of the so-called German Democratic Republic; no amount of talking can divert attention from this".

(5) The people of Berlin, "trusting in their friends throughout the world", would "continue to work in constructing the capital of

Germany and making their contribution toward ensuring the maintenance of legality and of the free democratic order in Berlin".

East German Support for Soviet Proposals

In a Note to the Soviet Government on Jan. 7, 1959 (in reply to the Soviet Note of Nov. 27), the East German Government announced its willingness "to recognize a demilitarized free city status for West Berlin" and its readiness "to assume appropriate pledges in common with other countries".

The Note stated that, "with the establishment of a demilitarized Free City of West Berlin, the German Democratic Republic would ensure West Berlin's communications with all parts of the world and take all necessary measures to guarantee unhampered passenger and goods traffic to and from West Berlin". It added: "The most essential and urgent steps to be taken to eliminate the centre of provocation which West Berlin represents are, in the opinion of the Government of the G.D.R., the ending of the illegally maintained occupation of West Berlin by the three Western Powers, the withdrawal of foreign troops from West Berlin, and the ending of the 'cold war' policy being pursued there against the G.D.R. and other Socialist countries. . . ."

After welcoming the Soviet decision to transfer its functions in Eastern Germany to the G.D.R., the Note said that the East German Government was "prepared to negotiate all matters related to the settlement of the West Berlin question". . . . The "democratic Magistrature of Greater Berlin" [i.e. the municipal authorities in East Berlin] was also prepared "to conduct negotiations with the West Berlin Senate and to conclude appropriate agreements".

Statement by Tass Agency

The Tass Agency had meanwhile issued a 4,000-word statement on Dec. 11, 1958, on behalf of the Soviet Government, reiterating that the U.S.S.R. would not agree to talks on German reunification "without the Germans and behind their backs", but at the same time stating that "the Soviet Union would not refuse to discuss the conclusion of a peace treaty, which, in its view, falls within the competence of the four Powers". It added that if the Western Powers "do not wish to co-operate with the U.S.S.R. in solving this problem, nothing remains for the Soviet Government but to relieve itself of the functions connected with maintaining the occupation régime in

Berlin and to conclude a corresponding agreement with the Government of Eastern Germany". An assurance was given that the Soviet Union "does not want to cause any damage to the prestige of the Western Powers" and that it was prepared, together with other Powers, "to guarantee [West] Berlin's free city status and non-interference in the political and economic affairs of western Berlin".

Geneva Conference of Foreign Ministers, 1959

Agreement having been reached between the four Powers on the holding of a Foreign Ministers' meeting in Geneva, such a conference took place between May 11 and June 20, 1959.

The conference was presented on May 14 with a detailed "Western Peace Plan" for a settlement of the Berlin question, German unification and European security. This plan was amplified on May 26 by detailed Western proposals providing for the unification of Berlin after free elections.

These proposals were followed by counter-proposals made by Mr. Gromyko, the Soviet Foreign Minister, on June 10, but these were immediately rejected by the Western Foreign Ministers.

The conference adjourned on June 21 without agreement having been reached.

The resumed Foreign Ministers' talks in Geneva on July 13–Aug. 5, 1959, were held in private, and the final communiqué stated:

"The Conference of Foreign Ministers considered questions relating to Germany, including a peace treaty with Germany and the question of Berlin.

"The positions of the participants in the conference were set out on these questions. A frank and comprehensive discussion took place on the Berlin question. The positions of both sides on certain points became closer.

"The discussions which have taken place will be useful for the further negotiations which are necessary in order to reach an agreement."

No such negotiations, however, took place in 1959–60, a Summit Conference of the Heads of Government of the Western Powers and the Soviet Union, scheduled to begin in Paris on May 16, 1960, breaking down at its very beginning in consequence of a strong Soviet protest against "U.S. reconnaissance flights over Soviet territory" arising out of the shooting down of a U.S. aircraft (U-2) in the Soviet Union on May 1.

7. EXCHANGES ON REUNIFICATION OF GERMANY, 1959

During a visit to Eastern Germany from March 4–11, 1959, Mr. Krushchev had discussions with Herr Grotewohl, Herr Ulbricht and other East German leaders. A joint communiqué on these talks issued on March 11 stated (1) that a peace treaty should be signed with both German States, or with a German Confederation, should it be formed; (2) that the German Democratic Republic was prepared to guarantee free access to West Berlin from both east and west, and to respect its status as a demilitarized Free City; (3) that the Soviet Union was prepared to join in guaranteeing the independence and security of West Berlin. Both Governments called for a summit conference with the participation of Poland, Czechoslovakia and the two German States.

Herr Ollenhauer, leader of the Social Democratic Party in Western Germany, had a meeting in East Berlin on March 9 with Mr. Khrushchev, at the latter's invitation. After his discussion with Mr. Khrushchev (held at the Soviet Embassy) Herr Ollenhauer said that they had agreed that all problems should be solved by peaceful negotiations, and were confident that acceptable solutions could be found given good will on both sides. Whilst there were differences on the question of German reunification, he had received the impression that Mr. Khrushchev was not prepared to go to war over Berlin and was seeking a peaceful solution.

Allied Declaration on German Reunification—
East German Proposal for German "Confederation"—
Rejection by Federal Republic

A 12-point declaration setting forth the common policy of the British, French, U.S. and Federal German Governments on the question of German reunification was issued in West Berlin on July 29, 1957. It was signed by the three Western Ambassadors to the Federal Republic and by Dr. von Brentano (the Federal Foreign Minister) as representing "the only Government qualified to speak for the German people as a whole".

The declaration said *inter alia* that "the reunification of Germany remains the joint responsibility of the Four Powers who in 1945 assumed supreme authority in Germany." . . . It reiterated the West German call for a freely elected all-German Government and for an all-German National Assembly. The Government of a reunified Germany, the declaration said, "should be free to determine its foreign policy and to decide on its international associations." . . .

The declaration also contained the following passages:

"The Western Powers have never required as a condition of German reunification that a reunified Germany should join the North Atlantic Treaty Organization. It will be for the people of a reunified Germany themselves to determine through their freely elected Government whether they wish to share in the benefits and obligations of the treaty.

"If the all-German Government, in the exercise of its free choice, should elect to join NATO, the Western Powers . . . are prepared to offer, on a basis of reciprocity, to the Government of the Soviet Union and to other countries of Eastern Europe which would become parties to a European security arrangement, assurances of a significant and far-reaching character. The Western Powers are also prepared, as part of a mutually acceptable European security arrangement, to give an assurance that, in the event of a reunited Germany choosing to join NATO, they would not take military advantage as a result of the withdrawal of Soviet forces.

"The reunification of Germany, accompanied by the conclusion of European security arrangements, would facilitate the achievement of a comprehensive disarmament agreement. Conversely, if a beginning could be made towards effective measures of partial disarmament, this would contribute to the settlement of outstanding major political problems such as the reunification of Germany. Initial steps in the field of disarmament should lead to a comprehensive disarmament agreement, which presupposes a prior solution of the problem of German reunification. The Western Powers do not intend to enter into any agreement on disarmament which would prejudice the reunification of Germany.

The declaration concluded: "The four Governments continue to hope that the Soviet Government will come to recognize that it is not in its own interest to maintain the present division of Germany. The Western Powers are ready to discuss all these questions with the Soviet Union at any time that there is a reasonable prospect of making progress. At such time there will be many points relating to the procedure for German reunification and the terms of a treaty of assurance which will require to be worked out by detailed negotia-

161

tion. In advance of serious negotiations, the Western Powers cannot finally determine their attitude on all points. Nor can they contemplate in advance the making of concessions to which there is no present likelihood of response from the Soviet side. . . ."

Two days before the Allied declaration was issued, the Prime Minister of Eastern Germany (Herr Grotewohl) had sent a memorandum to all diplomatic representatives accredited to the German Democratic Republic proposing that the two German States should enter into a contractual relationship as a "confederation", while at the same time retaining their present administrative arrangements. Herr Grotewohl laid down the following conditions as pre-requisites for such a "confederation": (1) the Federal Republic should withdraw from NATO and the Democratic Republic from the Warsaw Pact, armed forces in both parts of Germany should be strictly limited, and conscription should be abolished in the Federal Republic; (2) both German States should request the great Powers to arrive at a common agreement for the phased withdrawal of their forces from German territory; (3) no nuclear weapons should be stored in any part of Germany and all "nuclear war propaganda" should be strictly forbidden.

Herr Grotewohl reiterated the Soviet thesis that reunification could not be achieved through free all-German elections but only through a gradual *rapprochement* between Eastern and Western Germany. He proposed that the "confederation" should be established by treaty between the two German Governments, and that it should take the form of an All-German Council, recruited from both German Parliaments, which would endeavour to achieve conformity in matters of trade, currency, transport and communications, the status of Berlin and other matters of common concern. This Council would be an advisory body and would make recommendations to both German Governments, which could accept or reject them. The lifting of the ban on "democratic organizations" in Western Germany—i.e. the West German Communist Party and the Communist-controlled "Free German Youth" organization—was among the conditions mentioned by Herr Grotewohl as a pre-requisite for an all-German "confederation".

The East German proposals were rejected out of hand by all parties in the Federal Republic. Dr. Adenauer, in a statement on July 28, said that Herr Grotewohl's proposal for a "confederation" between Eastern and Western Germany was "absolutely out of the question" and that the Federal Government could never agree to a step which would "strengthen the slavery of 17,000,000 people in the Soviet zone".

The Soviet Tass Agency described the four-Power declaration on German reunification as "another scrap of paper added to the documents on the German question". It said that the Western Powers, "realizing that their proposals on the German question are unacceptable, want to exploit them as a counter-move to the Soviet disarmament proposals".

Social Democratic Plan for European Security and
German Reunification—Criticism by Federal Government—
Social Democrats reject East German Proposal for Joint Action

The national executive of the Social Democratic Party (the Opposition party) and the executive of the Social Democratic parliamentary group in the *Bundestag* unanimously adopted on March 18, 1959, a plan for the reunification of Germany and the relaxation of tension and security in Europe. The urgency of the proposals was stressed in the light of the Soviet demands concerning the status of West Berlin.

The Social Democratic plan was divided into three parts, dealing respectively with (1) military relaxation and European security; (2) the political and economic integration of Germany; (3) reunification.

On the political and economic integration of Germany the plan proposed that, as the restoration of German unity by a freely-elected National Assembly pre-supposed a gradual *rapprochement* in stages, joint organs should be set up, without, however, affecting the respective powers in both parts of Germany during the interim period. The necessary arrangements should be made either between the four great Powers, or by those Powers jointly with both parts of Germany within the framework of a peace treaty, or directly between the two German Governments within the framework of a settlement laid down by the four Powers. It was indispensable, however, that such arrangements should safeguard human rights and essential liberties in both parts of Germany pending the introduction of an all-German Constitution. Existing economic systems, foreign trade relations, and long-term treaties would remain unaffected for the time being unless expressly agreed otherwise. Both German Governments should subscribe to a policy of full employment and of guaranteeing social development.

The proposed political and economic phases were:

First Stage—Political integration would begin with an All-German Conference at which both German Governments would be equally represented. This conference would have the task of regulating internal affairs, without, however, affecting the functions of constitutional organs in either part of Germany. The All-German Conference would be informed of all legislative proposals presented in the West German *Bundestag* or the East German *Volkskammer*, and must give its opinion. An All-German Court would be set up by the Conference to safeguard uniformity in the interpretation of human rights and basic freedoms; it would be a supreme court and its decisions would be final.

Economic integration would begin with the creation of joint institutions on a basis of parity; the lifting of present embargoes and quota regulations for inter-zonal trade by the Federal Republic; expansion of inter-zonal commercial exchanges; and the opening of additional inter-zonal traffic routes.

An All-German Investment Fund would be set up, as well as a Bank for Inter-German Settlements. The fund would plan and finance investments in the sphere of transport and power or aimed at adjusting the two economies, whilst the bank—in addition to clearing payments between the two parts of Germany—would handle pensions and similar payments.

Second Stage—An All-German Parliamentary Council would be established on a basis of parity; its members would be separately elected in both parts of Germany and would enjoy parliamentary immunity throughout the country. It would legislate especially for railways, roads, inland navigation, posts and telegraphs, and increased production. It would also prevent the abuse of economic power and would regulate patents and trade-marks. Either German Government could appeal within a fixed period against any decisions of the Council, which would decide on such appeals and could overrule them by a two-thirds majority.

Economic integration would be accelerated by the development of an All-German Market and the introduction of an official rate of exchange for the East and West German currencies, as well as the abolition of import quotas for internal German trade by the German Democratic Republic.

Third Stage—The powers of the All-German Parliamentary Council would be increased to enable it to draft legislation on taxation and financial matters for the whole of Germany, on social legislation in both parts of the country, and for the creation of a Customs and currency union.

Provision would also be made for all-German referenda on legislative proposals if requested by at least one million electors. If either of the two Governments should object to the result of a referendum, there would be a second one a year later; if this confirmed the previous decision, the latter would be final. No referendum could be held if it aimed at restricting human rights and basic liberties, changes in property rights, or the abolition of the existing legislative or executive organs in either part of Germany.

The All-German Parliamentary Council would be empowered to enact legislation for the election of a National Constituent Assembly, which would require approval by a two-thirds majority of the votes cast. If such a majority in the Council was not forthcoming, legislation of this kind could be enacted by a referendum if approved by a two-thirds majority of the votes cast. The National Assembly, when formed, would supersede the All-German Parliamentary Council and would proceed to draft and adopt an all-German Constitution.

During the various stages Berlin would become the seat of the all-German institutions.

Reunification. After the all-German Constitution had come into force, there would be free and secret elections throughout Germany for an all-German Parliament, which would then form an all-German Government.

The Federal Government issued a statement on March 20 commenting on the Soviet Democratic plan for German reunification.

While promising that the Government would give the plan "careful examination", the statement made the following critical comments: (1) the proposed "military relaxation", without making it directly dependent on political advances, would weaken the defensive strength of the West and lead to the withdrawal of U.S. troops from Europe; (2) there was no controllable undertaking guaranteeing that each stage would be automatically followed by the next one, everything being left to the arbitrary discretion of the East German Government as far as the manner, extent and speed of reunification were concerned; (3) implementation of the plan implied recognition of the "Pankow régime" [i.e. the East German Government], contrary to numerous unanimous resolutions of the *Bundestag*; (4) the Federal Government was opposed to holding free all-German elections only after the framing of the new Constitution, since this would constitute a serious danger to the democratic development of a future all-German State.

The Federal Foreign Minister (Dr. von Brentano) reaffirmed in Washington on March 28 that the only way to bring about Germany's reunification was through free democratic elections; no other "stages of reunification" could be considered until such elections had taken place.

East German Proposal for Joint Action— Rejection by Social Democrats

The central committee of the East German Socialist Unity Party sent a letter to the West German Social Democratic Party on April 3 welcoming its proposals for a German peace treaty and German reunification, and appealing for "normal and comradely relations" between the two parties. The Social Democratic executive, however, decided on April 6 not to reply to the Socialist Unity Party and to reject any joint action with that party.

Social Democratic Leaders' Visit to Moscow

Professor Carlo Schmid, deputy chairman of the Social Democratic Party, and Herr Fritz Erler, deputy chairman of its parliamentary group, visited Moscow on March 11-16 for talks with Mr. Khrushchev and other Soviet leaders.

At a press conference in Bonn on March 18, Professor Schmid and Herr Erler quoted Mr. Khrushchev as saying that, once Soviet troops had withdrawn from Eastern Germany, they would not intervene if the East German population decided that it desired a different form of government, even if violence were used; this would not apply, however, if the West interfered in Eastern Germany or was "the cause of the trouble". As regards free elections or other all-German matters, Mr. Khrushchev had said that the U.S.S.R. would respect any agreements reached between the two German States. On the other hand, he was also quoted as saying that he was opposed to all-German elections at any time, because "fifty million West Germans would impose their will on seventeen million East Germans", which would mean that "the majority, but not freedom, would prevail".

Professor Schmid and Herr Erler indicated that Mr. Khrushchev was really pressing for two separate peace treaties with East and West Germany; these treaties could contain features in common, as well as other clauses suited to the different wishes of the two German States. Failing this, a treaty would in any case be signed between the Soviet Union and Eastern Germany. As regards reunification, the two Social Democratic leaders quoted Mr. Khrushchev as saying that "nobody really wants the reunification of Germany at this moment—nobody at all".

166

Herr Grotewohl's Letter to Dr. Adenauer

In a letter on April 8, the East German Prime Minister (Herr Grotewohl) appealed to Dr. Adenauer to agree to joint action by both Governments at the forthcoming four-Power conference at Geneva. The letter reiterated the East German proposal for a commission of representatives of both States which would work out a joint attitude towards a peace treaty, and suggested that representatives of the Democratic Republic and the Federal Republic should meet without delay to work out the necessary joint proposals.

A spokesman in Bonn stated on April 9 that no reply would be sent to Herr Grotewohl's letter.

8. THE BERLIN CRISIS OF 1961— EASTERN PEACE PROPOSALS

The East German Government announced on Aug. 30, 1960, that it had issued instructions about the access by West Germans to the Eastern sector of Berlin during the next five days. From midnight of Aug. 30-31 until midnight of Sept. 4-5 only those West German citizens with valid residence visas would be permitted to cross into the Eastern sector, and anybody attempting to contravene the order would be liable to the penalties provided under the East German criminal code. The restrictions, it was stated in the announcement, were to prevent the "misuse of the traffic links and territory of the German Democratic Republic for the organization and propagation of militaristic and revanchist meetings". This referred to rallies planned to be held in West Berlin from Sept. 1-4 by the German Association of Ex-prisoners of War and Missing Persons' Relatives and the German Federal Refugees' Association. The ban did not apply to citizens of West Berlin.

The announcement also contained a warning by the East German Government to the Western Powers not to permit "the misuse of the air corridors to West Berlin for the transport of military and revanchist elements".

Following talks with Herr Brandt, then Chief Burgomaster of West Berlin, the three Western Commandants in the city protested to General Zakharov, the Soviet Commandant, on Aug. 31 against the restrictions imposed by the East German Government, which they described as "a flagrant violation of the right of free circulation" within the city of Berlin and "a direct contravention" of the agreements of June 20, 1949, between the Western and Soviet Governments [i.e. the agreement ending the Soviet blockade of West Berlin]. After a Cabinet meeting in Bonn under the chairmanship of Professor Erhard, in the absence of Dr. Adenauer, a statement was issued on Aug. 31 condemning the East German action in Berlin as "illegal" and rejecting the allegations that the refugees' and ex-Servicemen's organizations due to hold rallies in Berlin were "militaristic" and "revanchist".

The restrictions were extended on Sept. 1 to the border between Eastern and Western Germany, where a number of West German citizens travelling to West Berlin were stopped because their papers showed that they had been born in the former German territories beyond the Oder-Neisse Line. Later the same day the West Berlin Senate announced, however, that anyone turned back at the zonal frontiers would be transported to West Berlin by air free of charge.

The temporary ban on the entry of West Germans into East Berlin was lifted on Sept. 5, 1960, but later the same day the official East German News Agency issued a statement asserting that the German Federal Government were planning "new provocations" in West Berlin, and describing a meeting due to take place on Sept. 9 between Professor Erhard and Herr Brandt as "an open challenge to the people of Berlin". The Agency's statement added that Herr Ulbricht (the East German Communist leader and Deputy Premier) had already declared that no representative of the Government in Bonn had "any business to be in Berlin".

This was followed by the imposition of new restrictions on free travel in Berlin on Sept. 8, when the East German Council of Ministers approved regulations under which West German citizens would in future need a permit for any entry into East Berlin. The permit, it was stated, could be obtained only by East Berlin citizens acting on a West German's behalf, or by the West German himself, and must be applied for at "the appropriate offices of the German People's Police" [i.e. the East German police]; three-monthly permits might be granted for repeated entry into East Berlin.

The East German News Agency, which announced that the order would come into effect at midnight on Sept. 8-9, said that the East

German Government, after discussing the "continued misuse of West Berlin for incitement for revenge", considered it "necessary to draw attention emphatically to the fact that under the Potsdam Agreement any Nazi, militaristic and revenge-seeking activity and propaganda was forbidden, and German militarism and Nazism should be eradicated. True to the Agreement, the State organs of the German Democratic Republic are taking the necessary measures, which are exclusively directed against West German and West Berlin revenge-seeking politicians, whose activities endanger peace".

On Sept. 13 the East German radio announced that the East German Government would no longer recognize the validity of the West Berlin passports held by citizens of West Berlin. An East German decree stated that West Berliners wanting to travel to Eastern Germany, as distinct from transit travel to the Federal Republic, would henceforth require an identity card with a special East German permit attached to it. A Government spokesman in Bonn described the East German measure as another "conscious and arbitrary barrier" likely to cause disquiet.

The Czechoslovak and Polish military missions in West Berlin stated on Sept. 15 that their countries had followed the East German example of no longer recognizing West Berlin passports held by West Berliners, and that the latter would have to possess visas on a paper attached to their West Berlin identity cards for visits to Czechoslovakia and Poland.

Herr Brandt stated on Sept. 8, 1960, that, during the earlier frontier restrictions from Sept. 1-4, 1,061 West Germans had been turned back by the East German police; of these, 610 had reached Berlin by air, and altogether there had been 4,000 more visitors to West Berlin than in the same period in 1959. Herr Brandt added that everything necessary to meet Communist pressure must be agreed in complete accord with all involved, including the Western Allies, and that if the Communists regarded their current pinpricking as a "dress rehearsal", the same must be true of Western counter-action.

Soviet Note to Federal Government

On Feb. 17, 1961, the Soviet Government sent a Note to the German Federal Government on the question of a German peace treaty and the Berlin situation.

After alleging that agitation for a revision of Germany's existing frontiers was growing in the Federal Republic, that "extensive military preparations" were on foot in Western Germany, and that West Berlin was being used "for subversive activities against the German Democratic Republic", the Note went on:

"As is known, Soviet proposals envisage the solution of the problem of West Berlin as a free city on the basis of a peace treaty with the German States. This opens for the German Federal Republic broad opportunities for safeguarding its interests in West Berlin, inasmuch as its representatives would appear as a party in the peace negotiations. In any case, the Soviet Government . . . is prepared to display maximum understanding of the wishes of the Federal Government and to take them into account during negotiations with all other parties concerned.

"An entirely different situation would arise if the Federal Government were to continue to insist on its negative position with regard to a peace treaty with Germany. By this very fact it would deny itself the possibility of direct defence of its interests. . . .

"Should no peace treaty with both States be concluded within the agreed time-limit, the Soviet Union, together with other nations wishing to do so, will sign a peace treaty with the German Democratic Republic. That will also mean ending the occupation régime in West Berlin, with all the attendant consequences. In particular, questions of communications by land, water and air passing through the territory of the German Democratic Republic will in that case be settled only on the basis of appropriate agreements with the German Democratic Republic".

Declaring that the U.S.S.R. had "no wish to dictate" to Western Germany and "stretches out the hand of friendship to the entire German people", the Note added: "The Soviet draft of a peace treaty with Germany is not an ultimatum. Should the Government of the Federal Republic disagree with any particular point of our draft, it is welcome to make its own suggestions or put forward a draft peace treaty of its own. The Soviet Government is prepared to discuss any constructive proposals of the Federal Government which would take account of the present situation and contribute to concluding a peace treaty. . . . Whether or not this problem will be adjusted with the participation of the German Federal Republic depends on the Federal Government alone. . . ."

Herr Brandt visited the U.S.A. from March 11-20 and discussed the Berlin question with President Kennedy on March 13; after the meeting Herr Brandt said that the President had "reiterated the determination of the United States, in co-operation with its Allies, to preserve and maintain the freedom of West Berlin, to which it is committed, and to defend the Allied position in the city, upon which the preservation of that freedom in large measure depends".

Mr. Khrushchev's Memorandum to President Kennedy in Vienna

On June 3–4, 1961, President John F. Kennedy had talks with Mr. Khrushchev in Vienna. Among other questions they also discussed the problems of Germany and Berlin. During their meeting Mr. Khrushchev presented to President Kennedy a memorandum dealing with the question of a German peace treaty and a settlement of the Berlin question.

The memorandum proposed the calling "without any delay" of a conference to conclude a peace treaty with the two German States; recapitulated the proposal to make West Berlin a "free demilitarized city", if necessary under U.N. guarantee; and reiterated that access to the proposed free city would have to be negotiated with the East German Authorities. In order "not to drag out the peace settlement", it was proposed that the two German States should "explore the possibilities of agreement on questions falling within their internal competence", the Soviet Government expressing the view that "a period not exceeding six months" would be adequate for such talks, should the two German States fail to reach agreement, "then measures will be taken to conclude a peace treaty with both German States or with one of them".

East German Reactions

The Soviet Government's proposals on Germany and West Berlin, as set out in the memorandum to President Kennedy, were conveyed to Herr Ulbricht on June 7 by the Soviet Ambassador in East Berlin. The Tass Agency stated that Herr Ulbricht had expressed "cordial gratitude to the Soviet Government for its consistent peace-loving policy on the settlement of the German problem in the interests of safeguarding and consolidating peace".

The restrictions imposed in August 1960 on West Germans entering East Berlin were lifted by the East German authorities from midnight of Feb. 15. The official announcement stated that the regulations under which West Germans had required special visas to enter East Berlin had been "simplified and eased", without giving details; it was understood, however, that visas would no longer be necessary and that West Germans entering the Eastern sector would only be required to produce their identity cards, as was the case before the restrictions were introduced.

At a press conference on June 15, Herr Ulbricht expressed confidence that the Berlin question would be settled within a year, declaring that "a peace treaty will come and West Berlin will be a free city with its neutrality guaranteed". In reply to questions, he said that the German Democratic Republic would control all communications with West Berlin after the conclusion of a peace treaty; that the Western Powers would have to negotiate on details of traffic arrangements; and that the G.D.R. was ready to give "realistic guarantees" of continued access to West Berlin by land, air and water.

West German Reactions

Speaking on June 11 at a Hanover rally of some 300,000 refugees from Silesia, Dr. Adenauer said that Mr. Khrushchev's memorandum to President Kennedy showed that the Soviet Government's sole concern was to maintain the situation in Europe resulting from the Second World War. Rejecting the Soviet proposal that the Federal Republic and Eastern Germany should reach an agreement within six months on a peace treaty, in default of which the U.S.S.R. would sign a separate treaty with Eastern Germany, Dr. Adenauer declared: "The Federal Government will never agree to this Russian demand; we want self-determination and freedom for the whole German people".

The German Federal Government's reply to the Soviet Note of Feb. 17, 1961 [see page 169], was presented in Moscow on July 12.

The West German Note declared that it was "an indisputable fact that, in spite of the events which have followed in the wake of the Second World War, the German people continue to exist as an entity. . . . Any policy that disregards this fact in attempting to settle the German problem cannot claim to be considered as realistic". After pointing out that the German people as a whole were still denied the possibility of a common national order, although the war had ended 16 years ago, the Note said that a "sober appraisal of the situation" led to the conclusion that this state of affairs could only be changed if the German people were allowed to exercise the right of self-determination.

With regard to the urgency of concluding a German peace treaty, as stressed in the Soviet Note, the Federal Government said that this "presupposes the existence of a Government capable of acting, and legitimized by a democratic decision of the German people, whose authority would apply to the entire German people. Such a Government can only be established by the German people if it has been enabled to exercise the right of self-determination through a free expression of its will. Hence the timing of the conclusion of a peace treaty with Germany depends upon the readiness of the U.S.S.R. to grant the German people the exercise of the right to self-determination".

After emphasizing that a separate peace treaty with only one part of Germany would violate the right of self-determination of peoples—a right recognized as one of the basic principles of the U.N. Charter, to which the Soviet Government had subscribed—the Note continued: "A peace treaty with a German Government generally recognized and formed on the basis of the right of self-determination of the German people would settle all problems concerning Germany, including that of the German frontiers. The question of Berlin . . . would also be settled, since Berlin could then fulfil its natural destiny as the capital of Germany." On the other hand, a peace treaty based on the partition of Germany would not help to lessen tension but would increase it, since it would perpetuate the division of the country.

As regards the Soviet Government's call for counter-proposals from the Federal Government [contained in the Soviet Note], the West German reply said that the U.S.S.R. would only regard proposals as "constructive" if they were based on the inevitability of the partition of Germany. Proposals founded on such a premise, however, could not be called "constructive" since they could never lead to a lasting peace; only proposals which did away with the partition of Germany could be regarded as a constructive contribution to a general peace settlement. Such proposals had been put forward by the Western Powers on many occasions, but without avail, the most recent being at the Geneva Foreign Ministers' Conference of 1959.

Continuing, the Federal Government declared its readiness to subscribe to any agreement on general controlled disarmament which might be reached by the great Powers; rejected the Soviet allegation that it was ready to use force to change the existing frontiers; and stressed that there were no nuclear weapons under the control of the Federal Republic, which had specifically abandoned by treaty the right to produce them. The Soviet allegations of militaristic intentions on the part of Western Germany (the Note added) were the less understandable inasmuch as all the *Bundeswehr* forces were integrated in NATO, which pursued no aggressive aims and was formed solely for the defence of the West.

In conclusion, the Federal Government reiterated its wish to achieve the reunification of the German people in peace and freedom exclusively by peaceful means, and declared that it had no intention in the forthcoming Federal elections of creating any feeling of enmity amongst the population towards the Soviet Union, as it was its basic policy to refrain from any action which might increase international tension.

Bundestag Declaration

A declaration appealing "to the world and before history" for a peace treaty based on the right of self-determination of the whole German people was read in the West German *Bundestag* on June 30 by its president, Dr. Gerstenmaier, in the presence of Dr. Adenauer, members of the Federal Cabinet, and representatives of the *Länder* Governments.

In presenting this declaration—issued with the support of all parties represented in the *Bundestag*—Dr. Gerstenmaier pointed out that all efforts at a solution of the German question had failed because the Soviet Union, "while speaking incessantly of a peace treaty, obviously only intends to sit down at the conference table when it is certain that the partition of Germany has . . . been made permanent and the recognition of Pankow [i.e. of the East German régime] achieved". Dr. Gerstenmaier emphasized that the right of self-determination was claimed for the entire German people, and not only for the 52,000,000 Germans in the Federal Republic.

Dr. Adenauer visited West Berlin on July 12 for talks with Herr Brandt and the West Berlin Senate. A communiqué was issued after the talks stating that there was complete identity of views between the Federal Government and the West Berlin authorities on the Berlin question, and emphasizing the following points: "(1) The presence of the Western Powers in West Berlin is based on an unaltered legal position and should be maintained; (2) West Berlin's integration in the economic, financial and judicial system of the Federal Republic represents a pivot of the city's independent existence; (3) there should be no restrictions on free access to or from West Berlin, nor any interference with the city's communications with the West; (4)

any agreement on Berlin must take into account the clearly-expressed wishes of the city's population; (5) Berlin should continue to be a meeting-place for all Germans."

East German "Peace Plan"

The East German *Volkskammer* unanimously adopted on July 6, 1961, a "German Peace Plan" presented by Herr Ulbricht, chairman of the East German State Council.

In a speech Herr Ulbricht said that the German Democratic Republic supported Mr. Khrushchev's memorandum to President Kennedy and was determined to follow the course outlined therein. After noting that the East German State Council had sent an urgent appeal to the Federal Government and the *Bundestag* for negotiations on a peace settlement and German reunification, he asserted that any further delay in concluding a peace treaty and making West Berlin a demilitarized free city represented "a growing danger for the German people, the Soviet Union, Poland, Czechosolvakia and all other European nations, as well as the American people". If the "Bonn Government" continued to resist a peace treaty and carried on its "policy of *revanche* and rearmament", the conclusion of a peace treaty with the German Democratic Republic alone would be "inevitable"; such a separate peace treaty would "confirm in law the existing frontiers, reinforce the international status of the G.D.R., including its admission to the United Nations, and lead to the removal of the centre of provocation in West Berlin and its abuse as a base in the cold war".

After alleging that the Western Powers had "violated" the Potsdam Agreement, which constituted "the basic charter for the aims of the occupation of Germany", and asserting that a right of occupation detached from these aims and extending for an indefinite period did not exist under international law, Herr Ulbricht said that the present "occupation régime" in West Berlin had neither in law nor in fact anything to do with the aims of the anti-Hitler coalition. A peace treaty would extinguish occupation rights under international law on the whole territory of the G.D.R., "i.e., also in West Berlin", and the G.D.R. was under no obligations deriving from the "anachronistic occupation law" in West Berlin which "the three Western occupation Powers have created for themselves".

Herr Ulbricht continued: "The freedom and security of the population in West Berlin will, under our proposals, be secured by the strongest imaginable international guarantees. For this it will be necessary, however, that West German militarism and the revanchist politicians from Bonn . . . are removed from West Berlin. The conclusion of a peace treaty with the G.D.R. would free the population of West Berlin of the obligations imposed by the separate occupation régime and enable it to decide its status within a demilitarized free city of West Berlin. . . . We have no intention of interfering with West Berlin affairs. I repeat . . . that the right of a demilitarized free city of West Berlin to determine its own order and freedom and to decide its own affairs will in no way be affected . . . and that we are willing to guarantee its communications with west, east, north, and south. However, we demand one thing—West Berlin must cease to be a base for the cold war.

"The G.D.R. is willing to negotiate a settlement of all questions arising from the ending of the occupation régime in West Berlin and the conclusion of a peace treaty, as far as they affect the sovereignty of the G.D.R. This is a concession by the G.D.R. . . . , and the Western Governments should reasonably accept that the G.D.R. will not tolerate a violation of its sovereignty."

The East German "Peace Plan" contained the following proposals:

(1) The setting-up of a German Peace Commission consisting of representatives of both German Parliaments and Governments, with the task of reaching agreement on all-German proposals for a peace treaty and on "a goodwill agreement aiming at an immediate improvement of their relations".

(2) (a) Such an agreement might contain the following provisions: (i) both German States would renounce nuclear arms and agree on the immediate ending of further rearmament; (ii) both would agree on the strength, armament and location of their defence forces pending the conclusion of a general disarmament agreement; (iii) both would suppress all "war and *revanche* propaganda"; (iv) neither of them would interfere in the social order of the other, and each would "regard the decision on the other's social order as an act of self-determination of the other's population"; (v) both would support a non-aggression treaty between the Warsaw Treaty countries and the NATO countries, as well as the creation of a nuclear-free zone in Central Europe; (vi) both would take measures to expand trade between them, foster cultural relations, and facilitate and improve traffic between the two German States.

(b) All discussions in the Peace Commission would be based on the principle that neither side would "impose its will on the other".

(3) A peace treaty should make it impossible for Germany ever to start a new war, but should also secure for the German people "permanent peace and full equality in the family of nations". German proposals for a peace treaty should therefore include the following:

(i) Both German States would undertake to renounce any threat

176

of force, or use of force, in their international relations, to settle international disputes by peaceful means only, and to follow a policy of peaceful coexistence between peoples and States;

(ii) both would support the creation of a militarily neutral Germany, the inviolability of this neutrality being guaranteed by the principal members of the anti-Hitler coalition. The treaty would regulate the strength, armament and location of the defence forces of both German States, who would renounce nuclear weapons and support general and complete disarmament;

(iii) the existing German frontiers would be confirmed and the inviolability and sovereignty of each German State guaranteed;

(iv) all "war and *revanche* propaganda" would be banned, all "Nazi, militaristic and revanchist organizations and associations" forbidden, and persons who had committed crimes against peace, crimes against humanity and war crimes would be banned from occupying leading posts in public life;

(v) the contracting parties would recognize the full sovereignty and self-determination of the German people, "including the right to bring about Germany's reunification as a peaceful State without foreign interference";

(vi) all contracting parties would support Germany's co-operation in UNO and other organizations on a basis of equality and, pending Germany's reunification, would support the admission of both German States to the United Nations;

(vii) both German States would be granted full freedom for the development of their economy, shipping and access to world markets.

(4) Until Germany's reunification, West Berlin would have the status of a neutral free city. No "espionage, diversionist and subversive activities or hostile propaganda against other States" would be permissible in West Berlin as a demilitarized free city, and "any kind of warmongering and any activity of militarist and Fascist organizations" would be banned. The people of West Berlin would be guaranteed the inviolability of the city's status as a neutral free city and freedom to decide on their internal and external affairs. Communications would be guaranteed through agreements with the German Democratic Republic.

(5) "Because of the existence of two German States with different social orders", reunification could only be achieved through the creation of a German Confederation "aimed at their co-operation on the basis of peaceful coexistence and creating the pre-requisites for reunification in a peaceful, democratic and neutral State". The organs of the German Confederation would make recommendations to the two German Governments, including the following:

(i) implementation of the provisions of a peace treaty throughout Germany;

(ii) the gradual ending of the obligations derived from membership of different military groupings, withdrawal from these alliances and withdrawal of foreign troops and bases;

(iii) agreement on the military neutrality of both States as the basis for a future neutral unified Germany;

(iv) general disarmament of both States "as a German contribution to world disarmament";

(v) the foreign relations of both States to be based on the U.N. Charter, and both to become members of international organizations and conventions;

(vi) aid to economically under-developed countries "without any form of colonialism";

(vii) extension of relations between both States in the spheres of economy and trade, culture, science and technology, and sports, and removal of obstacles to free traffic;

(viii) preparation of a democratic Constitution for a unified German State, and the holding of "general, free and secret democratic elections" for an all-German Parliament;

(ix) the formation of an all-German Government with Berlin as its capital.

In a telegram on June 28, the East German State Council had appealed to the *Bundestag* and the Federal Government to agree without delay to the opening of negotiations between representatives of both States on the questions of a peace settlement and reunification, so as to ensure jointly that the national interests of the German people would be safeguarded in a peace treaty.

The West German Government Bulletin commented on July 4 that the Soviet Union had rejected all constructive proposals made by the three Western Powers and the Federal Government with the aim of achieving a permanent and just peace settlement; that negotiations for a peace treaty could be carried out on the German side only by an all-German Government elected by a free decision of the whole German people; that "functionaries imposed on part of the German people by a foreign Power cannot speak on behalf of the German people or part of it"; and that a just settlement of the German question, ensuring peace in Europe, could only be achieved by granting the entire German people the right of self-determination.

Mr. Khrushchev's Broadcast on Germany and Berlin, August 1961

In a televised broadcast on Aug. 7, Mr. Khrushchev declared *inter alia* that West Berlin must "not be allowed to become another

Sarajevo" and called upon the Western Powers to "sit down sincerely at the conference table" and "clear the atmosphere". Mr. Krushchev spoke in part as follows:

"The conclusion of a peace treaty with Germany would make it possible to normalize the situation in West Berlin. . . . Should West Berlin be made a free city, that would not affect either the interests or the prestige of any State. We propose that it should be stipulated in the peace treaty that the free city of West Berlin be granted freedom of communications with the outside world. We agree to the establishment of the most effective guarantees for the independent development and security of the free city of West Berlin. We stand for the freedom of West Berlin, but not on the basis of the maintenance of the military occupation status. . . .

"Both the Yalta Declaration and the Potsdam Agreement clearly established that the occupation of Germany must help the German people to eradicate militarism and Nazism. The Western Powers violated all the principles agreed upon at Yalta and Potsdam. The conspiracy by the Western Powers in 1946 on the merger of the two occupation zones was the beginning of the division of Germany and the restoration of the power of the militarists and revenge-seekers in Western Germany. The Western Powers finally and unilaterally tore up the Potsdam Agreement by setting up a separate West German State, concluding the Paris Agreements, and including Western Germany in NATO. It is not accidental that a special tripartite occupation status was established for West Berlin in this connexion. By this tripartite occupation status the Western Powers themselves confirmed that they had destroyed the foundation of their occupation regime in West Berlin under international law and that this regime rests solely on armed force.

"If the Western Powers persist in refusing to sign a German peace treaty we shall have to settle this problem without them. The other day a conference of the first secretaries of the Communist and Workers' Parties of the Warsaw Treaty countries took place in Moscow. They exchanged views on matters involved in preparing for a German peace treaty. The communiqué says that if the Western Powers continue evading the conclusion of a German peace treaty, the States concerned will be compelled to conclude a peace treaty with the German Democratic Republic.

"It goes without saying that in that case the G.D.R. would attain full sovereignty and therefore the question of the use of communications with West Berlin running across its territory would have to be decided by agreement with the G.D.R. Government. As for the agreements between the U.S.S.R. and the Western Powers on the question of access to West Berlin concluded during the occupation period, they would become null and void.

"Some might say, however: 'But is it all that necessary to sign a peace treaty with Germany now? Why not wait another two or three years, or even more, for the conclusion of this treaty? Perhaps that would eliminate tension and remove the danger of war?' No, this line of action is impermissible. The truth must be faced: the Western Powers are refusing to conclude a peace treaty with Germany on an agreed basis. At the same time they threaten with war and demand that we should not conclude a peace treaty with the G.D.R. They want nothing more nor less than to impose their will on the Socialist countries.

"To them the question of access to West Berlin and the question of the peace treaty as a whole is only a pretext. If we renounced the conclusion of a peace treaty, they would regard this as a strategic break-through and would widen the range of their demands at once. They would demand the elimination of the Socialist system in the G.D.R. They would set themselves the task of annexing from Poland and Czechoslovakia the territories restored to them under the Potsdam Agreement. And were the Western Powers to attain all this, they would advance their main claim—the abolition of the Socialist system in all countries of the Socialist camp. . . . That is why the question of a peace treaty cannot be postponed. . . ."

East German Refugee Exodus to West Berlin

An immediate result of the Berlin crisis was a very great increase in the number of East German refugees seeking asylum in West Berlin, the exodus being on a scale unprecedented since the 1953 uprising in Eastern Germany. Thousands of refugees, the majority of whom registered at the Marienfelde reception camp, crossed into the Western sectors every day throughout July 1961, the total figure for the month being 30,444; some 15,000 more sought asylum in West Berlin during the first fortnight of August before the East German authorities sealed the Berlin border [see below].

[Figures published in July by the West German Ministry of Refugees showed that over 2,600,000 refugees had fled from East Germany between 1949 and June 30, 1961.

Over 300,000 refugees had fled from Eastern Germany during the 18-month period from Jan. 1960 to June 1961, prior to the exodus during July and the first part of August. In addition to many young people, they included large numbers of factory workers, former independent craftsmen and shopkeepers, farmers, policemen, doctors, dentists, lawyers, university professors and teachers, resulting—as admitted by the East German authorities—in serious labour shortages and in a severe shortage of skilled professional men, notably in the medical, dental, and teaching professions.]

The Berlin Wall

East German Authorities close Berlin Border

At 2:30 a.m. on Aug. 13, 1961, the East German authorities sealed off the border between East and West Berlin, and also between West Berlin and the surrounding East German territory, leaving only 13 official crossing-points open. A special broadcast said that these measures had been taken in agreement with a decision by the Political Advisory Council of the Warsaw Treaty Organization; that they would remain in force until the conclusion of a peace treaty; and that they had been taken "in the interests of peace in Europe and of the security of the G.D.R. and of the other Socialist States".

The East German decree imposing the above restrictions alleged *inter alia* that the "Adenauer Government" was "systematically carrying out preparations for a civil war with regard to the G.D.R."; that East German citizens visiting the Federal Republic were being "increasingly subjected to terroristic persecutions"; that "West German and West Berlin espionage organizations are systematically luring G.D.R. citizens and carrying out a regular slave traffic"; and that "the aim of this aggressive policy and sabotage is to extend the domination of the militarists from the G.F.R. to the G.D.R." For these reasons it had been decided to take the following measures:

(1) "To put an end to the hostile activities of the revanchist and militarist forces in Western Germany and West Berlin, the same control is to be introduced on the borders of the G.D.R., including the border with the Western sectors of Berlin, as is normally carried out along the borders of every sovereign State."

(2) Citizens of the G.D.R. would need special permits for crossing the border into West Berlin "until West Berlin is turned into a demilitarized neutral free city".

(3) West Berlin citizens might enter "Democratic Berlin" (i.e. the Eastern sector) on presenting West Berlin identity cards. Entry would be refused, however, to "revanchist politicians and agents of West German militarism".

(4) "As regards visits to Democratic Berlin by citizens of the G.F.R., former decisions on control remain in force. These decisions do not affect visits by citizens of other States" to East Berlin.

(5) "As regards travel abroad by West Berlin citizens along the

communication lines in the G.D.R., former decisions remain in force" (i.e. there would be no interference with communication routes linking West Berlin and the Federal Republic).

(6) The decree "in no way revises former decisions on transit traffic between West Berlin and West Germany via the G.D.R."

As a result of the closing of the border except for the official crossing-points, the flood of refugees from East Berlin dwindled to a trickle; nevertheless, some 1,500 succeeded in escaping into West Berlin during the day across backyards, gardens and bombed sites, and in some cases by swimming canals and the River Havel. Steel-helmeted East German border guards, People's Police, and factory "fighting squads" were strongly reinforced along the entire border, tanks and armoured cars brought up at some places, roads dug up with pneumatic drills and barbed-wire fences erected.

The Brandenburg Gate, one of the 13 official crossing-points still remaining open, was sealed by the East German authorities on Aug. 14, when armed People's Police accompanied by armoured cars took up positions on the East Berlin side of the Gate; the East German News Agency said that the measure was only "temporary" and had been taken because of "West Berlin provocations aimed at violating the border at the Brandenburg Gate". During the night of Aug. 17-18 a concrete barrier up to 6ft. high and topped with barbed wire was erected in the Potsdamer Platz by Communist "shock workers"; similar concrete barriers were raised at other points along the sector boundaries, apparently designed to fill in existing gaps between the crossing-points.

The following additional restrictions were imposed by the East German authorities during the night of Aug. 22: (a) the establishment of a "no-man's-land" of 100 metres' width on both sides of the border, coupled with a warning to West Berliners not to approach within that distance "in the interests of their own safety"; (b) reduction of the number of crossing-points to six (three for West Berliners, two for West Germans, and one for foreigners and diplomatists); and (c) an announcement that West Berliners would not be allowed to enter East Berlin without special visas, in order to prevent the entry of "spies and *provocateurs*" into the Eastern sector. It was stated that such visas would be issued at two offices to be opened at S-Bahn stations in West Berlin, but the West Berlin Senate announced that such offices would be immediately closed if attempts were made to set them up.

The Western Allied commandants immediately denounced the "no-man's-land" order as "effrontery", and on the following day about 1,000 U.S., British and French troops patrolled up to the sector boundaries within the 100-metre radius with tanks, armoured vehicles and anti-tank guns.

Meanwhile, however, the East German Government had proceeded to extend the concrete wall and barbed-wire fences so as to surround the whole of West Berlin, with the number of authorized crossing-points remaining strictly limited.

Reactions in Western Germany and West Berlin

Dr. Adenauer declared on Aug. 13: "Those in power in the Soviet zone have tonight begun, in open violation of the Four-Power agreements, to seal off West Berlin from its surroundings. This measure has been taken because the régime forced upon the people by a foreign Power is no longer able to master its internal difficulties. . . . The arbitrary action by the Pankow régime has created a serious situation. Together with our Allies we are taking the necessary counter-measures. . . ."

Herr Brandt wrote in a letter to President Kennedy on Aug. 16: "The measures taken by the Ulbricht régime . . . have almost entirely destroyed what remains of the four-Power status (of West Berlin). Whereas previously the commander of the Allied forces in Berlin protested against parades by the so-called (East German) People's Army, they have now had to be content with a delayed and not very forceful démarche following the occupation of East Berlin by the People's Army. The illegal sovereignty of the East Berlin régime has been tacitly recognized . . . I consider this a very grave stage in the post-war history of this city. . . .

"By means of the (East) German People's Army the Soviet Union has achieved half of its proposals for a Free City. The second half is only a question of time. . . ."

Herr Brandt went on to plead for the creation of a three-Power status for West Berlin, and also for a "demonstrative reinforcement" of the U.S. garrison in West Berlin.

Herr Brandt told a gathering of nearly 300,000 West Berliners on Aug. 16 that the situation was the most serious with which the city had been faced since the 1948 blockade.

Addressing great crowds outside the Schöneberg Town Hall (the City Hall of West Berlin), Herr Brandt declared that the Western commandants' protest was "good but not good enough", and disclosed that he had written to President Kennedy [see above] saying that "Berlin expects not merely words but political action". "What has happened in the past few days in Berlin," he said, "is a new edition of the occupation of the Rhineland by Hitler; in the coming weeks and months Berlin must not become another Munich".

The West German *Bundestag* held an emergency session on the Berlin situation on Aug. 18, when statements were made both by Dr. Adenauer and by Herr Brandt.

Dr. Adenauer said that by closing the Berlin borders the East German régime had given the entire world a "clear and unambiguous declaration" of its "political bankruptcy". Despite the "unending patience" shown by the Western Powers and the Federal Republic, the Soviet Government had shown that it believed existing problems could be solved by "illegal acts and threats". Western solidarity was essential in face of the common danger, and the North Atlantic alliance must counter the Soviet threats by preparing "measures which are necessary for the maintenance of our security and freedom"; in this connexion the Federal Republic would increase her own military preparedness within the NATO alliance to support and complement the efforts of the Western Allies, who had already taken such steps.

The Chancellor reiterated his Government's willingness to support all efforts for four-Power negotiations on Berlin and Germany; emphasized that the Federal Government had never held that the Berlin problem could be solved by military measures; expressed the hope that negotiations would soon begin on the Berlin problem; and, on behalf of the West German Government, appealed to the Soviet Union "to return to a realistic appraisal of things at this critical moment". He emphasized that the right of the German people to self-determination could constitute the only basis for a change of relations between the Soviet and German peoples, adding in this connexion that the mass flight of East Germans was indicative of what they really thought about their régime.

Herr Brandt said that "intervention by international institutions" had become necessary in face of the "flagrant breach of human rights" committed in Berlin by the East German régime. Urging "convincing non-military counter-measures" by the West, he declared: "The City Government of [West] Berlin believes it would be good if visible signs of the Allied presence and of Allied rights were to follow, and above all if political initiatives were taken. . . . The Soviet Union must not believe that it can strike us in the face and that we will keep on smiling." He emphasized that the West Berlin City Government was not addressing any reproaches to the Western Allies in demanding "convincing non-military counter-measures"; it would, however, "think nothing of counter-measures which would set off resounding laughter from the Potsdamer Platz to Vladivostok".

Statistics relating to Incidents at Berlin Wall

On the occasion of the 10th anniversary of the building of the Berlin Wall on Aug. 13, 1971, a West Berlin body known as the "Working Group 13th August" published various statistics relating to attempts by East Germans to escape into West Berlin and Western Germany.

According to these, 2,838 East Germans had been arrested while attempting to cross the Berlin Wall during the period of its existence, of whom some 1,500 had been imprisoned for attempting to flee from the G.D.R.; in the same period there had been 65 certified cases of people being killed by East German border guards along the West Berlin border. However, some 30,000 people had succeeded in crossing either the fortifications around West Berlin or the border between Eastern and Western Germany.

The working group also claimed that 45,000 members of the East German forces were at present engaged in guarding the borders, with 15,000 of them around West Berlin; since the erection of the wall, 2,314 members of the East German armed forces were claimed to have fled from Eastern Germany, and 526 of those who escaped in the period up to the end of June were said to have come to West Berlin.

Mr. Khrushchev's and Herr Ulbricht's Statements on Germany and Berlin

Mr. Khrushchev visited the German Democratic Republic in January 1963 for the sixth congress of the East German Socialist Unity Party, which was held in East Berlin on Jan. 15–21.

On the question of Germany and Berlin, Mr. Khrushchev said:

"It may appear at first glance that nothing has changed since we raised the question of a German peace treaty. . . . Four years have gone by, but there is no peace treaty. . . . Some people may be inclined to say that the time has been wasted, that the Socialist countries have gained nothing by raising the question of a German peace treaty. But those who think so fail to see, or do not understand, the changes that have occurred. . . .

"The position of the German Democratic Republic has grown stronger. For a long time your Republic did not have all the necessary resources to protect its sovereignty effectively. Its border with West Berlin was an open gate which subversive forces used without hindrance and with impunity, not only to squeeze the lifeblood out of you and rob the working people of the Republic of milliards of marks every year, but also to undermine the very foundations of Socialism. On Aug. 13, 1961 [the day on which erection of the Berlin Wall began]—a stop was put to these abuses. . . .

"The problem of the German peace treaty is not really what it was before the defensive measures were taken on the G.D.R.'s border with West Berlin. This does not mean, of course, that the Socialist countries have lost interest in concluding a peace treaty. On the contrary, the question is of vital importance. . . .

"The Socialist countries agree to a peace treaty being signed with the two German States or with one of them. They propose that West Berlin be granted the status of a free city under the peace settlement. They are willing to provide this free city with the most reliable guarantees of non-interference in its affairs—guarantees of freedom for the population of West Berlin to choose whichever social and political system they prefer. The United Nations should be the guarantor. It may be recalled that the German Democratic Republic, the Soviet Union, and their Socialist allies have even consented to foreign troops staying in West Berlin for a fixed period under the U.N. flag. . . ."

In his speech at the congress, Herr Ulbricht put forward a seven-point plan for the "normalization" of relations between the German Democratic Republic and the German Federal Republic. Admitting that the Western Powers had "certain prestige interests" in West Berlin which must be taken into account, he advocated—like Mr. Khrushchev—the conversion of West Berlin into a "peaceful, neutral free city" with the co-operation of the United Nations. On relations between the G.D.R. and the G.F.R., Herr Ulbricht proposed a pact between the two German States based upon the existence of differing social systems, and including the following clauses:

(1) Each German State should recognize the other, respect its political and social system, and renounce the use of force in any form.
(2) The two States should respect each other's existing frontiers and renounce any attempt to change them.
(3) Both States should renounce the possession and use of nuclear weapons.

(4) Rearmament should be halted and defence budgets frozen.

(5) Each State should recognize travel documents carried by citizens of the other as a precondition for the normalization of travel between the two German States.

(6) Normal cultural and sporting contacts should be restored.

(7) An agreement should be signed for the expansion of trade between the two States.

The congress adopted a new statute for the Socialist Unity Party which, unlike its predecessor, made no mention of German reunification but envisaged a confederation between two "equal and sovereign" German States and the "free city" of West Berlin.

President Kennedy's Berlin Speech

President Kennedy of the U.S.A., in the course of a visit to the German Federal Republic, visited West Berlin on June 26, 1963. After touring the city in the company of Dr. Adenauer and Herr Brandt, and inspecting the Berlin Wall, the President made a short speech at the Schöneberg Town Hall, saying:

"Two thousand years ago the proudest boast in the world was *Civis Romanus sum*. Today, in the world of freedom, the proudest boast is *Ich bin ein Berliner*.

"There are many people in the world who do not understand what is the great issue between the free world and Communism. Let them come to Berlin. And there are some who say in Europe and elsewhere that we can work with the Communists. Let them come to Berlin.

"Freedom has many difficulties and democracy is not perfect; but we never had to put up a wall to keep our people in. I know of no city which has been besieged for 18 years and still lives with the vitality, force, hope and determination of this city of West Berlin. While the wall is the most obvious and vivid demonstration of the failures of the Communist system, we take no satisfaction in it, for it is an offence not only against history but against humanity. . . .

"In 18 years of peace and good faith this generation of Germans has earned the right to be free, including the right to unite their family and nation in lasting peace with the goodwill of all people. When the day finally comes when this city will be joined as one in this great continent of Europe, the people of West Berlin can take great satisfaction in the fact that they were in the front line for almost two decades. . . ."

187

9. BERLIN PASSES AGREEMENTS OF 1963–66

Between 1963 and 1966 the West Berlin Senate and the East German Authorities approved several agreements on passes which enabled West Berliners to visit their relatives in East Berlin.

The first passes agreement was signed on Dec. 13, 1963, permitting the issue of passes valid for one day for Christmas or New Year visits to East Berlin between Dec. 20, 1963, and Jan. 5, 1964.

The second agreement, which was signed in East Berlin on Sept. 24, 1964, laid down that visits by West Berliners to their relatives in the Eastern sector of the city would be possible during four periods of 14-16 days each during the year. The agreement was subject to renewal after 12 months.

On March 10 and Sept. 8, 1964, the East German Government announced other concessions: (1) West Berliners travelling through Eastern Germany to a foreign country would be allowed to stay for up to 72 hours in some East German towns on the main railway routes. (2) Elderly East Germans were allowed to visit relatives in West Berlin and Western Germany.

On Nov. 25, 1965, a new passes agreement was signed in West Berlin, regulating the issue of visitors' passes on the lines of the 1964 agreement. The agreement also provided for additional family visits by West Berliners in cases of special "hardship" (death of a relative, serious illness, etc.). The validity of the new agreement was limited to March 31, 1966, but the agreement was later extended to June 30, 1966.

10. SOVIET PROTEST AGAINST FRANCO-GERMAN TREATY OF 1963

A Franco-German Treaty of Co-operation came officially into force on July 2, 1963, when Dr. Schröder, the German Federal Foreign Minister, and M. Roland de Margerie, the French Ambassador in Bonn, exchanged the documents of ratification, following parliamentary approval of the Treaty in both countries.

Notes protesting in strong terms against the Franco-German Treaty were handed by Mr. Gromyko on Feb. 5 to the French and West German Ambassadors in Moscow.

Extracts from the Note to Western Germany are given below:

"It is generally known that the Government of the German Federal Republic has for a number of years been stubbornly fitting keys to open nuclear arsenals. It makes no secret of the fact that it is ready to subscribe to any plan, whether it be the establishment of so-called 'multilateral NATO forces' or atomic partnership on another basis, if only it can get nuclear weapons at its disposal. . . . Regardless of the way in which nuclear weapons might come into the hands of the *Bundeswehr,* whether directly or indirectly, the Soviet Union would regard this as an immediate threat to its vital national interests and would be compelled to take the necessary measures dictated by such a situation. . . .

"The Soviet Government considers it necessary to dwell particularly on that part of the [Franco-German] Treaty which provides for the extension of its operation to West Berlin. This clause can only be regarded as deliberately provocative. . . . West Berlin is not and cannot be part of the territory of the Federal Republic. The jurisdiction of the authorities of the Federal Republic does not and cannot extend to that city, and the Federal Government has no right to speak on behalf of West Berlin in international affairs. . . .

"The attempt to bring West Berlin—which is situated on the territory of the German Democratic Republic—within the sphere of the Franco-West German Treaty cannot have any force in international law. But the fact that such an attempt is being made provides additional proof that the Government of the German Federal Republic is seeking allies, not for peace, but for complicity in satisfying its expansionist claims. . . .

"The fact that the German Federal Republic, 18 years after the Second World War, does not have diplomatic relations with many States of Eastern Europe—including Poland and Czechoslovakia, the first victims of Nazi rapine—emphasizes the entire falsity of the assurances regarding the desire of the Federal Republic for reconciliation with the peoples of States which were formerly enemies of Germany in the war.

"The Soviet Government . . . has more than once proposed to the Federal Republic that it should put an end to this mistrust engendered by the past. It has urged, and continues to urge, the Federal Government to march in step with the States which are guided in international affairs by the principles of peaceful coexistence, all-round co-operation and the peaceful settlement of disputed questions. But the Government of the Federal Republic unfortunately turns a deaf ear to these calls. . . ."

Rejection of Protest by Western Germany

The West German Government replied to the Soviet Note on March 29, 1963.

The Federal Government's reply declared *inter alia* that the Soviet Note "completely misunderstands the character, significance, and aims" of the Franco-German Treaty, which was "not directed against any people or any State" but expressed "the wish of the German and French peoples finally to remove the national differences between them". It rejected as "absurd" the Soviet statement that the Treaty had been concluded because of "the old unquenchable thirst for domination over other States and nations, for carving up the map of the world again after their own pattern", and described as "equally absurd" the allegation that Federal Germany was pursuing a "policy of unleashing a thermo-nuclear war and involving the principal NATO members in it on the side of the German Federal Republic".

The Note continued: "As should be known to the Soviet Government, the Federal Government voluntarily renounced in 1954, within the framework of the Western European Union, the production of atomic, biological or chemical weapons. She has placed all her fighting forces under NATO, which is a purely defensive alliance. In the circumstances the Soviet allegation that the Federal Government is planning a war for the restoration of the frontiers of the Hitler Reich appears particularly untruthful, all the more since it comes from a Government which disposes of a vast arsenal of atomic weapons, which has steadily refused to accept control of disarmament measures and nuclear tests, and which threatens the Federal Government with powerful and concentrated blows by its rocket and nuclear weapons."

After recalling that the German forces under NATO command could only be used for self-defence, that the Federal Republic had committed itself in 1954 to conducting its policy in accordance with the U.N. Charter, and that it had repeatedly undertaken to settle all differences with other countries by peaceful means, the Note declared: "The Federal Government refrains from refuting in detail the misleading, incriminating and insulting statements in the Soviet Note, of which there are too many." Rejecting the Soviet assertion that the Franco-German Treaty was a "deliberate provocation" because it also referred to West Berlin, the German Note stated that for a long time the Federal Government had provided for the application to Berlin of treaties concluded with other countries; this, however, was expressly made subject to the consent of the Allied authorities in Berlin in deference to Berlin's special status, "which the Soviet Union is flagrantly violating by her unilateral and illegal measures in East Berlin, especially through the construction of the Berlin Wall".

As regards the Soviet complaint that the Franco-German Treaty had been concluded without authority from the "so-called German Democratic Republic", the Note declared: "In concluding this Treaty . . . the Federal Government has in fact acted on behalf of the whole

German people. It would have been perfectly willing to ask the Germans in the so-called German Democratic Republic whether they desired this reconciliation, and it is absolutely certain that the overwhelming majority of them would have agreed to the Treaty. Unfortunately any consultation with those Germans living in the so-called German Democratic Republic is impossible under the régime supported by the Soviet Government."

The West German reply went on: "The Soviet Government acknowledges the rights and obligations conferred upon it by the four-Power agreements. In this connexion the Federal Government refers particularly to the responsibility of the four Powers to bring about the reunification of Germany by free elections, the achievement of which . . . the head of the Soviet Union had himself undertaken at the 1955 Geneva Conference. The Federal Government . . . regrets that the Soviet Government has evaded this obligation again and again in recent years. . . ."

In conclusion, the Note rejected the Soviet allegation that the Federal Government had disregarded appeals for co-operation and the peaceful settlement of differences, and declared that the Federal Government was willing to investigate any course which could improve relations between the two peoples.

11. CHANCELLOR ERHARD'S POLICY STATEMENTS, 1964–65

Dr. Adenauer resigned as Federal Chancellor at the age of 87 on Oct. 11, 1963, and was succeeded by Professor Ludwig Erhard who on Oct. 17 formed a new Cabinet composed of Christian Democrats (including members of the party's Bavarian wing, the Christian Social Union) and Free Democrats.

Dr. Erhard's New York Policy Statement, June 1964

The German Federal Chancellor's activities during the months from January to July 1964 included official visits to all the capitals of the six member-countries of the European Economic Community as well as to Canada, the United States and Denmark.

During his visit to New York Dr. Erhard addressed the Council of Foreign Relations on June 11, 1964, calling for:

(a) "Complete and free travel between East and West" supplemented by "exchange of publications" and in particular by intensified "economic and cultural contacts";

(*b*) Going "beyond the realm of ideologies" to foster contacts with "all thinking, open-minded people not addicted to dogma" in the countries behind Europe's Iron Curtain; and

(*c*) Elimination of "one of the most dangerous trouble spots" in Europe by permitting a divided Germany to reunite in peace and freedom.

The Chancellor said in the course of his speech: "German reunification through self-determination is in the best interest of the people; it is in the best interest of all East European peoples. At any rate, it offers better guarantees of security and prosperity than the current kind of imperialism based on terror and suppression still practised in the Soviet Zone of Germany. We hope, and there are beginning to be slight indications to justify this hope, that this conviction is gaining ground even in the Soviet Union."

On Czechoslovakia he said: "I state here clearly and explicitly—the Munich agreement of 1938 was torn to pieces by Hitler. The German Government has no territorial claims whatsoever with regard to Czechoslovakia and separates itself expressly from any declarations which have given rise to a different interpretation."

On Poland he said, after mentioning the disputed Oder-Neisse line: "The German Government feels that the German-Polish border should be established in a peace treaty in accordance with the Potsdam Agreement, a treaty that can only be concluded with an all-German Government. Poland and the Federal Republic of Germany have a common interest that this condition be established, which will make it possible for the two peoples to live together in peace."

Stressing that he wanted more, not less, relaxation of East-West tension, he suggested that the Soviet Union might extend the principle of peaceful coexistence by agreeing to a "coexistence of ideas". The Federal Government as well as the whole German nation, he said, was devoid of "cold war" concepts and ready for any meaningful talk. "Nobody," he declared, "is thinking of Germany going it alone. There will be no new 'Rapallo' just as there will be no new 'Munich'." [By concluding the Treaty of Rapallo with the Soviet Union in April 1922, for the mutual renunciation of reparations and the establishment of diplomatic and economic relations, the Republican Government of Germany had antagonized the Western Allies.]

The following joint communiqué (cross-headings inserted) was issued on June 12 after the talks in Washington between President Johnson, Mr. Dean Rusk (Secretary of State), Dr. Erhard and Dr. Schröder (the Federal Foreign Minister):

Germany and Berlin.—"Every suitable opportunity should be used to bring nearer the reunification of Germany through self-determination. So long as Germany remains divided, Europe will not achieve stability.

"The President and the Chancellor noted the Soviet Government's announcement that it signed today a treaty of friendship, mutual assistance, and co-operation with the so-called German Democratic Republic. They agreed that no unilateral move by the Soviet Union could in any way affect the rights of the three Western Powers or modify the obligations and responsibilities of the Soviet Union with respect to Germany and Berlin. They stressed that the Soviet Government would be solely responsible for the consequences of any attempt at interference with Allied rights that might result from implementation of the new treaty. They also reaffirmed that until Germany is unified, only the freely elected and legitimately constituted Government of the Federal Republic of Germany and no one else can speak for the German people.

"The President restated the determination of the United States to carry out fully its commitments with respect to Berlin, including the maintenance of the right of free access to West Berlin and the continued freedom and viability of the city.

Eastern Europe.—"The President and the Chancellor stressed the importance of improving relations with the nations of Eastern Europe. The President said that the United States fully supports the actions of the Federal Republic directed towards this goal. They also expressed the conviction that measures designed to reduce the threat of war and to bring about arms control serve to promote the goal of German reunification. . . ."

In Washington on June 13 Dr. Erhard stated his conviction that the question of German reunification was, to Washington, not just "a distant objective" but "a matter that had to be dealt with daily".

He discounted any suggestion of a new West German approach to the Soviet Union in the near future, saying: "We are all aware that this cannot be solved by any single action overnight and that it is part of a process."

Re-election of President Lübke—
Soviet Protest at Election in West Berlin

Dr. Heinrich Lübke was re-elected President of the German Federal Republic for a second five-year term at a meeting of the *Bundesversammlung* (the Federal Convention, consisting of the members of both Houses of Parliament) in West Berlin on July 1, 1964. The decision to hold the presidential election in West Berlin was the subject of Soviet protest Notes to Britain, France and the U.S.A. on June 26.

The Notes reiterated the Soviet view that West Berlin was not part of the Federal Republic, which fact had been recognized by the Western Powers when endorsing the Federal Constitution; described the holding of the election there as "a new provocation" on the part of the Federal Government; and said that "the claims laid by the authorities of the Federal Republic to West Berlin, which is an independent political entity, and their hostile activities in that city against the interests of other States" were "a direct and overt violation of international law" and "a manifestation of the dangerous policy pursued by the revenge-seeking circles. . . ." "No Parliament in history," the Notes added, "has ever left the bounds of its country to hold presidential elections abroad." After accusing the Western Powers of "ambiguity" in their policy as regards West Berlin and of "toeing the line of the West German authorities in this matter", the Notes reiterated the Soviet Government's commitments to "ensure the inviolability of the borders of the German Democratic Republic".

At the opening of the session the President of the *Bundestag*, Dr. Gerstenmaier, who also presided over the *Bundesversammlung*, said in reply to the Soviet protest that the election was taking place in Berlin "neither because of a wish to cause provocation nor through annoyance caused by the East German Communist régime's continued provocation". On the contrary, what had brought the *Bundesversammlung* to Berlin was "solely our loyalty to this city, to the whole people, and to our own history". Dr. Gerstenmaier described the Soviet claim that the presidential election was being held "abroad" as "an insult to the whole German people".

Dr. Erhard's Policy Statement of Nov. 10, 1965

In his first policy statement to the *Bundestag* on Nov. 10, 1965, after his re-election as Federal Chancellor, Dr. Erhard re-defined his Government's attitude on both foreign and domestic affairs, dealing in particular with the question of the reunification of Germany, East-West relations, the Western Alliance and disarmament.

194

Recalling the achievement of sovereignty by the German Federal Republic and its accession to NATO in May 1955, Dr. Erhard reviewed the changes which had occurred since then, notably (*a*) the achievement of independence by a large number of "young nations"; (*b*) the "loosening of the inner cohesion" of the two big Power blocs both in the East and in the West; (*c*) the emergence of Communist China as an independent political factor; and (*d*) a "softening-up" in the relationship between the two great Power groups, though as yet insufficient to be called "a genuine *détente*".

These changes, he continued, had not, however, affected the question of the continued division of Germany, and the establishment of diplomatic relations between the Federal and the Soviet Governments in 1955 had not led to "the restoration of a democratic German State", which had at that time been described as "the chief national problem of the entire German nation". After declaring that this was due solely to the fact that the U.S.S.R. did not want the reunification of the German people in freedom, Dr. Erhard pointed out that no effect had been given to the directive issued by the Heads of Government of the four Powers on July 23, 1955, which laid down that "the reunification of Germany by means of free elections shall be carried out in conformity with the national interests of the German people and the interests of European security".

Dr. Erhard expressed his views on Soviet policy with regard to German unification as follows:

In 1958 the U.S.S.R. had announced its intention of separating the city of Berlin from Western Germany and transforming it initially into a third independent part of Germany and later into part of "the Soviet-occupied Zone of Germany". This intention, however, had not been carried out because of "the firm stand of our Allies, our own firm will, and above all the gallant attitude of the Berliners". The future of Berlin would, he declared, rest on the following principles and demands: (*a*) "the presence of the three Allies in Berlin"; (*b*) "unrestricted free access to Berlin"; (*c*) Berlin's forming part of free Germany; and (*d*) respect for "the unequivocal will of the Berliners" as the basis of any agreement on Berlin.

The Chancellor maintained that the Soviet Union, while using the concept of peaceful coexistence, still intended to have the present state of affairs sanctioned, and that in particular (*a*) it aimed at the destruction of the Western security system by the use of offensive means; (*b*) it attempted to obtain recognition of the "Soviet Zone" [i.e. the German Democratic Republic] throughout the world; (*c*) it claimed that the German people's desire for reunification impaired a *détente* in international affairs; and (*d*) it described reunification as a matter to be settled between "the two German States" and intended to divest itself of its obligations as one of the four responsible Powers.

Announcing the forthcoming publication of a White Paper on the subject, Dr. Erhard re-defined his Government's attitude as follows:

"The Federal Government insists that the entire German people shall decide its destiny in self-determination and that the four Powers honour their obligation. . . .

"The Federal Government has repeatedly declared its readiness to the Soviet Union to take steps to improve mutual relations even if immediate agreement could not be reached on the most important problem between us and the Soviet Union—reunification. It has indicated that it would be prepared to talk about many things—among them, for instance, security guarantees in the event of reunification. I sought immediate talks with the Soviet leaders, and, in fact, ex-Chairman Khrushchev was ready to come to Bonn. However, the Soviet Government persists in its error that a divided Germany is of greater advantage to the Soviet Union than a reunified one. We want it to know, however, and we have stated it before, that the German people and any all-German Government will be ready to provide safeguards that no danger will arise to Russia and our Eastern neighbours from the reunification of Germany.

"The Federal Government will do everything in its power to consolidate the inner cohesion between the two parts of our divided people, but—let this be clear to everybody—will not pay any political price for it. In particular, we shall not be ready to agree to any measures calculated to impair the conditions for reunification in freedom. For we have to stand up for our countrymen in the [Soviet] Zone as well, and for their great hope that one day they may finally be able to live under a free and democratic system in a reunified Germany. We pay all the more tribute to our countrymen for their reconstruction achievements in the Zone, as those achievements were made under the most difficult conditions and under an unworthy and sterile social system.

"A régime which, to protect its own existence and to subjugate people, resorts to erecting a wall in the divided capital of Berlin and to surrounding itself with barbed wire and watch-towers condemns itself and cannot but meet with rejection and contempt.

"The Federal Government has, since its inception, upheld its right to be the sole representative of all Germans. That means that we would regard any recognition or international upgrading of the Zone as an unfriendly act directed against the restoration of German unity. We shall not slacken in our efforts to prevent such a development even at the risk of appearing here and there to be a disturbing element. How would other nations act if they were in our situation? I am sure that no nation with a history of its own would be ready to give up its unity and its right.

"Soviet propaganda holds against us that our wish that the Soviet Union should grant our countrymen the right of self-determination introduces an element of tension into world affairs. This agitation presents the facts the wrong way round. For, if the Soviet Union were to grant the Germans in the Zone the right of self-determination and thus make the reunification of our nation possible, it would indeed remove an essential obstacle to a lasting relaxation of tension between East and West. We do not want less *détente*, but more.

"It may be a long way; a way that may require privation and sacrifice. Yet we shall go it. At its end there will be a peace treaty, negotiated and concluded by a freely elected all-German Government. It is only by, and in, such a treaty that the final boundaries of Germany can and must be determined, since, according to valid legal authority, Germany continues to exist within her boundaries of Dec. 31, 1937, as long as a freely elected all-German Government does not recognize different boundaries. Reunification of Germany means peace in Europe."

Reaffirming his Government's wish to improve its relations with Eastern European countries, the Chancellor expressed his belief that "reunification policy, security policy and foreign policy are one" and that German security policy must be aimed at a "peaceful balance of interests".

IV. FROM DR. ERHARD'S PROPOSALS FOR RELAXATION OF TENSION TO HERR BRANDT'S "OSTPOLITIK" TREATIES, 1966–71

From 1966 onwards the Government of the German Federal Republic made efforts to enter into negotiations with countries in Eastern Europe in order to improve mutual relations.

The first of these efforts was made in March 1966 by the Christian Democratic Government of Dr. Erhard, but the standpoints of Western Germany on the one hand and the Soviet Union, Poland and Czechoslovakia on the other were still far apart.

The period of the Grand Coalition between Christian Democrats and Social Democrats from December 1966 to October 1969 was marked by the first attempts of the West German Government, with Dr. Kiesinger (CDU) as Chancellor and Herr Willy Brandt as Vice-Chancellor and Minister of Foreign Affairs, to negotiate with the German Democratic Republic (GDR) (or Eastern Germany) at ministerial level.

1. WEST GERMAN PROPOSALS OF 1966 FOR RELAXATION OF TENSION IN EUROPE

Identical Notes were sent by the German Federal Government on March 25, 1966, to all countries with which it had diplomatic relations, as well as to the countries of Eastern Europe, containing proposals for world peace, general disarmament, and the relaxation of international tension.

The West German Note contained six specific proposals, namely:

(1) All non-nuclear States belonging to military alliances in the East or the West should renounce the production of nuclear weapons and submit to international control.

(2) The Federal Government was ready to join any agreement for the staged reduction of nuclear weapons in Europe. Such an agreement would have to include all Europe and be linked with "the solution of political problems in Central Europe".

(3) The handing over of fissionable material to countries outside Euratom should be controlled by the International Atomic Energy Commission in order to prevent the use of the materials for the manufacture of nuclear weapons.

(4) The Federal Republic was ready to exchange formal declarations with the Soviet Union, Poland, Czechosolvakia and any other East European State whereby each side would give an undertaking to the other not to use force in the settlement of international disputes.

(5) To "dispel mistrust with regard to alleged German aggressive intentions", the Federal Republic also proposed bilateral agreements with the Soviet Union, Poland, Czechoslovakia, Hungary, Romania, and Bulgaria on the exchange of military observers to attend manoeuvres of armed forces.

(6) The Federal Government was prepared to participate "in a constructive spirit" in a world disarmament conference or any other such conference which promised success.

The West German Note also included the following passages.

Relations with Poland and Czechoslovakia.—"Despite the fact that the Federal Government has made particular efforts to cultivate relations with Poland, the country which suffered most of all among the East European nations in the Second World War, it has made but little progress in this direction. Although the Polish Government is obviously interested in more lively trade between Germany and Poland, it has hitherto not given any indication that it is interested in achieving a conciliation between the two nations. Rather does it hamper the cultural contacts we seek, stand for the continued division of Germany, and at the same time calls upon the Federal Government to recognize the Oder-Neisse line, though it is generally known that, under the Allied agreements of 1945, the settlement of frontier questions has been postponed until the conclusion of a peace treaty with the whole of Germany and that, according to international law, Germany continues to exist within its frontiers of Dec. 31, 1937, until such time as a freely elected all-German Government recognizes other frontiers.

"If, when the occasion arises, the Poles and the Germans enter into negotiations on frontier questions in the same spirit that led to the conciliation between Germany and her Western neighbours, then Poles and Germans will also find their way to agreement. For in this question neither emotions nor the power of the victor alone, but rather reason, must prevail.

"In recent years the Federal Government has established official relations with Poland, Romania, Hungary and Bulgaria. It is endeavouring to create such relations with Czechoslovakia as well and would welcome a renewal of more friendly relations between the people of that State and the German people.

"In the opinion of the Federal Government the Munich Agreement of 1938 was torn asunder by Hitler and no longer has any territorial significance. The Federal Government, therefore, does not assert any territorial claims against Czechoslovakia; it stresses that this is the official statement of German policy.

"The policy pursued by the Federal Government is neither revanchist nor restorative. It is looking forward, not backwards, and its aim is an equitable European order on the basis of peaceful agreements—an order in which all nations can live together freely and as good neighbours. . . .

The Soviet Attitude.—"The Government of the U.S.S.R. has announced time and again that it does not want war. The Federal Government presumes that the Soviet Union really means this, but the value of Soviet assurances is diminished by quite unambiguous and massive threats like those frequently made against the Federal Republic, as, for instance, in the Note communicated by the Soviet Government on Feb. 5, 1963, which states: 'It is not hard to imagine that in the event of a thermo-nuclear war the mighty and concentrated blows of rockets and nuclear weapons will inevitably come down over Western Germany and that that country would not survive a third world war.'

"Such language reveals a mentality which the Federal Government can only view with concern. And it has all the more reason as the Soviet Union does, in fact, possess the strongest ground forces in Europe and, furthermore, has at its disposal a very large arsenal of nuclear and hydrogen bombs, rockets, as well as a fleet of nuclear bombers and guided-missile submarines. . . ."

Reply of Soviet Government

The Soviet Government's reply to the West German Note was not presented in Bonn until May 17. Running to over 3,000 words, it described the Oder-Neisse frontier as "final and unalterable", said that it was "not by courtesy of the German Federal Republic that the European States and their frontiers exist", and described the Federal Government's "talk about the frontiers of other European States" as "absolutely senseless". After alleging that Western Germany was trying to create a "Bonn-Washington axis", the Soviet Note said that the whole policy of the German Federal Government was "subordinated to one purpose—to obtain the status of a nuclear Power and to try . . . to restore the German Reich with all its pretensions".

The Note stated in particular:

"Violating the obligations ensuing from the Potsdam Agreement, the Government of the German Federal Republic formed an army (the *Bundeswehr*), half a million strong, which is being adapted for nuclear missile warfare. It closely links its policy with the policy of a non-European State, the United States of America. . . .

"The G.F.R. ranks second among the NATO countries, after the United States, in the level of military expenditure. . . . Hundreds of openly Nazi, militarist and revanchist organizations are active in the Federal Republic. They receive ostentatious political, moral and material support from Government bodies and from highly-placed officials. Citizens of the Federal Republic are being poisoned literally from childhood with the venom of militarist and revanchist ideas, which also colour school syllabuses, literature, the Press, films and television. Hitler officers and generals bring up the soldiers of the *Bundeswehr* on those ideas. . . .

"Even in a Note which the Government of the G.F.R. would like to present as a 'peace initiative', it has . . . put forward a thesis . . . claiming that 'Germany continues to exist within the frontiers of Dec. 31, 1937'. This gives away the secret of the whole policy of the Government of the German Federal Republic. . . .

"The Government of the Federal Republic is quite familiar with the commitments undertaken by the U.S.S.R., the German Democratic Republic, Poland, Czechoslovakia, Hungary and other member-countries of the Warsaw Treaty to prevent new aggression by German militarism and to guarantee the stability of the frontiers that have taken shape. . . .

"The frontier along the Oder and Neisse, established by the Potsdam Agreement and in the Zgorzelec Treaty concluded between Poland and the German Democratic Republic, is final and unalterable.

"The Federal Government presents almost as a 'gesture of good will' its statement that the territoral provisions of the 1938 Munich Agreement now have no significance whatsoever. . . . However, it is worth noting that the Government of the G.F.R. obviously does not

201

want to denounce that document of coercion and aggression or to recognize its complete invalidity from the very outset. . . .

"The Government and people of the G.F.R. must be clearly aware that any encroachments on the frontiers of the German Democratic Republic, Poland or Czechoslovakia will meet with a crushing rebuff from the U.S.S.R., the German Democratic Republic, Czechoslovakia and the other European States that are allied with them. . . ."

After saying that the West German Note "does not say a single word about its attitude to the idea of concluding a treaty on the non-proliferation of nuclear weapons", the Soviet Note went on: "It is glaringly obvious that the Government of the G.F.R. is hushing up a possibility which non-nuclear States have for acquiring nuclear weapons—namely, through existing military groupings of Powers. This, of course, is not an accidental omission. It is common knowledge that the Government of the Federal Republic . . . wants . . . to find a loophole for access to nuclear weapons for the G.F.R."

As regards the West German proposal that mutual guarantees should be given not to resort to the use of force in solving international problems, the Soviet Note said: "In considering [this] offer the Soviet Government cannot but draw attention to the contradictory character of the pronouncements of the Federal Government. On the one hand it declares that it will never resort to force in settling the German problem. This can only be welcomed. Yet at the same time the Government of the G.F.R. stresses that there will be neither lasting peace nor security in Europe—or, in other words, that there will be war—until a settlement of the German issue in accordance with the demands of the G.F.R. . . ."

After saying that the Soviet Union "approaches the German national problem with understanding" and that the key to this problem was "in the hands of the two German States", the Soviet Note ended by setting out the Soviet Government's own proposals for "improving the international situation, strengthening peace, and developing peaceful co-operation among States". These proposals, in which it was hoped that Western Germany would co-operate, were:

(1) Immediate conclusion of a treaty on the non-proliferation of nuclear weapons, in accordance with U.N. decisions, which would "stop all loopholes to such proliferation".

(2) Dismantling of military bases on foreign territories and the withdrawal of foreign armed forces from those territories.

(3) Dissolution of military blocs, including both NATO and the Warsaw Pact. The Soviet Government would be ready to take part "in working out a system of reliable guarantees for the security of European States".

(4) The Soviet Government supported the East German proposal that both German States should renounce nuclear weapons and reduce their armed forces and armaments. It also supported the

Polish proposals (i.e. the Rapacki Plan) for a nuclear-free zone in Central Europe [see page 144].

(5) The easing of tensions between the States of Eastern and Western Europe by developing co-operation between them, thereby helping to end the "cold war" and creating "a climate in which it would be easier to solve urgent problems agitating the European peoples, including the German people".

(6) A conference of European States to discuss, on an all-European basis, "questions concerning European security, including military disengagement, the reduction of armaments, and the development of peaceful, mutually-beneficial contacts among all European States".

(7) The Soviet Government had approved the application of the German Democratic Republic for membership of the United Nations and would also support any application for U.N. membership by the German Federal Republic.

(8) A German peace settlement "taking due account of the situation that actually exists in Europe. . . . With a German peace settlement, a system of European security could also cover West Berlin, which is an independent political entity." . . .

Polish and Czechoslovak Replies

The Polish Government's reply to the West German Note was handed on April 29 by the Polish Ambassador in Copenhagen, Mr. Romuald Poleszczuk, to the West German Ambassador for conveyance to the Federal Government. Copies were sent to all Governments with which Poland had diplomatic relations.

Like the Soviet Note, that of the Polish Government emphasized that the Oder-Neisse frontier was final and beyond discussion. Saying that the German Federal Government had "had the boldness to ask Poland to renounce her sovereign rights to an important part of her territory", it accused the Federal Government of presenting the situation "in a way which is at variance with historical truth". Like the Soviet Note also, the Polish Note emphasized the suffering caused to the Polish people by the German invasion in 1939, declaring that the memory of the Second World War among the Polish people was "strong and ineffaceable". Extracts from the Polish Note are given below.

"The [West German] Note . . . contains the absurd argument that Germany continues to exist within her 1937 frontiers. The Government of the Polish People's Republic has repeatedly pointed out that such a position is devoid of any foundation, and once more rejects it categorically.

"The frontier on the Oder and Lusatian Neisse is final. It was established at the Potsdam Conference by the decision of the victorious Powers, on behalf of the anti-Nazi coalition, with the voice of Poland having been taken into consideration. That decision, constituting an act of historical justice, was immediately implemented, *inter alia*, through the realization of the provisions relating to the resettlement of the German population from the Western and Northern territories restored to Poland. As regards the peace conference—as incontestably follows from the wording of the Potsdam Agreement —it was left the task of only a formal confirmation of the Polish Western frontiers.

"It is today a universally known and recognized fact that the Polish Western and Northern territories are an integral part of Poland, just as Poland is part of Europe. The Polish-German frontier has been finally delimited on the basis of the agreement concluded in 1950 at Zgorzelec between Poland and her neighbour, the German Democratic Republic. This frontier cannot be the subject of any discussions or bargains and, therefore, of any claims by the German Federal Republic. . . ."

After saying that Poland was linked with the German Democratic Republic [Eastern Germany] "not only by an understanding but also by close ties of friendship and co-operation", the Polish Note said that conditions for the full normalization of relations between Poland and the German Federal Republic would only materialize when the G.F.R. "recognizes without reservations the existing frontiers of Poland on the Oder and Lusatian Neisse and renounces once and for all its claims to the Polish Western and Northern territories".

The Polish Note ended: "The renunciation of territorial claims against Poland; recognition of the frontier on the Oder and Neisse; recognition of the Munich Agreement as null and void, not because Hitler invalidated it by his perfidy and crimes, but because it sanctioned the rape of Czechoslovakia and was a stage in the policy of conquest; recognition of the existence of the German Democratic Republic as an equal German State and a partner for the unification of Germany; a clear answer to the question of what that unified Germany should be like; the renunciation of armaments and, in particular, the abandonment of the intention to gain access to nuclear weapons; a constructive approach to even partial and gradual solutions aimed at relaxation in Europe—that is the real and only road towards the consolidation of security and peace. . . ."

The Czechoslovak Government's reply to the West German Note was presented on May 6.

The Czechoslovak Government said that it had examined the German Note "particularly from the point of view as to whether and how far it constitutes a change in the policy hitherto pursued by the German Federal Republic" but had found that the Federal Government had "again made quite openly territorial demands against peace-loving European States and, without regard to the undeniable facts of post-war developments and international basic principles", had claimed the right to speak for the whole German nation. It continued:

"As long as the German Federal Republic bases its policy on the non-recognition of the German Democratic Republic as an independent and sovereign State, all its proposals lack any real substance. . . . If the Federal Government now declares that it desires good relations with all its neighbours, and if it contends that it has tried in various ways to improve its relations with the States and peoples of Eastern Europe, this contradicts its whole policy towards the Socialist countries."

After describing the attitude of the Federal Government to the Oder-Neisse border with Poland as "especially clear proof of the anti-peace, revanchist character and political aims of the German Federal Republic", the Czechoslovak Note went on: "Of basic importance is the Federal Government's attitude towards the so-called Munich Agreement. It continues to maintain that . . . [this Agreement] was legally concluded and had lost its validity only by the subsequent aggression of Nazi Germany, i.e. by the total occupation of Czechoslovakia in March 1939. It therefore again refuses to reject the Munich dictate morally, legally and politically as a criminal act of Nazi aggression. If the Federal Government wants to achieve a real improvement in the relations between Czechoslovakia and the German Federal Republic . . . then it must unconditionally condemn the so-called Munich Agreement and expressly recognize that it was invalid from the beginning."

After refuting the German proposals for disarmament measures as "being based on just as unrealistic conceptions as the whole policy of the Federal Government", the Note referred to continued efforts by the Government in Bonn to obtain access to nuclear weapons within the framework of NATO, and declared: "Numerous statements by Government officals . . . prove that the German Federal Republic regards a joint NATO nuclear force only as an interim stage on the way to the direct possession of nuclear weapons, to be used as a means to pursue its power policy with the principal aim of bringing about a revision of the results of the Second World War." In conclusion the Note alleged that the abnormal position in the mutual relations between the two countries was solely a result of the Federal Republic's policy, which had rejected Czechoslovak proposals and continued with its "negative attitude" towards the resumption of normal diplomatic relations.

An official spokesman in Bonn commented on May 6 that the Czechoslovak Note "evaded an objective discussion" of the concrete German proposals, but expressed the hope that an occasion would present itself for further elucidation of the German Note to the Czechoslovak Government.

1966 Exchanges between SPD and SED—
Unsuccessful Negotiations on Joint Meetings

Also during 1966, there were repeated but in the end unsuccessful efforts by the Socialist Unity Party (SED) and the Social Democratic Party (SPD), then in opposition in the Federal Republic, to arrive at a "dialogue".

Herr Ulbricht first invited Herr Brandt, chairman of the SPD and then Chief Burgomaster of West Berlin, on Feb. 8, 1966, to talks to be held both in Eastern and in Western Germany. The reply of the SPD, dated March 18, 1966, agreed in principle to discussions between all parties on both sides but raised a number of critical questions on the attitude of the SED; *Neues Deutschland*, the SED organ in East Berlin, published it on March 26, together with a reply from the SED proposing that public meetings should be held in May in Karl-Marx-Stadt (formerly Chemnitz) and in Essen, and be addressed by speakers of both parties.

The SPD replied on April 14 with the proposal that Herr Brandt and the SPD's deputy chairmen, Herr Fritz Erler and Herr Herbert Wehner, should speak in Karl-Marx-Stadt between May 9 and 13, and that the SED should send representatives to a meeting in Hanover between May 16 and 20.

The Federal Government agreed to this proposal on April 20 but reiterated that discussions between the two Governments were out of the question.

Herr Ulbricht explained on April 21 that his aim in the talks would be to pave the way step by step for a system of bilateral agreements between the G.D.R. and the G.F.R. with a view to eventual "confederation". However, at preparatory talks held between representatives of the two parties in Berlin on April 29-30, 1966, the SED asked for a postponement of the proposed meetings until after the *Land* elections in North Rhine-Westphalia in July, asserting that their delegates would be "endangered" by visiting the Federal Republic. Nevertheless, following further exchanges between the negotiators of the two parties, they announced in a joint communiqué on May 26 that they had agreed on meetings in Karl-Marx-Stadt on July 14 to be addressed by the SPD leaders, and in Hanover on July 21 to be addressed by SED representatives, and that both meetings would be extensively covered in the Press, radio and television on both sides.

Herr Brandt replied immediately, declaring that because some of the questions posed by the SPD had now elicited a negative reply from the SED it was all the more necessary to pursue all efforts to obtain easier conditions on the human level for Germans living in both parts of Germany, on the principle that even in a divided Germany "much could be done". Addressing the SPD congress in Dortmund on June 1, he declared that the Communist plans for a confederation were "of no help to those who wanted to achieve German unity in freedom", and that the Communists should "bury any hope they may still have" of inducing the SPD "to flirt with the 'popular front' tiger". He acknowledged that there had been "significant economic development" in Eastern Germany in recent years and, though he insisted on the continued responsibility of the four Powers for Germany, on the West German claim to sole representation of all Germans, and on non-recognition of the G.D.R., he said that this ought not to hamper an "internal German settlement" of problems. While rejecting the idea of confederation he said he favoured a policy of easing life in divided Germany step by step.

Herr Brandt, Herr Wehner, and Herr Erler, who should have addressed the meeting in Karl-Marx-Stadt on July 14, gave on that day on the West German radio and television an outline of their planned speeches, and on the following day Herr Brandt wrote a letter to all SPD members denouncing Communist plans "to by-pass the SPD leadership" and penetrate local SPD organizations in what they called "the second phase". The letter concluded: "The confrontation [with the SED] requires the firm unity of the party and, if it is to be successful, confidence in the SPD leadership."

Neues Deutschland on Oct. 22, 1966, published "six questions" by the SED Central Committee to the SPD, to which Herr Wehner replied the same day by putting four counter-questions, while also on Oct. 22 the SPD executive, Party Council and Control Commission approved a joint statement repeating that in the SPD's view the régime in the other part of Germany could be recognized neither as democratic nor as legitimate under international law, but emphasizing that the time was ripe for discussing in both parts of Germany the basic questions of German policy "openly and in public"; the party also remained ready to discuss with SED representatives "far-reaching technical arrangements" aimed at easing the effects of the country's division and means to overcome this. After this no further negotiations between the two parties took place.

2. KIESINGER GOVERNMENT'S EXCHANGES WITH EASTERN GERMANY, 1967–69

Formation of "Grand Coalition" by Christian Democrats and Social Democrats—Dr. Kiesinger replaces Dr. Erhard as Federal Chancellor

The two-party coalition of the Christian Democrats and the Free Democrats, which had endured for five years, came to an end on Oct. 27, 1966, with the resignation of all four Ministers of the Free Democratic Party. On Nov. 29 the Christian Democratic Union (CDU) approved a coalition between the CDU and the Social Democratic Party (SPD), and on Nov. 30 the SPD parliamentary party voted in favour of the coalition. On the same day Dr. Erhard tendered his resignation from the Chancellorship to President Lübke, who accepted it on Dec. 1.

The coalition between the Christian Democrats and the Social Democrats—described in political circles and in the West German Press as the "grand coalition"—was the first occasion in the 17-year history of the Federal Republic that the Social Democratic Party had been in power.

Dr. Kiesinger, the CDU leader, was elected Federal Chancellor on Dec. 1, while Herr Brandt, the leader of the SPD and Chief Burgomaster of West Berlin, was appointed as Foreign Minister in addition to taking the Vice-Chancellorship.

In a press statement, Dr. Kiesinger described himself as an "old European" and said that he would do all in his power to help bring about the unification of Europe as speedily as possible. As regards Eastern Europe, it was his intention "in all sincerity" to seek to create "the best and most peaceful relations with the countries of the East, but bearing in mind the difficult problem of the division of Germany".

Dr. Kiesinger made his first policy statement in the *Bundestag* on Dec. 13 in a lengthy speech which covered both domestic and internal policy. In the field of external affairs, Dr. Kiesinger dealt *inter alia* with relations with Eastern Europe, and in particular with Poland and Czechoslovakia. Extracts from Dr. Kiesinger's speech are given below (cross-headings inserted).

Germany and Eastern Europe.—"For centuries Germany was the bridge between Eastern and Western Europe. We would like to fulfil this role in the present age and are therefore interested in improving relations in all fields of economic, cultural and political life with our Eastern neighbours who have the same desire, and even of opening diplomatic relations with them whenever the circumstances allow it.

Germany and Poland.—"Wide sections of the German people have a lively desire for reconciliation with Poland, whose tragic history we have not forgotten and whose desire to live in a State with secure frontiers we understand better than before, in view of the present fate of our divided people.

"But the boundaries of a reunified Germany can be laid down only in an agreement concluded freely with an all-German Government, an agreement creating conditions approved by both peoples for a lasting and peaceful relationship of good neighbourliness.

Germany and Czechoslovakia.—"The German people would also like to reach agreement with Czechoslovakia. The Federal Government condemns the policy of Hitler, which aimed at the destruction of the Czechoslovak State. It agrees with the view that the Munich Agreement, which came into existence under the threat of force, is no longer valid.

"However, there are still problems requiring a solution, such as that of the right to nationality. We are aware of our duty to protect the Sudeten German people, like all refugees and expelled persons, and we take this duty seriously."

During 1968 the two parts of Germany, the German Federal Repubilc (G.F.R.) and the German Democratic Republic (G.D.R.), for the first time in their history both declared their readiness for talks at ministerial level. [Previous talks on interzonal trade, inland navigation, etc., had always been conducted at "technical level", i.e.

by officials.] An offer by Herr Horst Sölle, East German Minister for Foreign Trade, to meet Professor Karl Schiller, West German Minister of Economic Affairs, for talks on trade between the two sides had been accepted by Professor Schiller, who announced on Aug. 16 that he was ready to meet Herr Sölle in East Berlin or any other German city without any preliminary conditions for such talks. Dr. Kiesinger, the Federal Chancellor, had explained on Aug. 17 that such a meeting was in line with proposals previously made by him to the East German régime.

Herr Ulbricht's Proposals—Exchange of Letters between Dr. Kiesinger and Herr Stoph

These proposals had developed out of statements made on both sides from time to time, and an exchange of letters between Dr. Kiesinger and Herr Willi Stoph, chairman of the Council of Ministers of the G.D.R., during 1967.

Herr Ulbricht (Chairman of the Council of State of the G.D.R.) had proposed on Sept. 1, 1964, that "the two German States" should take some first steps towards a relaxation of tension between them, including (*a*) separate declarations rejecting the possession, production, testing, or stationing of nuclear weapons; (*b*) an application to the signatories of the Potsdam Agreement to declare the whole of Germany an atom-free zone and to withdraw any nuclear weapons stationed in Germany; and (*c*) a reduction in military Budgets. These steps, Herr Ulbricht said, could be followed by others, such as a solemn rejection of the use of force, urging the NATO and Warsaw Pact member-States to conclude a non-aggression agreement, support for the Polish proposal for freezing nuclear arms in Central Europe, and readiness to accept international control by representatives of NATO and the Warsaw Pact to supervise disarmament measures on German territory.

In his New Year message of Dec. 31, 1966, Herr Ulbricht stated that it was impossible to unite the Socialist G.D.R. and the Federal Republic, which he asserted was "dominated by monopoly capital", but that it was imperative that they should coexist peacefully with a view to later confederation. To this end he proposed 10 steps, as follows:

210

(1) The two German States should establish normal relations with each other.

(2) They should conclude a non-aggression treaty.

(3) They should solemnly recognize the existing frontiers in Europe.

(4) They should agree to halve arms expenditure.

(5) They should renounce nuclear weapons.

(6) They should encourage normal relations between all European States and the German States.

(7) They should make a declaration of neutrality, to be guaranteed by the great Powers.

(8) They should pledge themselves to respect West Berlin as a separate and independent territory.

(9) The G.D.R. and the West Berlin Senate should conclude a treaty in which the Senate would pledge an ending of the "cold war" against the G.D.R. and the G.D.R. would guarantee the transit routes through its territory to West Berlin.

(10) The two German States should establish a joint commission to investigate to what extent the clauses of the Potsdam Agreement guaranteeing peace and democracy in Germany had been implemented in each of them. This joint commission should make proposals for further measures which might be found necessary.

Dr. Kiesinger on his part issued a statement on April 12, 1967—shortly before the SED was due to hold its seventh congress in East Berlin—reiterating his previously expressed wish to achieve a relaxation of tension between East and West but, by implication, refusing any recognition of the G.D.R. as a separate State. His statement was supported by all parties in the *Bundestag*.

Dr. Kiesinger listed as immediate steps to be taken to that end between the two parts of Germany: (a) improvements in travel facilities, including pass arrangements in Berlin and between neighbouring areas on both sides, as well as easier payment transfers, receipt of medical supplies and of gifts, and family reunions; (b) an expansion of inter-German trade, partly by means of increased public guarantees and credits, and involving the exchange of power (in particular electricity), the establishment of new communications, and postal and telephone improvements, including the restoration of telephone services between East and West Berlin [then cut off by the East German régime] (c) agreement on trade, technical, and cultural exchanges; the removal of bureaucratic obstacles to contacts between universities, research institutes and scientific societies; and the gradual introduction of free exchanges involving books, periodicals, newspapers, youth visits, sports and cultural organizations.

The official East German news agency in a statement the same day criticized the proposals on the ground that they contained no indication that the Chancellor had abandoned his Government's claim to be the sole representative of all Germans or of its "intention to annex the G.D.R." Herr Ulbricht nevertheless said on April 16 that the proposals proved that sooner or later the two Governments would have to negotiate as equal partners—as had always been maintained by the Government of the G.D.R.—and at the opening of the SED congress on April 17 he proposed that Dr. Kiesinger and Herr Stoph should meet with delegations at a place to be agreed upon to discuss further steps and to conclude agreements.

On May 11, 1967, it was officially announced in Bonn that the Federal Government had received a letter from Herr Stoph. [No such announcement had previously been made in respect of earlier communications received from the East German Government.] It was disclosed the next day that Herr Stoph had, in his letter dated May 10, proposed a meeting with Dr. Kiesinger either in East Berlin or at the Chancellor's office in Bonn to "open direct negotiations with the aim of concluding agreements" on a number of points similar to those stated above by Herr Ulbricht.

After it had been officially stated in Bonn on May 12, 1967, that a reply would be sent to Herr Stoph, Dr. Kiesinger declared on May 14 that he would pursue his efforts to achieve negotiations with the object of improving conditions "on a human level". The *Bundestag* agreed on May 17 to the establishment of a special committee of Cabinet Ministers of both coalition parties to draft a suitable reply, and this was given on June 13 in the form of a letter to Herr Stoph personally, unanimously approved by the Cabinet the same day in respect of its form and contents. The principal parts of this letter read as follows:

"Dear Mr. Chairman: I have received your letter of May 10. Unfortunately it does not deal with my Government's statement of April 12. I enclose the text. The meaning and the purpose of this statement was: so long as basic differences of opinion prevent a just solution to the German question, we must, in the interests of peace of our people and of a relaxation of tension in Europe, seek internal

German arrangements which further as far as possible the human, economic and intellectual relations between Germans in East and West.

"But you say: all or nothing. You raise demands for the political recognition, in international law, of the division of Germany, a division which contradicts the will of the people in both parts of our Fatherland. You make acquiescence to these demands a condition for talks. If I were to adopt your procedure I would have to demand an immediate, secret and internationally controlled referendum. In the present situation, however, such a confrontation would lead us no further.

"On the other hand, I think it is necessary to have discussions on how we can prevent the Germans in a period of enforced partition from growing apart. . . . Life in divided Germany must be made more bearable. It is the duty of all responsible people to contribute to this with all their powers.

"The well-being of our people demands that the tensions in Germany should not be increased but lessened. . . . It is certainly not our purpose to exercise tutelage over the people in the other parts of Germany. Only so long as these people are prevented from expressing their will about the destiny of our nation without any doubt, is the free Federal Government obliged to speak for them."

Reiterating his Government's "solemn renunciation" of the use of force for the attainment of political ends, Dr. Kiesinger stressed that the other side would also have to renounce the use of force, and concluded: "The reality which you and I have to recognize is the will of the Germans to be one people. I therefore propose that emissaries, to be appointed by you and myself, should start talks, without preliminary political conditions, on such practical questions of co-existence among Germans as are contained in my statement of April 12."

Dr. Kiesinger's letter was not published in Eastern Germany, and it was not until Sept. 18, 1967, that Herr Stoph replied, restating the East German point of view and enclosing with his letter a draft treaty of six articles "to establish normal relations between the G.D.R. and the Federal Republic of Germany", worded as follows.

"*Article 1*. The G.D.R. and the G.F.R. establish normal relations with each other.

"*Article 2*. The relations between the Socialist G.D.R. and the G.F.R., which are the relations between sovereign States of the German nation striving for peaceful coexistence and gradual *rapprochement*, are based upon the generally recognized principles of international law.

The Governments of the two German States conclude an agreement on the renunciation of force.

The Government of the G.D.R. and the Government of the G.F.R. pledge themselves to base their relations upon the following principles:

Respect for sovereignty, equality of status, and non-intervention in internal affairs.

Respect for the territorial integrity of the States of Europe.

Recognition of the existing frontiers in Europe, including the Oder-Neisse frontier and the frontier between the G.D.R. and the G.F.R.

Recognition of West Berlin as an independent political unit.

Recognition of the nullity from the very beginning of the Munich Agreement [of 1938].

Renunciation by both German States of any form of access to nuclear weapons, or the stationing of nuclear weapons on their territories.

"*Article 3.* For the establishment and cultivation of normal relations between the G.D.R. and the G.F.R., such direct contacts shall be established as are normal between States.

"*Article 4.* On the basis of mutual advantage and with the aim of achieving a regularized peaceful coexistence, the necessary agreements shall be concluded in the fields of the economy, trade, posts and telecommunications, transport and other spheres.

"*Article 5.* The Government of the G.D.R. and the Government of the G.F.R. pledge themselves that the two German States shall make further contributions towards guaranteeing European security, in particular in the form of the renunciation of access to nuclear weapons in any form, and their stationing.

"*Article 6.* The Governments of the two German States declare their readiness to open negotiations aimed at a peaceful solution of the German problem, after they have normalized their relations, after the implementation of agreed disarmament, after the conclusion of an agreement on European security, and under the condition that militarism, neo-Nazism and the power of the monopolies have been overcome."

In his letter Herr Stoph proposed that Secretaries of State from Bonn and East Berlin should make "technical preparations" for a meeting of the Chancellor and himself. He repeated, however, that the unification of Germany could only be based on "an understanding between the two German States and their Governments in carrying out the task of overcoming militarism, neo-Nazism and the power of monopolies", and added that West German membership of the

214

European Economic Community was "diametrically opposed to this process of unification".

In a statement made on Sept. 29 the Federal Chancellor declared that he was in principle in favour of a plebiscite to be held throughout Germany, in which Germans would answer the question whether they wished to live in one or in two States.

Herr Stoph said the same day, with reference to Dr. Kiesinger's letter, that he was ready to start negotiations at the level of Secretaries of State for the purpose of dealing with the establishment of formal relations, the conclusion of a bilateral treaty renouncing the use of force, and recognition of the existing frontiers.

Neues Deutschland stated on Oct. 4, 1967, that Dr. Kiesinger's letter would not be published in the G.D.R., and reiterated the two conditions for any all-German talks: (*a*) final abandonment by the Federal Government of all claims to the sole representation of Germans and (*b*) acceptance of talks as between equal partners between the Heads of Government of both German States. Herr Ulbricht repeated on Oct. 9 that his Government was ready for talks on a treaty establishing normal ties between the two German States and on mutual renunciation of the use of force.

Dr. Kiesinger, however, said in Berlin on Oct. 11 that any recognition of the Communist German "part-State", whether step-by-step or immediate, constituted a "mortal danger", and denied that his coalition Government had any intention of moving in that direction.

Herr Otto Winzer, the East German Foreign Minister, said on Nov. 16, 1967, that the exchange of letters between Dr. Kiesinger and Herr Stoph did not of itself provide a basis for negotiations on terms of equality; that "the whole world—including Dr. Kiesinger— knows that a change in the territorial *status quo* cannot be achieved by peaceful means"; and that, although the Chancellor was talking of the "renunciation of force", his "clinging to the old revanchist targets" clearly implied war. *Neues Deutschland* stated on Dec. 20 that, while Western Germany was not to be regarded as a foreign country, there were "two States of the German nation".

Dr. Kiesinger declared in the *Bundestag* on March 11, 1968, *inter alia*: "The Federal Government is ready to negotiate with the Government in East Berlin, and the themes discussed could include the renunciation of force. I myself am ready to meet Herr Stoph. But the other side must abandon its attempts to couple such talks with the demand for recognition in international law."

Herr Ulbricht, in reply, rejected the Federal Government's point of view and attacked Dr. Kiesinger personally in a television statement on March 11.

The question of eventual West German recognition of the Oder-Neisse frontier was raised at an SPD conference in Nuremberg on March 18, when Herr Willy Brandt, the Federal Foreign Minister, said "present circumstances amounted to the recognition or respecting of" this frontier "pending a settlement through a peace treaty", this formula being approved by the conference on March 20.

Further East German Proposals

The State Council of the G.D.R. on June 25, 1968, addressed a declaration to the "people and Government of Western Germany" which largely repeated the earlier East German proposals, as follows:

(1) The Governments of the two German States undertake to accede immediately to the international Treaty on the Non-Proliferation of Nuclear Weapons, which serves to prevent a nuclear war.

(2) Conclusion of a treaty valid under international law between the Government of the G.D.R. and the Government of the G.F.R. which prohibits the storing of nuclear warheads on the territories of the two German States.

(3) Conclusion of a treaty valid under international law between the Government of the G.D.R. and the Government of the G.F.R. on the non-application of force in relations between the two German States.

(4) Conclusion of a treaty valid under international law between the Government of the G.D.R. and the Government of the G.F.R. on the recognition of the *status quo* and the existing frontiers in Europe.

The *Volkskammer* (the East German Parliament) authorized the G.D.R. Council of Ministers on Aug. 9 to conclude treaties on the basis of these proposals with the G.F.R. and to nominate a Secretary of State for the required negotiations. At the same time the *Volkskammer* approved a proposal by Herr Ulbricht for negotiations between the two countries' Ministers of Economic Affairs. It was as a

216

result of this decision that Herr Sölle offered to meet Professor Schiller [see above].

Herr Ulbricht's political proposals, approved by the *Volkskammer* at the same time, envisaged:

(*a*) The establishment of normal diplomatic relations among all European States, with the two German States being drawn in gradually with equal rights;

(*b*) The admission of "both German States" to the United Nations and its organizations;

(c) The signing of the Non-Proliferation Treaty by the Bonn Government;

(*d*) The conclusion of a single agreement on the renunciation of the use of force between the G.D.R. and the G.F.R.;

(*e*) The recognition of the existing frontiers in Europe and of the the *status quo*;

(*f*) The conclusion of a treaty on the normalization of relations between the two German States; and

(*g*) An exchange of properly authorized missions, provided the Federal Government abandoned (i) its claim to sole representation of all Germans, and (ii) the Hallstein Doctrine.

G.D.R. Claims for Postal and Railway Charges, and for Refund of Road Transport Tax

In addition to exchanges between Herr Ulbricht, or Herr Stoph, and Dr. Kiesinger, East German Ministers had individually approached their West German counterparts with a view to negotiations on specific East German financial demands.

Herr Rudolf Schulze, G.D.R. Minister of Posts and Telecommunications, wrote in October 1966 to Herr Richard Stücklen, then Federal Minister of Posts and Telecommunications, and Senator Schütz of West Berlin, demanding negotiations on posts and telecommunications involving payment to the G.D.R. of amounts claimed to be due for services in transit across G.D.R. territory. The Federal Government ignored this letter, regarding it as an attempt to achieve negotiations at ministerial level, which would involve recognition of the G.D.R., in a matter which in the West German view could be settled satisfactorily through the existing "technical" contacts.

After another letter dated April 26, 1967, from Herr Schulze to

217

Dr. Werner Dollinger, the new Federal Minister of Posts and Tele-communications, had been received but returned unopened by the latter Ministry on April 28 in terms of standing instructions dating from 1959, the Federal Government decided on May 17, 1967, that letters from G.D.R. Ministers should be accepted. On June 14, however, the Federal Government rejected the East German demand; it accepted the need for certain payments, but refused to recognize the territory of the G.D.R. as an independent postal area and maintained that payment could not be demanded at international rates.

Herr Siegfried Böhm, the Minister of Finance of the G.D.R., in a letter to Herr Strauss, the Federal Minister of Finance, demanded on Nov. 22, 1967, that the transport tax imposed by the G.F.R. on road transports should be abolished to the extent to which it also covered mileage in East German territory and that the amount hitherto levied (more than 120,000,000 East German marks) should be paid to the East German Finance Ministry. Herr Böhm wrote a similar letter to Herr Heinz Striek, the West Berlin Senator for Finance, claiming 110,000,000 East German marks. Herr Böhm's letters, however, received no reply.

New Interzonal Trade Agreement (1969-75) between Eastern and Western Germany—Settlement of Dispute over West German Fuel Tax

An agreement on interzonal trade between the two parts of Germany up to Dec. 31, 1975, was concluded on Dec. 6, 1968, through an exchange of letters in East Berlin between the negotiators on both sides, Herr Willy Kleindienst (Western Germany) and Herr Heinz Behrendt (Eastern Germany).

The Federal Minister of Economics, Professor Karl Schiller, announcing the conclusion of the agreement on that date, explained that it had been made possible by a decision of the Federal Cabinet on Dec. 4 to compromise with the East German régime on a number of controversial points, which had so far held up a settlement of the long-drawn-out negotiations. The four principal points of the agreement, which was also announced on the same day in East Berlin, were as follows:

(1) The Federal Government would pay to the German Democratic Republic over the clearing account 120,000,000 account units

(one unit being equivalent to DM 1 and the total of DM 120,000,000 being equal to U.S. $300,000,000) in two instalments of 60,000,000 a/u's each on Dec. 31, 1968, and Dec. 31, 1969, respectively. This payment was meant to compensate the East German régime for losses which it claimed to have incurred through a fuel tax imposed by Western Germany, which was said to have affected East German earnings from fuel deliveries to the Federal Republic.

In conjunction with this it was agreed that Eastern Germany would accept supplies of capital equipment and machinery from Western Germany up to the total amount of the compensation payment, and would moreover resume its fuel deliveries, under fresh annual quotas of DM 30,000,000 for diesel oil and DM 20,000,000 for petrol for which no West German compensatory payments would be made.

(2) The annual quotas for machinery, motor vehicles and electrical goods were increased by both sides to reach by 1975 double the quotas for 1968, the Federal Republic thus stepping up its deliveries from DM 300,000,000 in the latter year to DM 650,000,000 by 1975 by means of annual increases of DM 50,000,000; whilst the German Democratic Republic would also raise its deliveries by DM 50,000,000 annually from DM 200,000,000 in 1968 to DM 550,000,000 in 1975.

(3) The "swing" on the clearing account, hitherto fixed at 200,000,000 a/u's, would in future be adjusted to actual East German deliveries and would amount to 25 per cent of West German purchases in the previous calendar year, thereby facilitating credit arrangements for East German purchases.

(4) The existing provision under which any debit balance on the clearing account had to be settled as at June 30 of each year was dropped, with the intention of facilitating long-term arrangements in interzonal trade.

The West German initiative in proposing a compromise, to which the East German authorities responded positively, was considered to have political implications in addition to its economic aspects.

Professor Schiller said that in the exchange of letters Herr Kleindienst had emphasized the importance of the agreement. He [Professor Schiller] declared that new conditions had been created for long-term and continuing trade relations between both parts of Germany, and added: "We regard these arrangements as our contribution for an all-round improvement of relations, which is indispensable to the economy of both sides and for the unhindered settlement of their commercial exchanges. I think I may say that the Federal Republic has done its share in its efforts to assist internal German trade, which has created a new basis for business. It is now up to the other side to make the next move."

In East Berlin the agreement was also welcomed by *Neues Deutschland* as a step which would remove existing trade restrictions and was in the interests of the two commercial partners.

1968–69 Exchanges on Status of West Berlin

A protest from the Soviet Government to the U.S.A., Britain and France in February 1968 concerning certain activities of the German Federal Government in West Berlin was followed in March-June by a series of East German restrictions affecting the overland access routes to that city. These steps led to protests to the Soviet Union from the three Western Powers and to the imposition by NATO countries of counter-measures against East German citizens.

Soviet Protests against Federal Cabinet and Bundestag Meetings in West Berlin

Mr. Pyotr Abrassimov, Soviet Ambassador to the German Democratic Republic, in Notes of Feb. 14 to the U.S., British and French Ambassadors in Bonn alleged that in the past year the German Federal Government had "systematically extended" its "illegal activity" in West Berlin by holding "regular Parliamentary Weeks" and meetings of the Cabinet and *Bundestag* committees, establishing various Ministries and offices employing more than 20,000 civil servants, and planning to build an official residence for the Federal Chancellor. Furthermore, it had claimed the "exercise of the privileges of State power" in West Berlin, whose Chief Burgomaster, Herr Klaus Schütz, had been elected president of the *Bundesrat*.

"The Soviet Union," the Notes concluded, "will not tolerate West Berlin's integration in the Federal Republic in any form, or its utilization for purposes which cannot be reconciled with a normalization of the European situation and a strengthening of European security. . . . I hope that these considerations will be properly understood, and that the Western Powers will take the necessary measures to protect the status of West Berlin as a special political structure from the illegal attacks of the German Federal Republic."

Dr. Kiesinger, the Federal Chancellor, visited West Berlin on March 5-6 to attend a "Parliamentary Week", which had opened on March 4 and consisted of meetings of all *Bundestag* committees and the three parliamentary parties; on March 6 Dr. Kiesinger also presided over a Cabinet meeting.

Addressing the CDU parliamentary group on March 5, he stressed that the Federal Government had no intention of provoking a new crisis over Berlin. He also said that he had on March 1 told Mr. Tsarapkin, the Soviet Ambassador in Bonn, that the Federal Government rejected his accusations of "revanchist intentions to annex West Berlin"; that, on the contrary, it wished to maintain the present status of the city and respected the rights of its Western allies in West Berlin; and that the *Bundestag* was legally entitled to come to the city.

Mr. Abrassimov had on March 4 issued a press statement condemning the "Parliamentary Week" as unlawful.

The statement declared: "West Berlin is situated outside the territory of the Federal Republic, is not within the jurisdiction of its organs, and cannot be either a *Land* or a protectorate of the West German State. . . . By organizing provocations in West Berlin the Government of the Federal Republic is assuming full responsibility for all the possible undesirable consequences of these actions."

East German Restrictions on Travel and Goods Traffic to and from West Berlin

Under four decrees issued on June 11, 1968, the East German Government imposed the following additional restrictions on all West German and West Berlin citizens and goods:

(1) All West Germans travelling across Eastern Germany to West Berlin and *vice versa* would be required to possess a passport and a transit visa (the charge for the latter being raised to DM5 for each crossing).

(2) West Berliners travelling through East German territory to or from Western Germany would need an identity card and a transit visa (also costing DM 5).

(3) West Germans wishing to visit Eastern Germany would require a passport and entry and exit visas (costing DM5 each), but those on a day visit to East Berlin and carrying a passport would only need a day permit (costing DM 5).

(4) West Berliners wishing to visit Eastern Germany would require an identity card and an entry visa. [No provision was made for West Berliners visiting East Berlin for a day, as the previous pass arrangements for such visits on public holidays and on compassionate grounds had not been extended, the East German authorities having failed to react to West Berlin proposals for such an extension.]

(5) An "equalization tax" would be imposed from July 1 on the transport of goods to and from Western Germany and West Berlin by lorry, train or barge, the rate of tax varying according to the nature of the goods and the length of the transit route. Coach passengers would also be taxed.

(6) Goods accompanied by official documents referring to West Berlin as part of Western Germany would not be admitted.

(7) The transport through East German territory of printed matter issued by the National Democratic Party (NPD) or other "neo-Nazi material" was prohibited and East German Customs authorities were ordered to refuse access to motor vehicles carrying such material.

(8) The minimum amount which Western visitors were obliged to change into East German marks would be raised from DM 5 to DM 10 a day, except for day visits to East Berlin.

Colonel-General Friedrich Dickel (the Minister of the Interior), explaining the new measures to the *Volkskammer* on June 11, alleged that the passage of Emergency Laws in the Federal Republic had created "a new situation".

The East German Government issued an order on March 10 banning members of the NPD and other persons "engaged in any kind of neo-Nazi activity" from staying on, or travelling through East German territory.

The East German Minister of the Interior issued another order on April 13 extending the March 10 ban to Ministers and senior officials of the Federal Republic.

Herr Günther Diehl, the Federal Government's chief spokesman, denounced the East German measures on June 11 as "part of a long-term political plan which aimed at giving the [East German] régime the character of an independent sovereign State".

Meanwhile Dr. Kiesinger had visited West Berlin on June 13 for talks about the East German restrictions with Herr Klaus Schütz, the

Chief Burgomaster of West Berlin, and with members of the West Berlin Senate and the House of Deputies. Later the same day he told a press conference that Federal assistance to West Berlin would include improved financial aid on a permanent basis, incentives for industrial investment in the city, compensation for payments incurred in respect of East German visa charges and transport taxes and increased subsidies for an expansion of air flights between the Federal Republic and West Berlin which was under discussion with the Western Powers.

Herr Brandt's Talk with Mr. Abrassimov

Herr Brandt, who because of the East German measures had prematurely returned from an official visit to Yugoslavia, crossed from West to East Berlin on June 18, 1968, for an eight-hour talk with Mr. Abrassimov. Herr Brandt had told a press conference in West Berlin on June 15 that the Federal Government would make a direct approach to the Soviet Government over the latest East German traffic restrictions, and a Foreign Ministry official in Bonn stated on June 18 that the meeting, at which "questions of mutual interest" were discussed, had resulted from an invitation to Herr Brandt in his capacity as chairman of the West German Social Democratic Party from Mr. Abrassimov in his role as a member of the Central Committee of the Soviet Communist Party.

In a press statement in Bonn on June 19 Herr Brandt said that his talks with Mr. Abrassimov had covered Berlin and Soviet relations with Western Germany, but denied that the latest East German restrictions constituted a "new Berlin crisis". Earlier the same day, however, he had declared to members of the SPD parliamentary group that he had warned Mr. Abrassimov that the East German decree was "creating real damage and would place a heavy burden on efforts to reduce world tensions".

Federal Measures against East German Barge Traffic through Federal Territory

The Federal Minister for Transport, Herr Georg Leber, announced at a press conference on July 1 that the Federal Government had informed the East German authorities that no further East German barges would be allowed to pass through West German territory in transit to other countries until an agreement on transit traffic on German inland waterways had been concluded.

Soviet and East German Protests at Decision to hold West German Presidential Election in West Berlin— Dr. Heinemann elected President of Federal Republic

The decision of the then President of the West German *Bundestag,* Dr. Eugen Gerstenmaier—announced in Bonn on Dec. 18, 1968— to hold the 1969 West German presidential election in West Berlin, as had been done on three previous occasions, evoked strong protests from the Soviet and East German Governments, both to the Federal Republic and to the Governments of the United States, Britain and France, and led to repeated sporadic interference in the pre-election period with road traffic between Western Germany and West Berlin, which lies 110 miles inside the territory of the German Democratic Republic.

The date for the presidential election was subsequently fixed at March 5, 1969, by Herr von Hassel, the new President of the *Bundestag,* who announced the decision on Feb. 12 after consultations with Dr. Kiesinger, Herr Brandt, the parliamentary party leaders, and Herr Schütz.

The Foreign Ministry in Bonn received on Feb. 6 a lengthy teletyped Note from the East German Government—bearing no signature but only the address "Ministry for Foreign Affairs of the G.D.R."— protesting at what it described as the "misuse of West Berlin for the policy of annexation and revenge of the ruling circles in the Federal Republic", denouncing the holding of the presidential election in West Berlin as a "deliberate, serious provocation", and saying that if the election was held in Berlin the Federal Government would have to bear "full responsibility for the consequences that would follow the measures which the authorities of the G.D.R. would be forced to take". A communication in similar terms was received the following day by Herr Schütz; signed by Colonel-General Dickel, the East German Minister of the Interior, it described the proposal to hold the West German presidential election in West Berlin as "a flagrant violation of existing international agreements".

At the request of the G.D.R. Government, the East German Minister of the Interior issued a directive on Feb. 8, effective from Feb. 15, which (a) barred all members of the West German Federal Assembly (*Bundesversammlung*), the body which elects the West German Federal President, from travelling across the territory of the G.D.R. until further notice; (b) barred the transport through the G.D.R. of all working material (documents, etc.) for the proposed West German presidential election in Berlin; and (c) barred all members of the West German armed forces and members of the defence committee of the West German *Bundestag* from crossing G.D.R. territory to or from West Berlin until further notice. Accusing the German Federal Government of a "gross violation of the Potsdam Agreement", the decree stated that the proposal to elect the West German President in West Berlin "violates international law" and was fresh evidence of the Federal Republic's intention to "continue its aggressive actions to annex the independent political entity of West Berlin to the West German State".

Herr Günther Diehl issued a statement on Feb. 9 emphasizing that the East German authorities had no right under international law to challenge the agreed status of Berlin, which was under the quadripartite protection of the Soviet Union, the United States, the United Kingdom and France. The East German attempt to prevent the election of the President in West Berlin, Herr Diehl added, introduced "a new element of tension" into East-West relations and was "tantamount to a violation of the status of Berlin".

The Soviet Ambassador in Bonn, Mr. Tsarapkin, called on Feb. 13 on the Federal Chancellor, Dr. Kiesinger, and presented a strongly-worded statement by the Soviet Government protesting against what was termed the "provocative intention" of the Government of the German Federal Republic to hold the presidential election in West Berlin.

On Feb. 14 the Czechoslovak news agency (Ceteka) issued a statement by the Government in Prague likewise describing the proposed meeting of the Federal Assembly in West Berlin as "illegal and provocatory". A similar statement by the Polish Government on Feb. 11 had described the decision to choose the West German Head of State in "the separate political unit of West Berlin" as a "significant example of the efforts of West German cold war circles to increase tensions in Europe".

A new development occurred on Feb. 21 when *Die Wahrheit,* the party journal of the SEW (Socialist Unity Party of West Berlin)—the new name adopted by the former "SED West Berlin" on Feb. 15—published an interview with the chairman of that party, Herr Gerhard Danelius, in which the latter intimated that the G.D.R. Government was willing, in return for the cancellation of the Federal Assembly meeting in West Berlin, to permit the issue of passes for West Berliners enabling them to visit East Berlin at Easter. On the same day Herr Ulbricht, in his capacity as First Secretary of the central committee of the Socialist Unity Party (SED), sent a letter to Herr Brandt, in his capacity as chairman of the Social Democratic Party in the G.F.R., saying:

"We have heard that within the SPD the question is being discussed of raising in the [Federal] Government the question of transferring the Federal Assembly to a West German city. If the Social Democratic Ministers could bring about such a decision of the Federal Government and the President of the *Bundestag,* this would mean a relaxation of tensions. As West Berlin is a separate political entity, the West Berlin Senate might in this event approach the G.D.R. Government about the granting of facilities for West Berlin citizens to visit the capital of the G.D.R. [i.e. East Berlin] at Easter 1969. We are informed that the G.D.R. Government is willing to examine such a proposal in a positive manner."

In Herr Brandt's absence in the United States, the letter was received by his deputy, Herr Herbert Wehner, and immediately transmitted to Dr. Kiesinger and Herr Schütz.

On Feb. 22-23 Dr. Kiesinger and Mr. Tsarapkin had two meetings within 48 hours. At their first meeting, on Feb. 22, the Soviet Ambassador had received from the Federal Chancellor the West German Government's rejection of the Soviet statement of Feb. 15 protesting at the decision to hold the presidential election in West Berlin.

At the meeting on Feb. 23 the Soviet Ambassador indicated that, if the Federal Government abandoned its plan to hold the presidential election in West Berlin, the East German authorities would be prepared to issue passes to West Berliners at Easter for visits to relatives and friends living in East Berlin. Following the first Kiesinger-Tsarapkin meeting, the Chief Burgomaster of West Berlin had visited Bonn on Feb. 22 for talks with the Federal Chancellor, and after the second Kiesinger-Tsarapkin meeting Herr Schütz informed Dr. Kiesinger that the West Berlin Senate was ready to have discussions with the authorities in East Berlin.

The Federal Government's deputy spokesman, Herr Conrad Ahlers, indicated on Feb. 23 that although the Soviet offer was regarded as "encouraging", the Chancellor had made it clear that there could be no question of holding the presidential election elsewhere than in Berlin unless a "concrete result" was achieved which would include "lasting and positive arrangements" for the movements of Berliners between the two halves of the city.

From Christmas 1963 until Whitsun 1966, the East German authorities had issued passes to West Berliners allowing one-day family visits to East Berlin at special seasons—Easter, Whitsun, Christmas, and for a period in the autumn. Negotiations to reach a further agreement, however, broke down in 1966 (the last such arrangements were concluded in Easter and Whitsun of that year), and since then West Berliners had only been permitted to visit East Berlin in cases of special hardship, i.e. for urgent humanitarian and family reasons such as death, severe illness, etc.

Herr Brandt, in his reply of Feb. 25 to Herr Ulbricht's letter of Feb. 21, declared that no discussions were possible "between the SPD and you" on the Federal Assembly and the venue of its meeting but that, because of the importance of contributing to an understanding, his party fully supported the efforts of Herr Schütz to bring about a solution of the problems of the people of West Berlin. On the same day (Feb. 25) an exchange of letters took place between Herr Schütz and Herr Stoph, the East German Prime Minister, followed by a meeting in East Berlin on Feb. 26 between Herr Horst Grabert, head of the West Berlin City Government's Chancellery, and Dr. Michael Kohl, East German Under-Secretary of State. No agreement was reached, however.

At a special meeting of the West Berlin Senate earlier the same day Herr Schütz had formulated his views as follows: "(1) We are principally interested in reaching comprehensive arrangements which will alleviate the life of Berliners in the divided city. (2) It is therefore not only a question of passes for visits in the traditional sense, and an isolated discussion about this or that period by-passes the crux of the problem. (3) We do not aim at any short-term results but are concerned with bringing about a freer movement for the people of Berlin, and thereby a long-term stabilization. This would satisfy the interests of both sides and would be a practical contribution to the reduction of tensions in Germany and in Europe."

A statement by the East German Press Office after the meeting between Herr Grabert and Dr. Kohl quoted the latter as having repeated the willingness of the G.D.R. Government to issue Easter passes for visits by West Berliners to East Berlin, but as having insisted that its demand for the presidential election to be held elsewhere had to be met unconditionally. In reply to an invitation by Herr Grabert to Dr. Kohl for further talks in West Berlin on Feb. 27, Dr. Kohl wrote that any further discussions would serve no purpose unless the West Berlin Senate declared beforehand that the West German Federal Assembly was not going to take place in West Berlin.

Mr. Abrassimov presented a Note on Feb. 28 to the East German Foreign Minister, Herr Otto Winzer, accusing the West German authorities of "flagrant abuse of the communication routes" linking Berlin to the Federal Republic; requesting the G.D.R. authorities to "examine the possibilities of taking the necessary measures" to curtail such "unlawful activities"; and promising the support of the Soviet Union and all socialist countries for such action.

Further talks were held by Dr. Kiesinger on March 1, firstly with Mr. Tsarapkin and then with the ambassadors of the three Western Powers.

Dr. Kiesinger said afterwards on television that his talk with Mr. Tsarapkin had "unfortunately" been "without result", and gave a warning that "we will have to face the war of nerves which will continue strongly during the next few days".

Between March 1 and 4 the interzonal *Autobahn* was repeatedly closed by the East German authorities, while Soviet and East German troops were engaged in military manoeuvres in the area.

In East Berlin another meeting took place in the afternoon of March 4 between Herr Grabert and Dr. Kohl, at the latter's invitation, in an attempt to reach an eleventh-hour agreement between the East and West German authorities. According to subsequent statements by Herr Schütz and by the G.D.R. Press Office, the East German side had repeated its previous offer to grant West Berliners passes for one-day visits to relatives in East Berlin at Easter, and to discuss after Easter the possibility of further visits, provided the presidential election was not held in West Berlin. This offer, however, was again considered insufficient by the West Berlin Senate as well as by the Federal Government, Dr. Kohl being informed accordingly the same evening. It was pointed out in Bonn that only a "lasting solution" permitting free movement between the two parts of Berlin would have been regarded as acceptable.

On March 5, 1969, the Federal Assembly, which was held in Berlin as planned, elected Dr. Heinemann President of the German Federal Republic.

3. BRANDT GOVERNMENT'S TALKS
WITH EAST GERMAN REGIME, 1969–70

Ostpolitik of Brandt Government

In the sixth general election in the German Federal Republic held on Sept. 28, 1969, no party obtained an overall majority. Agreement on the formation of a coalition between the Social Democratic Party (SPD) and the Free Democratic Party (FDP) was announced on Oct. 3 by Herr Brandt and Herr Walter Scheel (the FDP leader)— a decision which meant that the Christian Democrats would go into Opposition for the first time in the 20 years of the Federal Republic.

On Oct. 21 the new *Bundestag* elected Herr Brandt as Chancellor of the German Federal Republic.

In a press statement after his election Herr Brandt said that one of the main tasks of his Government would be to react "positively" to the interest of the Polish Government in beginning talks, in which connexion "we should welcome it if we succeeded in opening diplomatic relations between the Federal Republic and Poland in the foreseeable future".

On Oct. 28 Herr Brandt made a statement of his Government's policy to the *Bundestag,* in which he outlined his policy towards Eastern Germany as follows:

"This Government," said Herr Brandt, "works on the assumption that the questions which have arisen for the German people out of the Second World War and from the national treachery committed by the Hitler régime can find their ultimate answers only in a European peace arrangement. However, no one can dissuade us from our conviction that the Germans have a right to self-determination just as has any other nation. The object of our practical political work in the years immediately ahead is to preserve the unity of the nation by ending the present deadlock in the relationship between the two parts of Germany.

"The Germans are one not only by reason of their language and their history, with all its splendour and its misery; we are all at home in Germany. And we still have common tasks and a common responsibility: to ensure peace among us and in Europe.

"Twenty years after the establishment of the Federal Republic of Germany and of the G.D.R., we must prevent any further alienation of the two parts of the German nation—that is, arrive at a regular *modus vivendi* and from there proceed to co-operation. This is not just a German interest: it is of importance also for peace in Europe and for East-West relations. . . .

"The Federal Government will continue the policy initiated in December 1966, and again offers the Council of Ministers of the G.D.R. negotiations at Government level without discrimination on either side, which should lead to contractually agreed co-operation. International recognition of the G.D.R. by the Federal Republic is out of the question. Even if there exist two States in Germany, they are not foreign countries to each other; their relations with each other can only be of a special nature.

"Following up the policy of its predecessor, the Federal Government declares that its readiness for binding agreements on the reciprocal renunciation of the use or threat of force applies equally with regard to the G.D.R.

"The Federal Government will advise the United States, Britain and France to continue energetically the talks begun with the Soviet Union on easing and improving the situation in Berlin. The status of the City of Berlin under the special responsibility of the Four Powers must remain untouched. This must not be a hindrance to seeking facilities for traffic within and to Berlin. We shall continue to ensure the viability of Berlin. West Berlin must be placed in a position to assist in improving the political, economic and cultural relations between the two parts of Germany. . . .

"The Federal Government will promote the development of closer political co-operation in Europe with the aim of evolving step by step a common attitude in international questions. Our country needs co-operation and co-ordination with the West and understanding with the East. The German people need peace in the full sense of that word also with the peoples of the Soviet Union and of the European East. We are prepared to make an honest attempt at understanding, in order to help overcome the aftermath of the disaster brought on Europe by a criminal clique. . . .

"In continuation of its predecessor's policy, the Federal Government aims at equally binding agreements on the mutual renunciation of the use or threat of force. Let me repeat: this readiness also applies as far as the G.D.R. is concerned. And I wish to make it unmistakably clear that we are prepared to arrive with Czechoslovakia—our immediate neighbour—at arrangements which bridge the gulf of the past. . . .

"Today the Federal Government deliberately abstains from committing itself to statements or formulae going beyond the framework of this statement, which might complicate the negotiations it desires. It is well aware that there will be no progress unless the Governments in the capitals of the Warsaw Pact countries adopt a co-operative attitude."

During the next four months there were a number of developments in connexion with the proposed negotiations between the two German States.

Herr Stoph on Relations between Eastern and Western Germany—Call for Normalization of Relations

In a speech on Nov. 12, 1969, Herr Stoph, the East German Prime Minister, said that the only way to break the deadlock on the German question was for the two German States to establish normal relations with each other, and declared that the Government of the G.D.R. was ready to negotiate with the Government of the German Federal Republic on this basis.

As a result of the West German *Bundestag* elections of September 1969, said Herr Stoph, a Government formed by the Social Democrats and the Free Democrats had come to power "for the first time in the history of the Bonn State". Although the new West German Government had expressed "contradictory and ambiguous views" about the policy it intended to pursue, some points had nevertheless emerged "which hint at a more realistic assessment of the situation created in Europe as a result of the Second World War".

"Willy Brandt," said Herr Stoph, "is the first West German Chancellor to speak, in a Government declaration, of the existence of two German States. Though this declaration appears to us to have been made some 20 years too late, it represents at least some progress. But words alone cannot convince us. Precise political deeds have to follow. The policy of the new West German Government can only be judged by whether it is prepared to respect the inviolability of the frontiers existing in Europe, to throw overboard completely the bankrupt 'Hallstein Doctrine', and to renounce once and for all the presumptuous claim . . . to be the sole representative of the German people. . . .

"Nobody can deny that the German Democratic Republic and the German Federal Republic are two independent States, which have existed side by side for more than 20 years. Consequently, their relations and their normal inter-State co-operation can only develop if they are free from any discrimination, that is, if they are based on the principles of international law. Consequently, the establishment of normal relations between the G.D.R. and the German Federal Republic is an indispensable necessity.

"Progress in this question can only be attained on the basis of political realities. The Government of the G.D.R. continues to be prepared to hold negotiations, on an equal basis, with the Government of the G.F.R. on the establishment of relations in international law.

"As far as the relations between the G.D.R. and the separate political entity of West Berlin are concerned, our attitude is sufficiently well known. It is above all in the interests of the citizens of West Berlin that the Bonn Government should renounce its interference in the affairs of this separate political entity, which has never belonged to the West German Federal Republic and will never belong to it."

East German Proposal for Negotiations
Correspondence between Herr Ulbricht and
President Heinemann—Proposed Draft Treaty

The East German *Volkskammer* passed a resolution on Dec. 17, 1969, in the following terms: "The German Democratic Republic advocates taking up relations with the West German Federal Republic on the basis of peaceful coexistence. The relations should be governed and secured by agreement valid under international law." It was added that the Council of State and the Council of Ministers had been authorized to "take the necessary measures" to this end.

On the following day, Dec. 18, two senior East German officials— Dr. Michael Kohl, a State Secretary, and Herr Hans Voss, a departmental head at the East German Foreign Ministry—arrived in Bonn bringing a personal letter from Herr Ulbricht, Chairman of the State Council of the G.D.R., to the West German Head of State, President

Heinemann. The latter's reply to Herr Ulbricht was conveyed to the East German representatives, and the text of the two letters was made public on Dec. 21, as follows:

Herr Ulbricht to President Heinemann.—In writing to President Heinemann, said Herr Ulbricht, he was "actuated by the desire to contribute to the securing of peace in Europe and to make possible the establishment of equal relations between the German Democratic Republic and the Federal Republic of Germany in conformity with the principles of peaceful coexistence". "Living next to each other peacefully," the letter continued, "and achieving good neighbourliness between the two German States, require that their relations be established on the generally recognized norms of valid international law. That can only be advantageous for the relaxation of tensions in the heart of Europe, for which the German Democratic Republic and the Federal Republic of Germany bear an especially high responsibility to their own citizens and to the people of Europe. Therefore I take the liberty of transmitting to you a 'Treaty Concerning the Establishment of Equal Relations between the German Democratic Republic and the Federal Republic of Germany', which has been approved as a draft by the State Council of the German Democratic Republic."

After stating that he had empowered Herr Stoph and Herr Otto Winzer (the East German Foreign Minister) to conduct the negotiations on behalf of the G.D.R. for the signing of the proposed treaty, and proposing that these negotiations should begin in January 1970 if possible, Herr Ulbricht concluded: "I voice the expectation that you, Mr. Federal President, and I will do what we can to ensure that the establishment of equal international relations between both German States be reached in businesslike negotiations."

President Heinemann to Herr Ulbricht.—After acknowledging the receipt of Herr Ulbricht's letter, President Heinemann replied: "I agree with you that we bear a high responsibility for relaxation of tensions in Europe. I, too, feel obliged, as does the Federal Government, to work for peace, relaxation of tensions and co-operation. It is in our mutual interest to protect the unity of the German nation. Therefore I welcome the readiness expressed by you to start negotiations.

"In conformity with the requirements of the Basic Law of the Federal Republic of Germany, I have sent your letter and its annex [i.e. the proposed draft treaty] to the Federal Government. It is for the latter to study your proposals and to take up a position thereon with the speed required by the issue."

The text of the proposed draft treaty between the G.D.R. and the G.F.R. annexed to Herr Ulbricht's letter was made public in East Berlin on Dec. 21 by *Neues Deutschland*. It consisted of nine Articles, as follows:

Article 1. "The treaty partners agree to the establishment of normal equal relations between the German Democratic Republic and the German Federal Republic, free of any discrimination and on the basis of generally recognized principles and norms of international law. Their mutual relations are based in particular on the principles of sovereign equality, territorial integrity, inviolability of State frontiers, non-interference in internal affairs and mutual advantage."

Article 2. "The treaty partners mutually recognize their present territorial existence within the existing borders, and the inviolability thereof. They recognize the frontiers which came into existence in Europe as the result of the Second World War, in particular the frontier between the German Democratic Republic and the German Federal Republic, and the frontier on the Oder and Neisse between the German Democratic Republic and Poland."

Article 3. "The treaty partners pledge themselves to renounce the threat and use of force in their mutual relationship, and pledge themselves to solve all disputes between themselves in a peaceful way and by peaceful means.

"Both sides pledge themselves to refrain from all measures contrary to the stipulations of Article 1 which would discriminate against the treaty partner; they will, without delay, repeal laws and decrees contrary to this treaty, and will revise relevant court decisions. They will in the future avoid any discrimination against the treaty partner."

Article 4. "The German Democratic Republic and the German Federal Republic renounce the acquisition of nuclear weapons or any form of control over them. They pledge themselves to take steps towards negotiations on disarmament. Neither chemical nor biological weapons may be produced, stationed or stockpiled on the territory of the two German States."

Article 5. "The German Democratic Republic and the German Federal Republic shall establish diplomatic relations with one another. They will be mutually represented in the capitals Berlin and Bonn by embassies. . . ."

Article 6. "Relations on specific questions will be agreed upon separately."

Article 7. "The German Democratic Republic and the German Federal Republic pledge themselves to respect the status of West Berlin as an independent political entity, and to regulate their relations with West Berlin in accordance with this status."

234

Article 8. "The German Democratic Republic and the German Federal Republic shall apply, without delay, . . . for admission as full members in the United Nations Organization. . . ."

Article 9. "The treaty shall be concluded for 10 years. It is subject to ratification, and comes into force one month after the exchange of the ratification documents. The treaty will be deposited with the Secretariat of the U.N. Organization for registration in accordance with Article 102 of the U.N. Charter."

In making public the text of the proposed draft treaty, *Neues Deutschland* said that it had done so because, it asserted, parts of the document had been disclosed by the West German Press "taken out of context or distorted".

Herr Brandt's Statement on Relations between Western and Eastern Germany

Relations between the German Federal Republic and the German Democratic Republic formed an important part of Herr Brandt's first Report on the State of the Nation submitted to the *Bundestag* on Jan. 14, 1970, in his capacity as Chancellor. Herr Brandt, who said that "there must, there can, and finally there will be negotiations between Bonn and East Berlin", spoke on this subject as follows:

"Twenty-five years after the unconditional surrender of the Hitler Reich, the concept of the nation is the bond around divided Germany. A nation combines historical reality and political will. It embraces and implies more than a common language and culture and more than a State and social structure. It rests on a people's enduring sense of solidarity. Nobody can deny that in this sense there is and will be one German nation as far as we can think ahead. The G.D.R. in its Constitution also professes itself to be part of this German nation.

"We must have a historical and political perspective when we discuss the state of the nation, when we reaffirm the German people's claim to self-determination. History, which has divided Germany through her own fault, will decide when and how that claim can be satisfied. But as long as the Germans muster the political will not to abandon that claim, the hope remains that later generations will live in a Germany whose political order all Germans can help to shape.

"In a European peace arrangement, too, the national components will play their role. But the path that leads to German self-determination within such a peace arrangement will be a long and thorny one. Its length and labours must not restrain us from seeking, in the present phase of history, if that is possible, regular neighbourly relations between the two States in Germany.

"However, the two State and social structures that have now been existing on German soil for more than two decades, reflect completely different and incompatible ideas of what the unity of Germany, what a common future, should look like and how it could be reached. Nobody should entertain the delusive hope of being able to evade the frictions that are unavoidable because Germany is not only divided as a State, but because there are two completely different social systems confronting each other on her soil. On this point we are agreed with Ulbricht—there can be no intermingling, no dubious compromise, between our own system and what has become a set order on the other side. . . ."

After repeating his Government's intention to reach a *modus vivendi* and subsequent co-operation with Eastern Germany, as declared in his policy statement of Oct. 28, 1969 [see above], Herr Brandt said:

"We are faced with a remarkable development. The States of the Warsaw Pact—except for the G.D.R.—have understood, though with some qualifications, the good will of the Federal Government. They have pointed out that words must be followed by deeds. It is our conviction that this rule should be complied with everywhere.

"There are leading elements in the G.D.R. who excel themselves in making ever new demands. One has to admit that they certainly do not lack obstinacy. Let me give three examples:

"(*a*) The G.D.R. Government demands of us recognition under international law. The other member-States of the Warsaw Pact expect us to conclude treaties with the G.D.R. which—naturally—must be just as binding as those concluded with them.

"(*b*) The G.D.R. demands of the Federal Government that it reconsider the Paris Agreements and that it reduce or even liquidate its commitments under the Atlantic Alliance. The Soviet Union and other Warsaw Pact States maintain that anyone who seeks to put the reduction or the dissolution of existing alliances on the agenda would block a European security conference. . . . I need not stress that as far as the Federal Government is concerned neither the Paris treaties nor our commitments under the Atlantic Alliance are matters for discussion.

"(*c*) The G.D.R. Government declares that it recognized the Oder-Neisse line definitively as a peace frontier 20 years ago, and that it did so 'on behalf of all Germans, that is, also on behalf of the West German population'. I do not know whether this declaration pleased the Government of Poland. Its logic would be that

Poland's western border is no subject for us. After all that I have heard, such is not the People's Republic of Poland's view. . . .

"There must, there can, and finally there will be negotiations between Bonn and East Berlin. . . . But on our part there are some guiding principles which cannot be renounced:

"Firstly, the right of self-determination;

"Secondly, the striving for national unity and freedom within the framework of a European peace arrangement;

"Thirdly, the ties with West Berlin without impairing the Four Powers' responsibility for the whole of Berlin;

"Fourthly, the Federal Government respects, and will continue to respect, the rights and responsibilities of the Three Powers as regards Germany as a whole and in Berlin. We have no thought of tampering nor of letting any one tamper with these rights and responsibilities. These include commitments both for the Federal Government and for the Governments of the Three Powers. I have worked in Berlin long enough to know that there are things for which our shoulders are too weak and regarding which the Federal Republic has no interest in claiming unrestricted sovereignty for itself. Nothing that we are trying to do in our relationship with the G.D.R. will touch the rights of the Three Powers referred to. . . ."

After pointing out that the German Federal Republic was firmly linked to the West, and the German Democratic Republic to the East, Herr Brandt continued: "I shall not . . . enter upon a futile debate as to why this has come about, and who is to blame for it. Most of us have their answer; some things will still occupy the historians. Governments have to proceed from the facts as they find them; they have to look ahead and study how today's conditions can be developed into a better future.

"In doing so, let us all realize that outside our nation there are not many people in this world who are enthused by the thought that the 60,000,000 and the 17,000,000 Germans—the economic potential of the one and of the other, let alone their armies—might merge. But there is no use in quarrelling about this now. I only want to make clear what I take to be the truth: despite everything, the unity of the nation exists. The unity of the Germans depends on many factors. It does not in the first place depend on what the Constitution says but on what we do. It does not in the first place depend on what the treaties provide but on how far we can win other States as our friends. It depends less on what was enacted at Potsdam in 1945 but rather on overcoming the division of Europe in the seventies, the eighties and—if need be—the nineties. . . .

"In this connexion there is no longer only one German question. Talking of Germany one must speak . . . of several German questions which must receive individual consideration, and not—as one tried to do in the fifties—be given one and the same answer. Nowadays each of these questions must receive its own answer, though not separate, and, above all, not isolated from one another.

"The fate of the Eastern provinces and of their people, the expellees, the people who have remained there, of those who have settled there and of those who have since been born there; the Soviet-occupied zone which became the G.D.R.; the three Western zones which came to be the Federal Republic of Germany—neither of them provisional creations any more, both of economic importance and most closely linked to one of the two super-Powers; and, not last, the reality of West Berlin, part of a four-Power city, subject to the Three Powers' unrestricted sovereignty. In addition, and on behalf of these Three Powers, the ties between West Berlin and the economic, financial and judicial system of the Federal Republic, as well as its representation abroad by the Federal Government.

"This, briefly sketched, is the position. . . . In the face of this situation the question arises: Which are the objectives towards which German policy should strive?

"The first answer is that those parts of Germany which today live in freedom must be kept free. . . . The second answer is that we must solve all problems only by peaceful methods. The third answer is that we must make our contribution in order that more human rights be granted and practised.

"Here, logically, the question arises: How can these objectives be achieved today by German policy? They cannot be attained any longer by the traditional means of the nation-State, but only in alliance with others. In future there will be no political settlements of significance outside of alliances, security systems or communities. In future German problems of importance can be dealt with not in terms of the nation-State and in traditional fashion, but only through gradual endeavours for a European peace arrangement. So it is a matter of seeing and respecting realities—not in order to put up with existing wrongs in resignation, but rather in order to remove the divisive character of Europe's frontiers. . . .

"The Federal Republic remains a Western State by its ties and conviction. The G.D.R. remains an Eastern State by its ties and the will of its leaders. These are the facts. They must not keep us from organizing neighbourly relations and from proceeding from confrontation to co-operation. This international objective implies an important task for the Germans both here and on the other side. The Federal Government is resolved to assume its share of the responsibility, with all ensuing consequences. . . .

"East Berlin has taken offence at our statement that the two German States cannot be foreign countries to each other. This, they contend, is of no consequence in international law. I do not now want to go any further into that. . . . After all, there are closer family ties between people living in Leipzig and Hamburg than between people living in Leipzig and in Milan or Warsaw. . . .

"The Government of the G.D.R. says that it is ready for negotiation. We, too, are ready, as we are ready for negotiations with other members of the Warsaw Pact. The Federal Government proposes to the Government of the G.D.R. negotiations on the exchange of declarations renouncing the use of force, such negotiations to take place on the basis of equality and non-discrimination. The exchange of views on this subject with the Soviet Union having begun, . . . we think it practical to enter upon appropriate negotiations also with the Government of the G.D.R. Such negotiations would provide a useful framework for a broad exchange of views on all questions relevant to an orderly relationship between the two sides. In this connexion it is not possible, of course, for one side to say—this is my draft treaty, take it or leave it. If that be the G.D.R.'s attitude, there could only be rejection.

"In our opinion it would serve an understanding if a direct exchange of views on all subjects of interest to either side took place prior to formulating details. Such is the customary practicable procedure which, for example, is used at the moment between the Federal Republic and the Soviet Union. Such an exchange of views or negotiations—however one likes to call them—could start soon. Each side must be free to bring up all points which it wishes to discuss. I shall soon make a corresponding proposal to the Chairman of the Council of Ministers of the G.D.R.

"The Federal Government will be guided in this by the following principles:

(*a*) Both States have the obligation to preserve the unity of the German nation. They are not foreign countries for one another.

(*b*) Furthermore, the generally recognized principles of international law must apply, especially exclusion of any distortion, respect for territorial integrity, obligation to settle all disputes peacefully and respect for each other's borders.

(*c*) This also includes the undertaking not to seek to change the social structure existing on the territory of the other contracting party by force.

(*d*) The two Governments and their plenipotentiaries should aim at neighbourly co-operation, especially in the technical field; understandings to facilitate such co-operation could become the object of governmental arrangements.

(*e*) The Four Powers' existing rights and responsibilities regarding Germany as a whole and of Berlin shall be respected.

(*f*) The Four Powers' endeavours to bring about arrangements for an improvement of the situation in and around Berlin shall be supported.

". . . In conclusion, I can state on behalf of the Federal Government that our attitude is determined by a dispassionate and realistic assessment of the situation. This means that the Federal Government enters upon the negotiations with the Soviet Union, Poland, the G.D.R. and others in the firm resolve to hold serious negotiations, and is desirous of the most positive development. It also means that it does not entertain any illusions concerning the difficulty of these negotiations, and that in view of the firm positions which it maintains and continues to maintain it cannot exclude the possibility of failure, although it certainly does not wish these negotiations to fail. The Federal Government, however, submits itself and the other Governments I have mentioned to the test of the earnestness of the efforts for *détente* and peace. . . ."

Correspondence between Herr Brandt and Herr Stoph on G.D.R.-G.F.R. Negotiations

Herr Brandt sent a letter to Herr Stoph on Jan. 22, 1970, suggesting that the Governments of the Federal Republic and the G.D.R. should open negotiations "on the exchange of declarations on the renunciation of force"; stating that the Federal Government was "willing to begin negotiations at any time"; and adding that Herr Egon Franke, the Federal Minister for Internal German Relations (*Innerdeutsche Beziehungen*), was available "for initial talks in which the course and progress of negotiations can be agreed".

"These negotiations," wrote Herr Brandt, "which should take place according to the principle of non-discrimination, should provide an opportunity for a wide-ranging exchange of views on the settlement of all outstanding questions between our two States, among them questions of equality in relations. Each side must be free to bring forward all those considerations, proposals, principles and drafts that in its view appear proper. Discussions and negotiations on these should be possible without any pressure of time."

Herr Stoph, in his reply to Herr Brandt (delivered in Bonn on Feb. 12), suggested that talks between them should take place on Feb. 19 or 26 "in the building of the Council of Ministers in the capital of the German Democratic Republic, Berlin" [i.e. in East Berlin].

The East German Prime Minister emphasized that "direct negotiations" should aim at bringing about "peaceful coexistence and a treaty on normal relations between the two German States on the basis of the generally recognized rules of international law". It was essential, however, for the G.D.R. and the G.F.R. to "recognize and respect each other for what they are, namely, sovereign subjects of international law with equal rights"; without such recognition the negotiations could have no positive results. Herr Stoph expressed regret that Herr Brandt had not taken up Herr Ulbricht's suggestion [made in the latter's letter to President Heinemann] for the conclusion of a treaty between the two German States.

Herr Brandt wrote to Herr Stoph on Feb. 18 accepting the latter's invitation to visit East Berlin for talks, but suggesting, in view of the Federal Government's commitments, that these should take place in the second or third week of March rather than on the dates in February proposed by Herr Stoph. Herr Brandt's reply was unanimously approved by the Federal Cabinet, and was sent after the Chancellor had had a meeting the previous day with his predecessor, Dr. Kiesinger, which was described as "very harmonious". The Christian Democratic Opposition announced on Feb. 18 that it supported the Federal Government's decision to enter into talks with the G.D.R. on all questions affecting the coexistence of Germans, including renunciation of force.

There ensued preparatory talks between high officials from both sides on March 2-12, during which it emerged that Herr Brandt intended to travel to East Berlin via West Berlin, where he planned to hold a press conference. The East German Government, however, took the line that a visit to West Berlin—which, it reiterated, was not part of the Federal Republic—by the Federal Chancellor would be "a mere provocation and as such unacceptable", and that it would burden or disturb the proposed Four-Power talks on the status of Berlin [see page 298].

In the circumstances the Federal Government proposed that the meeting between Herr Brandt and Herr Stoph should take place not in East Berlin but in Erfurt, and the East German Government agreed to this proposal.

First Brandt-Stoph Summit Meeting in Erfurt

Herr Willy Brandt, the German Federal Chancellor, and Herr Willi Stoph, Chairman of the Council of Ministers of the German Democratic Republic, met on March 19, 1970, in Erfurt (Eastern

Germany)—the first such meeting between the Heads of Government of the two States since their foundation after the end of World War II.

After crossing the East German border at Gerstungen, where Herr Brandt was formally welcomed by G.D.R. Government officials, the train carrying the Chancellor and his party arrived in Erfurt at 9.30 a.m. on March 19, being welcomed by Herr Stoph. Some 2,500 people, mostly young, were waiting outside the station, and as both leaders were crossing the station forecourt and entering the Erfurter Hof hotel opposite the station the onlookers broke through the police barriers shouting "Willy, Willy, Willy Brandt". When the crowd continued to call for him, Herr Brandt briefly appeared at an upper window to acknowledge their welcome.

Some 40 Western press representatives had arrived with the Chancellor, but the East German authorities, who stated that they had issued press permits to 350 correspondents from 42 countries, refused them to the majority of the Western pressmen.

During the opening session of the talks, which lasted until 12.30 p.m., Herr Stoph and Herr Brandt read lengthy prepared statements [see below]. Resumed at 3 p.m., the talks were interrupted an hour later when Herr Brandt, accompanied by the East German Foreign Minister, Herr Otto Winzer, left to visit the former concentration camp at Buchenwald, where he laid a wreath at the memorial to those killed by the Nazi régime. On his return Herr Brandt and Herr Stoph conferred privately for two hours.

Statement by Herr Stoph

In his opening statement Herr Stoph proposed that both sides should enter into discussions on the draft treaty between the G.D.R. and the G.F.R. which Herr Ulbricht had sent to President Heinemann in December 1969 [see above], and that they should consider the following seven questions of principle:

(1) The establishment of normal diplomatic relations between the German States on a basis of equality and non-discrimination. The G.F.R. should abandon any claim to represent all Germany.

(2) Non-intervention in the foreign relations of other States and the formal renunciation of the "Hallstein Doctrine".

(3) Agreement on the renunciation of the use of force between the G.D.R. and the G.F.R. and, on the basis of international law, recognition of their territorial integrity and the inviolability of their existing national frontiers in accordance with Article 2, Section 4 of U.N. Charter.

(4) Both German States to seek membership of the United Nations.

(5) Renunciation of any attempt to acquire or control nuclear weapons in any form. Renunciation of the production, use or stockpiling of biological and chemical weapons. Reduction of armaments expenditure by 50 per cent.

(6) Discussions to be held on residual matters arising out of the Second World War.

(7) Settlement by the G.F.R. of all debts and restitution obligations to the G.D.R.

Before listing the above demands, Herr Stoph, after welcoming Herr Brandt, expressed regret that the talks were not being held in Berlin "as originally agreed", and continued: "Our meeting is undoubtedly an event of political importance. For the first time since the establishment of the G.D.R. and the G.F.R. the two Heads of Government have met to consider the normalization of relations between their two independent sovereign States. . . . Both Governments have the responsibility of ensuring that never again does a war begin on German soil. . . . On behalf of the G.D.R. I can assure you that our entire policy is directed to the maintenance of peace, and towards this end the Chairman of the State Council of the G.D.R., Herr Ulbricht, sent to President Heinemann of the G.F.R. on Dec. 17, 1969, a draft treaty designed to establish equality of rights and non-discrimination between us based on international law. This draft treaty offers an opportunity to establish at last a relationship of equality and peaceful coexistence.

"Over the last 20 years we have repeatedly taken various initiatives, but . . . successive Federal Governments have failed to respond or have brusquely rejected them. The Federal Republic believed that by accelerating rearmament, and by undermining the G.D.R., it could achieve its aim of reversing the results of the Second World War. This policy has failed, and we hope that the sole remaining opportunity of establishing a relationship of peaceful coexistence based on international law will be used and this chance not be wasted again. . . . We are not here to discuss secondary or tertiary matters, as the present abnormality in the relations of our States is very dangerous. . . . In our draft treaty we require from you no more than we offer. This is real equality and non-discrimination. To say that it would be a matter of the capitulation of one side or the other is a complete twisting of the truth, nor does prestige enter into it. It is a matter of ensuring peace. Barriers and obstructions designed to support a policy aimed at changing the *status quo,* the alteration of frontiers and the revision of the results of World War II must be removed.

"In the change of government and the defeat of the CDU/CSU coalition we have seen the rejection of this dangerous policy by the broad mass of the West German people, and we hope that your Government will give heed to this expression of will. . . . The development of the G.D.R. as a modern socialist State cannot, and will not, be stopped. . . . You yourself have stated in the *Bundestag* that arrangements cannot be made with the members of the Warsaw Pact without also coming to an arrangement with the G.D.R. on the basis of equality of rights and non-discrimination. It would correspond to this realization if normal international, that is to say diplomatic, relations between us were now to be established, which would be in the European interests of both the G.D.R. and the G.F.R. . . .

"In your letter of Jan. 22, 1970, you expressed your willingness to negotiate with the G.D.R. on the basis of equality of rights and non-discrimination. It should follow from this that both States in their relations should recognize themselves for what they are, namely sovereign entities under international law. . . . This should lead to the recognition of the sovereign equality of the G.D.R. being expressed in a treaty valid in international law. . . . I therefore wish to ask you in the name of the G.D.R. whether you, on behalf of the Federal Government, are ready to take this step and begin negotiations on the basis of our draft treaty for the establishment of normal diplomatic relations, with the aim of signing such a treaty as soon as possible. . . .

"We cannot ignore, and are very concerned, that concurrently with expressions by Federal representatives of the desire to lessen tension and regulate relations, dangerous and aggressive military plans directed against the G.D.R. and other socialist States are being made and perfected . . . [by] the Federal generals and the Federal Minister of Defence. . . . And when Herr Schmidt, the Minister, urges more rapid rearmament, the G.D.R. and her allies cannot ignore such a development. This . . . is a matter of war or peace. . . . There can be no true peace until policies aimed at the revision of the *status quo* and of European frontiers are abandoned. . . . What can we make of statements made in the Federal Republic that recognition of the results of the Second World War must await a peace treaty? . . . Those who await a peace treaty, and at the same time prevent its negotiation, and yet in 1970 still refuse to recognize existing frontiers, can only intend to keep the door open for their revision. . . .

"Although you refer to 'internal German affairs' and indeed have a Ministry with that name, such a term has become meaningless after the division [of Germany] and your signature of the Paris Treaties, and it reveals political intentions incompatible with a normal relationship on a basis of equality between our States. Internal German relations cannot exist after the integration of the Federal Republic in the NATO system under the Paris Treaties . . . , the acceptance of which had not only an anti-national but an imperialist character. Article 2 of the Treaty on Germany retained for the Western Powers their rights and responsibilities for Germany as a whole, and Article 7 proclaimed as the aim of the signatories the integration of the G.D.R. into the monopolistic social system of the Federal Republic and into the Western imperialist pact system. . . . Equally untenable is the Federal Republic's stand on four-Power responsibility for the G.D.R. and its capital, Berlin. The G.D.R. is neither a four-Power nor a three-Power responsibility, but an independent sovereign socialist State. The phrase 'internal German relations' implies the old claim to subject the G.D.R. to tutelage. . . . This is unacceptable to us and cannot be discussed . . . [and] you had better cease such attempts to treat us in this manner. . . .

"Until the Federal Government became integrated with NATO, we kept open our border with the West in the hope that a realistic policy would be followed by the G.F.R. But the abuse of this open border for the unscrupulous fight against the G.D.R. cost our citizens more than DM 100,000,000,000 (£ 10,000,000,000) . . . , and we trust the Federal Government will understand that payment of its debt and the settlement of its obligations for compensation to the G.D.R. are an indispensable condition.

"Relationships between any two States always have a special character, as witness those between the G.F.R. and Austria or Switzerland, which are different from its relations with France. But the general rules of international law are the fundamental basis of relations between all States, and this applies equally to relations between the two independent and sovereign German States. . . . We are not simply 'all Germans'. . . . There are now two German States, whose citizens live under completely different conditions . . . and fundamentally incompatible social systems. . . . You yourself have said that there could be 'no mixing, no foul compromise' between the opposing social systems in the G.D.R. and the G.F.R. Indeed the two States cannot be united . . . , and mutual acceptance of this fact could help in the establishment of internationally valid relations between the G.D.R. and the G.F.R. Naturally, as socialists we are interested in the victory of socialism in all countries and thus in the Federal Republic. . . . But this is not a question of today or tomorrow . . . , and in the given circumstances there is no other way to ensure peace than the establishment of peaceful coexistence on the basis of international law.

"In a recent speech you referred to a *modus vivendi* between us, but this very term infers only a provisional agreement, based on the assumption that the existing situation—that is, the present balance of power between socialist and imperialist countries—makes it impossible to achieve more far-reaching aims and intentions . . . — a sort of interim solution under which one accepts *pro tempore* the existence of a socialist State but continues the hostile policy against the G.D.R. and waits for a change in the international climate in order to cross non-recognized frontiers. This is neither realistic nor a policy of peace. . . .

"Further, one cannot talk of normalization of relations when it is the practice of your Government to damage the G.D.R. and discriminate against it on the international level. Instructions are officially issued by your Foreign Minister to your representatives aimed at obstructing relationships between other States and the G.D.R., and even preventing the setting up of commercial offices . . . ; attempts are made to exclude the G.D.R. from international organizations . . . [such as] the World Health Organization; and your Government carries out discrimination against the G.D.R. by calling for the continued existence of the 'Allied Travel Office in West Berlin', even against the wishes of some NATO States. . . . The maintenance of the claim of being the sole representative of the German people and of the Hallstein Doctrine contradicts your declared intention that you would no longer discriminate against the G.D.R. . . . This claim must be finally and unconditionally dropped. Please note that the G.D.R. and its allies will act against all attempts by the Federal Government to prevent the G.D.R. from developing its international relations and to exert pressure on other States [in this respect]. . . ."

After saying that if the draft treaty put forward by his Government were concluded it would be "the first step in the right direction for 25 years", Herr Stoph proposed that the treaty be discussed "with the aim of establishing international relations between the G.D.R. and the G.F.R. on a basis of equality". He proposed that they should also discuss the above-mentioned seven points and continue their talks at a further meeting in the G.F.R. near the East-West German border.

Statement by Herr Brandt

Herr Brandt in his statement spoke as follows:

"No one need be surprised if I view many things quite differently from what has been said. . . . In a few weeks 25 years will have passed since the National Socialist régime of violence ended in the collapse of the German Reich. This event unites us round this table, whatever else may divide us. . . . Many will regret that after 1945 the German people could not go forward as one nation, but we cannot

246

undo the past. The situation demands that we make progress towards peace and seek ways of improving the lot of the human beings in Germany. . . .

"German policy after 1945 flowed from the differing policies of the Powers which had defeated and occupied Germany. The East-West confrontation overshadowed Germany and divided Europe. We cannot redress this division, but we can strive to lessen its worst effects and actively help in a development which aims to fill up the ditches which divide us in Europe and thereby in Germany. Although I consider myself free of the nationalism of earlier times, I nevertheless believe in the continuing and living reality of the German nation. Bonds of a common history, language, culture, family ties, and all the other imponderables which give us a sense of belonging, are themselves a reality. A policy which denied their existence would fail. This fact is just as basic as the fact that within the actual frontiers of Germany in 1970 there exist two German States which must live together. There are deep differences between us on social organization, but this should not prevent us from seeking—in the perspective of a European peace order—a regulated form of peaceful coexistence. . . .

"It should be our task to harmonize the interests of our two States, as well as those of the Powers with which our States are allied, in a way which will benefit peace and the people. The present relationship between us is the more regrettable in that dealings between ordinary people in both German States are depressed well below the level normally existing between foreign States and their citizens. This negative situation ought to be loosened up and, if possible, overcome. My Government's aim is *détente* instead of tension, ensuring peace instead of military confrontation. . . .

"It is unusual as between States that we should meet today without the normal preparation by officials and start with summit talks, but the problems before us are so great that only at governmental level can a start be made. This shows our joint responsibility: for whatever we do or do not do, we can no longer shelter behind history in general or Hitler in particular. . . . It is clear that the situation between East and West cannot be materially improved while tension continues in the heart of Europe . . . , and I hope that the Government of the G.D.R. is prepared to look forward and avoid becoming a prisoner of our dark past.

"It cannot be denied that a relationship of a very special character exists between the inhabitants of our two States such as does not normally exist between other friendly or allied States. . . . Our differences are also different from those between foreign peoples, and stem from the basic unity of the nation. There are other joint features. Both the G.F.R. and the G.D.R. are members of highly armed and opposing Pact systems facing each other heavily armed on German soil. They help to bring about an equilibrium of force in Europe, which has prevented the outbreak of war over the years and has given a measure of security. But true peace, and security of a lasting nature, can only be assured through a European peace order which would end the confrontation of the two blocs and the mutual antagonism of the two German States. . . . We are both equally determined that no future war should start from German soil again. Neither German State has either the right, or the possibility, of using force, or the threat of force, to achieve any ends. A democratic, peace-loving, united Germany can never be brought about through war or civil war. . . .

"There is a further matter on which there should be no misunderstanding. No agreements between our two States can affect, or replace, the existing rights of the Four Powers under the Four-Power Agreement on Germany of 1944. The same applies to our agreements with the Three Powers as it does to those of the G.D.R. with the Soviet Union. . . . These agreements, however, need not and should not prevent us from reducing the existing barriers between us.

"My reference to the Four-Power Agreement, and our agreements with the Three Powers, is made specifically in reference to Berlin. We have no wish to change the existing status of Berlin as long as the German question remains unresolved. . . . The fact that West Berlin is not administered by the Federal Republic has not prevented the Three Powers from delegating certain tasks to the Federal Government, for example the representation of West Berlin abroad, and the fostering of its economic viability. In effect West Berlin does not differ in economic, financial, legal and cultural matters from the Federal Republic, and neither the Three Powers, nor the Federal Republic, nor the ordinary Berliner would want to see any change in the status of West Berlin as defined by the Four Powers. . . . It is up to the Four Powers to decide how they will exercise their supreme powers in Berlin. Should an agreement between them lead to an improvement in the present position, we would welcome it. But I must make it crystal clear that, as far as my Government is concerned, all efforts to normalize relations and reduce tension in Central Europe are inextricably bound up with the normalization and reduction of tension in and around Berlin.

"The Federal Government has examined the draft treaty forwarded on Dec. 18, 1969, by the Chairman of the State Council of the G.D.R. to the Federal President, though we are opposed to the publication of draft treaties, particularly when there has been no previous discussion of the articles they contain. The Federal Government wants to try to enter in the first instance into an exchange of views, and for this reason has not produced a counter-draft. The goal of this preliminary exchange of views should be to determine whether a basis for negotiations exists, at the end of which there would be an agreed settlement of our relations. . . .

"My ideas about the nature and objectives of any negotiations to be conducted between us were transmitted to you in my letter of Jan. 22, 1970, as follows:

(1) Both States have a duty to preserve the unity of the German nation. They are not foreign to each other.

(2) The normal recognized principles of law between States should apply, in particular those of non-discrimination, respect for territorial integrity, peaceful settlement of all disputes, and respect for each other's frontiers.

(3) This includes the obligation not to seek to alter the social structure of the other by force.

(4) The two Governments should aim at good-neighbourly co-operation, particularly through collaboration in the technical and professional spheres.

(5) The existing rights and responsibilities of the Four Powers for Germany as a whole, and for Berlin, should be respected.

(6) The efforts of the Four Powers to reach agreements on the improvement of the situation in and around Berlin should be supported.

"I also informed you on Jan. 22 that we should agree on the mutual renunciation of the use of force, and that we should jointly declare that in their mutual relations and in questions of European and international security our two States would be guided by the general principles and aims of the U.N. Charter. We would therefore have to settle our differences solely by peaceful means. We should also commit ourselves, in accordance with Article 2 of the U.N. Charter, not to use force or the threat of force in questions of European security and in our mutual relations. Consolidation of the relations between our two States on a contractual basis would assuredly help to bring about a conference for the furtherance of security and collaboration in Europe.

"In your draft treaty there is a point concerning the participation of both States in international organizations. In my policy statement of Oct. 28, 1969, I had already announced that the Federal Government planned to participate more actively in other international organizations, and I also said that our and our friends' attitude towards the international relations of the G.D.R. would depend on the attitude of the G.D.R. Government itself. I propose that we discuss these matters in the course of our meetings later on. Progress in this respect would serve to utilize more than hitherto the capabilities of our people, our economy and our science for the benefit of peace, development, and the fight against hunger in many parts of the world. In order to be able to help effectively in this respect we should also aim at a balanced reduction of forces and weapons in the East and the West. . . .

"More than documents is required to normalize relations. Normalization must bring benefits to the ordinary man on either side. . . . We must first and foremost do all that is in our power to relieve human hardship. To quote two examples: we must find ways and means to unite children and parents still separated; we should enable engaged couples separated by the border to get married. The decline in our mutual trade has, much to my satisfaction, been stopped, but we should instruct our departments concerned not to be satisfied with the figures achieved. We should also strive for greater economic and technical exchanges; co-ordinate our planning for the construction of trunk roads; open additional frontier crossing-points; and provide other facilities in communications such as a speeding-up of passenger trains, creation of uniform freight-handling arrangements with through tariffs, improved technical collaboration of the two railway authorities, and improvements in inland navigation. To help improve communications between persons and firms with their partners in the other part of Germany we should arrange for the extension of telephone, telegraph and telex facilities and overcome existing difficulties with clearing accounts.

"Finally, I think of the numerous practical and administrative problems arising from the existence of the border and creating local problems. It would certainly be an improvement if ordinary visits, cultural exchanges and sports meetings between the two German States and in Berlin could take place at least to the extent that already exists between Federal Germany and several East European States. This would be a modest beginning, but we must begin somewhere if we seriously think of a normalization and if treaties are not to be mere words. Beyond this I state quite openly that it is my view that a real normalization must contribute to the breaking down of frontier barriers and walls, which symbolize the deplorable special character of our situation."

After declaring that he could not accept Herr Stoph's views on various aspects of the Federal Republic's internal development, on certain political groups and personalities, and on the role of the G.F.R. in the Atlantic alliance, as well as the particular role played by Herr Schmidt, the Federal Minister of Defence, Herr Brandt went on: "We are a loyal member of the Alliance to which we belong, as you are on your side. There is unlikely to be any change in our position in this regard until the Western and Eastern alliances produce changes in attitude affecting Europe—as I hope they will.

"You have twice asked whether I am prepared to begin formal treaty negotiations. I have replied that we are prepared to examine whether the time has come to negotiate—and I hope it has—on all matters which either side has raised, or will raise, during these talks. My starting-point is that our relations must be built on the basis of non-discrimination and equality. None of us can act for the other,

250

and none can represent the other abroad. . . . It must be the goal of both States to aim at a specially close relationship. . . .

"I have not come to Erfurt to demand the loosening of any ties the G.D.R. has with others, nor to demand any change in its social system. I would naturally reject any similar demands on the G.F.R. The Constitutions of both our States envisage the possibility of a unitary German State. This is also reflected in the treaties which we have with the three Western Powers and which you have with the Soviet Union. . . . It should be quite clear that nothing in these treaties nor in our intentions and aims should alter this perspective, which derives from the right of self-determination. Thus I remain convinced that expressions such as 'recognition based on international law' and 'non-intervention in internal affairs' are out of place in the context of a relationship of equality between the G.F.R. and the G.D.R.

"Your statement and mine show there is a long and arduous road to travel. . . . We cannot ignore what separates us, but we should place in the foreground those areas where agreement might be possible. That we should have exchanged such formal preparatory statements is an indication of the extraordinary circumstances which have brought the Heads of Government of the two German States together for the first time. However, we should perhaps now exchange our views in a more confidential manner, which experience shows does help matters. . . . This would also conform with the method used by both the Soviet and Polish Governments in their discussions with the Federal Government."

In conclusion, Herr Brandt invited Herr Stoph to a meeting in the Federal Republic in May for further discussions and suggested the nomination of delegates to prepare for this, to examine the proposals made by both sides, and to draw up a list of questions to be considered at the second meeting. This list, Herr Brandt said, might form the basis for discussing the further procedure, especially the future tasks of their delegates or commissions.

A joint communiqué published at the end of the talks announced that Herr Stoph had accepted Herr Brandt's invitation for a further discussion in Kassel (Western Germany) on May 21, 1970.

Second Brandt-Stoph Summit Meeting in Kassel

Statement by Herr Brandt

The Kassel meeting, held at the Wilhelmshöhe Schlosshotel, opened with a statement by the Federal Chancellor, who in the course of his speech outlined a 20-point treaty which, he proposed, should be concluded between the Federal Republic and the German Democratic Republic on a basis of equality.

Herr Brandt expressed the hope that "in spite of all our differences of opinion we shall be able to achieve progress both in matters of principle and on practical questions". Addressing Herr Stoph, he went on:

"Our meeting in Erfurt was without doubt an event of political significance, as you, Mr. Chairman, said in your opening statement at the time. It was keenly followed by our population, and attracted much attention in all those countries who take a special interest in what happens in Germany. This places a great duty and responsibility on us. We can only meet it if, as I said in Erfurt, we continue to search for areas where it will be possible to achieve progress for peace and for the people in Germany. . . .

"We both know that the way to a settlement of our relations will be long and arduous. We should not render it even more difficult by making unfounded reproaches and accusations, as has frequently been the case since Erfurt. The fact that we are meeting here today—something that we have both equally helped to bring about—should be proof enough that on both sides the will to reduce tensions is not lacking.

"I do not think it would be right to burden our meeting with polemical statements. I therefore confine myself to assuring you that the insinuations and imputations cast on my Government almost every day will neither be helpful nor make us abandon our convictions. . . . My Government has never concealed the fact that its attitude to the G.D.R.'s international relations is conditional upon the development of relations between the two parts of Germany. . . .

"Our attitude implies neither tutelage nor presumption. It reflects our efforts to improve the relationship between the two States in Germany step by step. Certainly, it would have been useful if in Erfurt we had agreed to appoint representatives and come to initial arrangements. But it is not too late to do that now.

"I have repeatedly proposed to you, Mr. Chairman, that we open negotiations for a contractual settlement of relations between our two States on a basis of equality. And I have also said that any mutual discrimination should be excluded by such arrangements. I formally underline this readiness. But if there is so much talk about discrimination . . . it must be mentioned that the G.D.R. has constantly tried to thwart the Federal Government's efforts to improve its relations with the countries of Eastern Europe.

"As I pointed out in Erfurt, the Constitutions of the two German States are based on the unity of the nation. Neither of them envisages division as a permanent state. I feel that we cannot achieve a meaningful arrangement of relations with each other without making allowance for these constitutional principles. This brings me to our actual task.

"I see no point in telling each other that one cannot take the second step before the first, and in arguing what the second or third should be before having taken the first one. To me it is in each case the next possible step that matters. As things stand at present, that next step can only be negotiations between our two Governments on practical and also political problems—and that in itself would be a great deal.

"The purpose of such negotiations ought to be to place relations between the two States in Germany on a contractual basis, both in the interest of the people and of peace and for the sake of the future of the nation. The Federal Government is prepared to do so. Naturally, such a treaty . . . can only be concluded on the basis of equality and non-discrimination. . . .

"In Erfurt I expounded on the matters to be settled. I left no doubt that contractual arrangements must be consistent with the special situation prevailing between our two States, but legally they must be as binding as similar agreements which each party concludes with third States. I also made it clear that we intend neither to bypass the rights of the Four Powers, which continue to have effect, nor to recognize the division of Germany under international law.

"However, I cannot believe that the demand for formal recognition is all that the Government of the G.D.R. can contribute to our negotiations, especially as it has failed to this day to indicate more specifically how it visualizes these relations. If the G.D.R. had nothing to offer other than charges and accusations, demands and conditions, then we would not be living up to the significance of this meeting, to the expectations of our people, and to our far-reaching task.

"In the hope and the assumption that this is not the case, I suggest that we today reach agreement on the opening of negotiations and on details of procedure. The arrangements I have in mind should include a treaty forming the basis for the relationship between our two States."

After referring to the proposed draft treaty between the G.D.R. and the G.F.R. which Herr Ulbricht had sent to President Heinemann in December 1969, and to the principles which he [the Federal Chancellor] had elaborated in his letter to Herr Stoph in January and at Erfurt, Herr Brandt set out the Federal Government's "concepts of the principles and elements of a treaty regulating relations between the Federal Republic of Germany and the German Democratic Republic on a basis of equality", as follows:

(1) The Federal Republic of Germany and the German Democratic Republic, "whose Constitutions are oriented to the unity of

the nation", would conclude a treaty regulating relations between the two States in Germany, improving contacts between the populations of the two States, and helping to eliminate existing disadvantages.

(2) The agreement should be submitted to the respective legislative bodies of both sides for approval.

(3) Both sides should "proclaim their desire to regulate their relations on the basis of human rights, equality, peaceful coexistence and non-discrimination".

(4) Both sides should undertake "not to use or threaten to use force against each other, and to resolve all existing mutual problems by peaceful means. This includes respect for each other's territorial integrity and frontiers."

(5) Both sides should respect the independence and autonomy of each of the two States in matters relating to their internal sovereignty.

(6) Neither of the two German States could act on behalf of or represent the other.

(7) "The two contracting parties declare that war must never again originate in Germany."

(8) They would undertake to refrain from any actions likely to disturb the peaceful coexistence of nations.

(9) The two sides should "reaffirm their intention to support all efforts to achieve disarmament and arms control that will enhance European security".

(10) The treaty "must proceed from the consequences of the Second World War and the particular situation of Germany and the Germans, who live in two States, yet regard themselves as belonging to one nation".

(11) "Their respective responsibilities towards the French Republic, the United Kingdom of Great Britain and Northern Ireland, the United States of America, and the Union of Soviet Socialist Republics, which are based on the special rights and agreements of those Powers with respect to Berlin and Germany as a whole, shall remain unaffected."

(12) "The four-Power agreements on Berlin and Germany will be respected. The same applies to the links that have grown between West Berlin and the Federal Republic of Germany. Both sides undertake to support the Four Powers in their efforts to bring about a normalization of the situation in and around Berlin."

(13) The two sides would "examine the areas where the legislation of the two States collides", and would "endeavour to eliminate such collision so as to avoid creating disadvantages for the citizens of the two States in Germany". In doing so they would "start from the principle that the sovereign authority of both sides is limited to their respective territories".

(14) The treaty should provide for increased possibilities for travel between the two States and for freedom of movement.

(15) A solution should be found for the problems arising from the separation of families.

(16) The local authorities in the border areas should be enabled to solve existing problems on a good-neighbourly basis.

(17) Both sides should reaffirm their readiness to intensify and extend their co-operation in various fields, e.g. transport and travel, posts and telecommunications, exchanges of information, science, education, culture, environmental problems and sport, to their mutual advantage, and to open negotiations to this end.

(18) As regards mutual trade, the existing agreements, commissions and arrangements would continue to apply. Trade relations should be further developed.

(19) The two Governments should appoint plenipotentiaries with the rank of Minister, and with permanent representatives, who would be "given working possibilities at the seat of the respective Governments and be afforded the necessary facilities and privileges".

(20) On the basis of the treaty to be concluded between them, the Federal Republic of Germany and the German Democratic Republic would make the necessary arrangements for their membership of and participation in international organizations.

"These proposals," Herr Brandt added, "together with the draft treaty proposed by the G.D.R. and other statements and suggestions that we have both put forward or intend to put forward, should be the subject of our further exchanges of views. . . ."

Statement by Herr Stoph

Herr Stoph spoke as follows: "We have come to the Federal Republic in order, for our part, to do everything once and for all to bring about relations between the G.D.R. and the G.F.R. on a basis of equal status and validity under international law, and in doing so to make a significant contribution to peace and security in Europe." Addressing Herr Brandt, he went on:

"Since my meeting with you in March, Mr. Chancellor, the standpoint of the German Democratic Republic has gained new and lasting support. . . . Additional States have entered into diplomatic relations with the G.D.R. It is apparent that the chances of the defenders of the 'Hallstein Doctrine' are fading. In the Federal Republic, too, there are growing numbers of people who are speaking up, with good reason, for the establishment of relations under international law between the G.F.R. and the G.D.R. . . .

"We have come to Kassel to receive a clear answer to the question of whether the Government of the G.F.R. has studied thoroughly our concrete, constructive proposals, and whether it is now ready to conclude with the Government of the G.D.R. a treaty on the establishment of equal relations on the basis of international law. In the name of the Council of Ministers of the German Democratic Republic I declare that we are ready to prepare and to sign such a treaty without delay. This would be the most suitable way to ensure relations between our States which could lead to the establishment of peaceful coexistence between the German Democratic Republic and the Federal Republic of Germany.

"It stands in contradiction to the most elementary interests of European peace when a State in the heart of our continent refuses to give international recognition to a neighbouring State, when it ignores its sovereign equality, when it questions its frontiers, and when it wishes to alter the territorial *status quo*. I should like to stress most strongly that recognition of the G.D.R. under international law and of the *status quo* in Europe is not simply a legal question, or a question of the prestige of the G.D.R., but a basic condition for peace and security in Europe. . . .

"Let us call a spade a spade. Those who refuse to accept international law as the basis for the relationship with another sovereign State obviously pursue aims which are contrary to international law and to the elementary principles of humanity. The refusal to recognize the G.D.R. and its frontiers under international law forces us to conclude that the intention is to keep the way open for aggressive acts against the frontiers of the G.D.R. and against its social system. . . .

"The slogan about 'liberating the Soviet Zone' which has been enunciated by others, and not only by Christian Democratic politicians, still echoes in our ears. After 20 years of a hostile policy by the G.F.R. with regard to the G.D.R., words alone about understanding and equal rights, promises about peaceful intentions, are not sufficient to bring about normal relations.

"Now a word with regard to West Berlin. In the past weeks the Government of the G.F.R. has emphasized in a sharpened form its illegal claim to West Berlin. Here it must be clearly stated that the independent political entity of West Berlin, which lies in the middle of the G.D.R. and in its territory, has never been a part of the G.F.R. and never will form a part of the G.F.R.

"The Governments of the three Western Powers have also repeatedly confirmed that West Berlin is not a province of the Federal Republic, and that it may not be governed by the Federal Government. If your Government, Chancellor Brandt, believes that it can bargain with or about West Berlin, then I must remind you that the Federal Government has no sort of rights or responsibilities in and for West Berlin; and that it therefore has nothing to bargain about in this matter. . . .

"At our first meeting in Erfurt, and in the subsequent weeks, you, Chancellor Brandt, have repeatedly spoken about equality and non-

256

discrimination. However, what has happened, particularly in the field of international relations, can only be described as a campaign for non-equality and discrimination against the G.D.R."

Herr Stoph then went on to criticize what he alleged to be West German opposition to the G.D.R.'s full participation in the World Health Organization and also in the work of the U.N. Economic Commission for Europe. As regards Herr Brandt's assertion that the G.D.R. had repeatedly tried to hinder the Federal Government's attempts to improve its relations with East European countries, Herr Stoph declared: "If anybody is disturbing relations between the G.F.R. and the socialist States, it is your Government itself. It is the Federal Government which refuses to recognize the results of the Second World War; which refuses to recognize the final nature of the Oder-Neisse frontier; which refuses to recognize that the Munich Agreement of 1938 was invalid *ab initio*."

Herr Stoph continued: "These specific cases raise the question as to what the Federal Government really means by 'equality'. Does it understand as equality that the Federal Republic should regard only itself as a subject of international law, while it refuses the same right to the sovereign G.D.R.? Does it regard it as equal that the Federal Republic should claim all the rights of a sovereign State in its international relations, but at the same time should attempt to deny the G.D.R. the same elementary rights? Does it understand it as equal that it should . . . cling to the claim to be the 'sole representative of Germany', even if it does not use this phrase?

"We should like to have your answer, Chancellor Brandt, to the following questions:

"Are you ready to give your active support to the preparation of a European Security Conference in which all States of our continent may participate with equal rights?

"Are you ready to recognize, finally and without reservations, the *status quo* in Europe and the frontiers of Europe, and to conduct your international policy on the principle of non-intervention?

"Are you ready to abandon the claim to sole representation [of the German people] and instead to act in accordance with the principle of equality?

"Are you ready to aid peace and security in Europe by agreed steps towards disarmament?

"Are you, above all, ready to conclude a treaty on the establishment of equal relations under international law between the G.D.R. and the G.F.R.? . . .

"The G.D.R. stands by its constructive proposals. Our proposals have been tabled and I should like to declare once again: We are ready immediately to conclude a treaty on the establishment of equal relations under international law between our States. . . . The G.D.R. would consider it most regrettable if an uncomprehending 'no' from the Federal Government were to make it impossible at the present time to establish such relations between the G.D.R. and the G.F.R. . . ."

There were formal sessions between the West and East German delegations during the day, as well as personal meetings between Herr Brandt and Herr Stoph. The Kassel meeting, like that at Erfurt, ended, however, without any agreement on the political issues dividing the two German States, no communiqué being issued.

At a news conference in Bonn on May 22 Herr Brandt said that he and Herr Stoph had agreed to continue their exchange of views at a later date; "that no concrete agreements emerged" [at Kassel], the Chancellor added, "shows once more how deep is the gulf that separates the two parts of Germany, and how much patience we must exercise". Herr Brandt pointed out, however, that the Kassel talks should not be seen in isolation, but in the wider context which included the negotiations in Moscow and Warsaw [see below].

Other 1970 Developments in East-West German Relations

Between the Erfurt and Kassel meetings of the German Federal Chancellor, Herr Brandt, and the Chairman of the East German Council of Ministers, Herr Stoph, in March and May several smaller steps were taken by the Federal Government to improve the general climate between the two countries.

Agreement on Postal Payments and Telecommunications

Negotiations held in Bonn between the Federal Ministry of Posts and the East German Ministry for Posts and Telecommunications resulted on April 29, 1970, in a partial agreement under which:

(a) The Federal Post Administration undertook, retroactive to Jan. 1, 1967, and until 1973, to pay to the East German authorities DM 30,000,000 as an annual lump sum compensation for the costs of inter-German postal communications as well as those from Western Germany through the G.D.R. to other East European countries; two earlier West German payments of DM 16,900,000 and DM 5,000,000 would be set against this total. The question of compensation for the period before 1967 remained open. In earlier

258

abortive negotiations in 1967, the East Germans had demanded total payments of DM 1,800,000,000 [see above, page 217].

(b) The number of telephone lines between Eastern and Western Germany would be increased from 34 to 74, and of telex lines from 19 to 35. Details of the improvement of communications between East Berlin and West Berlin remained unsettled, although Herr Georg Leber, the Federal Minister of Communications, expressed the hope that the effect of the new arrangements would also benefit Berlin.

West German Measures to balance Inter-German Trade

The Federal Government decided on April 30 to take the following measures to reduce the large West German surplus in trade with Eastern Germany:

(a) With effect from July 1, sales to Eastern Germany were made less profitable by the imposition of a value-added tax of 6 per cent; hitherto no such tax was levied on such sales.

(b) With effect from May 1, purchases of industrial goods from Eastern Germany were made cheaper by raising tax preferences from 5 per cent to 11 per cent.

It was hoped to achieve thereby more speedily a balance in inter-German trade, which had hitherto shown a rapidly growing deficit for the G.D.R. and a corresponding surplus for the G.F.R., the total imbalance accumulated to the end of 1969 having reached about DM 500,000,000.

West German Revocation of "Safe-Conduct" Law

The Act of 1966 granting safe-conduct in the Federal Republic to certain representatives of the East German Socialist Unity Party who might have been previously connected with the prevention of flights of Germans from the G.D.R. to the West (a punishable act under West German law) was formally abolished under legislation approved by the Bundestag on May 7, with the CDU/CSU members abstaining, and by the Bundesrat on May 15, with Bavaria abstaining.

The 1966 Act, which had been passed in connexion with the abortive proposal that SPD leaders should address an SED meeting at Karl-Marx-Stadt (Chemnitz) and SED leaders an SPD meeting at Hanover, had aroused strong hostility on the part of the East German and Soviet Governments.

4. TREATY BETWEEN WESTERN GERMANY
AND THE SOVIET UNION, AUGUST 1970

After prolonged negotiations between the West German and Soviet Government, a treaty on the renunciation of force was signed in Moscow on Aug. 12, 1970, by Herr Brandt and Mr. Kosygin, the Soviet Prime Minister.

Herr Brandt had first called for the conclusion of such a treaty in October 1967, when he was Foreign Minister in the Kiesinger Government.

Speaking on Oct. 8, 1967, at the Free University of Berlin, Herr Brandt called for "sincere friendship" between the German Federal Republic and the Soviet Union and, on behalf of the Federal Government offered to conclude a treaty on the mutual renunciation of force. Four days later Mr. Tsarapkin proposed to Herr Brandt an exchange of mutual renunciation-of-force pledges between the German Federal Republic and the German Democratic Republic.

In a Note on Nov. 21, 1967, however, the Soviet Government claimed that, as a member of the anti-Hitler coalition of World War II, it possessed, under Articles 53 and 107 of the U.N. Charter, the right of intervention in Western Germany in the event of the "resumption of aggressive policies by a former enemy State", The relevant paragraphs of the Soviet Note said *inter alia*:

"The U.N. Charter contains a number of passages dealing specifically with the rights and duties of the States of the former anti-Hitler coalition. Article 107 of the Charter states: 'Nothing in the present Charter shall invalidate or preclude action, in relation to any State which during the Second World War has been an enemy of any signatory of the present Charter, taken or authorized as a result of that war by the Governments having responsibility for such action'.

"In addition Article 53, Paragraph 1, which deals with enforcement action for the maintenance of peace by the Security Council, states that this does not affect 'measures against any enemy State as defined . . . in Article 107, or in regional arrangements directed against renewal of aggressive policy on the part of any such State'.

"Thus the acts undertaken by the States of the anti-Hitler coalition and the agreements concluded by them retain their full validity under the U.N. Charter. As a result relevant measures can be taken against the resumption of aggressive policies by a former enemy State."

In a statement sent on Dec. 8, 1967, not only to the West German Ambassador in Moscow but also to the Ambassadors of the United States, Britain and France, the Soviet Government demanded that Western Germany should recognize the existing frontiers in Europe; abandon its claim to represent all Germans; renounce all access to nuclear weapons; renounce the claim that West Berlin was part of the Federal Republic; and recognize that the Munich Agreement of 1938 was null and void *ab initio*. The Note also accused the Federal Government of fostering a "rebirth of fascism and militarism" in Western Germany. The Soviet accusations were rejected by the West German Government on Dec. 22, 1967, and by the three Western Powers on Dec. 29, 1967.

The West German reply recalled the repeated criticisms of the Federal Republic's internal and foreign policies expressed by the Soviet Government, which the Federal Government had "not deemed to require an answer" as in its view mutual polemics would not lead towards a relaxation of tension. The Federal Government expressed regret that the Soviet statement should give an "utterly distorted picture" of German internal policies and of the Federal Government's principle of seeking to achieve its aims by peaceful means only, as was well known throughout the world.

The West German Government had meanwhile asked the Soviet Government on Dec. 14, 1967, in an *aide-mémoire*, whether it was still interested in a continued exchange of ideas on the mutual renunciation of force, and reaffirmed its willingness to take part in further discussions. In its reply, handed to the Foreign Ministry in Bonn by Mr. Tsarapkin on Jan. 29, 1968, the Soviet Government stated that the answers received from the Federal Government to the Soviet proposals had not gone to the root of the matter because they had not been based on acceptance of the Soviet demands [see above]. The Soviet Government insisted that a renunciation-of-force agreement would have to be concluded between Western and Eastern Germany on the same basis as with the other socialist countries, and accused the Federal Government of underestimating the threat of neo-Nazism in Western Germany.

The Federal Government's reply, handed to Mr. Tsarapkin on April 9, 1968, set out proposals for negotiations with "every member-State of the Warsaw Pact", including "the other part of Germany", on an exchange of declarations on the renunciation of the use of force for the settlement of outstanding problems. The non-aggression pacts thus concluded, it said, while not to be regarded as a final settlement of European issues, would prepare the ground for a peaceful solution of these problems. The Federal Government also declared itself ready to sign a nuclear non-proliferation treaty; to negotiate with the Czechoslovak Government on the Munich Agreement; to oppose firmly all right-wing extremism; and to continue to respect the four-Power status of Berlin. On the other hand it repeated its earlier stand that Germany's eastern frontier could only be established by a final peace treaty concluded with a united German Government, and rejected Soviet assertions that the U.S.S.R. had a right to intervene in Western Germany on the basis of provisions of the Potsdam Agreement and the U.N. Charter [see above], as these, in the Federal Government's view, had been overtaken by the effluxion of time.

In a further *aide-mémoire* presented in Bonn on July 5, 1968, the Soviet Government said that if the German Federal Government was seriously interested in an agreement on the renunciation of force it must recognize the existing frontiers in Europe, "draw the necessary conclusions from the fact that two independent German States exist", abandon claims to nuclear weapons, and recognize the invalidity of the Munich Agreement *ab initio*. The Soviet Government described the Federal Government's Note of April 9 [see above] as an attempt "to avoid the question of concluding a settlement binding in international law on the renunciation of force in relations with the German Democratic Republic" and to "evade recognizing the existing frontiers in Europe". The *aide-mémoire* also claimed that "under the terms of the Potsdam Agreement the Oder-Neisse frontier was laid down once and for all and cannot be the subject of any discussion or bargaining".

Without notifying the German side, and in disregard of the arrangement to treat the exchanges as confidential, *Izvestia* published all the Soviet documents on July 11-13, 1968. The German Federal Government thereupon published its own proposals to the Soviet Union on the mutual renunciation of force on July 12, 1968.

Herr Brandt, in a press statement on the latter date, declared in reply to Soviet suspicions that "everybody should know that after what has happened the whole German people desires nothing more than the disappearance for all time of violence or threats of violence in relations between States". The Soviet Government, he went on, seemed to hold the view that such a renunciation of force and of the threat of force could not be agreed as long as the G.F.R. did not accept unconditionally all the unilateral Soviet demands. In its *aide-mémoire* the Soviet Government had demanded the right, even after a solemn mutual renunciation of force and the threat of force, to use force unilaterally against the partner of such a renunciation, on the basis of "long superseded provisions of the U.N. Charter on the relations between the victors and the vanquished in the Second World War". Expressing regret that the *aide-mémoire* "practically ignored" the arguments of the German Federal Government, Herr Brandt said that, "instead of a quiet and factual discussion of the problems", it contained "long polemical sections attacking the Federal Government, the unjustifiability of which is clearly shown in the documents now published". He added: "We reject violence as a means in international and internal German disputes. We are and we will remain ready to affirm this unconditionally by solemn mutual commitments *vis-à-vis* each member of the Warsaw Pact."

The protracted "dialogue" between the Federal Republic and the

Soviet Union was temporarily interrupted by the Soviet and Warsaw Pact intervention in Czechoslovakia in August 1968, but on Sept. 4, 1968, Mr. Tsarapkin presented another Soviet *aide-mémoire* which demanded *inter alia* that the Federal Government should abandon its previous East European policy and recognize the German Democratic Republic. Dr. Kiesinger, who was visiting Afghanistan at the time, said at a press conference in Kabul on Sept. 13 that "after the Czechoslovak adventure" the Soviet Government wanted to compel the Federal Republic to recognize the G.D.R. and to abandon all idea of a reunified Germany.

In a speech on the same day (Sept. 13, 1968) Herr Brandt declared that the Soviet thesis of a right of intervention in Western Germany in terms of Articles 53 and 107 of the U.N. Charter—previously put forward by the Soviet Government in its Note of Nov. 21, 1967 [see above], and repeated by Moscow Radio on Sept. 11, 1968—was "without substance" both juridically and politically, as the provisions of those Articles of the U.N. Charter had been superseded by the fact that Western Germany was a member of NATO. Herr Brandt described the Soviet reference to these Articles as "a massive attempt at intimidation".

Mr. Gromyko, however, in a speech to the U.N. General Assembly on Oct. 3, 1968, while reiterating the Soviet criticisms of West German policy, again returned to the proposal for talks between the two Governments on the conclusion of an agreement for the renunciation of the use of force. Dr. Kiesinger replied to this proposal in a speech at Ludwigshafen on Oct. 6, 1968, in which he offered to resume the "dialogue" with the Soviet Union which had been interrupted by the invasion of Czechoslovakia. In his speech Dr. Kiesinger rejected the allegation that his Government's policy was directed against the vital interests of the Soviet Union; stressed that only a peaceful understanding with the Soviet Union could solve the problem of the division of Germany; and declared that the Federal Republic was prepared to make every constructive contribution towards peace in Europe "as long as the unconditional capitulation of the German people is not demanded". In a subsequent statement in the *Bundestag* on Oct. 16, 1968, Dr. Kiesinger reiterated that "we want to continue our peace policy towards the countries of Eastern Europe in spite of all disappointments".

The next positive step, however, did not take place until July 5, 1969, when Herr Georg-Ferdinand Duckwitz, State Secretary in the West German Foreign Office, handed to Mr. Tsarapkin a document which related to the "dialogue" between the two countries and contained a reply to the Soviet *aide-mémoire* of July 5, 1968; no statement was issued on the contents of the document.

In a statement to the Supreme Soviet in Moscow on July 11, 1969, Mr. Gromyko said that the Soviet Union had repeatedly made it clear that the German Federal Republic had the same opportunities as other countries to bring about normal relations with the Soviet Union. "The difficulties," he went on, "are not created by us. The point is that the G.F.R. wants to obtain an improvement in our relations by making us abandon the principles of our European policy. But this is out of the question. Our people, like other peoples in Europe, will remember for a long time what aggressive German imperialism inflicted on them during the Second World War."

"A change in our relations," Mr. Gromyko continued, "is only possible if the G.F.R. follows the road of peace. For this, revanchist plans will have to be replaced by the realization that the future of the G.F.R. . . . lies in peaceful co-operation with all countries, including the Soviet Union. On this basis the Soviet Government is willing to continue the exchange of views with the G.F.R. on the renunciation of force, as well on other questions affecting Soviet-German relations. . . . It goes without saying that in such exchanges the Soviet Union will fully take into account the interests of our allies. . . ." After reiterating the Soviet stand on the question of West Berlin, Mr. Gromyko added: "We will take no steps which will effect the just interests of the German Democratic Republic and the special status [of Berlin]."

Following the formation of Herr Brandt's Government and the new Chancellor's statement on his wish to bring about an understanding with the Soviet Union, Dr. Helmut Allardt, the West German Ambassador in Moscow, on Nov. 15, 1969, presented a West German Note proposing the resumption of talks in Moscow on the renunciation of force by the two countries. It was announced in Bonn on Dec. 7, 1969, that the Soviet Government had agreed to a West German proposal that talks should begin in Moscow on the following day. An initial 90-minute meeting accordingly took place on Dec. 8 between Mr. Gromyko and Dr. Allardt, no statement being issued.

In a statement on Dec. 10 the West German Foreign Minister, Herr Scheel, said that the meeting on Dec. 8 between the Soviet Foreign Minister and Ambassador Allardt had "served to clarify a number of questions arising from previous exchanges on a renunciation-of-force agreement", and that German-Soviet discussions on this subject would continue.

Mr. Gromyko and Dr. Allardt had two further meetings on Dec. 11 and Dec. 23, on which no official statements were issued. On Jan. 27,

264

1970, Herr Conrad Ahlers (the Federal Government spokesman) announced in Bonn that Herr Egon Bahr, State Secretary in the Federal Chancellor's office, had been appointed to conduct on the German side "a very special phase" of the Moscow talks which, it was hoped, would "carry the somewhat broad discussions into concrete negotiations".

The Soviet-West German negotiations were continued in Moscow on Jan. 30, when a six-hour meeting took place between a Soviet delegation headed by Mr. Gromyko and a West German delegation headed by Herr Bahr and including Dr. Allardt. Herr Bahr had two further meetings with Mr. Gromyko on Feb. 3 (a three-hour talk at which Mr. Semyonov, the Soviet Deputy Foreign Minister, was also present) and on Feb. 6, again for over three hours. On Feb. 13 Herr Bahr had a meeting with Mr. Kosygin, the Soviet Prime Minister, lasting about an hour and a half.

On his way for a visit to India, Thailand and Singapore, Herr Scheel made a stopover in Moscow on Feb. 12 to discuss with Herr Bahr the progress of the German-Soviet talks; he was also welcomed by Mr. Semyonov and other members of the Soviet delegation taking part in the talks.

On March 22 a communiqué was issued stating that from Jan. 30 to Feb. 18 and from March 3 to March 21 an exchange of views had taken place in Moscow between the two delegations.

Herr Bahr visited Moscow on May 11, 1970, for a third round of exploratory talks with Mr. Gromyko, which lasted from May 12 to May 22 and which were partly conducted with Mr. Valentin Falin, head of the European department in the Soviet Foreign Ministry. On leaving the Soviet capital on May 22, Herr Bahr told journalists that all remaining problems in connexion with the preparatory talks had now been settled, that both sides were in a position to start formal negotiations, and that he would be making a "positive report" in Bonn on the progress of his discussions in Moscow. The official communiqué issued on the same day said that the exchanges of views between the two Governments on the question of a treaty on the mutual renunciation of force continued.

Guidelines for negotiating renunciation-of-force agreements with the Soviet Union as well as with other East European countries were approved by the German Federal Cabinet on June 7 at a special session. The official spokesman, Herr Ahlers, stated that the Federal

Government would seek negotiations based on observance of the following principles:

(1) "Relations between the German Federal Republic and the U.S.S.R. shall be based on the principle of the renunciation of both the use and the threat of force in exactly the same way as is already the case between the G.F.R. and the three Western Powers. This also applies to the inviolability of the territorial integrity of all States and their frontiers. The threat of force or the use of force will also have to be excluded with regard to differences of views or disputes which continue to exist after the conclusion of a treaty renouncing force."

(2) "The Federal Government's attitude on the question of Berlin remains unaffected. It proceeds from the assumption that the four-Power negotiations about Berlin will affirm the close ties between Western Germany and West Berlin, as well as unhindered access to West Berlin. Without such a safeguard a treaty on the renunciation of force will not be able to come into effect."

(3) "Existing treaties and agreements with third countries will not be affected by the envisaged agreement. This also applies to the German Treaty" [i.e. the London and Paris treaties on Western Germany].

(4) "The Germans' right of self-determination would not be affected by the non-aggression pact. The [Federal Republic's] Basic Law, including its preamble [which envisages all-German elections], remains outside the negotiations."

(5) "The Federal Government proceeds from the assumption that the agreements at which it aims with the Soviet Union, Poland and other Warsaw Pact countries, especially the settlement of its relations with the G.D.R. on the basis of the 20 points proposed by it at Kassel, will lead to the establishment and development of normal relations, and regards this policy for a better co-existence of the peoples and the security of peace in Europe as one whole."

(6) "The Federal Government notes with satisfaction that this policy is being approved and supported by the three Western Powers and the member-countries of the Western European Union."

On June 5 a deputy Federal Government spokesman, Herr Rüdiger von Wechmar, had made the following statement in reply to a question by the opposition Christian Democrats (CDU/CSU):

"The Federal Government is firmly of the view that renunciation-of-force agreements should not prejudice the material premises of existing points of dispute. . . .

"The Federal Republic is clear about the current goals of the

Soviet Union's policies for Germany and Europe. For its part, the Soviet Union knows—the Federal Government left no doubt about it during the discussions in Moscow—that there can be non-aggression agreements only in so far as our renunciation of force cannot be presented by the Soviet side as a renunciation of our efforts to bring about a just and lasting peace arrangement in Europe; to realize the German people's right of self-determination and of free political development, as is self-understood in a democracy. . . .

"It must not be possible to characterize our declared peaceful goals as territorial claims and as an infringement of the renunciation-of-force agreement."

The following written statement on behalf of the Federal Government was issued at the same time (i.e. on June 5), in response to a question by the Christian Democratic opposition, regarding the Soviet Union's reservation of unilateral intervention rights *vis-à-vis* the Federal Republic:

"Mutual renunciation of force may not be qualified, let alone made valueless, by one side's reservation of force. In our judgment of the legal situation, the Soviet Union possesses no intervention rights *vis-à-vis* the Federal Republic of Germany. The three Western Powers have expressed their joint agreement that none of the victorious Powers has unilateral intervention rights *vis-à-vis* the Federal Republic of Germany. And the Soviet Union has never expressly asserted that it possesses unilateral intervention rights *vis-à-vis* the Federal Republic of Germany, even though it has expressly stated that Articles 53 and 107 of the U.N. Charter are valid and applicable.

"The basis for the bilateral relationship between the Federal Republic of Germany and the Three Powers is contained in the Final Act of the London Conference, in which the Three Powers, without mentioning Articles 53 and 107, following a corresponding commitment by the Federal Republic of Germany, state that they 'will, in their relations with the Federal Republic, adhere to the principles contained in Article 2 of the U.N. Charter'. The Three Powers made this statement only after the establishment of a contractually settled relationship of confidence with the Federal Republic."

Finally, the statement said that there was "nothing to be added" to a declaration made by Chancellor Brandt to the *Bundestag* on Jan. 16, 1970, "to the effect that the Federal Government, in its relations with the Soviet Union, is striving for a status similar to the status we have by virtue of the interpretations and assurances on the part of the Western Powers".

The preparatory talks having been concluded, it was announced in Bonn on July 16 that both Governments had agreed to open formal negotiations on the treaty in Moscow on July 27. On the latter date Herr Scheel, the West German Foreign Minister, arrived in the Soviet capital, where he was received by Mr. Gromyko, the chief Soviet negotiator.

Opening their discussions on July 28, 1970, the Soviet and West German delegations continued their negotiations on the treaty for 10 days at a number of full meetings, as well as *tête-à-tête* talks between the two Foreign Ministers. Final agreement on the treaty was reached on Aug. 7, when it was initialled at a private ceremony by Mr. Gromyko and Herr Scheel, the latter returning the same day to Bonn. It was announced in that city on Aug. 9 that Herr Brandt had accepted a Soviet invitation to visit Moscow for the formal signing of the treaty.

Dr. Kiesinger, the CDU leader, said on Aug. 9 that there should be "no hectic rush" in signing the treaty and that the Opposition should be given sufficient time to examine it.

Herr Brandt, accompanied by Herr Scheel, arrived in Moscow on Aug. 11—the first visit of a West German Chancellor to the Soviet capital since that of Dr. Adenauer in 1955. During a three-day stay in Moscow (Aug. 11-13) Herr Brandt signed the treaty in the Kremlin on Aug. 12, Mr. Kosygin being the Soviet signatory; had a meeting with Mr. Brezhnev and talks with Mr. Kosygin; laid a wreath at the Tomb of the Unknown Soldier near the Kremlin Wall; and attended a dinner given in his honour by the Soviet Government.

The following communiqué was issued on the talks between Herr Brandt and Mr. Kosygin:

"The two sides are convinced that the treaty they have signed opens up favourable prospects for the successful development of peaceful co-operation between the U.S.S.R. and the Federal Republic of Germany in various fields, in the interests of the peoples of both States.

"They expressed confidence that the treaty would help to strengthen security in Europe, to solve problems existing there, and to establish peaceful co-operation among all European States, irrespective of the difference in their social systems. The Governments of the U.S.S.R. and the Federal Republic of Germany will contribute towards the realization of steps which serve these aims.

"The two sides also had a detailed exchange of views on a number of current problems of the present international situation.

"Both sides found it desirable to continue the exchange of views on questions of mutual interest at appropriate levels."

Finally, the communiqué stated that Mr. Kosygin had "gratefully accepted" an invitation by Herr Brandt to visit the Federal Republic, and that this visit would take place at a date to be arranged later.

Provisions of the Treaty

The treaty consisted of five Articles preceded by a preamble. Its text was as follows:

"The High Contracting Parties;
"Seeking to promote the consolidation of peace and security in Europe and throughout the world;
"Convinced that peaceful co-operation among States on the basis of the purposes and principles of the Charter of the United Nations accords with the aspirations of the peoples and the general interests of international peace;
"Noting that the agreed measures previously taken by them, in particular the conclusion on September 13, 1955, of the agreement on the establishment of diplomatic relations [see page 119], have created favourable conditions for new important steps directed towards the further development and strengthening of their mutual relations;
"Desiring to express in contractual form their determination to improve and extend co-operation between them, including economic relations as well as scientific, technical and cultural contacts, in the interests of both States;
"Have agreed as follows:
Article 1. "The Union of Soviet Socialist Republics and the Federal Republic of Germany regard the maintenance of international peace and the achievement of the relaxation of tension as a major objective of their policies.
"They affirm their desire to promote the normalization of the situation in Europe and the development of peaceful relations between all European States, and in so doing proceed from the actual situation existing in this region.
Article 2. "The Federal Republic of Germany and the U.S.S.R. shall be guided in their mutual relations, as well as in matters concerning the safeguarding of European and international security, by the aims and principles set out in the Charter of the United Nations. Accordingly, they will settle their disputes exclusively by peaceful means and undertake, in accord with Article 2 of the U.N. Charter, to refrain from the threat of force or the use of force in any matters affecting security in Europe and international security, as well as in their mutual relations.

Article 3. "In conformity with the foregoing aims and principles set out above, the U.S.S.R. and the Federal Republic of Germany share the realization that peace in Europe can only be maintained if no one disturbs the present frontiers.

"They undertake to respect the territorial integrity of all States in Europe within their existing frontiers;

"They declare that they have no territorial claims whatsoever against anybody, and will not assert such claims in the future;

"They regard as inviolable now and in the future the frontiers of all States in Europe as they are on the date of the signing of this treaty, including the Oder-Neisse line, which forms the western frontier of the Polish People's Republic, and the frontier between the Federal Republic of Germany and the German Democratic Republic.

Article 4. "The present Treaty between the U.S.S.R. and the Federal Republic of Germany does not affect any bilateral or multilateral treaties and agreements previously concluded by them.

Article 5. "The present Treaty is subject to ratification and shall come into force on the date of exchange of the instruments of ratification, which will take place in Bonn."

The treaty was drawn up in the Russian and German languages, both texts being equally authentic.

Herr Scheel's Letter to Mr. Gromyko—
Federal Government's Letter to Western Powers

The texts were also made public on Aug. 12 of (*a*) a letter by Herr Scheel to Mr. Gromyko on the question of German unity, and (*b*) a letter sent by the German Federal Government to the U.S., British and French Governments. Herr Scheel's letter to the Soviet Foreign Minister was worded as follows:

"In connexion with today's signature of the Treaty between the Federal Republic of Germany and the Union of Soviet Socialist Republics, the Government of the Federal Republic of Germany has the honour to state that this Treaty does not conflict with the political objective of the Federal Republic of Germany to work for a state of peace in Europe in which the German nation will recover its unity in free self-determination."

The German Federal Government's letter to the three Western Powers read:

270

"The Government of the Federal Republic of Germany has the honour, in connexion with the forthcoming signing of the Treaty between the Federal Republic of Germany and the Union of Soviet Socialist Republics, to state the following:

"The Federal Foreign Minister has, in connexion with the negotiations, disclosed the viewpoint of the Federal Government with regard to the rights and responsibilities of the Four Powers towards Germany as a whole and Berlin.

"As a peace treaty settlement is still outstanding, both sides have worked on the basis that the intended Treaty does not affect the rights and responsibilities of the French Republic, the United Kingdom of Great Britain and Northern Ireland, the Union of Soviet Socialist Republics and the United States of America.

"The Federal Foreign Minister has declared in this connexion:

'The question of the rights of the Four Powers is in no way connected with the Treaty which the Federal Republic of Germany and the Union of Soviet Socialist Republics intend to conclude, and is not affected by it.'

"The Foreign Minister of the Union of Soviet Socialist Republics has declared in this connexion:

'The question of the rights of the Four Powers will also not be affected by the Treaty which the Union of Soviet Socialist Republics and the Federal Republic of Germany intend to conclude. This is the attitude of the Soviet Government in this matter.' "

The U.S., British and French Governments, who had been apprised by Bonn of the contents of the treaty, delivered identical messages to the West German Government on Aug. 11 approving the treaty which was to be signed in Moscow between the Federal Republic and the Soviet Union.

West German Opposition's Objections

The *Bundestag* Opposition's main objections to the treaty were listed in a communiqué issued by the CDU presidium on Aug. 26, 1970, as follows:

(*a*) The Germans' right to self-determination was endangered; (*b*) the determination of frontiers must be reserved for a peace treaty; (*c*) concrete improvements in inter-German relations—in particular greater freedom of movement for people and ideas—had not as yet been guaranteed; (*d*) the question of the security of West Berlin and its future remained unclarified; and (*e*) the Government's policy, which was at the basis of the treaty, was threatening the foundations of Western integration and the policy of the Western Alliance.

5. TREATY BETWEEN WESTERN GERMANY AND POLAND, NOVEMBER 1970

Steps towards Normalization of Relations— Polish Insistence on Finality of Oder-Neisse Frontier

The appointment of Herr Brandt as Chancellor of the German Federal Republic was followed by a West German initiative for the normalization of relations between the G.F.R. and Poland, as stated above. Herr Brandt told the new *Bundestag* in his policy statement on Oct. 28, 1969, that the Federal Government intended to transmit to the Polish Government a proposal for the opening of talks between the two countries, "thereby responding to the comments made by Wladyslaw Gomulka on May 17, 1969". In Mr. Gomulka's statement of the latter date, to which Herr Brandt referred, the Polish leader had expressed the readiness of the Polish Government to conclude an agreement with the German Federal Republic provided the G.F.R. "recognizes without any reservations the existing Polish frontier on the Oder and Neisse as final and inviolate".

Speaking in Warsaw on May 17, Mr. Gomulka had referred to the Budapest appeal for an all-European conference on collective security and peace which had recently been made by the Warsaw Pact Powers. He accused successive West German Governments of having "stubbornly blocked for many years every initiative aimed at *détente* and at lasting peace and security in Europe"—citing in this respect the fate of the Polish proposal for an atom-free zone in Central Europe, and of the Soviet proposal for a non-aggression pact between NATO and the Warsaw Treaty countries.

Nevertheless, Mr. Gomulka continued, there had for some time been "tendencies in certain circles of the German Federal Republic which seem to indicate an intention to give a slightly different direction" to Bonn's eastern policy. He had in mind "certain statements made by the leaders of the West German Social Democratic Party" at that party's congresses in Bad Godesberg (April 1969) and Nuremberg (March 1968), "particularly those made by Willy Brandt, Vice-Chancellor of the G.F.R. and chairman of that party".

After emphasizing that "the touchstone of the policy of the German Federal Republic is, will be, and always has been the attitude of the

West German Government to the recognition of the existing frontiers in Europe, including the frontier of the Oder and Neisse, as final, and to the recognition of the German Democratic Republic as a sovereign German State with equal rights", Mr. Gomulka went on:

"In his speech at the Social Democratic Party congress in Nuremberg on March 16, Willy Brandt is reported to have said that he regards it as necessary to recognize or respect the Oder-Neisse line until a settlement in a peace treaty. This meant, he explained, that his party wanted to renounce the use of force and to be reconciled with Poland, even before the peace treaty if this was possible. . . . The substance of Brandt's attitude to the question of the frontier on the Oder and Neisse was also reiterated in a resolution by the Nuremberg congress. . . . One cannot fail to appreciate the fact that . . . the formula of the Social Democratic Party on the recognition by the German Federal Republic of the Oder-Neisse frontier constitutes a step forward compared to the stand taken on this issue by all previous Governments of the G.F.R. . . ."

Nevertheless, Mr. Gomulka continued, "even if one were to assume that the Bonn Government will accept Vice-Chancellor Brandt's Nuremberg formula, this would in fact change nothing in the present state of affairs. A change can only occur when the Government of the G.F.R. recognizes without any reservations the existing Polish frontier on the Oder and Neisse as final and inviolate. . . ." After saying that the G.F.R. was seeking to avoid recognizing the existing frontier as definitive because the Potsdam Agreements laid down that final delimitation of Poland's western border would have to await a peace conference, Mr. Gomulka declared:

"There are no obstacles of a legal nature to the recognition by the German Federal Republic of the existing Polish western frontier as final. We are ready to conclude such an inter-State agreement with the G.F.R. at any time, just as we concluded such an agreement with the German Democratic Republic 19 years ago. If, however, the Government of the G.F.R. maintains that the conclusion of such a treaty with Poland would be in contravention of the Potsdam Agreements, we suggest that it should ask the Governments of the Soviet Union, France, Great Britain and the United States whether the German Federal Republic has the sovereign right to conclude a treaty with Poland in which the existing Polish frontier on the Oder and Neisse is recognized as final. If Western Germany wants to exist peacefully with other European countries, if it wants real reconciliation with the nations of Europe, it must recognize the present political map of Europe. . . ."

The Chief Burgomaster of West Berlin, Herr Schütz, visited Poland in mid-July, and on returning to Berlin wrote an article for the Hamburg weekly *Die Zeit* advocating the normalization and progressive expansion of relations between Poland and the German Federal Republic; while in Poland Herr Schütz visited Warsaw, where he had talks with the Polish Foreign Minister, Dr. Stefan Jedrychowski; he also visited Cracow, the Poznan International Fair and the site of the Nazi extermination camp at Oswiecim (Auschwitz), where he laid a wreath in memory of the 2,000,000 Jews murdered there in the Second World War. On Sept. 1, the 30th anniversary of the German attack on Poland which started World War II, President Heinemann appealed in a television broadcast for "a new start" in relations between Poland and the G.F.R., saying that "that which has been achieved to our great satisfaction with our former historic enemy, France, remains an unfulfilled task in the case of our eastern neighbours, and especially Poland".

On Nov. 25, 1969, following Herr Brandt's assumption of the Chancellorship the head of the West German trade mission in Warsaw, Dr. Heinrich Böx, handed a Note to the Polish Deputy Foreign Minister, Mr. Jozef Winiewicz, which, it was understood, offered "comprehensive negotiations" between the West German and Polish Governments. The contents of the Note were not published, but it was described in West German and Polish press comments as a follow-up to Herr Brandt's policy statement to the *Bundestag* and also as a response to Mr. Gomulka's speech of the previous May.

The Polish Government's acceptance of the West German offer of talks between the two Governments was conveyed to the West German Foreign Ministry on Dec. 22 in a note handed over by Mr. Waclaw Piatkowski, head of the Polish trade delegation in Bonn; like the West German Note to Poland, its contents were not made public. On the same day (Dec. 22) the Polish Prime Minister, Mr. Cyrankiewicz, told the *Seym* of Poland's willingness to enter into talks with Bonn, but reiterated that the "starting-point for a process of normalization of relations" between the two countries was "recognition of the Oder-Neisse frontier as final".

The Negotiations

Herr Scheel, the West German Foreign Minister, announced on Jan. 27, 1970, that the Polish Government had agreed to a proposal by the German Federal Government that talks should open between the two countries "on all questions of interest"; he added that the talks would begin in Warsaw on Feb. 5 and that the Federal German delegation would be led by Herr Georg Ferdinand Duckwitz, State Secretary in the Federal Foreign Ministry [in which Herr Duckwitz was the second-ranking official].

Talks between the Polish and West German Governments—the first high-level negotiations between Poland and Western Germany since the Second World War—accordingly took place in the Polish capital on Feb. 5-6, the West German delegation being led by Herr Duckwitz and the Polish delegation by Mr. Jozef Winiewicz, the Deputy Foreign Minister. It was stated in Bonn that the talks had been "frank, factual and useful" and that they would be continued in Warsaw in the second week of March.

Herr Duckwitz and Mr. Winiewicz met for a second round of talks in Warsaw on March 9-11; a third round, also in the Polish capital, on April 22-24; and a fourth round in Bonn on June 8-10. No statements on these talks were issued, but after the Bonn discussions in June a joint communiqué said that the conferees had "concluded the phase of exploratory exchanges of opinion" and that the talks would be continued in July.

Herr Duckwitz and Mr. Winiewicz accordingly held another round of talks in Warsaw on July 23-25, followed by a further round in Bonn on Oct. 5-7. A joint communiqué after the latter meeting said that the negotiations had reached an advanced stage and that Herr Scheel, the Federal Foreign Minister, would visit Warsaw at the beginning of November for final talks with the Polish Foreign Minister, Dr. Jedrychowski.

At a meeting in Bonn on Oct. 26 of the parliamentary party executive of the Christian Democratic Union (CDU) and the Christian Social Union—the Bavarian wing of the CDU—it was decided not to accept the Federal Government's invitation to send an observer to Warsaw in November for the negotiations to be carried out between Herr Scheel and the Polish Foreign Minister. [The CDU/CSU had also refused an invitation to be represented in the West German delegation which negotiated the treaty with the Soviet Union—see above.] Dr. Rainer Barzel, chairman of the CDU/CSU parliamentary group, said there were three reasons why the party had declined the invitation to be represented at Warsaw: (1) the Federal Government had obviously already determined its policy towards the treaty with

Poland; (2) there was not the necessary degree of common outlook between the Government and the Opposition; (3) the Federal Government had committed itself so firmly in the treaty with the Soviet Union that it had no room for negotiations in the Warsaw talks.

The CDU/CSU parliamentary group had previously issued a statement on Oct. 15 which, while emphasizing the necessity for an understanding and reconciliation with Poland, declared that "future European solutions must not be obstructed by the political cementing of demarcation lines and borders" and that "everything must be done to make them gradually less rigid" [an obvious reference to Poland's western border on the Oder-Neisse line, although this was not specifically mentioned]. The statement added: "Until a freely agreed and enduring settlement is achieved, Poland can rely on being secure in its present form so far as the Federal Republic is concerned. Peace treaty settlements must not be anticipated either intrinsically or formally; the whole German people must be able to act in free self-determination." After saying that a policy of reconciliation and understanding should include the security of human and minority rights—a clear reference to the "ethnic Germans" still living in Poland—the statement advocated the early establishment of diplomatic relations between the Federal Republic and Poland, intensified contacts between the two countries in the economic, cultural and other spheres, and the creation of a Polish-West German chamber of commerce.

Commenting on the CDU/CSU statement, the Polish newspaper *Trybuna Ludu*, organ of the United Workers' (Communist) Party, said that it reiterated the "bankrupt thesis of the allegedly temporary character of our western frontier", and emphasized that recognition of the Oder-Neisse border was essential to a normalization of relations between Poland and Western Germany. Without recognition of this border as final, said *Trybuna Ludu*, there could be no diplomatic relations between Warsaw and Bonn.

Early in November Warsaw Radio declared, in reply to the argument by some quarters in Western Germany that under the Potsdam Agreements the German borders could be recognized only by an all-German Government, that this had not prevented the Federal Government from recognizing, by treaty and under international law, the western frontiers of Germany, e.g. with Belgium in 1956 and with the Netherlands in 1960.

Herr Scheel arrived in Warsaw on Nov. 2 for the final stages of talks on the treaty, which began on Nov. 3 and concluded on Nov. 14. During his 11 days in the Polish capital Herr Scheel had a number of meetings with Dr. Jedrychowski, both in private and in plenary sessions, the detailed provisions of the treaty being worked out by delegations which included Herr Duckwitz on the West German side and Mr. Winiewicz on the Polish side. At the conclusion of the meetings on Nov. 14 the Polish Government's spokesman, Mr. Romuald Poleszczuk, told journalists that the negotiations had been successfully concluded and that "the text of a treaty on the foundations for the normalization of relations between the Polish People's Republic and the German Federal Republic has been finally agreed". He added: "The talks were intensive and difficult, but their successful conclusion has confirmed the will and desire of the two sides to . . . prepare foundations for the opening of a new stage in mutual relations between the two countries." A statement in broadly similar terms was made by the German Federal Government's spokesman, Herr Rüdiger von Wechmar.

While in Poland Herr Scheel visited on Nov. 8 the site of the Auschwitz (Oswiecim) extermination camp. In signing the memorial book at Auschwitz, Herr Scheel wrote: "In the face of these horrors, this inhumanity, it must be our task to preserve the highest values— the dignity of Man, and peace between nations."

Herr Scheel returned to Warsaw on Nov. 18 to initial the treaty on behalf of the German Federal Republic, while Dr. Jedrychowski initialled it on behalf of Poland. Speeches were made by both Foreign Ministers at the ceremony.

Dr. Jedrychowski expressed the Polish Government's conviction that the treaty would be "a lasting foundation for the normalization of mutual relations" between the two countries, and that it would open "a new, successful and fruitful era for both sides in the relations between the two countries and societies". He went on: "At the same time, the treaty is a contribution by our two States to the cause of strengthening security and peace in Europe. It will promote the normalization of European relations based on co-operation, understanding and mutual advantage of the European nations, irrespective of the political differences and differences of system existing between them.
"During the negotiations agreement was reached on a number of specific problems involved in the initiation of the process of normalization after the treaty comes into force. These are difficult problems because they stem from a particularly difficult past. But on these

problems, too, mutual understanding has been reached and results have been achieved which, I think, will contribute to the building of normal relations between our countries. . . ."

Herr Scheel said that the Federal Government also regarded the treaty as "a decisive step in German-Polish relations which should make possible the overcoming of the painful past and the development of normal friendly relations between our two countries". He went on: "There has been hard bargaining on the wording of individual clauses. At the same time, however, these German-Polish negotiations have been carried out, by and large, with the intention of achieving results acceptable to both parties and of respecting their points of view and interests. They have been carried out with the awareness that what was involved has been a historical turning-point in the relations between our two States and that a smoothing of the way towards a lasting settlement between our peoples is important for all Europe. . . .

"A hard struggle is ahead," said Herr Scheel, "before the treaty receives the approval of the competent parliamentary bodies of the Federal Republic of Germany and of the German public. . . . I regard this as a normal procedure vital for a genuine German-Polish reconciliation. The Federal Government will continue its present policy undeterred; and I am confident that it has the approval of a broad majority of our people. . . ."

At the end of his speech Dr. Jedrychowski announced that the treaty, which, he said, was "of tremendous importance" to both countries, would be signed by the two Heads of Government, Herr Brandt and Mr. Cyrankiewicz.

The Treaty Provisions

The provisions of the treaty between Poland and the Federal Republic of Germany were published simultaneously in Bonn and Warsaw on Nov. 20. Under Article 1 both countries expressed their mutual agreement that the existing boundary-line on the Oder and the western Neisse constituted the western frontier of Poland; they also reaffirmed "the inviolability of their existing frontiers now and in the future" and declared that they had no territorial claims against each other. Article 2 pledged both countries to settle any disputes between them exclusively by peaceful means and not to resort to the threat or use of force.

Consisting of a preamble and five Articles, the text of the treaty was as follows:

"The Federal Republic of Germany and the People's Republic of Poland,

"Considering that more than 25 years have passed since the end of the Second World War, of which Poland became the first victim and which inflicted great suffering on the nations of Europe;

"Conscious that in both countries a new generation has meanwhile grown up to whom a peaceful future should be secured;

"Desiring to establish durable foundations for peaceful coexistence and the development of normal and good relations between them;

"Anxious to strengthen peace and security in Europe;

"Aware that the inviolability of frontiers and respect for the territorial integrity and sovereignty of all States in Europe within their present frontiers are a basic condition for peace;

"Have agreed as follows:

Article I

"(1) The Federal Republic of Germany and the People's Republic of Poland state in mutual agreement that the existing boundary line, the course of which is laid down in Chapter IX of the Decisions of the Potsdam Conference of Aug. 2, 1945, as running from the Baltic Sea immediately west of Swinemünde, and thence along the Oder River to the confluence of the western Neisse River and along the western Neisse to the Czechoslovak frontier, shall constitute the western State frontier of the People's Republic of Poland.

[The Polish text defined Poland's western frontier as "running from the Baltic Sea immediately west of Swinoujscie and thence along the Odra River to the confluence of the Lusatian Nysa river and along the Lusatian Nysa to the Czechoslovak frontier".]

"(2) They reaffirm the inviolability of their existing frontiers now and in the future and undertake to respect each other's territorial integrity without restriction.

"(3) They declare that they have no territorial claims whatsoever against each other and that they will not assert such claims in the future.

Article II

"(1) The Federal Republic of Germany and the People's Republic of Poland shall in their mutual relations, as well as in matters of ensuring European and international security, be guided by the purposes and principles embodied in the Charter of the United Nations.

"(2) Accordingly they shall, pursuant to Articles 1 and 2 of the U.N. Charter, settle all their disputes exclusively by peaceful means and refrain from any threat or use of force in matters affecting European and international security and in their mutual relations.

Article III

"(1) The Federal Republic of Germany and the People's Republic of Poland shall take further steps towards full normalization and a comprehensive development of their mutual relations, of which the present treaty shall form the solid foundation.

"(2) They agree that a broadening of their co-operation in the sphere of economic, scientific, technological, cultural and other relations is in their mutual interest.

Article IV

"The present treaty shall not affect any bilateral or multilateral international arrangements previously concluded by either Contracting Party or concerning them.

Article V

"The present treaty is subject to ratification and shall enter into force on the date of exchange of the instruments of ratification, which shall take place in Bonn."

The treaty was drawn up in the German and Polish languages, each text being equally authentic.

Polish Statement on "Ethnic Germans" in Poland— West German Notes to Western Powers

On the same day on which the treaty was initialled, the Polish Government communicated to the German Federal Government a statement on "measures for a solution of humanitarian problems", referring specifically to the position of ethnic Germans, or those who considered themselves to be such, still resident in Poland.

Recalling that in 1955 the Polish Government had recommended the Polish Red Cross to conclude with the Red Cross of the German Federal Republic an agreement on the reunion of families, the statement said: "Under that agreement roughly a quarter of a million people left Poland up to 1959. Between 1959 and 1969 an additional 150,000 people departed from Poland under normal procedures. In carrying out measures to reunite families, the Polish Government has been guided above all by humanitarian motives. However, it could not, and still cannot, agree that its favourable attitude regarding

280

such reunions be exploited for the emigration of Polish nationals for employment purposes.

"To this day, there have remained in Poland for various reasons (e.g. close ties with their place of birth) a certain number of persons of indisputable ethnic German origin and persons from mixed families whose predominant feeling over the past years has been that they belong to that ethnic group. The Polish Government still holds the view that any persons who, owing to their indisputable ethnic German origin, wish to leave for either of the two German States may do so subject to the laws and regulations applicable in Poland.

"Furthermore, consideration will be given to the situation of mixed and separated families as well as to such cases of Polish nationals who, either because of their changed family situation or because they have changed their earlier decision, express the wish to be reunited with near relatives in the Federal Republic of Germany or in the German Democratic Republic. . . .

"According to the inquiries so far made by the Polish authorities, some tens of thousands of people may fall under the criteria possibly entitling them to leave Poland for the G.F.R. or the G.D.R. The Polish Government will therefore issue appropriate instructions for careful examination of whether the applications submitted are justified, and for their early consideration.

"The Polish Government will authorize the Polish Red Cross to receive from the Red Cross of the G.F.R. lists of the persons whose applications are held by the German Red Cross in order that they may be compared with the lists held by the appropriate Polish authorities and carefully examined.

"Co-operation between the Polish Red Cross and the Red Cross of the G.F.R. will be facilitated in any way necessary. The Polish Red Cross will be authorized to receive from the German Red Cross explanatory comments on the lists, and will inform the German Red Cross of the outcome of examinations by the Polish authorities of transmitted applications. The Polish Red Cross will further be authorized to consider jointly with the Red Cross of the G.F.R. all practical questions that might arise from this action. . . .

"As regards the traffic of persons in connexion with visits to relatives, the appropriate Polish authorities will, after the entry into force of the treaty, apply the same principles as are customary with regard to other States of Western Europe."

The German Federal Government on the same day (Nov. 18) presented *Notes verbales* to the British, U.S. and French Governments pointing out that in the negotiations between the Federal Republic and Poland it had been made clear by the G.F.R. that the

281

treaty "does not and cannot affect the rights of the French Republic, the United Kingdom of Great Britain and Northern Ireland, the Union of Soviet Socialist Republics and the United States of America reflected in the known treaties and agreements" [on Germany, i.e. the Potsdam Agreements]. The Federal Government also pointed out that it could "only act on behalf of the Federal Republic of Germany".

In identical replies on Nov. 10 the three Western Powers noted with approval the initialling of the treaty and agreed with the Federal Government that "the treaty does not and cannot affect the rights or responsibilities of the Four Powers" with regard to Germany.

Herr Brandt on the Treaty—Statement by Parliamentary Opposition

The West German Chancellor, Herr Brandt, made the following statement on the treaty in a radio and television broadcast on Nov. 20:

"The treaty between the Federal Republic of Germany and the People's Republic of Poland is a moving document for both peoples. It is to close a dark chapter of European history. It is to open a new one. The time has come to draw a line and start anew.

"More than 30 years have passed since the Second World War began with the German attack. The Polish people had to endure untold suffering. The war and its consequences have imposed infinite sacrifices on both nations, on us Germans too. Now it is a matter of shaping a peaceful future for our two countries and peoples.

"Those who have lost relatives, those who have been deprived of their homeland, will find it hard to forget. And we others must understand and respect a burden they carry for all of us.

"Yet, in this very hour, I must ask those of our countrymen who have been expelled from their native homes not to persist in bitterness but to look ahead to the future. It means a great deal that many families now have the prospect of receiving in their midst relatives from whom they have been separated for many years, and that it should be possible for them to revisit the birthplaces and graves of their ancestors in their former homeland.

"I am in favour of the treaty with the People's Republic of Poland because it creates the foundation for a peaceful future. It offers us the chance for understanding and co-operation. To the Polish people the treaty gives the assurance that they can live within secure boundaries. And as far as we are concerned, it should enable the principle of renunciation of force to be applied to all of Europe.

282

"Only history will tell whether, as we hope, this will mark the beginning of real reconciliation such as, in the West, we have fortunately achieved with our neighbour France.

"The treaty does not of course mean the retrospective legitimation of injustice. It does not, therefore, mean the justification of expulsion. What we want, a quarter of a century after the war, is to make a serious attempt at putting a political end to the chain of injustice.

"And as regards Poland's western frontier: there can be neither *détente* nor secure peace in Europe unless—and without affecting the rights of the Four Powers with regard to Germany—we proceed from the situation as it is, as it has now been for 25 years.

"It is not that, today, our nation is abruptly required to make a sacrifice. It had to make it long ago as a consequence of Hitler's crimes.

"We can only hope that this treaty will constitute an inspiring step towards a better Europe; a Europe where frontiers will no longer separate. That is what the youth of our countries expect. We wish to spare them, if possible, the burden of the past. For their sake, we want to begin anew."

The CDU/CSU parliamentary group on Nov. 25 issued a statement defining its attitude to the treaty.

It re-emphasized that the policy of the CDU/CSU was aimed at achieving understanding and reconciliation with Poland, but expressed the view that the treaty appeared to be in conflict with the Basic Law (the Federal Constitution), the agreements with "our allies", and the Federal Republic's responsibility for the rights and the destiny of the whole of Germany, and that "a final frontier settlement" for "both German States" would in fact decide this question for the whole of Germany and thus confirm its division into two States. The statement also referred to a declaration by Mr. Gomulka on Nov. 24, according to which the speed of "the normalization of relations between the Federal Republic and the Socialist countries" was in part dependent on the recognition by the Federal Republic of the German Democratic Republic as a State with equal rights and on the admission of both German States to the U.N.; the CDU/CSU therefore asked the Federal Government to clarify whether "normalization of relations" with Poland would depend on or presuppose recognition of the G.D.R. The CDU/CSU went on to ask "the people of Poland and all our European neighbours" to understand "our duty and resolve to insist on the German people's right to free self-determination and a settlement for the whole of Germany by means of a peace treaty".

The CDU/CSU *Bundestag* group on Dec. 4, 1970, unanimously approved a resolution which was laid before the *Bundestag* on the same day. This contained provisions for a suggested treaty with Poland, which, based on the Oder-Neisse line and without prejudice to a peace settlement for the whole of Germany, would create a *modus vivendi.*

Such a treaty would cover (*a*) obligations binding under international law for the settlement of all disputes by exclusively peaceful means; (*b*) freedom of encounter for people of all social classes, as well as the binding and concrete settlement of all humanitarian questions with the aim of formally and materially safeguarding human rights and the rights of groups (in terms of the European Convention on Human Rights); (*c*) increased exchanges in the fields of culture, art and science, the expansion of trade, and the intensification of technological and economic co-operation; and (*d*) the assumption of full diplomatic relations, with the Federal Republic also representing West Berlin.

Signing of the Treaty

Herr Brandt flew to Warsaw on Dec. 6, 1970, for the signing of the treaty, accompanied by a West German delegation which included representatives of the Social Democratic and Free Democratic parties (the parties of the governmental coalition) and church, youth and trade union representatives; the Christian Democratic Union, though asked to join the official delegation, again refused to do so, though reiterating its desire for reconciliation and understanding with Poland.

The treaty was formally signed on Dec. 7 at the Radziwill Palace —the seat of the Polish Council of Ministers—by Herr Brandt and Mr. Cyrankiewicz, among those attending the ceremony being the two Foreign Ministers, Dr. Jedrychowski and Herr Scheel.

Prior to the signing ceremony Herr Brandt had laid wreaths at the Tomb of the Polish Unknown Soldier and at the monument commemorating the Jewish rising in the Warsaw ghetto during the wartime Nazi occupation. [The ghetto was razed to the ground after a three-weeks' siege and all Jews still remaining alive were sent to the gas-chambers.] During his visit to the ghetto memorial Herr Brandt fell on his knees and remained kneeling for half a minute before rising; after his return to Bonn he explained that by his gesture "I wanted to ask pardon in the name of our people for a million-fold crime which was committed in the misused name of the Germans".

While in Warsaw Herr Brandt had talks with Mr. Cyrankiewicz and Mr. Gomulka and took part in a joint press conference with the Polish Prime Minister after the signing ceremony; Mr. Cyrankiewicz said at this press conference that the treaty represented "a mutual victory over the past" and "a victory for peace and security in Europe". Before Herr Brandt flew back to Bonn a joint communiqué was issued stating that (1) Poland and the Federal Republic of Germany would raise their respective trade missions in Bonn and Warsaw to the status of embassies when the treaty had come into effect upon ratification; (2) Mr. Cyrankiewicz would visit Bonn at a date to be determined; (3) both Governments would "normalize" their relations still further by increasing economic, scientific, technological and cultural co-operation between them.

6. RATIFICATION OF WEST GERMAN TREATIES WITH SOVIET UNION AND POLAND, 1972

The procedure for the ratification by the German Federal Parliament of the treaties between the Federal Republic of Germany on the one hand and the Soviet Union and Poland on the other was rendered difficult for the coalition Government of Social Democrats (SPD) and Free Democrats (FDP) by the persistent unwillingness of the Opposition Christian Democratic Union and Christian Social Union (CDU/CSU) to accept the treaties in their existing form and by the fact that the Opposition held a majority of seats in the *Bundesrat* (Upper House of the Federal Parliament), while the Government had only a slender majority in the *Bundestag* (Lower House).

First Reading of Ratification Bills in Bundesrat

Drafts of the ratification Bills were submitted to the *Bundesrat* on Dec. 13, 1971, together with various supporting documents.

The latter included four "declarations in the context of the treaty" made by Mr. Gromyko, the Soviet Foreign Minister during the negotiations in Moscow which preceded the signature of the treaty with the U.S.S.R. According to the text of these statements, dated July 29, 1970, Mr. Gromyko had declared that (*a*) the concept of recognition (of present frontiers) had been dropped; (*b*) if two States (i.e. the two German States) voluntarily decided to unite or to correct their frontiers, it would not occur to the Soviet Union to criticize, since this was a question of sovereignty; (*c*) on the question of the possible future reunification of Germany both sides' positions were clear, and "we could make a treaty which would bury all plans for the reunification of Germany", in which case "any utterance about reunification would be in conflict with the treaty"; and (*d*) as regards the settlement of disputes, the word "exclusively" [by peaceful means] stood in the text of the treaty and "we have not envisaged any exceptions".

The first reading of the ratification Bills in the *Bundesrat* took place on Feb. 9, when a resolution introduced by those *Länder* Governments headed by the CDU/CSU [i.e. Baden-Württemberg, Bavaria, Rhineland-Palatinate, Saarland and Schleswig-Holstein] was also passed, by 21 votes to 20 (the Opposition's majority in the Upper House), in which the final decision was made dependent on clarification by the Federal Government of a number of doubts and objections. Among those speaking in the debate were both Herr Brandt and Herr Walter Scheel, the Minister of Foreign Affairs.

Herr Scheel referred to improvements in relations between the Federal Republic and the Soviet Union and between the Federal Republic and Poland since the signature of the treaties, alluding in particular to the conclusion of the four-Power agreement on Berlin [see page 298], the avoidance of the recognition in international law of frontiers, and the establishment by treaty of the renunciation of the use of force as the basis of Western Germany's relations with the Soviet Union. Herr Scheel also warned against distorted interpretations of the significance of the treaties by those opposed to them and the damaging effect which such interpretations would have. With regard to the question of the "recognition" of the European Economic Community by the Soviet Union, he said that this had nothing to do with the treaties; anyone who wished to do business with the EEC would necessarily have to enter into agreement with it.

Dr. Helmut Kohl (CDU), the Premier of Rhineland-Palatinate, announced in the name of the CDU/CSU *Länder* Governments that they would reject the ratification Bills in the *Bundesrat* if, as hitherto, the Federal Government were unable to give a clarification of the points at issue. He maintained that the current public discussion of the treaties was being falsified to an increasing degree by the

Federal Government's argument that any rejection or criticism of the treaties, however objectively based, would involve incalculable risks and dangers. Dr. Kohl admitted that a failure to ratify the treaties would temporarily involve difficulties but said that responsibility for this risk must be borne by the Federal Government and the parties which formed it. In his opinion the treaties suffered from ambiguity, and out of responsibility for peace one could not agree to treaties which clearly carried in themselves the germ of future conflicts.

Herr Brandt, dealing with the alleged ambiguity of the treaties, stated that the Soviet Union naturally had a different conception of the future of Europe from that held in Bonn but denied that there was any reservation on the part of the U.S.S.R. or any open or concealed disagreement. Nobody, the Chancellor said, who compared the text of the treaty with the Soviet Union with the demands made in the Soviet Government's memorandum of November 1967 and its *aide-mémoire* of July 1968 would be able to maintain that account had been taken exclusively of Soviet demands.

The resolution passed by the *Bundesrat* listed 12 principal objections to the treaties, which were answered by the Federal Government in a statement approved at a Cabinet meeting held on Feb. 16; the statement was submitted to the *Bundestag* together with the resolution of the *Bundesrat,* the ratification Bills, and accompanying documents.

First Reading of Ratification Bills in Bundestag

The ratification Bills and supporting documents were first debated by the *Bundestag* on Feb. 23-25; no vote was taken at the end of the debate, which was opened by Herr Scheel after Herr Brandt had delivered the "Report on the State of the Nation, 1972".

Herr Scheel said that the treaties had already stood the first test: without them there would have been no Berlin settlement. Commenting on the provisions of the treaties, he maintained *inter alia* that the undertaking to abstain from the use of force contained in both of them meant that the Soviet Union was no longer able to invoke an alleged right of intervention under Articles 53 and 107 of the U.N. Charter; furthermore, no legal bases for existing frontiers were created by the treaties, nor was any view on the frontiers' origin expressed in them.

On the question of German reunification Herr Scheel stated that a policy aiming at a state of peace in Europe in which the German people would recover its unity in free self-determination did not violate the provisions of the German-Soviet treaty; this followed from the letter on German unity which Herr Scheel had addressed to the Soviet Foreign Minister at the time of the signing of the treaty, and which had been accepted by the Soviet side without contradiction. Herr Scheel also referred to the provision in both treaties whereby treaties previously concluded by the contracting parties would not be affected; this included the 1952 Bonn Convention on Relations between the Three Powers and the Federal Republic of Germany [see page 87], in which the signatory States set out their agreement that "an essential aim of their common policy is a freely negotiated peace settlement for the whole of Germany" and that "the final determination of the boundaries of Germany must await such a settlement".

Dr. Barzel said that in the event of a rejection of the treaties the Opposition did not fear a "disaster", because not only did NATO safeguard peace and democracy but it was known in Moscow, as in Washington, London and Paris, that the agreements could be approved as a *modus vivendi* by the Opposition, subject to (*a*) a positive attitude by the Soviet Union towards the EEC; (*b*) the inclusion of the right to self-determination in the agreements; and (*c*) the agreed intention, which would be binding on both sides, to restore freedom of movement in Germany by stages. Dr. Barzel accused the Government of presenting for parliamentary approval a set of agreements which was incomplete because it neither settled nor solved the core of the problem—the situation of the Germans in Germany; he also asserted that the agreements gave the Soviet Union, Poland and the G.D.R. all or almost all that they wanted, but brought about "no progress for the Europeans and the Germans".

Dr. Gerhard Schröder (CDU), a former Minister of Foreign Affairs, accused the Government of dropping the Eastern and German policies jointly pursued by the parties up to 1969, though he conceded agreement with regard to the affirmation of the right of self-determination of all Germans, peaceful relations, understanding and co-operation with Eastern Europe including the Soviet Union, and abstention from the threat or use of force. Dr. Schröder rejected Herr Scheel's contention that the Government had chosen precisely the point in time which was the most suitable for the achievement of a result acceptable for both sides, and maintained that the Government could have negotiated longer with greater patience instead of hastily seizing what little was being offered.

Dr. Schröder referred to "not only differences but opposed viewpoints" in the interpretations of the treaties by the Government and by their treaty partners; though the Government had claimed that the treaties should lead to a *modus vivendi,* they were represented in the East and also to some extent in the West and in the Third World as a recognition of the *status quo* and thereby of the division of Germany. In Dr. Schröder's opinion, the commitment of the three Western Powers in the German Treaty [i.e. the 1952 Bonn Convention] that they would contribute to a peaceful solution of the German question was not increased but diminished by the new treaties, and he also expressed fears as to the long-term effect of the Government's *Ostpolitik* on the solidarity of the West, the balance of power in Europe, and the security of Germany.

Herr Helmut Schmidt, then Minister of Defence, declared that since 1969 the Western Alliance had set its mind on linking defence with a policy of *détente*; by rejecting the treaties the Federal Republic would put itself in opposition to its allies. Denying Dr. Schröder's assertion that a rejection of the treaties would be without substantial consequences, Herr Schmidt maintained that such a course would lead to difficulties in the Alliance and the danger of a crisis of confidence with the Soviet Union, resulting in a renewed Berlin conflict.

At the end of the debate the ratification Bills were referred for examination to the foreign affairs and legal committees of the *Bundestag*.

The foreign affairs committee of the *Bundestag* approved the treaties on April 25, following (i) a ruling of the legal committee on April 12 that the treaties conformed to the Constitution, and (ii) an opinion transmitted by the inter-German affairs committee on the same day that the positive effects of the signing of the treaties were already obvious and that this gave reason to expect that ratification would lead to a further *détente* in Europe, and thereby favourably affect the development of relations with the G.D.R.

Federal Government's Majority in *Bundestag* reduced by Defections—Soviet "Concessions"

Under Article 77 of the Federal Republic's Basic Law (Constitution), legislation not approved by the *Bundesrat* could be enacted only after it had obtained an absolute majority in the *Bundestag*.

As the result of a number of defections, both from the FDP and from the SPD, during the early part of 1972, it appeared uncertain whether the Government would obtain the necessary 249 votes in the *Bundestag* for approval of the treaties' ratification.

During March and April 1972 the Soviet Government took a number of steps which were generally interpreted in the West as concessions made in the interest of assisting the ratification of the treaties in Western Germany. Nevertheless the Soviet clarifications did not fundamentally change the *Bundestag* Opposition's attitude.

At a session of the *Bundestag* foreign affairs committee on March 16, Herr Brandt announced that in the course of the ratification procedure in the U.S.S.R., the Supreme Soviet would take "official note" of Herr Scheel's letter on German unity handed over at the time of the signature of the German-Soviet treaty; the Chancellor also revealed that the Soviet Union was prepared, after ratification of the treaties by Bonn, provisionally to sign a renewal of the Soviet-West German trade agreement which had lapsed in 1964, and that the new version would include West Berlin. This trade agreement was subsequently initialled in Moscow on April 7.

Pravda on Feb. 20 published an article in which it was asserted that, contrary to the view expressed by opponents of the West German-Soviet treaty that there were discrepancies between its Russian and German texts, both versions were equally valid. Furthermore, in a speech before a trade union congress in Moscow on March 20 Mr. Brezhnev stated: "The Soviet Union by no means ignores the situation which has come into being in Western Europe, including also the existence of such an economic grouping of capitalist countries as the Common Market. . . . Our relations with the members of this grouping will depend on the extent to which they for their part recognize the realities which have arisen in the socialist part of Europe, in particular the interests of the Comecon countries." [Recognition of the EEC had been one of the demands made by the Opposition in Bonn—see above.]

Narrow Defeat of "Constructive Vote of No Confidence"

The CDU/CSU *Bundestag* group, following a decision by the presidium and executive of the CDU, decided on April 24 to enter against Herr Brandt a "constructive vote of no confidence" which simultaneously proposed the election of Dr. Barzel as Federal Chancellor. This was the first occasion in the history of the Federal Republic that the Opposition had decided to attempt such a move, made under Article 67 of the Constitution.

The reasons for moving the vote of no confidence were primarily the Government's *Ostpolitik*, which was alleged to be endangering the security of the Federal Republic, but also the condition of the Federal finances; it was moreover maintained that the outcome of a *Landtag* election in Baden-Württemberg [in which the Christian Democrats secured an overall majority] had conclusively shown that the Government had no majority in the country and that the treaties could not be ratified in their present form.

The "constructive vote of no confidence" took place on April 27 in the course of a debate in the *Bundestag* which had begun on April 26.

Herr Brandt, speaking on the first day of the debate, accused the Opposition of "excessive polemics" and repudiated the CDU/CSU interpretation of the Baden-Württemberg election result. He said that his Government's foreign policy was "the attempt—certainly not easy but, I think, successful—to bring German policy into line with the prevailing international tendencies"; the Federal Republic's policy towards the Eastern bloc was closely interlocked with the policy of her Western allies, and therefore created "not less but more security for our people". With specific reference to the treaties, Herr Brandt denied the existence of any secret agreements and criticized the use made by the Opposition of alleged extracts from the negotiating records relating to the Moscow treaty, which had been sent anonymously to a number of CDU/CSU deputies earlier in the month.

Dr. Barzel said with regard to the alleged extracts that it was the Government which through its spokesman had first commented on the contents of these papers. He maintained that the Soviet Government's willingness for further talks on the treaties was as incontestable as its determination to come to an arrangement with the Federal Republic, and reaffirmed the Opposition's belief in the importance of improving relations with the Soviet Union, Poland and Czechoslovakia through treaties on the renunciation of the use of force.

Herr Brandt described the vote of no confidence on April 27 as an attempt on the part of the Opposition to emerge from "the irresponsibility of [giving] a sterile 'no' to the vital questions of our people" but with the risk of a bitter responsibility for the Opposition if it should succeed. . . . After referring to a traffic treaty with Eastern Germany, which had been completed the previous night, and asking if anyone wished to endanger what had been achieved in inter-German relations, Herr Brandt affirmed his conviction that the Government would continue in office after the vote and alluded to the possibility of an attempt to define areas of common responsibility with the Opposition.

The "constructive vote of no confidence" taken on April 27 fell short by only two votes of the necessary absolute majority of 249 votes; 247 votes were cast in favour of the motion and 10 against, with three abstentions.

Formulation of Joint Resolution

Between April 28 and May 10 a number of discussions were held between representatives of the three political parties, while in the latter part of this period the Soviet Ambassador in Bonn, Mr. Valentin Falin, was also consulted. These discussions led to agreement on a joint resolution to be adopted by the *Bundestag* [see below].

Following consultations on May 3 to examine the demands of the CDU/CSU for "recognition" of the EEC by the Soviet Union, incorporation of the right of self-determination in the agreements, and binding agreements on freedom of movement between the two German States, Herr Brandt and Dr. Barzel agreed on May 4 to postpone the ratification debate until the following week, and a group of experts drawn from the three parties was formed to draw up a draft of a joint text of the proposed resolution.

It was agreed on May 5 that the negotiating documents covering the discussions with the Soviet Union might be inspected by Herr Kurt Birrenbach, a CDU deputy, who was received at the Foreign Ministry on the evening of May 5 and again on May 6.

On May 9 confusion was caused by a report that the Soviet Government had refused to accept two passages in the text of the resolution, the first of which stated that "the treaties do not anticipate a peace settlement for Germany by treaty and do not create any legal basis for the frontiers existing today", and the second that "the rights and responsibilities of the four Powers with regard to Germany as a whole and to Berlin are not affected by the treaties" [see below].

However, during the night of May 9-10 the Soviet Ambassador was received for talks at the Foreign Ministry, after which a Foreign Ministry spokesman stated that the Soviet Union was prepared to accept the joint resolution in the formulation agreed by all parties; in an overnight letter to Dr. Barzel, Herr Scheel confirmed that all Soviet doubts had been resolved and that the entire text of the resolution would be accepted by the Soviet Government without alteration.

Second Reading of Ratification Bills in *Bundestag*—
Text of Joint Resolution

In spite of these developments, the CDU/CSU moved in the *Bundestag* on May 10 that the ratification debate should be postponed. In the ballot—in which the Berlin deputies also participated (as this was a procedural matter)—259 votes were cast in favour and 259 against, but under the rules of the *Bundestag* the motion was thereby rejected. However, it was decided by inter-party agreement later in the day that the vote on the ratification Bills should in fact be postponed for a week until May 17.

Herr Brandt said during the debate on May 10 that when the treaties came into effect the Federal Republic would be able to pursue an Eastern policy on the same terms as other Western countries; the immediate result would be that the Berlin agreement would come into effect and humanitarian improvements would be achieved in relations with the G.D.R., while there could also be an agreement with Czechoslovakia, as well as diplomatic relations with Hungary and Bulgaria and greater economic, technical and cultural co-operation with the Soviet Union.

The Chancellor thanked the Opposition for its efforts to reach agreement with the Government, and stated that there were no longer any differences of opinion with the Soviet Union on the text of the joint resolution. In the course of his speech he also assured the Soviet and Polish Governments that the passage in the resolution in which it was stated that the treaties created no legal basis for existing frontiers did not devalue the recognition of the Oder-Neisse frontier by the Federal Republic contained in the Moscow treaty.

On May 15 the CDU presidium approved by 27 votes to one, with one abstention, a statement which listed the clarifications which had been achieved with regard to the treaties and affirmed that the joint resolution was clear in its meaning and that "we act in accordance with the treaties if we base our policy on this resolution". However, the CSU parliamentary group in a meeting held on the same day voted unanimously in favour of a rejection of the treaties, and, if necessary, a vote against them in the ballot. At the end of a meeting which began on May 16 and continued on the following day the CDU/CSU parliamentary group finally voted by a large majority in favour of a proposal, supported by Dr. Barzel and originally put forward by Professor Walter Hallstein, that the Opposition should abstain in the vote on the treaties.

In an introductory report Dr. Barzel had recommended approval of the treaties on the ground that earlier objections had been met as a result of the Opposition's efforts, but this viewpoint was rejected by Herr Strauss, speaking on behalf of the CSU, and it was reported that on the evening of May 16 it was apparent that important sections of the CDU/CSU, including the entire CSU, wished to vote in favour of the joint resolution but against the treaties.

In the course of the same meeting Dr. Kohl promised that he would advise the CDU/CSU *Land* Governments not to raise objections to the treaties on the second reading of the ratification Bills by the *Bundesrat*.

Voting on the ratification Bills and on the joint resolution took place in the *Bundestag* on May 17, the results being as follows:

	For	Against	Abstentions
Treaty with Soviet Union	248	10	238
Treaty with Poland	248	17	231
Joint Resolution	513	—	5

In the voting on the joint resolution all 518 members of the *Bundestag* were permitted to take part, whereas on the treaties themselves the 22 Berlin deputies were not allowed to vote.

The text of the joint resolution was as follows:

"In connexion with the voting on the treaty between the Federal Republic of Germany and the Union of Soviet Socialist Republics of Aug. 12, 1970, and the treaty between the Federal Republic of Germany and the People's Republic of Poland concerning the basis for the normalization of their mutual relations of Dec. 7, 1970, the German *Bundestag* declares:

"(1) One of the determining aims of our foreign policy is the preservation of peace in Europe and of the security of the Federal Republic of Germany. The treaties with Moscow and Warsaw, in which the contracting parties solemnly and wholly renounce the use and the threat of force, are intended to serve these aims; they are important elements of the *modus vivendi* which the Federal Republic of Germany seeks to establish with its Eastern neighbours.

"(2) The Federal Republic of Germany has assumed in its own name the obligations which it undertook in the treaties. In this respect the treaties proceed from the frontiers as existing today, the unilateral alteration of which they exclude; the treaties do not anticipate a peace settlement for Germany by treaty and do not create any legal basis for the frontiers existing today.

"(3) The inalienable right to self-determination is not affected by the treaties. The policy of the Federal Republic of Germany, which aims at a peaceful restoration of national unity within the European framework, is not inconsistent with the treaties, which do not prejudice the solution of the German question. By the demand for the realization of the right to self-determination the Federal Republic of Germany does not make any territorial claim or a claim for an alteration of frontiers.

"(4) The German *Bundestag* states that the continuing and unrestricted validity of the Bonn Conventions and of the related arrangements and declarations of 1954, as well as the continued validity of the agreement concluded on Sept. 13, 1955, between the Federal Republic of Germany and the Union of Soviet Socialist Republics, are not affected by the treaties.

"(5) The rights and responsibilities of the four Powers with regard to Germany as a whole and to Berlin are not affected by the treaties. The German *Bundestag*, in view of the fact that the final settlement of the German question as a whole is still outstanding, considers as essential the continuance of these rights and responsibilities.

"(6) As regards the significance of the treaties, the German *Bundestag* furthermore refers to the memoranda which the Federal Government has submitted to the legislative bodies together with the Bills for the ratification of the Moscow and Warsaw treaties.

"(7) The Federal Republic of Germany is firmly embedded in the Atlantic Alliance, upon which, now as before, its security and freedom depend.

"(8) The Federal Republic of Germany, together with its partners in the [European] Community, will unwaveringly pursue the policy of European unification, with the aim of developing the Community progressively into a political union. In this connexion the Federal Republic of Germany proceeds on the assumption that the Soviet Union and other socialist countries will enter into co-operation with the E.E.C.

"(9) The Federal Republic of Germany confirms its firm resolve to maintain and develop the ties between Berlin (West) and the Federal Republic of Germany in accordance with the four-Power agreement and the German supplementary agreements. It will also in the future ensure the city's viability and the welfare of its people.

"(10) The Federal Republic of Germany advocates the normalization of the relationship between the Federal Republic of Germany and the G.D.R. It proceeds on the assumption that the principles of *détente* and good neighbourliness will be fully applied to the relationship between the people and institutions of both parts of Germany."

The action of the *Bundestag* in approving the ratification Bills was welcomed on May 18 by, *inter alios*, leaders of both Eastern Germany and Czechoslovakia.

Herr Erich Honecker, First Secretary of the East German Socialist Unity Party, described the approval by the *Bundestag* as an important step for the success of movements towards *détente* in Europe; with the ratification of the treaties, he said, the results of the Second

World War and of post-war developments had been embodied in international law. Dr. Gustav Husak, First Secretary of the Czechoslovak Communist Party, declared that the time had now come for the restoration of "normal neighbourly relations on our western frontier".

Second Reading of Ratification Bills in *Bundesrat*— Signature of Legislation by President Heinemann

The foreign affairs committee of the *Bundesrat* on May 18 passed a resolution recommending the Upper House to allow the Bills to go through without an appeal to the mediation committee and also to endorse the joint resolution of the *Bundestag*. This course of action was followed by the *Bundesrat* on the following day, the representatives of SPD or SPD/FDP *Länder* Governments voting against an appeal and those of the CDU/CSU *Land* Governments abstaining (20 votes in favour, with 21 abstentions); the joint resolution was endorsed unanimously.

President Heinemann on May 23 signed the ratification Bills which came into force 24 hours after their publication in the Official Gazette on the following day. Previously on May 19, the joint resolution of the *Bundestag* had been handed by Herr Scheel to the Ambassadors of the Soviet Union, the United States, the United Kingdom and France, while the Polish Government was also notified.

Ratification of Treaties in Soviet Union and Poland— Exchange of Instruments of Ratification

The Presidium of the Supreme Soviet on May 31 unanimously ratified the treaty between the Soviet Union and Western Germany, the foreign affairs committee of both Chambers of the Supreme Soviet having unanimously recommended ratification on April 17.

In a statement before the Presidium on behalf of the Soviet Government on May 31, Mr. Gromyko said that the main significance of the treaty lay in the fact that it drew a line under a long period of strain in Soviet-West German relations. He stated that "of special importance is the recording of the commitments of the two sides concerning the existing State frontiers in Europe, which is the basic question of European security", and that "of basic importance is the problem of establishing normal relations between the Federal Republic of Germany and the G.D.R. in line with generally recog-

296

nized international standards". A positive solution to the problem of the admission of both the Federal Republic and the G.D.R. to the United Nations, he said, "would make it easier to settle many complex problems essential for improving the situation in central Europe".

The Polish Council of State unanimously ratified the treaty between Western Germany and Poland on May 26.

Mr. Stefan Olszowski, the Polish Minister of Foreign Affairs, said at a joint meeting of the foreign affairs and justice committees of the *Seym* (Parliament) on May 25 that in the treaty Western Germany had recognized the Oder-Neisse frontier as being inviolable and final; it constituted, he maintained, "a final recognition in international law", while "from the viewpoint of international law—as well as with regard to the obligations resulting from the treaty—none of the reservations contained in the unilateral *Bundestag* resolution has binding force".

The treaties came into force with the exchange of the instruments of ratification in Bonn on June 3 between Western Germany and the Soviet Union and between Western Germany and Poland.

7. AGREEMENTS ON STATUS OF WEST BERLIN, 1971

Four-Power Agreement on Status of and Access to West Berlin

*Western Proposals for Four-Power Talks
on Improving the Situation in Berlin*

Identical Notes were presented on Dec. 16, 1969, by the British, French and U.S. Ambassadors in Moscow to the Soviet Government proposing four-Power discussions on improving the situation in Berlin, and in particular guaranteeing free access to the city. It was understood that the proposal, which was made after full consultation with the West German Government, called for talks to be held first of all at official [i.e. less than ambassadorial] level at a place and time to be agreed on with the Soviet Union. Press reports made it clear that the Western aim was to improve movement both between Berlin and Western Germany and between the two parts of Berlin itself.

This move followed an earlier similar approach by the three Western Powers to the Soviet Government on Aug. 7, 1969, when the

British, French and U.S. Ambassadors, after consultation with the German Federal Government, proposed talks with the Soviet Union on improving the situation in Berlin and the problems arising out of the division of the city, access to West Berlin and relations between Western and Eastern Germany in general. This step had been prompted by a statement of Mr. Gromyko, the Soviet Foreign Minister, made on July 10, 1969, to the Supreme Soviet, in which he said that if Russia's former wartime Allies were to make an approach on the problem of Berlin, taking into account the interests of European security, "they would discover on the part of the Soviet Union a readiness to exchange opinions with the object of eliminating now and forever complications around West Berlin".

A Government spokesman in Bonn on Aug. 7 described the new Allied approach as a test of whether the Soviet Union was really prepared to talk about these issues. The Allies, he said, had indicated that the Federal Government was ready to initiate talks with Eastern Germany on ways of improving relations between them if the East Germans agreed, and the Federal Government hoped that the Government in East Berlin could now be persuaded to open talks on an improvement of relations between the two parts of Germany and the two parts of Berlin.

The Soviet reply, given to the three Western Ambassadors on Sept. 12, agreed that the question of Berlin should be discussed by the four Powers, but did not suggest a time and place or make any proposals. The Western recommendation that West and East German representatives should meet to improve road and rail access to the city and communications generally was merely "noted".

Conclusion of Agreement

Talks on problems relating to Berlin between the British, French and U.S. Ambassadors to Western Germany and the Soviet Ambassador to the German Democratic Republic eventually took place from March 1970 onwards, and at the 33rd meeting on Aug. 25, 1971, it was announced officially that the draft text of a settlement had been agreed upon.

The principal points of this quadripartite agreement, the official text of which was released on Sept. 3, 1971, were as follows:

(1) The four Governments declared that they "will strive to promote the elimination of tension and the prevention of complications in the relevant area. . . . There shall be no use or threat of force and disputes shall be settled solely by peaceful means. . . . The four Governments will mutually respect their individual and joint rights and responsibilities which remain unchanged."

(2) With regard to the question of free access to West Berlin the Government of the U.S.S.R. announced that "transit traffic by road, rail and waterways through the territory of the German Democratic Republic of civilian persons and goods between the Western sectors of Berlin and the Federal Republic of Germany will be unimpeded. It will receive the most simple, expeditious and preferential treatment provided by international practice."

(3) The Government of the U.S.S.R. declared: "Communications between the Western sectors of Berlin and areas bordering on these sectors will be improved. Permanent residents of the Western sectors will be able to travel to and visit such areas for compassionate, family, religious, cultural or commercial reasons, or as tourists, under conditions comparable to those applying to other persons entering these areas. . . ."

(4) On the status of West Berlin the three Western Powers agreed as follows:

"(a) The ties between the Western sectors of Berlin and the Federal Republic of Germany will be maintained and developed, taking into account that these sectors continue not to be a constituent part of the Federal Republic of Germany and not to be governed by it. The provisions of the Basic Law of the Federal Republic of Germany and of the Constitution operative in the Western sectors of Berlin which contradict the above have been suspended and continue not to be in effect.

"(b) The Federal President, the Federal Government, the *Bundesversammlung* [joint session of Parliament], the *Bundesrat* [Upper House] and the *Bundestag* [Lower House], including their committees and *Fraktionen* [Parliamentary party groups], as well as other State bodies of the Federal Republic of Germany, will not perform in the Western sectors of Berlin constitutional or official acts which contradict the provisions of paragraph (a).

"(c) The Government of the Federal Republic of Germany will be represented in the Western sectors of Berlin to the authorities of the three Governments and to the Senate by a permanent liaison agency."

(5) On the question of diplomatic representation the three Western Powers declared:

"The Governments of the French Republic, the United Kingdom and the United States of America maintain their rights and responsibilities relating to the representation abroad of the interests of the Western sectors of Berlin and their permanent residents, including those rights and responsibilities concerning matters of security and status both in international organizations and in relations with other countries.

"The three Governments will authorize the establishment of a Soviet consulate-general in the Western sectors of Berlin accredited to the appropriate authorities of the three Governments."

(6) In a final Quadripartite Protocol the four Governments agreed that they would proceed on the basis that the agreements and arrangements concluded between the competent German authorities would enter into force simultaneously with the quadripartite agreement.

The Protocol itself would enter into force on the date of signature.

The final protocol was signed on June 3, 1972, at a ceremony at the former Allied Control Council in West Berlin by the U.S. Secretary of State, and by the British, French and Soviet Foreign Ministers.

After the signing of the final protocol Mr. Gromyko paid an official visit to Bonn on June 3-4—the first such visit to Bonn by a Soviet Foreign Minister since the establishment of diplomatic relations between the Soviet Union and Western Germany in 1955.

Herr Brandt's Visit to the Soviet Union, September 1971

Following the signing of the quadripartite agreement on Berlin, Herr Brandt had talks with Mr. Brezhnev, the Soviet leader, at the Crimean resort of Oreanda, near Yalta, on Sept. 16-18, 1971.

A joint communiqué was issued on Sept. 18 stating that "in a spirit of complete loyalty to their allies" the two sides had discussed a wide range of international problems. The treaty between Western Germany and the Soviet Union, it was stated, "already . . . facilitates an improvement of the political climate between the two States and is exerting a favourable influence on the entire course of European affairs".

Reference was also made in the communiqué to the signing of the quadripartite agreement on Berlin described as "a major step along the road of easing European and international tensions", and to the prospects for the normalization of relations between Western and Eastern Germany, which "today appears to be possible and of much importance". In this latter context, the two leaders said that the entry of both German States into the United Nations and other international institutions would be an important step towards *détente* in Europe.

The development of bilateral relations between the Soviet Union and the Federal Republic of Germany had also been thoroughly discussed between Herr Brandt and Mr. Brezhnev, both sides coming to the conclusion that "extensive possibilities" existed for co-operation between the two countries "in the most diverse fields"; agreements on an expansion of trade relations and scientific, technical, cultural and sports ties, as well as exchanges between youth organizations, were foreseen, whilst it was stated that a joint commission would be set up to develop economic co-operation.

In conclusion it was affirmed that both sides believed that "the practice of exchanging views and of consultations at various levels, now taking shape between the Soviet Union and the Federal Republic both on questions of bilateral relations and on international problems, is useful and should be continued".

In an interview given to *The New York Times*, Herr Brandt said that it was incorrect to assume that the Federal Republic was developing a special relationship with the Soviet Union, and he declared: "We have not become friends of the Soviet Union or of its system, but rather have become partners in a businesslike contract, just as other Western States who are treaty partners of the Soviet Union."

West Berlin Agreement between Eastern and Western Germany, 1971

Herr Stoph's Proposals for Political Settlement rejected by West Berlin—Breakdown of Talks on Easter Passes for West Berliners—Partial Restoration of Telephone Links

Herr Stoph, the G.D.R. Prime Minister, announced during a meeting on Feb. 4, 1971, with Herr Danelius, chairman of the West Berlin Socialist Unity (Communist) Party, that his Government was prepared to conclude an agreement with the West Berlin Senate guaranteeing the access routes on condition that the Federal Republic's "political presence" in the city was abolished.

An official statement issued after the meeting said that particular attention had been paid to the normalization of relations between the G.D.R. and West Berlin, and that it had been emphasized that the interests of European security demanded the recognition of the special status of West Berlin, "which does not belong to the Federal

Republic and cannot be ruled by it". Noting "the existence of conditions which, if utilized, would make it possible to change West Berlin from a centre of constant conflicts and tension into a city which could contribute towards the strengthening of peace", Herr Stoph and Herr Danelius had stressed the great importance of the four-Power talks; emphasized their determination to contribute towards peace and *détente* and to bring about a situation which would "accord with the needs of the West Berlin population and the legitimate interests and sovereign rights of the G.D.R."; and agreed that the fundamental condition of any improvement in the West Berlin situation was the ending of the Federal Republic's "political presence" and the cessation of all "revanchist, militarist and anti-peace activities" in the city.

Herr Stoph, the statement continued, had declared that strict compliance with the status of the "independent political entity of West Berlin" could bring about a positive change in the relationship between the city and the G.D.R., making possible "mutually advantageous agreements in the fields of trade, science, transport and other areas which would be of particular benefit to the West Berlin population". Under the "appropriate circumstances" the G.D.R. Government would be ready to examine the question of concluding the necessary agreements with the West Berlin Senate, which would allow for economic, scientific, technical and cultural links between West Berlin and all States, including the Federal Republic. Moreover, the G.D.R. Government would then be able to allow West Berlin citizens to visit the G.D.R., including East Berlin, in accordance with the legal stipulations. The G.D.R. Government would also be ready to conduct negotiations with the West Berlin Senate on the mutual transit of persons and goods and, in accordance with the usual international norms and practices, to conclude a regular agreement on the following questions: guarantees for the transit traffic of West Berlin citizens and goods to and from all States; the greatest possible simplification of transit traffic, including arrangements for sealing freight in transit through the G.D.R.; and frontier regulation, which could apply, amongst other points, to the little enclave of Steinstücken, an isolated part of West Berlin situated a few hundred yards inside the G.D.R.

In an exchange of letters published in West Berlin on Feb. 16, Herr Danelius wrote to Herr Schütz suggesting a meeting between them to discuss Herr Stoph's proposals, but Herr Schütz replied that there was no need for an intermediary if the G.D.R. Government was serious about wishing to talk to the West Berlin Senate, and reiterated his view that the Senate continued to look for reasonable settlements within the framework of the four-Power talks.

As his next step, Herr Stoph, in a letter to Herr Schütz on Feb. 24, suggested the opening of direct talks between his Government and the West Berlin Senate on visits by West Berlin citizens to the G.D.R. The text of the letter was as follows:

"The Government of the G.D.R. attaches great importance to the present efforts to bring about *détente* in the centre of Europe, and to normalize the situation of West Berlin. . . . Some questions connected with a possible settlement affect directly the relations of West Berlin with the G.D.R. Naturally the G.D.R. Government and the West Berlin authorities must primarily see to it that these questions are settled in the most favourable manner.

"In the name of the G.D.R. Government I propose to you the opening of negotiations between the G.D.R. Government and the West Berlin Senate on the question of visits by the citizens of your city to the G.D.R., including its capital [i.e. East Berlin]. Understandably, an agreement on this question can [only] be implemented in case agreements on other questions regarding West Berlin, which are being discussed in relevant negotiations, come into force.

"The concrete conditions for an agreement could be discussed by our representatives at the negotiating table. However, the G.D.R. Government declares its readiness to solve the questions of visits in such a way that West Berlin citizens would enjoy the hospitality of the G.D.R. on the same basis as other visitors to the G.D.R.

"If the negotiations on all questions relating to West Berlin have not been concluded by Easter, the G.D.R. Government will consider the question of making it possible for West Berliners to visit the G.D.R. before, during and after Easter. This is naturally on the assumption that the West Berlin authorities, for their part, make efforts to guard the city from unnecessary complications which would make more difficult such investigation. . . ."

Herr Schütz, replying on Feb. 25, said that the West Berlin Senate was interested in a normalization of relations, and hoped that the four-Power talks would reach a successful conclusion. His letter to Herr Stoph continued:

"To this end, the Senate is ready to participate in the negotiations proposed by you on visits by West Berliners in the framework of the competence of the Senate and with the agreement of the three Powers. These negotiations could begin in the general interest, and taking into consideration the bigger issues, as soon as the current four-Power negotiations, which cannot be forestalled, have reached an appropriate stage." Welcoming the suggestion that West Berliners might be able to visit the G.D.R. during the Easter period, Herr Schütz suggested that talks between the two sides should begin as soon as possible.

The talks opened on March 6 with a five-hour meeting in East Berlin between Herr Günter Kohrt, State Secretary in the G.D.R. Foreign Ministry, and Herr Ulrich Müller, head of chancellery of the West Berlin Senate.

A second meeting between full delegations led by Herr Kohrt and Herr Müller respectively took place in West Berlin on March 12 and was followed by a statement by Herr Schütz.

According to *Die Welt,* Herr Schütz said that the G.D.R. delegation had aimed at reaching a "general and lasting settlement" but that the West Berlin side had only been "able, willing and in a position to discuss a settlement for Easter". Longer-term arrangements, Herr Schütz added, could only be made when the Powers responsible for Berlin had themselves reached an agreement in principle on the Berlin question.

The third meeting again took place in East Berlin on March 27, it being agreed to continue the talks in West Berlin, but in a surprise announcement on April 2 the East German Government Press Office stated that the G.D.R. would not grant any facilities for visits by West Berliners to East Berlin and the G.D.R. during the Easter holidays.

The statement put the responsibility for this on the West Berlin Senate and said that the East German proposals for a general agreement on relations, including visits by West Berliners to the G.D.R. and East Berlin, were being maintained.

Herr Schütz on the same day expressed regret at the East German refusal to permit visits to relatives over Easter. In recent weeks, he said, he had stated time and again that he was not willing to undermine the four-Power negotiations, but that West Berlin continued to be ready for special arrangements. He hoped that it was now clear both in East Germany and in the Soviet Union that the Senate "could not be blackmailed" and that nobody would be permitted "to interfere in West Berlin's internal affairs", including the ties between West Berlin and the Federal Republic, which were "unrenounceable".

304

In spite of this development, a fourth meeting between Herr Kohrt and Herr Müller was held in West Berlin on April 17, on a proposal by Herr Kohrt on April 5, which was accepted by the West Berlin side.

Meanwhile, based on an agreement of July 31, 1970, between the G.D.R. and West Berlin, telephone links between the two parts of Berlin were restored on Jan. 31, 1971, for the first time since May 1952, the new service comprising five lines in each direction. This was increased by the installation of 10 further telephone lines on either side on April 8.

Talks between East and West German Governments on Mutual Relations

Talks had meanwhile opened in East Berlin on Nov. 27, 1970, between the State Secretary at the Federal Chancellor's office, Herr Egon Bahr, and the State Secretary of the Council of Ministers of the G.D.R., Dr. Michael Kohl, on the basis of an agreement between the two Governments which had been announced in Bonn and East Berlin on Oct. 29, 1970, and provided for "an official exchange of views on questions the settlement of which would help towards a *détente* in central Europe and would be of interest to both States".

The deputy spokesman of the Federal Government in Bonn, Herr Rüdiger von Wechmar, stated on Oct. 29 that the agreement was the result of discussions in Bonn on Oct. 28-29 between two East German Government delegates and Professor Horst Ehmke, Minister without Portfolio for special duties at the Federal Chancellery; that the East German delegates had also been received by Herr Brandt, the Chancellor; and that the exchanges of views would presumably take place "at the middle level". It was still undecided which concrete subjects would be dealt with, but the Federal Government was taking as its starting-point the 20 points enumerated at the Kassel meeting between Herr Brandt and Herr Stoph.

The Federal Government spokesman, Herr Conrad Ahlers, explained on Nov. 2 that in view of Mr. Gromyko's [the Soviet Foreign Minister's] talks in East Berlin and with Herr Scheel in Frankfurt on Oct. 29-30, the four-Power talks on Berlin, and the Erfurt and Kassel meetings of Herr Brandt and Herr Stoph, the Federal Government considered it quite possible to enter into a discussion of the Berlin question with the G.D.R. Government even before the four-Power talks had ended, provided the Western Powers would give them a mandate for this. Stressing the close co-operation between the Western Powers and the Federal Government on the Berlin talks, he said that in the proposed discussions between Bonn and East Berlin it was intended to find out the extent of the difficulties and problems between them in a way similar to the preparations for the Moscow Treaty between Federal Germany and the Soviet Union and the then projected West German-Polish Treaty; this meant that competent officials from East Berlin and Bonn would prepare what, at a later stage, might be dealt with in ministerial negotiations. Herr Ahlers reiterated, however, that there was a restriction of the subjects which could be discussed with the G.D.R., though this did not exclude talks on traffic to and from West Berlin, but any negotiations in connexion with the four-Power discussions on Berlin could only take place when the four Powers or the three Western Powers considered such negotiations between the Federal Republic and the G.D.R. as "feasible".

Following initial discussions on Oct. 29, Herr Bahr and Dr. Kohl had nine further confidential talks, held partly in East Berlin (Dec. 16-23, 1970; Jan. 26, 1971; Feb. 17; March 8; and March 31) and partly in Bonn (Jan. 15; Feb. 3; Feb. 26; and March 17). After the first and second talks Herr Bahr and Dr. Kohl were assisted by other officials of their Governments, several of the talks lasting from five to nearly seven hours. After the 10th talk Herr Bahr said that they had dealt with traffic between the F.R.G. and the G.D.R., including traffic on inland waterways crossing the G.D.R. and traffic through the F.R.G. of importance to the G.D.R. for its communications with Western countries. Berlin transit questions had not been discussed, as the Federal Government had to wait for the "green light" from the three Western protecting Powers negotiating with the Soviet Union.

Herr Brandt's Reaffirmation of Link between Berlin Settlement and West German Ratification of Treaties with U.S.S.R. and Poland

In reply to Opposition criticisms of his Government's *Ostpolitik,* Herr Brandt, on the occasion of his visit to West Berlin and his talks with Herr Schütz [see above], issued a statement on Jan. 30, 1971, reaffirming that the Federal Government regarded a satisfactory Berlin settlement as "an essential, even a decisive, element for effective *détente* in Europe".

There was, Herr Brandt said, complete agreement between the Federal Government and its Western partners and allies, especially the three protecting Powers, on the criteria for a Berlin settlement, and the co-operation between the four Western Governments worked "excellently". The Chancellor stressed that the Federal Government had from the beginning made it clear to the Soviet Union, "unmistakably and beyond doubt", that an indissoluble link existed between a satisfactory Berlin settlement and the ratification of the Moscow treaty—a link which had been made equally clear to the Soviet Government by the chairman of the *Bundestag* foreign affairs committee, Dr. Gerhard Schröder (CDU), during a visit to Moscow. Referring to the hindrances to traffic between Western Germany and West Berlin, Herr Brandt said that a Berlin settlement must contain not only the right of unhindered access to, but also of unhindered assembly in, West Berlin.

In an interview published by *Der Spiegel* on May 24 Herr Brandt again referred to the link between a satisfactory settlement of the Berlin question and the Federal Republic's ratification of the Moscow treaty with the Soviet Union, frequently referred to in Western Germany as the "Berlin *Junktim*", saying in this connexion: "Perhaps as a Government we have not done enough to contradict that ambiguous word. We have never created what you [the interviewer] call a *Junktim,* certainly not a legal *Junktim* and not one in the sense that a State such as the Federal Republic of Germany could lay down pre-conditions for the improvement of relations *vis-à-vis* the Soviet Union. We have made all this perfectly clear in Moscow, but we have equally clearly and honestly pointed to the internal link between the [German-Soviet and German-Polish] treaties and a satisfactory Berlin settlement. We did this even before signing the [Soviet] treaty, and at the time it was quite understood [by the other side]. If it should not be possible to reach an understanding on Berlin . . . this would, unfortunately, only show that there can also be no decisive progress in other matters, especially as far as questions connected with a European security conference are concerned."

Agreements
between West and East German Governments and
between West Berlin Senate and East German Government

During the talks which led to the four-Power agreement on Berlin of Sept. 3, 1971 [see page 298], negotiations continued between Herr Bahr, the Federal State Secretary, and Dr. Kohl, the East German State Secretary.

After the conclusion of the four-Power agreement, these negotiations dealt with the facilitation of transit traffic between West Berlin and Western Germany, while parallel talks were held between Herr Günter Kohrt, State Secretary at the G.D.R. Foreign Ministry, and Herr Ulrich Müller, head of the Chancellery of the West Berlin Senate, on the access of West Berliners to East Berlin and the G.D.R. and the problem of West Berlin enclaves in East German territory.

Three agreements were eventually initialled in Berlin on Dec. 11, 1971, viz:

(a) "Agreement between the Government of the Federal Republic of Germany and the Government of the German Democratic Republic on the Transit Traffic of Civilian Persons and Goods between the Federal Republic of Germany and Berlin (West)."

The agreement laid down, *inter alia*: "Transit traffic will be facilitated and unimpeded . . .

"Transit travellers will be issued with visas at the border crossing points of the G.D.R."

For transit traffic of civilian goods, conveyances would be fitted with seals before departure.

The G.D.R. authorities would confine themselves to the examination of the seals and accompanying documents.

Misuse of the agreement would be deemed to have occurred if a transit traveller while using the transit routes "unlawfully and culpably violates the generally applicable regulations of the G.D.R.".

Western Germany would pay to the G.D.R. an annual lump sum covering the cost of maintaining roads, facilities and installations used for transit traffic, as well as visa fees, tax compensation and compensation for the G.D.R.'s loss of certain revenues. The annual lump sum for the period 1972-75 was fixed at DM 234,900,000 (about £28,000,000).

(b) "Agreement between the Senate and the Government of the

308

G.D.R. on Facilitation and Improvement of Travelling and Visiting",
containing the following main provisions:

Permanent residents of West Berlin would be able to visit East
Berlin and Eastern Germany for a total of 30 days per year on one
or several occasions.
Visits in excess of 30 days might be permitted "for urgent family
and humanitarian reasons".

(c) "Agreement between the Senate and the Government of the
G.D.R. on the Settlement of the Question of Enclaves by Exchange
of Territory."

Five areas totalling about 15.6 hectares (about 39 acres) were
to be given by West Berlin to the G.D.R. in exchange for three areas
aggregating about 17.1 hectares (approximately 42 acres).
Rights of private individuals and corporations to land, buildings
and installation in the areas to be exchanged would not be affected
by the agreement; claims for compensation would be settled by the
side on whose territory the lands, buildings and installations were
situated prior to the exchange of territory.

In addition, new agreements on postal services and telecommunications, signed in East Berlin on Sept. 30, 1971, by the Ministries of
Eastern and Western Germany provided *inter alia* as follows:

(1) The agreement concluded on April 29, 1970, whereby the
West German Government agreed to pay the East German authorities
an annual lump sum totalling DM 30,000,000 (about £3,600,000)
as compensation for the costs of inter-German postal communications
would be extended to 1976, while for the period prior to that covered
by the 1970 agreement a lump sum of DM 250,000,000 (about
£30,000,000) would be paid as compensation, this sum also covering the East German claims against the West Berlin Senate.
(2) The number of telephone lines between Eastern and Western
Germany was to be increased by 30 lines in each direction by Dec. 31,
1971, and by a further 16 lines by March 31, 1972; in the case of
telephone lines to and from West Berlin a further 60 lines in each
direction were to be brought into operation by Dec. 15, 1971, in
addition to the existing 15 in each direction. By Dec. 31, 1974,
subscriber trunk dialling would be gradually installed between Eastern
and Western Germany and a partial introduction of this system was
also foreseen for telephone links with West Berlin.

In an explanatory note to the agreements as published by the Federal Press and Information Office it was stated that they were the first settlement between the competent German authorities as defined by the quadripartite agreement.

All these agreements concluded between the West and East German Governments and between the West Berlin Senate and the East German Government entered into force simultaneously with the four-Power signature of the final protocol on June 3, 1972 [see page 300].

8. TRAFFIC TREATY BETWEEN WEST AND EAST GERMAN GOVERNMENTS, 1972

As the result of further negotiations conducted between Jan. 20 and April 26, 1972, a Treaty between the Federal Republic of Germany and the German Democratic Republic on Questions of Traffic was initialled in Bonn on May 12 and signed in East Berlin on May 26, 1972.

Under the treaty, the contracting States undertook "to the greatest possible extent to allow, to facilitate, and to organize as expeditiously as possible the traffic in and through their sovereign territories, corresponding to normal international practice on the basis of reciprocity and non-discrimination". The traffic would be subject to the law of the State in which it occurred, as far as the treaty did not provide otherwise.

For rail traffic, the International Agreements on Rail Passenger and Luggage Traffic and on Rail Goods Traffic, together with their supplementary agreements, would apply to the conveyance of travellers and luggage and to goods traffic respectively.

For inland navigation, on the basis of mutual agreement, permission for the use of waterways would not be required. Differences of opinion which might arise as to the application or interpretation of the treaty would be clarified by a joint commission, delegations to which would be led by authorized representatives of the Ministries of Transport of both States.

The treaty would remain in force for an indefinite period, although it could be terminated five years after its entry into force provided notice was given three months before the end of the calendar year in question.

The text of the main treaty was supplemented by protocol notes, an exchange of letters between Herr Bahr and Dr. Kohl, and a "Notification of the G.D.R. on Travel Facilitations".

Protocol Notes.—These stated that the proposed commission could "at the proper time also discuss questions of the further facilitation and expeditious organization of passenger and goods traffic. Suggestions to that effect require the decision of the Governments or their relevant authorities or organs." It was also affirmed that the Federal Republic and the G.D.R. agreed to take up negotiations "at the proper time" on air traffic agreement [a question which had been specifically excluded from the current traffic treaty].

Exchange of Letters.—In these it was stated that after the signing of the treaty the Federal Republic would apply for accession to the international rail traffic agreements mentioned above, which would not be applied until membership with equal rights of the Federal Republic and the G.D.R. in these agreements had been achieved. The legal position of the railway lines in West Berlin [which are run by the East German authorities] would be unaffected by membership in the agreements, as would existing agreements of the Federal Republic.

Notification of the G.D.R. on Travel Facilitations.—This notification stated that at the request of G.D.R. citizens the relevant authorities of the G.D.R. would allow the visit several times a year of relatives and friends from Western Germany; West German citizens could also visit Eastern Germany for commercial, cultural, sporting, religious or other reasons, provided that there existed invitations from the corresponding institutions or organizations of the G.D.R. Furthermore, tourist journeys by citizens of Western Germany into the G.D.R. would be made possible by agreements between the tourist offices of the two States.

The use of passenger cars for journeys into the G.D.R. would be allowed to a greater degree than hitherto, and the limit of duty exemption on presents taken on journeys into Eastern Germany would be raised. It was also stated that the G.D.R. Government would make possible travel to Western Germany by G.D.R. citizens in "urgent family matters"—a phrase which Dr. Kohl defined at a press conference at the time of the signing of the treaty as including births, deaths, weddings and serious illnesses.

In their declarations at the signing of the treaty both Secretaries of State said that the terms of the treaty were to be applied analogously to West Berlin.

After approval by the West German *Bundestag* and the East German *Volkskammer* the treaty was to come into force by an exchange of Notes; a corresponding Bill was approved by the Council of Ministers of the G.D.R. on May 31, 1972.

Easter and Whitsuntide Visits of West Berliners to East Berlin and Eastern Germany

The ADN news agency on Feb. 22 published a decision of the East German Socialist Unity Party Politburo and Council of Ministers "as a gesture of good will" temporarily to put into effect at Easter (March 29-April 5) and Whitsun (May 17-24) the agreements on transit traffic and on the access of West Berliners to East Berlin and Eastern Germany, which had been concluded in implementation of the four-Power agreement on Berlin.

At the office of the Chief Burgomaster of West Berlin it was announced on April 10 that according to information received from the G.D.R. authorities 449,597 West Berliners had visited East Berlin or Eastern Germany during the Easter period, of whom 264,959 paid visits lasting several days; the East German authorities requested DM 4,900,000 (about £600,000) as lump-sum payment by the West German Government for the visits. After the Whitsuntide visits the G.D.R. authorities revealed that 626,009 West Berliners had visited East Berlin and Eastern Germany during the period, and asked for an overall payment in return of DM 7,160,295 (about £870,000).

The Easter visits were the first which West Berliners had been allowed to make to East Berlin for six years and to Eastern Germany for more than 20 years.

SUBJECT INDEX

314

315

INDEX OF NAMES